"This book offers excellent contributions to the area of cultural tourism. The importance of heritage and cultural tourism has significantly increased in today's highly specialized tourism service economy. This book emphasizes further the importance of themed tourism with policy and development implications. The scope of the coverage is broad with examples from different international settings. It is a must reading for both students of tourism and also practitioners of tourism managing and marketing destinations."

– Associate prof. Albert G. Assaf, Isenberg School of Management, University of Massachusetts

"These 17 chapters on *Cultural Heritage* make this edited text an excellent resource that contributes to academic and practitioner understanding of the main themes that underpin the topic, and also provides fascinating insights into real-world cases, and examples of the consumption, management, and marketing of cultural heritage from a wide variety of perspectives."

– Dr. Heather Skinner, Chair: Corfu Symposium on Managing & Marketing Places and Chair: Visiting Places Special Interest Group – Institute of Place Management

"This comprehensive and timely compendium brings together the best international scholarship on cultural heritage from various disciplines. The editors solicited a synthesis of research exploring a variety of themes ranging from authenticity, values, place concepts to conservation, and dark heritage sites. Scholars and practitioners alike will appreciate the breadth and scope of this insightful anthology which stimulates and contributes to the current debates surrounding cultural heritage."

– Dr. Nicole Koenig-Lewis, Cardiff University's Business School

"This anthology provides a novel and valuable interdisciplinary examination of cultural heritage. Through a diversity of theoretical and empirical perspectives, its chapters illuminate current topics in cultural heritage such as values, authenticity, place branding, commercialisation, looting and dark sites, economic and technological aspects. This anthology is a highly welcomed contribution to the field of cultural heritage."

– Associate prof. Ana María Munar, Director Center for Leisure and Culture Services, Copenhagen Business School

Cultural Heritage

Cultural Heritage is a systematic, interdisciplinary examination of cultural heritage, which provides an up-to-date view of the field by drawing on various disciplines. The book offers a thorough, structured review of extant literature on heritage in tourism and pertinent challenges for cultural heritage.

This book offers new ways of looking at cultural heritage assets against a backdrop of increasing economic and environmental pressures. It comprises a number of sections that each examine cultural heritage from the perspective of ethics and values, community relations and development, cultural entrepreneurship, economic viability and conservation, methodologies, impacts of tourism research, consumption, and urban and immaterial heritage.

Encompassing global research perspectives from public management, visual culture, environmental management, and cultural entrepreneurship, *Cultural Heritage* is a crucial text for those working or interested in the heritage field.

Dr Adriana Campelo is Director of Resilience for the Municipal Government of Salvador and Chief Resilience Officer under the 100 Resilient Cities pioneering project by the Rockefeller Foundation. She holds a PhD in Marketing Management from the University of Otago in New Zealand and has published in many academic journals.

Laura Reynolds is in the final stages of an ESRC-funded PhD at Cardiff Business School. Her thesis is a critical exploration of the city branding process. Her main research interests include city branding, brand governance, and heritage tourism.

Dr Adam Lindgreen is Professor of Marketing at Copenhagen Business School where he heads the Department of Marketing. He is also Extra Ordinary Professor at the University of Pretoria's Institute of Business Science. Dr Lindgreen received his PhD from Cranfield University. He has published in the *California Management Review*, *Journal of Business Ethics*, *Journal of Product and Innovation Management*, *Journal of the Academy of Marketing Science*, and *Journal of World Business*, among others.

Dr Michael Beverland is Professor of Marketing at the University of Sussex. He is an Associate Editor for the *Journal of Marketing Management*. His research primarily focuses on marketplace authenticity and has been published in (among others) the *Journal of Advertising*, *Journal of Consumer Research*, *Journal of Management Studies*, *Journal of Product Innovation Management*, and *Journal of the Academy of Marketing Science*. A summary of his work can be found in *Building Brand Authenticity: 7 Habits of Iconic Brands* (Palgrave MacMillan 2009/2016).

Cultural Heritage

Edited by
Adriana Campelo, Laura Reynolds,
Adam Lindgreen, and Michael Beverland

Routledge
Taylor & Francis Group
LONDON AND NEW YORK

First published 2019
by Routledge
2 Park Square, Milton Park, Abingdon, Oxon OX14 4RN

and by Routledge
52 Vanderbilt Avenue, New York, NY 10017

Routledge is an imprint of the Taylor & Francis Group, an informa business

British Library Cataloguing-in-Publication Data
A catalogue record for this book is available from the British Library

Library of Congress Cataloging-in-Publication Data
A catalog record has been requested for this book

ISBN: 978-1-138-09282-2 (hbk)
ISBN: 978-1-315-10726-4 (ebk)

Typeset in Bembo
by Deanta Global Publishing Services, Chennai, India

MIX
Paper from responsible sources
FSC® C013056
FSC www.fsc.org

Printed and bound in Great Britain by
TJ International Ltd, Padstow, Cornwall

For Vicente and Lais who gave me "wings" to fly to many cultures and to learn about places and people.

—Adriana

For Patricia and Michael, whose encouragement and support has given me the confidence to take the road "less travelled by, And that has made all the difference".

—Laura

For Jørgen, Palle, Svend, and Wolf, discussions with you have contributed immensely to my work on methodological issues in genealogy, accounts of population development, and particular family lineages.

—Adam

For my colleagues past and present.

—Michael

Contents

Figures

Tables

About the editors

Adriana Campelo holds a PhD in marketing management from the University of Otago, an MA in management from the Federal University of Bahia, a specialization in economics from University Unifacs, and a law degree from the Catholic University of Salvador. She was a lecturer and researcher in marketing at Cardiff University's Business School from 2012 to 2015. She has published in journals such as *Journal of Macromarketing*, *Journal of Marketing Management*, and *Journal of Travel Research*. Her research interests include place marketing and consumer behaviour, particularly in relation to the uses of marketing and branding for economic development and urban regeneration. She is Former Deputy Secretary for Economic Development, Labour and Employability for the city of Salvador, Brazil. Currently, she is Chief Resilience Officer for the city of Salvador, as part of the 100 Resilient Cities pioneered by Rockefeller Foundation, and she serves as a special advisor for the municipal government of Salvador. In addition, she is a dissertation advisor for the management degree programs at the University of Liverpool Online.

Laura Reynolds is a PhD candidate in Cardiff University's Business School, specializing in marketing. Her research, funded by the Economic and Social Research Council (ESRC) and Cardiff University's Business School, focuses on the role of stakeholders in creating holistic city identities. She holds an MSc in social science research methods from Cardiff University (2014), an MA in marketing from Keele University (2012), and a LLB in law with history from Keele University (2009). Her main research interests include city branding, stakeholder management, heritage tourism, and consumer behaviour. She previously has undertaken research on the brand personality of the National Trust, as well as the importance of authenticity for the Blaenavon World Heritage Site. While pursuing her PhD, she has worked as a research assistant on several research projects analyzing acculturalization in buyer behaviour, mapping consumer misbehaviour, and investigating the confounding effects of occupational stress in small business management.

Adam Lindgreen after studies in chemistry (Copenhagen University), engineering (the Engineering Academy of Denmark), and physics (Copenhagen University), Professor Adam Lindgreen completed an MSc in food science and technology at the Technical University of Denmark. He also finished an MBA at the University of Leicester. He received his PhD in marketing from Cranfield University. His first appointments were with the Catholique University of Louvain (2000–2001) and Eindhoven University of Technology (2002–2007). Subsequently, he served as Professor of Marketing at Hull University's Business School (2007–2010); University of Birmingham's Business School (2010), where he also was the research director in the Department of Marketing; and the University of Cardiff's Business School (2011–2016). Under his leadership, the Department of Marketing and Strategy at Cardiff Business School ranked first among all marketing departments in Australia, Canada, New Zealand, the United Kingdom, and the United States, based on the hg indices of senior faculty. Since 2016, he has been Professor of Marketing at Copenhagen Business School, where he also heads the Department of Marketing. Since 2018, he also is Extra Ordinary Professor with the University of Pretoria's Gordon Institute of Business Science and a Visiting Professor with Northumbria University's Newcastle Business School.

Adam Lindgreen has been a visiting professor with various institutions, including Georgia State University, Groupe HEC, and Melbourne University. His publications have appeared in *Business Horizons, California Management Review, Entrepreneurship and Regional Development, Industrial Marketing Management, International Journal of Management Reviews, Journal of Advertising, Journal of Business Ethics, European Journal of Marketing, Journal of Business and Industrial Marketing, Journal of Marketing Management, Journal of the Academy of Marketing Science, Journal of Product Innovation Management, Journal of World Business, Psychology & Marketing*, and *Supply Chain Management: An International Journal*, among others.

Adam Lindgreen's books include *A Stakeholder Approach to Corporate Social Responsibility* (with Kotler, Vanhamme, and Maon), *Managing Market Relationships, Memorable Customer Experiences* (with Vanhamme and Beverland), *Not All Claps and Cheers* (with Maon, Vanhamme, Angell, and Memery), and *Sustainable Value Chain Management* (with Maon, Vanhamme, and Sen).

The recipient of the "Outstanding Article 2005" award from *Industrial Marketing Management* and the runner-up for the same award in 2016, he is Co-Editor-in-Chief of *Industrial Marketing Management*. His research interests include business and industrial marketing management, corporate social responsibility, and sustainability. He has been awarded the Dean's Award for Excellence in Executive Teaching.

Adam Lindgreen is a member of the International Scientific Advisory Panel of the New Zealand Food Safety Science and Research Centre (a partnership between government, industry organizations, and research institutions), as well as of the Chartered Association of Business Schools' Academic Journal Guide (AJG) Scientific Committee in the field of marketing.

Beyond these academic contributions to marketing, Adam Lindgreen has discovered and excavated settlements from the Stone Age in Denmark, including the only major kitchen midden—Sparregård—in the south-east of Denmark; because of its importance, the kitchen midden was later excavated by the National Museum and then protected as a historical monument for future generations. He is also an avid genealogist, having traced his family back to 1390 and published widely in scientific journals (*Personalhistorisk Tidsskrift, The Genealogist*, and *Slægt & Data*) related to methodological issues in genealogy, accounts of population development, and particular family lineages.

Michael Beverland is Professor of Marketing at the University of Sussex. Previously, he held positions in business schools at the University of Bath, RMIT, University of Melbourne, and Monash University. Primarily known for his work on marketplace authenticity, his current work examines the creation of brand culture in post-colonial New Zealand. His research has been published in journals including *Design Management Review, Journal of Advertising, Journal of Consumer Research, Journal of Macromarketing, Journal of Management Studies, Journal of Product Innovation Management, Journal of the Academy of Marketing Science*, and *Marketing Theory*. His previous books include *Building Brand*

Authenticity: 7 Habits of Iconic Brands and *Redesigning Manufacturing* (both with Palgrave MacMillan). His textbook on co-creating brand meaning is forthcoming in 2018 (Sage). He currently serves as an area editor for brand management with *Journal of Marketing Management* and is an editorial review board member for *Journal of Product Innovation Management*. He also serves as an associate editor for Bloomsbury for its global fashion business teaching case series. When he is not working, he enjoys cycling, analog photography, wildlife watching, drinking coffee, and drawing.

About the contributors

Erik Braun is a Senior Researcher and Lecturer in Urban Economics, Place Marketing, Tourism, and Real Estate at Erasmus University Rotterdam. His current place marketing research interests involve the application of marketing and branding concepts by cities and regions. His research has been published in books, book chapters, and academic journals, including for example *Cities, Environment and Planning C, Public Administration Review, Tourism Management*, and *Urban Studies*.

Stephen Brown is Professor of Marketing Research at Ulster University. He has written numerous books, including *Postmodern Marketing* (Routledge, 1995), *Free Gift Inside* (Capstone, 2003), and *Brands & Branding* (Sage, 2016). His articles have been published in the *Harvard Business Review, Journal of Consumer Research, Journal of Marketing*, and many others.

Simon Darcy is Professor in Management at the UTS Business School, University of Technology Sydney. He is an interdisciplinary researcher with expertise in developing inclusive organizational approaches for diversity groups, social impact, and volunteer management. His work is characterized by implementing the outcomes of his research to change practices by business, government, and the not-for-profit sector.

Brian Egloff is an Adjunct Professor of Cultural Heritage Studies at the University of Canberra. From 1999 to 2009, he served as the President and resuscitated the ICOMOS International Scientific Committee on Archaeological Heritage Management. Together with Kristin Kelly and Thongsa Sayavongkhamedy, he has published *Sacred Caves of Tam Ting (Pak Ou): Mystery, Splendor and Desecration*.

Audrey Gilmore is Professor Emerita of Services Marketing at Ulster Business School. Her teaching and research interests involve strategic marketing, service marketing management, and SME/entrepreneurial marketing. She has published in journals such as *European Journal of Marketing, International Business Review, Journal of Marketing Management*, and *Tourism Management*, as well as written three books and many book chapters on these themes. She has supervised 14 doctoral candidates to successful completion. She was joint-editor of *European Journal of Marketing* for 14 years and is a member of editorial boards for a number of marketing and small business journals. Currently, she is a member of the Academy of Marketing's (UK) Executive Committee, of the Academy of Marketing Research Committee, and of the Advisory Board of the GRME (Global Research in Marketing and Entrepreneurship, formerly known as the American Marketing Association's Marketing and Entrepreneurship Interface Group). She was appointed an Honorary Fellow of the Academy of Marketing and

Life Member in 2017 in recognition of extraordinary and distinguished services to the Academy. She has carried out research and consultancy for a number of start-up companies, social enterprises, and growing firms in the United Kingdom and has advised on quality service management issues with Stena Line.

Lina Lourenço Gomes has a PhD in economics (quantitative methods applied to economics) from the University of Minho (2010). Previously, she completed an MSc in economics from the University of Coimbra (2006) and a BSc (1999) in economics from the University of Trás-os-Montes and Alto-Douro (UTAD). She is an assistant professor in the Department of Economics, Sociology, and Management at UTAD and a researcher in the Centre for Transdisciplinary Development Studies (CETRAD) at the same university. Her main research interests include applied microeconomics, cultural economics, and economic valuation of non-market goods. She has presented papers at both national and international conferences and has published in international journals.

Torgrim Sneve Guttormsen is an archaeologist and researcher at the Norwegian Institute for Cultural Heritage Research (NIKU). Since the 1990s, he has participated in and directed numerous archaeological field surveys in Norway, as well as archaeological field works and heritage projects in Greece, Italy, and Oman. Since joining NIKU in 2001, he has conducted various projects related to environmental monitoring, spatial planning, and cultural heritage values. In 2013, he completed a PhD in archaeology from the University of Gothenburg. His doctoral thesis combines historiography and heritage studies by analyzing public blends of professional, political, and popular uses of the past. He has directed the master's program in archaeological resource management at the University of Oslo (2014), and from 2013 to the present, he has supervised students and given guest lectures in heritage studies that reflect the interfaces of heritage management/politics, public archaeology, and memory studies. His previous and on-going research and publications feature the theory of heritage, heritage politics and management, heritage routes, memorials, monument studies, difficult heritage, urban heritage, and immigrant heritage. His interests also cover political heritage research aimed at studying conflicts and diplomacy. He is the co-editor of *Heritage, Democracy and the Public. Nordic Approaches* (Routledge, 2016) and is leading his institute's strategic research program on Heritage Politics (2016–2020). He coordinates the Norwegian Chapter of the Association of Critical Heritage Studies and is a senior representative for Northern Europe in the Council of World Archaeological Congress.

Zara H. Hosseini holds a master's degree in business administration/marketing from IA University-North Tehran. Her current research interests include consumer and tourist behaviour, international and intercultural marketing, and tourism marketing.

Alexander Josiassen is Professor of International Consumer and Tourist Behavior at Copenhagen Business School. His current research interests include international marketing, tourist behaviour, tourist decision making, and firm performance. He has received several prestigious international awards in marketing and tourism. He has a practical background in management and regularly consults with major companies.

Florian Kock is an Assistant Professor of Marketing at Copenhagen Business School. His research interests include international and intercultural marketing and consumer behaviour; consumers' attitude structure, change, and psychological processing of market entities such as brands and tourist destinations; the role of emotions in consumer and tourist behaviour and decision making; and the role of prejudice and stereotyping in consumer behaviour. He conducts quantitative studies in the areas of marketing, tourism, management, and psychology involving the conceptual development, operationalization, and empirical validation of new constructs and scales, as well as nomological networks.

Mateja Kos Koklič is an Associate Professor of Marketing at the Faculty of Economics, University of Ljubljana. She received her PhD in marketing from University of Ljubljana's Faculty of Economics in 2007. Her primary teaching responsibilities include undergraduate and graduate courses on consumer behaviour, consumer psychology, and marketing. Her research focuses on consumer behaviour, particularly in digital piracy and sustainable consumption contexts. Her work has been published in *Behavior & Information Technology*, *Computers in Human Behavior*, *Journal of Business Ethics*, *Journal of Business Research*, and other outlets. She regularly presents at various national and international conferences, such as the European Marketing Academy's regional conference, the American Marketing Association conference, and the International Management Conference. She has been an ad hoc reviewer for *Behavior & Information Technology*, *Computers in Human Behavior*, *Electronic Commerce Research Journal*, and other journals.

Tomaž Kolar is an Associate Professor at the Faculty of Economics, the University of Ljubljana. His interests and research work mainly focus on consumer behaviour and strategic marketing issues, examined across various service domains such as leisure, tourism, culture, and play. In particular, he is interested in exploring consumer experiences with and managerial implications of diverse contemporary and traditional phenomena, socio-cultural contexts, and entrepreneurial practices. He has published in journals such as *Current Issues in Tourism*, *Evaluation Review*, *International Journal of Contemporary Hospitality Management*, *Journal of Business Research*, *Marketing Intelligence and Planning*, and *Tourism Management*.

Turgay Kerem Koramaz graduated in 1999 from Istanbul Technical University's Department of Urban and Regional Planning, Faculty of Architecture. He received his MSc degree in urban design and his PhD degree in urban and regional planning with a dissertation on the perception of urban historic sites through computer-aided three-dimensional representation and visualization techniques. He was visiting scholar in Royal Institute of Technology, Graduate School of Built Environment and Architecture, Stockholm in 2008. He has worked in Istanbul Technical University's Department of Urban and Regional Planning, Faculty of Architecture since 2000. He has published on spatial analysis, internal migration in Turkey, urban conservation, and renewal. He also teaches systems approaches to urban planning, planning methods, information and communication technologies, and research methods in urban design. He is involved in academic research and professional activities pertaining to spatial analysis in urban planning, urban conservation, and regeneration.

Maria Lichrou is a Lecturer in Marketing at the University of Limerick. At present, she is a visiting researcher at the University of Brighton. Her research focuses predominantly on narratives of place and generally adopts an emic perspective to understand the connections among place, tourism, and consumption. Together with colleagues in Brighton and Limerick, she is researching heritage consumption and memories of migration.

Roxana Magee recently obtained her PhD degree from Ulster University. Her most recent study focuses on service management, specifically, servicescape management and co-creation marketing in the heritage tourism sector. Her research interests include services marketing, co-creation marketing, and tourism industry marketing.

Lisa O'Malley is a critical marketing scholar. Her research considers the impact of marketing relationships on the co-creation of value and the role and impact of marketing within society (sustainability, family life, and individual agency). Current work involving tourism explores consumers' search for meaning and authenticity, opportunities (and challenges) for value co-creation, and the impact of such processes on the production and consumption of place.

Aggelos Panayiotopoulos is a Lecturer at the University of Brighton. His research focuses on tourism development, with a critical perspective. Drawing on political discourse theory, his work unpacks the political, cultural, and spatial aspects of tourism and the impacts on places and people. He is currently researching the phenomenon of overtourism in a post-socialist context and is involved in research on heritage consumption and memories of migration, exploring intrapersonal and interpersonal processes in the (re)construction of heritage experiences.

Anthony Patterson is Professor of Marketing at the University of Liverpool's Management School. Much of his research aims to provide a snapshot of current cultural practices, to explore how these phenomena affect consumer behaviour. His other research interests include digital consumption, nation branding, and book marketing. His publications have appeared in *Journal of Consumer Research*, *Journal of Service Research*, and *Psychology & Marketing*, among others.

Maurice Patterson is an interpretive consumer researcher at the University of Limerick. Maurice's key research interest centres on the relationship between consumption, embodiment and identity, and his work uncovers the connections between body-related consumption, individual identity projects and marketplace cultures. His work on tourism largely focuses on narratives of place. Recent work investigates how creolised sonic ecologies resonate with people alternately and simultaneously as tourists, shoppers and music fans on the streets of New Orleans.

João Rebelo was awarded his PhD in economics in 1993 from the University of Trás-os-Montes and Alto Douro (UTAD). He is Professor in Microeconomics and Econometrics at the same university. He undertakes his research within the Centre for Transdisciplinary Development Studies, where he researches and publishes on scale and scope economies, efficiency and productivity analyses, governance and property rights, market and organizations, consumer behaviour, and discrete choice models.

Cristina Ribeiro holds an MSc in Applied Statistics (2015) and a BSc in Mathematics (2006), both from the University of Trás-os-Montes and Alto-Douro (UTAD). She has participated in several research projects, principally through statistical data analyses with a special focus on multivariate analysis techniques, namely, categorical principal components analysis and cluster analysis.

Thongsa Sayavongkhamedy studied architecture and archaeology in Lao PDR and overseas in France and Australia before becoming the Director of the Department of National Heritage, Ministry of Information, Culture, and Tourism, in 2010.

He fostered the World Heritage listing of Wat Phu and Luang Prabang, while undertaking groundbreaking archaeological research at the Plain of Jars and studying the broader prehistory of Laos. Currently, he is the Heritage and Cultural Adviser to H.E. Minister of Information, Culture, and Tourism.

Stephen Schweinsberg is a senior lecturer in sustainable management at the UTS Business School. His research has been published *Journal of Sustainable Tourism* and *Tourism Management*. A recent co-authored monograph, *Marketing National Parks for Sustainable Tourism* (with Stephen Wearing and John Tower), was published by Channel View. His research interests focus on the sustainable management of tourism in national parks and other protected areas.

Joel Taylor graduated from Cardiff University in archaeological conservation with a BSc (honours) in 1996. He worked for the National Museums and Galleries of Wales and English Heritage as a practitioner before joining the University College London's Institute for Sustainable Heritage, initially as a researcher, before taking on the directorship of the master's program in sustainable heritage in 2008. During this time, he completed a part-time PhD in preventive conservation and developed research interests in heritage studies and heritage values. Upon moving to Norway in 2011, he worked for the University of Oslo before joining the Norwegian Institute for Cultural Heritage, where he worked on various projects related to conservation and heritage studies, including the Heritage Values Network (H@V). He currently works at the Getty Conservation Institute in California on an initiative to apply sustainable approaches to conservation practices through experimental studies, fieldwork, and teaching. He has published on assessment methods, conservation theory, heritage values, intangible heritage, preventive conservation, and sustainability in heritage, drawing on fields as diverse as archival studies, building science, cognitive psychology, cultural studies, digital humanities, engineering, intergenerational justice, moral philosophy, physics, and political science. He is an associate editor of *Studies in Conservation*.

Marilena Vecco is an Associate Professor in Entrepreneurship at Burgundy Business School. She holds a PhD in economic sciences from University Paris 1, Panthéon Sorbonne, a PhD in economics of institutions and creativity from the University of Turin (I), and an MBA executive in international arts management from the University of Salzburg Business School in collaboration with Columbia College, Chicago. Between 1999 and 2010, she was head of research of the International Center for Arts Economics and a research fellow and an adjunct professor of cultural economics and art markets at the University Ca' Foscari of Venice. Her research focuses on cultural entrepreneurship and management with a special focus on cultural heritage (tangible and intangible) and art markets. In 17 years of academic and professional experience as a researcher, lecturer, and consultant, she also has researched and consulted for several public and private organizations, including the OECD; Centre for Entrepreneurship, SMEs, and Local Development; the World Bank; and the European Commission. She is the author of several books including (with E. Konrad) *The Power of Partnerships: Necessity or Luxury in the Cultural and Creative Sectors?* and (with L. Lazzeretti) *Creative Industries and Entrepreneurship: Paradigms in Transition from a Global Perspective*, as well as articles published in journals such as *Creativity and Innovation Management*, *Journal of Cultural Economics*, *Journal of Cultural Heritage*, and *Journal of Economics Behaviour and Organisations*. She is a board member of the European network on cultural management and policy.

Stephen Wearing is a Conjoint Professor at the University of Newcastle. His research and projects relate to leisure and tourism studies, and his PhD research focused on sustainable forms of tourism. His early work was in the area of leisure and feminist theory; he has made contributions in other areas as well, including ecotourism, volunteer tourism, community development, and the importance of community-based approaches for leisure, recreation, and tourism sectors. His practical experience as a town, environmental, and park planner at local, state, and international levels provided him with real-world experiences that he leverages in his teaching and research. He co-founded and ran a volunteer tourism group (Youth Challenge Australia/Volunteers in Community Engagement), which started in 1992 and has worked in nine countries on over 500 community-based projects, many of them with women's groups in small, remote, and rural communities.

Leanne White is a Senior Lecturer in the College of Business at Victoria University in Melbourne. Her research interests include national identity, commercial nationalism, popular culture, advertising, destination marketing, and cultural tourism. She is the author of more than 50 book chapters and refereed journal articles. She is the editor of *Commercial Nationalism and Tourism: Selling the National Story* (2017) and co-editor of *The Palgrave Handbook of Dark Tourism Studies* (2017); *Advertising and Public Memory: Social, Cultural and Historical Perspectives on Ghost Signs* (2017); *Wine and Identity: Branding, Heritage, Terroir* (2014); *Dark Tourism and Place Identity: Managing and Interpreting Dark Places* (2013); and *Tourism and National Identities: An International Perspective* (2011). She lectures in undergraduate and postgraduate marketing while also supervising doctoral students. She is an occasional keynote speaker, regular reviewer of journal articles, thesis examiner, and member of professional associations dedicated to tourism, marketing, and sport.

Vesna Žabkar is Professor of Marketing at the University of Ljubljana's Faculty of Economics, where she also is a vice-dean for research and doctoral studies. A visiting scholar at Northwestern University (Fulbright Grant) and visiting professor at University of Vienna (Chair of International Marketing), she provides courses on marketing communications, strategic marketing analysis, marketing for managers, and digital marketing. Her research interests pertain to marketing communications, green marketing, and tourism marketing. Her work has been published in *Annals of Tourism Research*, *Journal of Business Research*, *Tourism Management*, and other outlets.

Sebastian Zenker is an Associate Professor at Copenhagen Business School. His current research interests mainly involve measures of place brands and place brand perceptions, as well as the relationship between residents and tourists. His work has been presented at various international conferences, as book chapters, and in peer-reviewed journals including *Cities*, *Environment and Planning A*, *International Journal of Research in Marketing*, and *Tourism Management*.

Foreword and acknowledgement

This systematic, interdisciplinary examination of cultural heritage seeks to provide an up-to-date view of the field by drawing on various disciplines. The 17 chapters in this anthology, thus, address a variety of issues pertaining to cultural heritage.

To start, Zara H. Hosseini, Florian Kock, and Alexander Josiassen offer "Heritage and Tourism: A Literature Review." In providing a thorough, structured review of extant literature on heritage in tourism, this chapter spans definitions and practical topics related to heritage management and tourism, along with various research perspectives and key trends and themes pertaining to both supply and demand aspects.

Rather than key trends, Stephen Brown considers pertinent challenges for cultural heritage in his chapter, "Poets Know It: Cultural Heritage and the Great Divide." An existing argument holds that culture is Great Britain's principal industry and greatest export, which requires marketing support. Yet culture and commerce are separated by a "Great Divide" that opened in the mid-nineteenth century and has become so deeply entrenched that it constitutes part of cultural industries' heritage. To bridge the gap, marketing should link to its own cultural heritage of artistic achievement, and the poetics of branding in particular.

The following three chapters all focus on values. In "Value and Values of Cultural Heritage," Marilena Vecco explores the values of cultural heritage, combining cultural and economic approaches, in an effort to clarify the concept and thereby identify appropriate methodologies and tools to assess heritage values, as part of an integrated, sustainable conservation process. She argues that these values are contingent and not objective; rather, they get "produced" by interactions of an object with its surroundings. Thus, cultural heritage values cannot be understood without reference to the social, historic, political, and cultural context.

By describing options for "Using Contestation to Elicit Values for Heritage Planning: The Case of the Urban Park at Ekeberg in Oslo, Norway," Torgrim Sneve Guttormsen and Joel Taylor outline how public heritage values can be elicited through planning and how contestation contributes significantly in multifunctional, poly-vocal spaces. They present Ekeberg Park in Oslo as an example of how multi-layered, contested public values get negotiated among various stakeholders. The park offers a democratic arena for discussions of societal issues, because it embodies various heritages and values, across different periods. Through an assessment based on distinct, valid heritage valuation methods, they determine that the different approaches provide varied representations of those values and potentially lead to unique implications for the park's future. The discussion about the park embodies a Bakhtinian idea of the marketplace as "Carnivalesque"—where low and high culture create friction—and a public space that reflects the multi-vocality of place. Recognizing complex, dynamic discourses thus is a valuable means to represent multi-layered values for public spaces.

Leanne White examines Australian popular culture, as represented in the Australian Icons segment of the closing ceremonies for the Sydney 2000 Olympic Games. With "Marketing Australia's Cultural Heritage: The Sydney Olympic Games Closing Ceremony," she explores key social and cultural aspects of Australia, broadcast strategically for tourism marketing and other purposes. Although the closing ceremony often gets overlooked in sport event tourism, studying it offers a new perspective on a significant global event. The chapter, thus, enhances understanding of the complex relationship among three discourses of nationalism, as an important subject of investigation.

Another set of three chapters relates to authenticity. First, Tomaž Kolar, Mateja Kos Koklič, and Vesna Žabkar argue that sustainability has replaced authenticity as a central tourism concern, but cultural heritage initiatives still require managerial models to depict authenticity. Therefore, in "Managing Sustainable Consumption of Cultural Heritage: The Key Role of Existential Authenticity," they identify existential authenticity as a key conceptual and managerial lever to encourage sustainable tourism consumption. Noting the "micro" conceptual relationships among existential authenticity and sustainability, the authors propose two basic mechanisms to reinforce sustainable consumption: self-affirmation and self-transcendence. With a broader conceptual model, they also predict how other relevant concepts relate to existential authenticity and sustainable consumption. The model and its resulting propositions provide foundations for managerially relevant measures and help fills this gap for sustainable cultural heritage tourism.

Second, with "Heritage as Embodied Co-Creation: 'Living the History' of the Titanic in Cobh," Aggelos Panayiotopoulos, Maria Lichrou, Lisa O'Malley, and Maurice Patterson cite the case of the Titanic Experience in Cobh, Ireland, to explore emerging understandings of heritage consumption and authenticity. To detail the role of authenticity in heritage tourism, they trace a shift from object authenticity to experience-based authenticity. Drawing (mainly) on auto-ethnographic observations, they also explicate the nature of their own interactions with specific elements of the experience and how it engaged them, in terms of the personal nature of the quest, transference and imagination, evocation and (re)construction of personal and collective memories, and ambivalence. The embodied experiences and interactions enable the co-creation of meaning relative to heritage consumption, such that it is necessary to acknowledge the combined roles of embodiment processes, sensations, and interactions to facilitate meaningful heritage experiences.

Third, building on the notion of "hot" (existential) and "cool" (objectivist) authentication, Laura Reynolds, Adam Lindgreen, and Michael Beverland demonstrate the importance of networks of stakeholders that co-create authenticity in the fore- and backgrounds of cultural heritage efforts. The intensive case study of Blaenavon's World Heritage Site (WHS) in "The People and Processes Underscoring Authentication of the Blaenavon World Heritage Site: Mediating 'Hot' and 'Cool' Authentication" details the benefits of partnerships and coordination efforts, particularly with the United Nations Educational Scientific Cultural Organization, and the practical and performative processes adopted by stakeholders in Blaenavon's visitor economy, local community, voluntary community, and local authority. Coordination is insufficient to relieve tensions among competing stakeholder claims, which instead requires its combination with symbolic and visible performative acts. In addition to specifying the importance of networks of stakeholders, this chapter accounts for stakeholder agency, especially among host-community volunteers and their significant impacts on authenticating the Blaenavon WHS. As guardians and ambassadors of cultural heritage, they transcend cool and hot authentication and instead provide sustainable, symbolic, supplementary input to the authentication process in this financially strained cultural heritage setting.

In a consideration of place concepts, Sebastian Zenker and Erik Braun then describe "Cultural Heritage as a Blessing and Curse for Branding Urban Destinations." City branding affects all place customers—residents, companies, tourists—and in this process, cultural heritage has a specific role. Branding often relies on simplified messages, but the effectiveness of such strategies for complex brands, like city brands, is questionable. Residents and business customers with specific knowledge of the place likely disagree with a simplified, touristic destination brand. Furthermore, the path dependency of place brands means that important prior developments remain relevant; their cultural heritage continues to inform perceptions among not only tourists but all stakeholders. The authors, thus, challenge "one-size-fits-all" city brands and instead call for more advanced brand management strategies that acknowledge target group-specific sub-brands. Such a strategy enables tourism experts, urban policymakers, marketing researchers, and (place) marketers to address place branding and appropriately integrate cultural heritage into their branding efforts.

A second chapter pertaining to place deals more with sensory perceptions. That is, Adriana Campelo argues in "Immaterial Heritage and Sense of Place" that people's senses connect them to the world and mediate perceptions of the sense of place. Therefore, sensory perceptions are part of the immaterial heritage of places. This chapter proposes including sensory knowledge in research agendas, with sensory capital as a key dimension to develop in place branding and marketing.

With her second contribution to this anthology, Marilena Vecco joins the theoretical debates about the economics of cultural heritage conservation. Focusing on built cultural heritage, she offers in "The Economic Calculation of Conservation" a detailed economic analysis of different meanings of conservation (re-use, restoration, and preservation) and their economic implications. Decision-making processes are key, especially when conservation objectives compete with other market interests or more valuable options for using the cultural heritage resource. To be sustainable in the medium and long term, an economic analysis must be integrated into heritage conservation discourses and narratives.

In an effort to define the abilities and functions of information and communication technologies for cultural heritage management, Turgay Kerem Koramaz presents "Information and Communication Technologies in Cultural Heritage Management." In addition to a comprehensive literature review, reflecting chronological, theoretical, and empirical perspectives, this chapter suggests ways to use information and communication technology tools for cultural heritage management, specifying some related policies and strategies for highlighting communication skills and membership in an information society. Widening the meaning of cultural heritage can facilitate the ability to respond to technological advances too.

With two chapters, this anthology also focuses, particularly, on the market. João Rebelo, Lina Lourenço-Gomes, and Cristina Ribeiro describe "Visitor Segments for the Alto Douro Wine Region Cultural Heritage Site: A Multivariate Approach." Adopting a demand-side approach to determine optimal provisions of cultural heritage goods, the first chapter identifies homogeneous groups—in their socioeconomic characteristics, cultural consumer experience, and travel/visit behaviour—who travel to a Portuguese world heritage site, the Alto Douro Wine Region. The univariate and multivariate statistical data analyses of a novel dataset reveal three main groups: same-day visitors, cultural visitors, and individual mass visitors.

Then with "Consuming our National Parks: Cultural Heritage in a Consumer Culture," Stephen Wearing, Stephen Schweinsberg, and Simon Darcy address how natural cultural heritage, exemplified by national parks, gets consumed through a neo-liberalist treatment of nature. Consumers' complex relationships with national parks have long encompassed economic use values, recreation and tourism interests, as well as conservation and cultural preservation forces. Commercialization of recreation and travel experiences enhances income generation, but the propensity toward commodification of park environments, by individual operators and a politically organized tourism industry, requires new means to align park marketing initiatives with cultural forces. This chapter concludes with some preliminary observations.

Finally, three chapters lift the covers to investigate looting and dark sites. First, Anthony Patterson proposes to "Let It All Fall Down: Delighting in Anti-Heroes, Alternative Heritage and Ruination." Cultural heritage operators embrace preservation and conservation, seemingly leaving little room for the purposefully cultivated squalor that marks alternative heritage. With a literary-inspired method, the author makes a case for ruination, contemplating the peculiar appeal of decaying, neglected places. The audience for such reifications of these desires may be larger than is generally assumed, marked by three common qualities: an interest in retroscendence, impoverished enrichment, and catharsis. Therefore, instead of rushing to impose preservation orders, heritage protectors might allow for a patina of decrepitation and brokenness to develop.

Second, in covering the "Conservation and Looting of the Tam Ting Caves and Its Impact on Lao Heritage Values," Brian Egloff and Thongsa Sayavongkhamedy provide a graphic example of the trade in illicit cultural property in South-East Asia. The Tam Ting caves in the Luang Prabang Province of the Lao People's Democratic Republic (Laos) hosted sculptures that underwent conservation and inventorying between 1992 and 1997. Then in 2010, as the extent of their looting became known, Tam Ting entered the World Monuments Watch. The full extent of the looting was determined in 2011; some 666 sculptures went missing. Empirical data document the unchecked illegal trade in cultural property in South-East Asia.

Third, different meanings get attached to dark heritage sites, and Audrey Gilmore and Roxana Magee describe this process in relation to concentration camps in "Re-thinking Places: From Dark Heritage Sites to Socially Symbolic Scapes." The concentration camps used to torture and murder Jews and other minority groups in the 1930s and 1940s are sites of death and dark events; until recently, visitors mainly were people with strong personal ties to the sites. But site managers need to shift existing perceptions of these places to engage with new, younger visitors who have no such personal ties. With an evaluation of site managers' and visitors' perceptions, the authors determine that rather than being dark places, the sites are meaningful places that offer society a space to strengthen its commitment to humanitarian values, re-think moral codes, and learn from the atrocities of the past.

Closing remarks

We extend a special thanks to Routledge and its staff, who have been most helpful throughout this entire process. Equally, we warmly thank all of the authors who submitted their manuscripts for consideration for this anthology. They have exhibited the desire to share their knowledge and experience with the anthology's readers—and a willingness to put forward their views for possible challenge by their peers. We also thank the reviewers, who provided excellent, independent, and incisive consideration of the anonymous submissions.

We hope that this compendium of chapters and themes stimulates and contributes to the ongoing debate surrounding cultural heritage. The chapters in this anthology can help fill some knowledge gaps, while also prompting further thought and action pertaining to the multiple aspects surrounding cultural heritage.

Adriana Campelo, PhD
Salvador, Brazil

Laura Reynolds, M.Sc.
Cardiff, Wales

Adam Lindgreen, PhD
Copenhagen, Denmark
Pretoria, South Africa

Michael Beverland, PhD
Sussex, UK

1 Heritage and tourism

A literature review

Zara H. Hosseini, Florian Kock and Alexander Josiassen

Introduction

According to the United Nation World Tourism Organization, tourism ranks as the world's third largest export category after chemicals and fuel and ahead of automotive products and food. International tourist arrivals (overnight visitors) in 2016 have reached a total of 1,235 million worldwide, an increase of 46 million over the year before, and the seventh year of uninterrupted growth in international tourism (UNWTO Tourism Highlights, 2017).

Today, visiting heritage sites and cultural areas are among the most popular purposes behind traveling (Timothy, 2011). Many destinations thus count on their culture and heritage for their tourism performance, and even the destinations not known as heritage destinations offer some components of culture and heritage to the visitors as a part of their product mix (Timothy, 2011). However, profit is not the only value heritage adds to the local communities. Heritage can also provide cultural and educational benefits for destinations, or create local or national identity and pride (Alazaizeh, Hallo, Backman, Norman, & Vogel, 2016). It is thus not surprising that there is a large and growing body of literature on heritage. The purpose of this chapter is to provide an extensive review of seminal works in the field of heritage and heritage tourism.

First and foremost it should be clarified what we are referring to when talking about heritage. United Nations Educational, Scientific, and Cultural Organization (UNESCO) classifies heritage into two main categories: Cultural heritage and natural heritage.

Cultural heritage

The first aspect is cultural heritage. Cultural heritage encompasses the legacy of physical artifacts and intangible attributes of a group or community that are inherited from previous generations, maintained in the present and conserved for the future (UNESCO, 2017). Cultural heritage is further divided into tangible and intangible forms:

- Tangible cultural heritage: Tangible heritage has many variations and can exist in different scales "from single buildings to entire cities and, arguably, countries" (Mckercher & Ho, 2005). In UNESCO's classification, tangible heritage is divided into three categories:
  - movable cultural heritage (paintings, sculptures, coins, manuscripts)
  - immovable cultural heritage (monuments, archaeological sites, and so on)
  - underwater cultural heritage (shipwrecks, underwater, ruins and cities)

- Intangible cultural heritage: Includes but not limited to oral traditions, customs, performing arts, ways of life, social practices, rituals, festive events, or the knowledge and skills to produce traditional crafts (UNESCO's Intangible Cultural Heritage document).

Natural heritage

The second category in UNESCO's classification is natural heritage, which involves natural sites with cultural aspects such as cultural landscapes, physical, biological, or geological formations.

By reviewing the existing literature on heritage, we can find different examples of heritage from tangible heritage in the museums (Hede, Garma, Josiassen, & Thyne, 2014; Hede & Thyne, 2010; Poria, Reichel, & Biran, 2006) and built heritage sites such as the Petra archaeological parks (Alazaizeh et al., 2016), to intangible heritage such as Flora Macdonald Scottish Highland Games (Chhabra, Healy, & Sills, 2003) and flamenco dance (Gonzalez, 2008) as the case or location of scholars' studies.

However, other examples of heritage can be found in the literature as researchers' case studies that are not specifically named in the UNESCO's classification of heritage. War heritage, intangible archeological heritage, and contemporary tourism heritage are three examples for the limits of the UNESCO heritage classification. War heritage involves artifacts and areas associated with war and other armed conflicts (Timothy & Boyd, 2003). The battlefield of Gettysburg (Chronis, 2005, 2012) and Kinmen battlefield (Zhang, 2017) are among war heritage areas that have been under scholars' examination within the heritage field of study. The second group of heritage which is not placed in UNESCO's classification is intangible archaeological heritage. In their study, Ross, Saxena, Correia, and Deutz have defined intangible archaeological heritage as "knowledge emanating from actors' own interpretation of archaeological sites that have either become physically inaccessible or been destroyed since initial exploration" (2017, p. 1). Further, they point out that this type of heritage should not be confused with intangible cultural heritage which involves customs and oral traditions inherited from previous generations. The third example of heritage type is acknowledged by Weaver (2011) as 'contemporary tourism heritage'. Contemporary tourism heritage is examined by Weaver and acknowledged as a valid form of heritage that has been mostly ignored by scholars as well as industry professionals (2011). According to Weaver (2011), contemporary tourism heritage includes the local heritage of tourism cities, created through the contemporary mass tourism industry. He provides evidence from Las Vegas and the Gold Coast, two famous tourist cities in the world for supporting his argument. For instance, he uses the 'Welcome to Fabulous Las Vegas' highway sign as an example of tourism heritage, belonging to a recent past and at the same time legitimate for being acknowledged as tourism heritage and ultimately being safeguarded.

On the one hand, as discussed above, there are some forms of heritage, mostly recognized in recent years, which are not clearly placed in UNESCO's category of heritage. On the other hand, the division between heritage categories is unnatural and out of date (Alvarez, Go, & Yuksel, 2016). Similarly, Kirshenblatt-Gimblett (2005) notes that the division between cultural and natural or tangible and intangible heritage is "arbitrary, though not without its history and logic" (p. 2). For instance, it can be discussed that many of the sites considered as world natural heritage sites have been in fact affected and reshaped by the interaction between humans and nature through time (Kirshenblatt-gimblett, 2005). As a result, considering the uncertainty of UNESCO's heritage classification and the complexity of heritage, in this chapter we use the term 'heritage' in the broad sense, encompassing these different types of heritage.

In this chapter, our aim is to offer a better understanding of heritage as it relates to tourism. The chapter is structured as follows: First, we examine the various definitions suggested by scholars for heritage. We then provide a comprehensive review of existing literature on heritage, addressing the following key topics: Heritage production, heritage management, heritage tourism, and heritage tourism motives.

Heritage definition

As stated by Timothy and Boyd (2003), heritage should not be regarded as synonymous with history. While history is the recording of the past as exactly as possible, heritage is an "archive of selective stories" of the past that communities choose to tell about themselves (Bryce, Murdy, & Alexander, 2017, p. 3). Accordingly, "heritage is not simply the past, but the modern-day use of elements of the past" (Timothy & Boyd, 2003, p. 4). These two qualities of presentness having a linkage to the past are in fact common between some of the other existing definitions of heritage as well. Kirshenblatt-Gimblett (1995) for instance, define heritage as; "a mode of cultural production in the present that has recourse to the past" (p. 4).

The notion of heritage, as also acknowledged by UNESCO, has broadened over the last century and now covers a wider range of elements. Accordingly, a shift from viewing heritage as something that is 'already there' to the perspective of seeing heritage in a "state of becoming" (Zhang, 2017, p. 1) can be seen in the literature. Chhabra et al. (2003) for example argue that heritage is being "created and re-created from surviving memories, artifacts, and sites of the past to serve contemporary demand." Alvarez et al. (2016) take this argument further to the extent which they state that heritage can be produced in any place, at any time, as long as there is a market for it.

Literature review

While attempts at defining heritage are continued by many scholars, others implicitly follow Garrod and Fyall's (2001) approach, suggesting that instead of getting caught up in defining things, researchers should spend more time studying the practical importance of those concepts. This is also well stated by Timothy and Boyd (2003); "the significance and value that lie within heritage are not in how it is defined, but in how it is used to create meaningful experiences for tourists" (p. 281). Accordingly, we also move beyond definitions and investigate the studies which have discussed heritage in practice. A summary of the key academic articles in the heritage field can be found in Table 1.1.

Heritage production

As mentioned earlier, "the commercialisation of history overflows the fixities of traditional heritage stuff to include active and creative (re)production of heritages by local communities" (Zhang, 2017, p. 1). According to Chhabra et al. (2003), staging entails relocation of cultural production from one place to another and making adjustments to suit new conditions of time and place. Today, heritage production and reproduction play an important role in supplying heritage for tourist. One of the recent studies in the field of heritage production is the work of Chronis (2012), investigating tourism imaginaries in the battlefield of Gettysburg. He notes that "commercial staging is both

Table 1.1 A summary of notable studies on heritage

Author(s), (date)	*Case study and location*	*Purpose of study*
Aas, Ladkin, & Fletcher (2005)	Luang Prabang, Laos	To explore the relationship between heritage management and tourism development through stakeholder collaboration
Alazaizeh, Hallo, Backman, Norman, & Vogel (2016)	Petra Archaeological Park, Jordan	Understanding tourists' value orientations in order to achieve sustainability in heritage tourism
Bruner (1994)	Lincoln's New Salem Site, USA	To discuss staging and reproduction from a constructivism perspective
Bryce, Murdy, & Alexander (2017)	27 different sites, Scotland	To explore ancestral tourism experiences
Caton & Santos (2007)	Route 66, USA	Exploring tourists' experiences visiting and traveling along the Route 66 and examining the role of nostalgia in their experiences
Chhabra, Healy, & Sills (2003)	Flora Macdonald Scottish Highland Games, USA	To analyze and measure perceived authenticity among visitors at a staged cultural event
Chronis (2005)	Gettysburg battlefield, USA	Introducing a coconstruction model for culture production at heritage sites
Chronis (2012)	Gettysburg battlefield, USA	Understanding and theorizing tourism imaginaries
Garrod & Fyall (2000)	Different built heritage sites, UK	Investigating different aspects of heritage management and their important roles in achieving sustainability in heritage tourism.
Garrod & Fyall (2001)	N/A	To respond to Poria, Butler and Airey's (2000) comment on Garrod & Fyall (2000)
Gonzalez (2008)	Japanese flamenco, Japan	Examining the relationship between intangible heritage tourism and personal identity
Kirshenblatt-Gimblett (1995)	N/A	Theorizing heritage
Kirshenblatt-Gimblett (2005)	N/A	Understanding the notion of heritage
Masberg & Silverman (1996)	USA	Understanding visitors' perspectives on the experience of visiting heritage attractions
Massara & Severino (2013)	Three World Heritage Sites, Italy	Exploring heritage tourism experience and introducing the concept of psychological distance into heritage studies
McCain & Ray (2003)	Venezuela, Ecuador, Costa Rica, the Provence region of France, and Alaska.	To explore a sub-segment of heritage tourism identified as legacy tourism
Mckercher & Ho (2005)	Hong Kong	Examining the relationship between tourism and cultural heritage management
Moscardo (1996)	N/A	To introduces the notion of mindfulness and to develop a model for designing effective interpretation at heritage sites.

(continued)

Table 1.1 Continued

Author(s), (date)	*Case study and location*	*Purpose of study*
Poria, Butler, & Airey (2001)	N/A	To comment on Garrod and Fyall's (2000) paper "Managing Heritage Tourism"
Poria, Butler, & Airey (2003)	Israel	To investigate the relationships between tourists' motives, behavior, and perceptions with their perception of the heritage sites.
Poria, Reichel, & Biran (2006)	Anne Frank House, the Netherlands	Investigating the link between tourists' perceptions and their motives for visiting a heritage site.
Richards (1996)	9 European countries	To explore the demand and supply aspects of cultural tourism
Richards (2002)	43 cultural attractions in Europe and 3 in Australia	Exploring cultural tourism attraction system
Ross, Saxena, Correia, & Deutz (2017)	N/A	Rethinking the archeological tourism framework from a creative perspective
Silberberg (1995)	N/A	Conceptualizing cultural tourism aspects
Timothy (1997)	N/A	Outlining the role of personal attachment to the heritage in tourists experiences
Weaver (2011)	Las Vegas, USA and Gold Coast, Australia	To explore contemporary tourism heritage
Zhang (2017)	Kinmen	Rethinking the concept of heritage in post-conflict tourism

narrative (storytelling) and material (statues, markers, memorials, and museum artifacts)" (p. 15). Stories that are attached to a place have the potential to convert it into a unique tourism destination. He highlights this point and continues to argue that tourism narratives are imaginary and it is through commercial staging that otherwise unnoticeable places being staged as narrative places become attractive tourism destinations. (Chronis, 2012) Similarly, Kirshenblatt (1995) asserts that 'actuality' and 'virtuality' are different approaches in heritage production. She argues that "we travel to actual destinations to experience virtual places...this is one of the several principles that free tourism to invent an infinitude of new products" (p. 12).

Heritage management

Several scholars have studied heritage management issues such as heritage conservation and sustainable tourism (e.g., Alazaizeh et al., 2016; Garrod & Fyall, 2000; Waligo, Clarke, & Hawkins, 2013), and the relationship between tourism and heritage management (e.g., Aas, Ladkin, & Fletcher, 2005). Management of heritage is multifaceted and challenging. When developing management and marketing strategies, decision-makers should take different stakeholders' benefits into consideration. They should not forget that the heritage and culture that is being presented to tourists is the heritage of the native people as well and it is thus necessary to assure them that by sharing their heritage with visitors they are actually gaining some sort of benefits and their voices are being heard by the management (Timothy & Boyd, 2003).

One of the other challenges faced by heritage site management is related to the balance that should be kept between conservation and contemporary use of heritage (Garrod & Fyall, 2000). The relationship between the tourism and heritage industries has been always a complicated one. Kirshenblatt-Gimblett (1995) view heritage and tourism industries as 'collaborative industries' considering that heritage transforms locations to destinations, and tourism makes them financially feasible by attracting visitors to those locations. However while heritage tourism, as a flourishing industry, can be considered as a source of profit and opportunities for many destinations, at the same time it can be viewed as a threat source, concerning the potential destruction of the heritage assets (Aas et al., 2005).

As Garrod and Fyall (2000) assert, there is a group who look into heritage management from a sustainability perspective and value the preservation of heritage properties for the future generations. The other group though, argues that limiting the present generation's access to heritage properties, in the purpose of saving the heritage for the future, will just prevent the heritage from being a part of the current generation's heritage (Garrod & Fyall, 2000). Therefore, the challenge for the management of heritage sites is to achieve sustainability by managing tourists in a way that enhances the quality of their experience and at the same time conserves heritage properties and resources for the future (Alazaizeh et al., 2016).

According to Mckercher and Ho (2005), the key to successful heritage tourism is creating a mature relationship between two groups of stakeholders; heritage management and tourism management. The tension between these two groups of stakeholders is derived from the fact that heritage organizations' main purpose is to protect and conserve heritage, whereas tourism management's main focus is on turning the heritage to a profitable business (Aas et al., 2005). Mckercher & Ho (2005) define the desired mature relationship as a relationship in which "both sets of stakeholders have a realistic appreciation of the tourism value of the asset, the need to conserve its core cultural values, an overriding acceptance that each stakeholder has a legitimate interest in the asset and each has a clearly defined role to play in promoting cultural tourism" (p. 8).

While the importance of involving different stakeholders, from heritage managers to tourism managers (Mckercher & Ho, 2005) and local people (Timothy & Boyd, 2003; Alvarez et al., 2016), in managing heritage attractions has been emphasized in the literature, one group of stakeholders has been mostly ignored; tourists (Alazaizeh et al., 2016). Alazaizeh et al. (2016) point out that to achieve sustainability in heritage tourism it is essential to involve and understand value orientations of different stakeholders including tourists in decision-making.

Heritage tourism definition

The continuous growth of visits based on cultural and heritage interests has led to a growing body of literature on heritage tourism. Accordingly, there are several different definitions of heritage tourism in the literature, however, as stated by McCain and Ray (2003), they are nowhere near being consistent. Perhaps the most general definition accepted by many researchers is "tourism related to what we have inherited" (McCain & Ray, 2003, p. 1).

Yet other scholars suggest more specific definitions. Some, for instance, rely on tourists' motives in their definitions of heritage tourism (e.g. Poria et al., 2001, 2003; Poria et al., 2006; Silberberg, 1995). Silberberg (1995) defines cultural tourism as "visits by persons from outside the host community motivated 'wholly or in part' by interest in the historical, artistic, scientific, or lifestyle/heritage offerings of a community, region, group, or institution" (p. 1). Poria et al. (2001) define heritage tourism by a smaller margin, considering personal heritage tourism as the core of heritage tourism by stating "…to clarify the nature of heritage tourism as a phenomenon which, at its core, has not the heritage attributes of a specific site, but rather the motivation to visit it, both in relation to that site's attributes and the tourists' perception of their own heritage" (p. 1). They draw attention to the fact that heritage tourism and historic tourism should be distinguished from each other based on visitors' motivations. Historic tourism is defined by them as visits based on historic attributes of the place. Heritage tourists can always be considered as historic tourists, however, the reverse cannot always be accurate. (Poria et al., 2001).

Chhabra et al. (2003) define heritage tourism from two perspectives; the demand and the supply points of view. They note that on the demand side, heritage tourism is based on contemporary tourists' wish to experience and consume a variety of past and present heritage landscapes, cultural performances, foods, handicrafts, and engaging activities. In terms of supply, however, heritage tourism is mostly viewed as a tool for destinations' economic development and it is mainly encouraged and supported by governments.

It is worth mentioning that the heritage tourism concept is an "overlapping concept" having common characteristics and mutual landscapes with nature tourism (ecotourism), urban tourism, and mostly with cultural tourism (Timothy & Boyd, 2003, p. 9). The overlap and vagueness of the division between heritage and cultural heritage have led to the usage of the terms interchangeably (e.g. McCain, & Ray 2003; Timothy, 2011) in the literature or using one term as an umbrella term surrounding the other one. Cultural tourism is mostly used to refer to people visiting and engaging in cultural performances, built heritage, living cultures, art, and other contemporary culture components based on people's motivation to culturally educate themselves or satisfy their cultural needs (Timothy, 2011). As noted by Timothy (2011), no significant difference can be identified between cultural tourism and heritage tourism characteristics, since "consuming living and built culture in rural or urban contexts and their own personal experiences, including education and cultural edification, are an important part of the heritage tourism experience" (p. 5). Accordingly, in this chapter, we use heritage tourism and cultural tourism terms interchangeably.

Heritage tourist characteristics

Scholars classify the heritage market based on their demographic characteristics. Demographic characteristics provide heritage suppliers and marketers with generalized information that help them to understand heritage tourists' needs and desires (Timothy & Boyd, 2003).

According to scholars, on average, heritage visitors have high education levels (e.g. Richards, 1996; Silberberg, 1995; Timothy & Boyd, 2003). In his study based on a survey of 6,400 participants, Richards (1996) indicate that cultural tourists are generally highly educated and belong to higher socioeconomic groups. Furthermore, the survey's results showed that 29% of the specific cultural tourists – tourists who have traveled to a place specifically for its cultural offerings – had an occupational link with the cultural industries (Richards, 1996). In terms of gender, it is suggested that cultural tourism includes more women than men (Richards, 1996; Silberberg, 1995). Concerning age, studies suggest different assumptions. Timothy and Boyd (2003), for instance, note that heritage tourists tend to be in younger age categories in comparison to other tourists. However, the exact opposite view has been stated by Silberberg (1995).

Heritage tourism motives

Among the researchers studying heritage tourism, many emphasize the importance of tourists' motivation for visiting heritage sites in their studies and suggest different motives such as; search for knowledge and learning about the past (Bruner, 1994; Richards, 2002), personal meanings (Massara & Severino, 2013; Poria et al., 2001, 2003; Poria et al., 2006; Timothy, 1997), to feel connected to ancestors (Bryce et al., 2017; McCain & Ray, 2003), and nostalgia (Bruner, 1994; Chhabra et al., 2003) for visits to heritage sites.

Poria and his colleagues examine the relationship between tourists and the heritage visited in several studies (Poria et al., 2001; 2003; Poria et al., 2006). They identify three categories of heritage visit motives; the desire to feel connected to the history presented, the desire to learn, and motives not linked with the historic attributes of the site (Poria et al., 2006). They highlight the point that "there are differences between heritage tourists and tourists at heritage places" (Poria et al., 2003, p. 12), and the difference mainly lies in the tourists' perception of heritage settings, meaning whether they perceive it as part of their own heritage (Poria et al., 2001).

Earlier the notion of personal heritage was used by Timothy (1997) as one of the different levels of heritage tourism experience including world, national, local, and personal experience. While millions of people travel to historic destinations without feeling a need for finding a personal attachment to the sites, millions of other people travel to those places with the purpose of experiencing a "heritage of a more personal nature" (Timothy, 1997, p. 1). Later on, McCain and Ray (2003) introduced the term 'Legacy tourism' in their study on personal heritage tourism. They define "Legacy tourists" as those who travel to "engage in genealogical endeavors, to search for information on or to simply feel connected to ancestors and ancestral roots" (p. 1).

As stated by Richards (1996) not every tourist visiting a cultural or heritage attraction can be considered as a cultural or heritage tourist. Silberberg (1995) suggests different degrees of motivation for cultural tourism; 'greatly motivated by culture', 'motivated in part by culture', those whom culture is an 'adjunct to another main motivation', accidental cultural tourists, and, finally those who would not attend a cultural attraction at all. The first group involves tourists who travel to a destination because they are particularly interested in its cultural offerings. The second segment includes tourists who travel to a city motivated by the city's cultural offerings as well as any other motivation such as visiting friends or family. The third category in Silberberg's cultural tourism market segmentation involves those whose main travel motivation does not involve culture, but they still plan to include cultural attractions in their visit. The fourth segment, which is called accidental cultural tourists, are those who do not have any intention to visit any cultural site or event while visiting a city, however, they somehow happen to visit one. Finally, there is a group of tourists and local residents who would not visit any cultural attractions under any circumstances. This group is not considered as a part of the cultural tourism market by Silberberg. (1995)

A group of scholars (e.g. Chhabra et al., 2003) gives the centrality to nostalgia as the main motivation for heritage tourism, or consider nostalgia as one of the major elements of the tourists' experience (e.g. Bruner, 1994). Bruner (1994) states that many tourists view the heritage sites with a sense of nostalgia for a bygone age when people were living simpler and more natural. Chhabra et al. (2003) refer to nostalgia as a global "catchword for looking back" (p. 4). In their study, they indicate that nostalgia plays an important role in the participants' heritage visit satisfaction. People are in search of nostalgic feelings and they want to relive the bygone days through tourism (Chhabra et al., 2003).

Yet others consider heritage tourism experiences as more complex than nostalgia theory would suggest (e.g. Caton & Santos, 2007). Caton & Santos (2007) argue that tourists experience at heritage sites is complex and multifaceted or in Masberg and Silverman's (1996) sense, multidimensional, thus it cannot be explained simply by the nostalgia theory. Caton and Santos (2007) emphasize the importance of tourists' perceptions of their experiences in their research on tourists traveling along Route 66, One of America's first transcontinental highways, and in their findings they reveal a number of meaningful elements of the tourists' experiences identified by tourists themselves, including; historical education, interaction with diverse landscapes, interaction with hosts, and personal growth. They draw attention to the fact that in their study tourists experiences did not appear to be characterized by nostalgia, as it is conceptualized in the tourism literature.

Conclusions

Having adopted a broad-based approach, in this chapter we review the literature across key topics in the field of heritage as it relates to tourism. Dominant definitions for heritage and heritage tourism from the literature have also been presented. Overall, this chapter gives an overview and understanding of the key areas involved in heritage tourism.

References

Aas, C., Ladkin, A., & Fletcher, J. (2005). Stakeholder collaboration and heritage management. *Annals of Tourism Research*, *32*(1), 28–48. https://doi.org/10.1016/j.annals.2004.04.005

Alazaizeh, M. M., Hallo, J. C., Backman, S. J., Norman, W. C., & Vogel, M. A. (2016). Value orientations and heritage tourism management at Petra Archaeological Park, Jordan. *Tourism Management*, *57*, 149–158. https://doi.org/10.1016/j.tourman.2016.05.008

Alvarez, M. D., Go, F. M., & Yuksel, A. (2016). *Heritage Tourism Destinations Preservation, Communication and Development*. USA: CAB International.

Bruner, E. M. (1994). Abraham Lincoln as Authentic Reproduction: A Critique of Postmodernism. *American Anthropologist*, *96*(2), 397–415.

Bryce, D., Murdy, S., & Alexander, M. (2017). Diaspora, authenticity and the imagined past. *Annals of Tourism Research*, *66*, 49–60. https://doi.org/10.1016/j.annals.2017.05.010

Caton, K., & Santos, C. A. (2007). Heritage Tourism on Route 66: Deconstructing Nostalgia. *Journal of Travel Research*, *45*(4), 371–386. https://doi.org/10.1177/0047287507299572

Chhabra, D., Healy, R., & Sills, E. (2003). Staged authenticity and heritage tourism. *Annals of Tourism Research*, *30*(3), 702–719. https://doi.org/10.1016/S0160-7383(03)00044-6

Chronis, A. (2005). Coconstructing heritage at the Gettysburg storyscape. *Annals of Tourism Research*, *32*(2), 386–406. https://doi.org/10.1016/j.annals.2004.07.009

Chronis, A. (2012). Between place and story: Gettysburg as tourism. *Annals of Tourism Research*, *39*(4), 1797–1816. https://doi.org/10.1016/j.annals.2012.05.028

Garrod, B., & Fyall, A. (2000). Managing Heritage Tourism. *Annals of Tourism Research*, *27*(3), 682–708.

Garrod, B., & Fyall, A. (2001). Heritage tourism: a question of definition. *Annals of Tourism Research*, *28*(4), 1049–1052. https://doi.org/10.1016/S0160-7383(00)00068-2

Hede, A.-M., Garma, R., Josiassen, A., & Thyne, M. (2014). Perceived authenticity of the visitor experience in museums. *European Journal of Marketing*, *48*(7/8), 1395–1412. https://doi.org/10.1108/EJM-12-2011-0771

Hede, A. M., & Thyne, M. (2010). A journey to the authentic: Museum visitors and their negotiation of the inauthentic. *Journal of Marketing Management*, *26*(7–8), 686–705. https://doi.org/10.1080/02672571003780106

Kirshenblatt-Gimblett, B. (2005). From ethnology to heritage: The role of the museum. *History*, 1–8.

Kirshenblatt-Gimblett, B. (1995). Theorizing Heritage. *Ethnomusicology*, *39*(3), 367–380.

Masberg, B. A., & Silverman, L. H. (1996). Visitor experiences at heritage sites: a phenomenological approach. *Journal of Travel Research*, *34*(4), 20–25. https://doi.org/10.1177/004728759603400403

Massara, F., & Severino, F. (2013). Psychological distance in the heritage experience. *Annals of Tourism Research*, *42*, 108–129. https://doi.org/10.1016/j.annals.2013.01.005

McCain, G., & Ray, N. M. (2003). Legacy tourism: The search for personal meaning in heritage travel. *Tourism Management*, *24*(6), 713–717. https://doi.org/10.1016/S0261-5177(03)00048-7

Mckercher, B., & Ho, P. S.Y. (2005). Relationship between tourism and cultural heritage management: evidence from Hong Kong $, *26*, 539–548. https://doi.org/10.1016/j.tourman.2004.02.018

Poria, Y., Butler, R., & Airey, D. (2001). Clarifying heritage tourism. *Annals of Tourism Research*, *28*(4), 1047–1049. https://doi.org/10.1016/S0160-7383(00)00069-4

Poria, Y., Butler, R., & Airey, D. (2003). The core of heritage tourism. *Annals of Tourism Research*, *30*(1), 238–254. https://doi.org/10.1016/S0160-7383(02)00064-6

Poria, Y., Reichel, A., & Biran, A. (2006). Heritage site management: Motivations and expectations. *Annals of Tourism Research*, *33*(1), 162–178. https://doi.org/10.1016/j.annals.2005.08.001

Richards, G. (1996). Production and consumption of European cultural tourism. *Annals of Tourism Research*, *23*(2), 261–283.

Richards, G. (2002). Tourism attraction systems: Exploring cultural behavior. *Annals of Tourism Research*. https://doi.org/10.1016/S0160-7383(02)00026-9

Ross, D., Saxena, G., Correia, F., & Deutz, P. (2017). Archaeological tourism: A creative approach. *Annals of Tourism Research*, *67*, 37–47. https://doi.org/10.1016/j.annals.2017.08.001

Silberberg, T. (1995). Cultural tourism and business opportunities for museums and heritage sites. *Tourism Management*, *16*(5), 361–365. https://doi.org/10.1016/0261-5177(95)00039-Q

Timothy, D. J. (1997). Tourism and the personal heritage experience. *Annals of Tourism Research*, *24*(3), 751–754. https://doi.org/10.1016/S0160-7383(97)00006-6

Timothy, D. J. (2011). Cultural Heritage and Tourism An introduction. Bristol, United Kingdom: Channel View Publication Ltd.

Timothy, D. J., & Boyd, S. W. (2003). Heritage Tourism. England: Pearson Education Limited.

UNESCO. (2017). Tangible Cultural Heritage. Retrieved October 2017. From https://en.unesco.org/

UNESCO Intangible Cultural Heritage. Retrieved October 2017. From https://ich.unesco.org/doc/src/01851-EN.pdf

UNESCO. (2006). Towards sustainable strategies for creative tourism: Discussion report of the planning meeting for 2008 international conference on creative tourism (CLT/CEI/CID/2008/RP/66). Retrieved from http://unesdoc.unesco.org/images/0015/001598/159811e.pdf

UNWTO. (2017). UNWTO Tourism Highlights: 2017 Edition. Retrieved October 2017. From http://mkt.unwto.org/publication/unwto-tourism-highlights

Vidal Gonzalez, M. (2008). Intangible heritage tourism and identity. *Tourism Management*, *29*(4), 807–810. https://doi.org/10.1016/j.tourman.2007.07.003

Waligo, V. M., Clarke, J., & Hawkins, R. (2013). Implementing sustainable tourism: A multi-stakeholder involvement management framework. *Tourism Management*, *36*, 342–353. https://doi.org/10.1016/j.tourman.2012.10.008

Weaver, D. B. (2011). Contemporary tourism heritage as heritage tourism: Evidence from Las Vegas and Gold Coast. *Annals of Tourism Research*, *38*(1), 249–267. https://doi.org/10.1016/j.annals.2010.08.007

Zhang, J. J. (2017). Rethinking "heritage" in post-conflict tourism. *Annals of Tourism Research*, *66*, 194–196. https://doi.org/10.1016/j.annals.2017.06.005

2 Poets know it

Cultural heritage and the great divide

Stephen Brown

This is the way the world ends
Not with a Bing but a Twitter.

—Anonymous[1]

Alternative Ulster

Established in 1929, the Ulster Museum is the principal repository of cultural heritage in Northern Ireland. Among other things, its thirty-three airy galleries tell the tales of human habitation – and associated material culture – from prehistory to the present. Starting with the first subsistence settlements of Stone Age hunters and gatherers, through the affluent agriculturalists of the bedazzling Bronze Age, past the gilded glories of Celtic culture in the early Christian era, to the majestic steam hammers, water mills and linen looms of the Industrial Revolution, the Ulster Museum is a repository of outstanding Irish accomplishment.[2]

In addition, the museum contains a fairly small but beautifully formed collection of oil paintings by eminent British and Irish artists (including Bridget Riley, Francis Bacon and Jack B. Yeats); it boasts resplendent shards from King Philip II's ill-starred Spanish Armada (which floundered around Ireland's north coast in September 1588); and, as befits a museum with eminent Victorian forebears, it possesses all sorts of bizarre bits and pieces (including Takabuti, a much-loved ancient Egyptian mummy, as well as four massive Qianlong Emperor bronze bells, which stand sentinel outside the former main entrance). Recently refurbished at a cost of £17 million, the new and improved Ulster Museum is one of the top five visitor attractions in Northern Ireland and won the UK's Museum of the Year award in 2010 (ahead of the Ashmolean).

A few years ago, to coincide with the post-remodelling relaunch, I was asked to contribute to a promotional venture. The basic idea was that 26 professional writers from Northern Ireland would be allocated a "treasure" from the Ulster Museum's collection and tasked with penning a 62-word summary – a prose poem, in effect – about the artefact. Paired with 26 graphic designers, who'd provide a visual version of the narrative, the ensuing works and the artefacts themselves would form the basis of a month-long museum exhibition, complete with the requisite glossy catalogue.[3]

For my sins, which are manifold and various, I was entrusted with a Stone Club. Approximately eight thousand years old, the cudgel came from a Mesolithic settlement in the Bann Valley, one of the earliest human habitations in the north of Ireland. As a lapsed archaeologist, albeit more of a Mohenjo-daro, Çatal Höyük, Cuneiform B kind of guy, I was thrilled with the treasure I'd been awarded. Along with my equally enthusiastic graphic designer, we zoomed off to Gallery Fourteen (Early Peoples) to get a feel for our beat-on-the-brat Ulster bludgeon.

Two things immediately struck me. First, the stone club looked brand new, almost as if it had been picked up off the streets of inner city Belfast after a 21st-century recreational riot.[4] It was a fantastic sight. Formidable rather. My mind was already racing with prose poem possibilities. Second, we weren't allowed to touch it, hold it, to get a sense of its heft in the hand. Yes, we asked for the display case to be opened. Naturally, we offered to wear protective gloves or whatever was considered necessary. Heck, I'd have donned a biohazard suit if that's what it took to get a proper feel for the thing. But no. Touching wasn't allowed. Look all you like. Take all the flash photographs you need. Touching's prohibited, though. The curator says no.

And it wasn't just me, he or she said no to. All 26 of us, 52 if the designers are added, were denied access to the artefacts we'd agreed to encapsulate – for free – on behalf of the museum's rebranding exercise. Some of the writers, what's more, were very well-known figures in the Irish arts community who were giving of their time so unstintingly. They too were given the look-don't-touch treatment.

All became clear, however, when one of the head honchos from the museum finally descended from his eyrie to thank us for our participation. His body language and general demeanour – to say nothing of the anodyne accompanying remarks – made it blindingly obvious that he loathed marketing, promotion, PR and anything, basically, that smacked of spin. I couldn't help feeling that he detested the people he'd (almost) entrusted his treasures to. If I'd had a stone club in my hand at the time, I might have been tempted to try it out for size…

Anyway, the exhibition went ahead as planned; the glossy catalogue was published as promised; and the event was very well attended, I'm reliably informed. I chose not to go myself, largely on account of the museum's anti-marketing attitude. My 62 words on the cudgel made it clear what I'd choose to do with the artefact had I been granted access as requested. Meanwhile, my designer decided to daub the club with (photoshopped) graffiti. So I guess he felt the same way as well.

The Great Divide

On reflection, I realize I should've known better. The curatorial cabal, in my long and painful experience, don't like grubby marketing types messing with their collections of marvels. Akin to Gollum with his "precious", they are overprotective to the point of madness. A few years ago, while working with colleagues on the *Titanic* brand, we interviewed a prominent movie producer who recounted all sorts of horror stories concerning his dealings with the custodians of Ulster's *Titanic* archive.[5] I myself once interviewed the marketing managers of several open-air heritage museums and, without exception, they spoke of the anti-marketing mentality within their organizational hierarchy. In one case, the curators had insisted that all signage be removed from the buildings – a collection of reconstructed farmhouses from different eras – because there were no signs on them back in the eighteenth century. Contemporary signage, therefore, was impermissible. Visitors to the attraction, needless to say, were utterly bamboozled by this peremptory decision. I stood and watched them staring at their guidebooks, trying to work out where they were, while turning their sitemaps round and round in order to identify the benighted building before them.[6]

I feel much the same way when thinking about marketing in the cultural industries. At a time of steep budget cuts and ever-rising cost pressures on arts organisations, they need marketing as never before. The recent digitized disintermediation of the sector means that "each artist, regardless of temperament, must become his or her own producer, promoter, and publicist".[7] The business community, conversely, is less hostile to artistic types than it used to be. The importance of creativity, imagination, innovation and out-of-the-box thinking is appreciated more than ever by managers. And artists, if nothing else, are founts of creativity who'd never dream of descending to a dreadful clanking cliché like out-of-the-box thinking.[8]

Yet for all that, the so-called Great Divide between culture and commerce is as evident as ever.[9] According to the *Economist*, "most businesspeople assume that artists are a bunch of pretentious wastrels...and seldom take the arts seriously".[10] On the opposite side of the chasm, meanwhile, there's Adele. When the multi-platinum-selling chanteuse was asked about her personal "brand", the soulful torch singer threw a strop, insisting that "I am not going to act, not going to release an autobiography, not going to release a perfume, not going to design a range of clothing. I don't want to be a brand".[11]

In a similar vein, Jason Statham, the go-to tough-guy in many popcorn blockbuster movies, is equally adamant that he isn't a brand.[12] When asked, in *Details* magazine, whether he viewed himself as a brand, he politely replied "F*** no, why should I?" Indeed, he said he couldn't understand why people kept describing him as a brand. "F*** 'em," he spat, in keeping with his USP as Hollywood's hard man of the moment, "I'm not a brand. Kim Kardashian's a f***ing brand".[13]

Even something as innocent as Arthur's Day, an annual celebration of the sainted Arthur Guinness – the man who crafted the eponymous Irish brew – has fallen into the Great Divide. After six years working together successfully, several prominent Irish musicians, including the great Christie Moore, complained bitterly about creeping commercialisation.[14] Huh? Given that the event was invented by Guinness, and that the musicians were well paid to participate, and that the brewery had previously sponsored many of their tours, this was as clear a case of biting the hand that feeds you as it is possible to imagine.

Our heritaged age

The divide between art and mart may not be as great as it was when Bill Hicks, an acerbic stand-up comedian, was urging despicable marketing types to kill themselves ("There is no excuse for what you do. You are Satan's little helpers. You are Satan's scum filling the world with bile and garbage. Kill yourselves."), or for that matter when Jim Morrison, the debauched rock star, was taking a sledgehammer to Buicks on-stage (since GM had the temerity to use a Doors' song in its TV advertising). Both sides now (reluctantly) recognize that they need one another, not least because we live in a heritaged age. These days, developed countries like Great Britain increasingly depend on exporting cultural products rather than the iron and the steel and the widgets and the worsted that once characterized the world's workshop. As Sandbrook explains in *The Great British Dream Factory*, Britain has morphed from a country that used to lead the world in making things into a country that has the most successful popular culture in the world.[15] And the proof, Goodwin goes on, is in the gigantic pudding of stupendous sales figures where "only Shakespeare and the King James Bible have sold more copies than Agatha Christie, *The Lord of the Rings* remains the second bestselling book after *A Tale of Two Cities*, the Beatles are still the most popular band of all time, Harry Potter has sold more copies than any other children's series, and no film franchise has lasted as long as 007".[16]

Just as culture is commerce these days, so too the past is present, the vintage is in vogue, the old-fashioned is new-fangled and history is bucks not bunk. We live in a world, according to Wilson[17] and Lowenthal[18], where sustainability, recycling, nostalgia, retrospection, restoration and wall-to-wall heritage loom large. In *Retromania*, his compendious companion to contemporary popular culture, Reynolds contends that the first decade of the 21st century comprised nothing but remakes, reboots, reissues, reinventions, rereleases, and non-stop nostalgia.[19] Although, he observes, retro is most prevalent in popular music...

> ...there's also retro toys (crazes for everything from the View-Master to the Blythe Doll of the early seventies) and retrogaming (playing and collecting old-school computer, video and arcade games from the eighties). There's retro food (sandwich chain Pret A Manger offers "Retro Prawn on Artisan", a sort of poshed-up sandwich version of that seventies fave the Prawn Cocktail) and there's also retro interior design, retro candy, retro ring-tones, retro travel and retro architecture. You even get retro-style commercials on television now and then, like the one for Heinz Baked Beans that mega-mixes snippets from vintage UK ads from the sixties, seventies and eighties, capped off with the imperishable slogan Beans Meanz Heinz.[20]

So popular has heritage become that it sometimes seems as if every other blockbuster movie is a prequel or sequel or reboot or set in the dim and distant past (*Star Wars*, *Spectre* and *The Man From Uncle* among them), every other big-name sports brand sells a range of heritage sneakers (such as the once futuristic now anachronistic Nike Air Max), every other famous fashion label is rifling through its archive, à la Dior and YSL, or taking its cue from nostalgic television series like *Poldark*, *Sherlock*, or *Downton Abbey*; and every fast moving consumer good with a long-tailed legacy has either disinterred its former logo or resurrected long-dead taglines or rebirthed half-forgotten mascots or reconsecrated an old-fashioned brand name, as the recent reinvention of Old Spice bears brilliant witness.[21]

The cultural heritage of consumer society is paralleled, arguably, by the cultural heritage of the cultural industry. That is, by the continuation of the Great Divide. Nowadays, there is no logical reason for the culture–commerce chasm. Everyone knows that artists have to make money to keep making their art. Everyone knows that business needs canny, creative, commercially-minded culturepreneurs. Yet the chasm is always there, like death and taxes and Starbucks.[22] It keeps yawning away before us when its mouth should surely be closed in a mannerly manner. In the cultural sphere, indeed, the word "brand" is normally enclosed by inverted commas, as a kind of distancing device or contamination prevention measure.

Why is that? And what can we do about it?

Why, oh why?

Creatives' antipathy to commerce is conventionally dated to the rise of the Romantic Movement in the 19th century. Appalled by the excesses of the Industrial Revolution, and the attendant disruption of traditional communities, families, working practices and so forth, Romantic artists celebrated the wondrous countryside, lionized the agricultural labourer and deliberately distanced themselves from the money-grubbing, city dwelling, unutterably philistine bourgeoisie. According to one self-appointed authority, "the archetype of the unappreciated artistic genius toiling without reward in an insalubrious garret dates from the romantic epoch, as does the elitist disdain felt towards those who prostitute their talent by pandering to the tastes of the petit bourgeois hordes".[23]

This thumbnail sketch of Romanticism's revolutionary impact – and the part it played in the propagation of the anti-commercial artistic ethos that lingers like a spectre at the feast – is of course a convenient caricature. Romanticism was a richly variegated movement that emerged at different times in different countries and whose distinguishing features were so diverse as to defy description.[24] The Lakeland Poets and their anti-industrial ilk were fairly important but far from representative. Lord Byron and Sir Walter Scott, to name but two of Romanticism's leading lights, were very canny businesspeople.[25] Byron not only penned advertising slogans for a proprietary brand of boot polish (anonymously admittedly) but later burnished his personal brand to such a shine that its lustre remains undimmed. Scott lived by his pen, sold books by the bucketload and, alongside Burns, concocted Scotland's still extant place brand – the triumvirate of tartan, thistles and tam o' shanters. His novels were the deep-fried Mars bars of their day. Lord Byron, by contrast, was more of a deep-fried Russell Brand.

The reality, Rowland shows, is that:

> ...the romantic period witnessed the emergence of the modern "free" market in artworks. The patronage of the aristocratic few was replaced, for the first time, by the capricious demands of a mass audience. Many of the literati, moreover, actually hailed from, or had close connections with, the trading classes. Blake was an engraver by profession, Southey the son of a draper, Keats came from a family of ostlers and Coleridge was sponsored by those celebrated proto-marketers, the Wedgwoods... Many romantics were torn between "giving the customers what they want" and remaining true to their calling, their inner light, their vision, their muse.[26]

If not the romantics themselves, where does the archetype of the penurious artist in a garret come from? What's the root cause of artists' elitist disdain for those who prostitute their creative powers by selling out? A strong case can be made for Bohemianism. As Nicholson recounts in her detailed account of the emergence and spread of Bohemian lifestyles, "Bohemia" was an enchanting imaginary country.[27] It was a wonderful place where artistic, aesthetically-minded escapees from the repressive rules, morals and mores of the Victorian era could find relief among like-minded people. The prototype of the Bohemian lifestyle was laid down in Henry Murger's influential novel of 1845, *Scenes de la Vie de Boheme*, later immortalized by Puccini in *La Bohème*. Murger's artistic lifestyle – wild, free, reckless, feckless, exuberant, ostentatious, anarchistic – proved enormously appealing to the golden youth of the Gilded Age, who descended on Montmartre's ramshackle studios with immortality in mind.[28] All too often, however, their undiscovered artistic genius remained undiscovered and death rather than glory was their unfortunate fate:

> Bohemians felt they were inheritors of a kingdom where the rich man cannot penetrate. Being penniless qualified one for a higher form of life than that offered by Victorian society. It is arguable that the very label Bohemian, with its romantic echoes of far-off lands, was adopted to give status to the poor who might otherwise have sunk without trace into the gutter. And the direr their Bohemian distress, the more it sanctified the conviction that art was worth making sacrifices for. Contempt for money was the extension of this position. If poverty is an imperative for the artist –

as many believed it to be – then wealth was to be derided, regarded as sordid and corrupting to the integrity of the artist. Bohemia on the whole felt a psychic distaste for Mammon.[29]

The idea of the outsider artist – someone implacably opposed to the machinations of The Man – thus emerged in the mid-nineteenth century. And it has informed every subsequent avant-garde movement in the arts, including impressionism, post-impressionism, fauvism, cubism, imagism, vorticism, surrealism and abstract expressionism (not to mention the monstrosities that are modernism, postmodernism and post-postmodernism). Bohemianism is integral to the artistic mind-set. It is inculcated by art colleges and perpetuated in innumerable BoHo enclaves from Greenwich Village to St Ives. It is made manifest in manifesto after manifesto after manifesto after manifesto, all determined to oust the establishment, defenestrate the bourgeoisie and inaugurate a brave new world where money doesn't matter and art for art's sake obtains.[30]

What can we do about it?

The Great Divide, then, is an important aspect of the cultural industries' cultural heritage. And it's unlikely to disappear anytime soon. Far from being a pose struck by exhibitionist narcissists – a lifestyle choice of sorts – it is nothing less than an ideology.[31] It is a deep-seated belief system that can't be cast off like last year's fast fashion, let alone an Aquascutum trench coat. It's impervious to gentle persuasion or authoritarian diktat. As for rational argument, forget about it! The Great Divide, akin to the Great Wall of China, is implacable, impregnable, imperishable, impervious to imposition, imploration or importunity.

So what should marketing do? The obvious answer is absolutely nothing, because Bohemianism is good for business. As Thomas Frank shows in his classic text *The Conquest of Cool*, countercultural consumers have long been a lucrative market.[32] You want to rebel? We'll sell you the tie-dyed tee-shirt and artfully distressed jeans, as well as the beads, bangles, sandals and suchlike that every self-respecting non-conformist needs. The final scene of *Mad Men*, where Don Draper envisages "Hilltop", the iconic Coca-Cola ad that taught the hippy-dippy world to sing in perfect harmony, exemplifies the rebel sell.[33] The BoHo look, Nicholson likewise notes, remains a steady seller. The sub-culture's influence is felt in many realms of contemporary consumer society ranging from apparel and travel to entertainment and interior design. We are all Bohemians nowadays.

This let-sleeping-artists-lie attitude is all very well. It forms the basis of Brooks' much-debated BoBo argument, whereby bohemians are becoming ever more bourgeois and the bourgeoisie is embracing bohemianism like it's going out of fashion.[34] The Great Divide, in other words, is slowly closing. Artists increasingly appreciate that, just as sisters are doing it for themselves, so too screenwriters, songwriters, storytellers and suchlike must do marketing too.[35] Art plus mart is smart. So stop the rot. Close the gap. Top the chart. Or the shopping cart at least.

Unfortunately, the art-for-art's-sake ideology is far too deeply embedded. It is certain to remain so as long as high-profile acts like Adele and Jason Statham – hardly the most avant of the avant-garde – parrot their adherence to the prehistoric party line. Branding is bad. Marketing is malevolent. Advertising is the spawn of Satan. The disdain heaped on E.L. James for having the temerity to write a mega-selling series of pornographic novels and Banksy's Disneyesque Dismaland, a post-apocalyptic critique of extortionate American theme parks, are a testament to the continuation of artists' anti-commercial ethos.

If, however, cultural heritage is crucial for the economic health of the nation, then hands-off needs to be taken in hand.[36] A helping hand is necessary.[37] As Thompson and Tian show in their study of counter-memory in the southern states of America, the best way to combat ideology is not through critique or condemnation (i.e., "You artistic types need to get your act together. Shape up and start selling!"), but by articulating an alternative ideology that somehow rings true.[38]

The most obvious candidate in this regard is artists' entrepreneurial instincts. The old idea that business is bad to the bone is belied by ample evidence of poet-preneurship, painter-preneurship, playwright-preneurship or any other artist-prefixed, preneurship-suffixed neologism you prefer.[39] Whether it be Madonna or Taylor Swift or Damien Hirst or Jeff Koons or J.K. Rowling or James Patterson, or indeed the highest of the high modernists, such as Samuel Beckett, James Joyce, Ezra Pound and W.B. Yeats, there's never been a shortage of commercial nous in the artistic community.

There's a famous story told about Picasso, for example, where an affluent American admirer visited his Parisian studio while the great man was working on a baffling abstract canvas. "What's it about?" the befuddled plutocrat inquired. "About forty thousand dollars," Picasso replied. Picasso, as Muñiz et al. make clear, was a painter-preneur par excellence.[40] He didn't just paint canvasses, he canvassed canvasses as well.

Consider also T.S. Eliot, often regarded as the absolute epitome of the avant-garde artist pouring scorn on the noisome bourgeoisie. The reality, however, was that he was a very astute operator, a commercially minded authorpreneur with business in his blood. He was the youngest son of a successful Midwestern industrialist, who built the Hydraulic Press Brick Company into a thriving regional brand. He began his first business venture at the age of eleven, a self-published magazine called Fireside, which contained spoof advertisements for popular brands of patent medicine. His first published poem, "The Love Song of J. Alfred Prufrock", was named after a department store in his home town of St. Louis and his later oeuvre is replete with matters mercantile, to say nothing of ample brand name-dropping. As everyone knows, furthermore, Eliot was not only employed by Lloyds Bank of London but promoted to high office therein. He was, in the words of his most recent biographer, "a poet with a business brain".[41]

The mote in marketing's eye

Despite abundant evidence of artistpreneurship – Dickens was a demon marketing man, Shakespeare lived or died by his box-office, Mozart sold his musical wares on subscription – it remains to be seen whether creative artists will wake up from their marketing slumbers. Artists' seeming determination to dismiss their more successful rivals as sellouts, bread-heads, media-whores, etc. might hold water when directed at the likes of Madonna or Kiss, the cartoonish hard rock band, both of whom make no bones about their move-the-merchandise mind-sets. However, it's hard to deny T.S. Eliot's or Pablo Picasso's artistic accomplishments, much less Shakespeare's.

Part of the problem, I reckon, lies with us. We marketing types not only lack artistic credibility, but we're hypocrites to boot. That is to say, we're happy to lecture artists on the benefits of brand building and business planning even as we deny our own artistic patrimony. Marketing sees itself as a rigorous social science, for the most part. It hides its cultural heritage under a cloak of multivariate statistics and psych-lab experimentation. The ancient "art or science" debate was convincingly lost by the former.[42] True, there is a small group of scholars clustered around CCT (Consumer Culture Theory) who adopt an aesthetically-aligned approach to the subject. However, they are very much a marginalised minority, an anti-managerial coterie with a critical chip on their collective shoulder.

Marketing must change if it wants creative types to take it seriously. It needs to get in touch with its inner artist and take cognizance of its cultural heritage. Consider, for instance, the poetics of branding. When it comes to brand names, the more poetic they are, the more memorable and powerful they prove to be.[43] Kodak, Kindle, Kinkos, Kickers, Kit-Kat, Coca-Cola, Calvin Klein, Krispy Kreme, Kimberly-Clark, Kellogg's Corn Flakes, the Kardashian Kollection – to name but a few voiceless velar plosives – catch the ear, trigger the synapses and trip off the tongue, not unlike Pentium, Amazon, Airbus, Oreo, Twitter, Tumblr, Swiffer, Under Armor, Dunkin Donuts, Reese's Pieces, Sweaty Betty, Black & Decker, I Can't Believe It's Not Butter.

Poetic resonance is equally apparent in slogans, taglines and jingles, the last of which hark back to the earliest days of poetry when odes were sung and epics chanted.[44] Syncopated slogans sell well, what's more: I Like Ike, J'Adore Dior, Intel Inside, Must See TV, Beanz Meanz Heinz, Less Flower More Power, Loose Lips Sink Ships, Camel Tastes Good Like a Cigarette Should, Chocolate Heaven Since 1911, Let the Train Take the Strain, Tetley Makes Teabags Makes Tea, A Mars a Day Helps You Work, Rest and Play, You Can't Fit Quicker than a Quik-Fit Fitter.

Longer-form advertising copy also adheres, on occasion, to the rules of poetic rhetoric. Doggerel, indeed, was de rigueur in the ad campaigns of the early twentieth century, when H.G. Wells was waxing lyrical about the poetry of commerce and consumer behaviour both:[45]

Once Beauty bore a sunshade large
To shield her soft white skin
And o'er her charming features fair
An envious veil did pin.

But now in old Sol's burning rays
She dares to sweetly slumber
For Beetham puts her all to rights
With Glyc'rine and Cucumber!

It was equally evident in the 1950s, when television advertising made its memorable debut:[46]

Double your pleasure, double your fun
With double good, double good, Doublemint Gum.
Double delicious, double smooth too,
Doublemint's double delightful to chew.
So double your pleasure, double your fun
Get double everything rolled into one.
Oh, double your pleasure, double your fun
With double good, double good, Doublemint Gum.

And it's just as popular today. Big, blue-chip brands like McDonald's, Santander, Virgin Media, BBC Radio, McCain's Oven Chips, Cathedral City Cheese and the Nationwide

Building Society have employed – or are employing – poetry for promotional purposes. To good effect, apparently. Recitation enriches. Sonnets sell.

Pedagogy can be poetic as well. Apart from eminent educators with a flair for clever coinages – "marketing myopia" (Theodore Levitt), "niches are riches" (Philip Kotler), "tales make sales" (Sidney Levy) – poetry can communicate meaningful marketing messages (and research findings) in an expressive, invigorating manner.[47] The field's fondness for acronyms, acrostics and alliterative aides memoir is similarly indicative of its poetic inclination. SWOT, PEST, STP, USP, the 3Cs, the 4Ps – 5Ps? 6Ps? – the seven Ss, the eight Es, the thirty Rs of relationship marketing that riddle student textbooks and research reports both, may have become ridiculous and risible through overuse. But that doesn't diminish their poetic power.

Poetry, in fact, is ideally suited to the short-form forms of marketing communication – tweets, texts, hashtags, et al – that prevail in today's Netflixed, Dropboxed, Facebooked, Instagrammed, Buzzfed, iTuned, eBayed, Linkedin, Ubertous, Snapchatty, selfie-centred, app-for-that, iPhone-a-friend society. It's a society where learned academic articles go unread and voluminous research reports gather dust on the shelves of corner offices worldwide. Poems, by contrast, pack a lot into a little.[48] They are a better and more original metaphor for 21st-century branding than the onions, icebergs, pyramids, prisms, wheels and what have you that continue to appear in our reputedly rigorous marketing textbooks. As Clive James observes, advertising copywriters and marketers more generally are blessed "with every poetic gift except the ability to live on a pittance".[49]

It seems to me that just as artistic types need to wake from marketing slumbers, so too marketing types need to raise themselves from the scientific sepulchre.

Hell's bells

The chances of marketing coming to its senses, renouncing pseudo-science and embracing the artist within are of course slim verging on anorexic. However, stranger things have happened. I used to live quite close to the Ulster Museum and walked past its imposing exterior on my way to work. The great bronze Chinese bells that stood outside were endlessly fascinating to begin with but soon blurred into the background of my rush-to-work routine. Then, one day, all hell broke loose. Two of the mighty bells had been toppled in the night. They lay there on their sides like beached whales in burnished bronze. Commuters stopped and stared, wondering who or what had done the dirty deed and whether it was an omen of end times. The earth hadn't moved in the night – it never did for me back in those days – nor was Belfast's often-inclement weather responsible for the heinous act of aesthetic anarchy. The only possible explanation was that they'd been overthrown by human hand. But the bells weighed a ton. Several tons more like. They say, of course, that drunks have the strength of ten men and Irish drunks have twice that. I presume therefore that an Irish drunk, or ten, took the bells in hand and hurled them over. Maybe they used a lever. An old stone club, perhaps. Wonder where they got it from?

The museum, as I recall, was packed with visitors for the next few days, all keen to see the fallen idols. A cherry-picker was called in due course – when visitor numbers had dwindled, naturally – and order was finally restored. I wonder, though. I sometimes wonder whether it was a publicity stunt all along. Or indeed the work of a wannabe guerrilla marketer who just happened to live nearby.[50]

Notes

1 FYI, I am Anonymous. I'm also Spartacus on occasion. But that's our little secret.
2 Bourke, M. (2011), *The Story of Irish Museums 1790-2000: Culture, Identity and Education*, Cork: Cork University Press. BTW, I'm aware that the old tripartite trajectory, Stone Age, Bronze Age, Iron Age, is out of favour with the archaeological establishment. However, it's still widely used in everyday discourse.
3 Simmons, J. (2012), *Twenty-six Treasures: 4 National Museums, 104 Objects, 62 Words Each*, London: Unbound.
4 The term recreational rioting was coined by a Northern Irish police officer to describe the high jinks that some young people get up to during Ulster's combustible "marching season".
5 Brown, S., McDonagh, P. & Schulz, C.J. (2013), "Titanic: consuming the myths and meanings of an ambiguous brand", *Journal of Consumer Research*, Vol. 40, No. 4, pp. 595-614.
6 Brown, S., Hirschman, E.C. & Maclaran, P. (2000), "Presenting the past: on marketing's re-production orientation". In S. Brown & A. Patterson, (Eds.), *Imagining Marketing: Art, Aesthetics and the Avant-Garde*: pp. 145-191. London: Routledge.
7 Timberg, S. (2015), *Culture Crash: The Killing of the Creative Class*, New Haven: Yale University Press, (p. 7).
8 The Economist (2014), "Philosopher kings: business leaders would benefit from studying great writers", *The Economist*, October 4, p. 80.
9 Huyssens, A. (1988), *After the Great Divide: Modernism, Mass Culture, Postmodernism*, Basingstoke: Macmillan.
10 The Economist (2011), "The art of management: business has much to learn from the arts", *The Economist*, February 19, p. 70.
11 Sherwin, A. (2011), "The secret of Adele's success? No festivals, tweeting or selling out", *The Independent*, May 24, www.independent.co.uk, accessed 29 April 2014.
12 Statham appears in anything, basically, featuring fast cars, heavy weapons, kick-ass action and brain-dead dialogue. Not that I'd say it to his face, admittedly.
13 Solotaroff, I. (2012), "Jason Statham: the king of action films", *Details*, April 1, www.details.com, accessed 29 April 2014).
14 Fleming, D. (2013), "Irish Arthur's Day condemned", BBC News Northern Ireland, September 25, www.bbc.co.uk, accessed 15 October 2015.
15 Sandbrook, D. (2015), *The Great British Dream Factory: The Strange History of our National Imagination*, London: Allen Lane.
16 Goodwin, D. (2015), "Britain's got talent", *Sunday Times Culture*, October 4, pp. 38-39.
17 Wilson, J.L. (2005), *Nostalgia: Sanctuary of Meaning*, Lewisburg, PA: Bucknell University Press.
18 Lowenthal, D. (2015), *The Past is a Foreign Country Revisited*, Cambridge, Cambridge University Press.
19 Reynolds, S. (2011), *Retromania: Pop Culture's Addiction to its Own Past*, London: Faber.
20 If Reynolds were writing today, he might be tempted to add "And All Because the Lady Loves Milk Tray", an advertising tagline that's been resurrected by Cadbury's some forty-seven years on from its first appearance.
21 Iezzi, T. (2010), *The Idea Writers: Copywriting in a New Media and Marketing Era*, New York: Palgrave Macmillan.
22 The words "Starbucks" and "tax" should never be placed in the same sentence, since the omnipresent coffee chain takes great exception to taxes. But there's a first time for everything.
23 Yes, I am that self-appointed expert. Brown, S. (1998), "Stoning the romance: on marketing's mind-forg'd manacles". In S. Brown, A.M. Doherty & B. Clarke (Eds.), *Romancing the Market*, pp. 1-21. London: Routledge.
24 Day, A. (1996), *Romanticism*, London: Routledge.
25 Richards, T. (1990), *The Commodity Culture of Victorian England: Advertising and Spectacle, 1851-1914*, Stanford: Stanford University Press.
26 Rowland, W.G. (1996), *Literature and the Marketplace: Romantic Writers and their Audiences in Great Britain and the United States*, Lincoln: University of Nebraska Press. Paraphrased in Brown (1998), op cit.
27 Nicholson, V. (2003), *Among the Bohemians: Experiments in Living 1900-1939*, London: Penguin.
28 Roe, S. (2014), *In Montmartre: Picasso, Matisse and Modernism in Paris, 1900-1910*, London: Fig Leaf.
29 Nicholson, op cit., p.7.
30 Cottington, D. (2013), *The Avant-Garde: A Very Short Introduction*, Oxford: Oxford University Press.

31 Eagleton, T. (2007), *Ideology: An Introduction*, London: Verso.
32 Frank, T. (1998), *The Conquest of Cool: Business Culture, Counterculture and the Rise of Hip Consumerism*, Chicago: University of Chicago Press.
33 Heath, J. & Potter, A. (2004), *Nation of Rebels: How Counterculture Became Consumer Culture*, London: HarperCollins. Colin Campbell, the eminent sociologist, analogously argues (in *The Romantic Ethic and the Spirit of Modern Consumerism*) that contemporary consumer society is a direct consequence of the Romantic Movement, still seen by many as a forerunner of the anti-bourgeois avant-garde.
34 Brooks, D. (2001), *BoBos in Paradise: The New Upper Class and How They Got There*, New York: Simon & Schuster.
35 Timberg, op cit.
36 Sandbrook, op cit.
37 A light touch helping hand, I should say. Berating artists about branding will only prove counterproductive. As Timberg (op cit., p. 21) ruefully observes, quoting a disillusioned creative writer, "I've seen a lot of people go into marketing, or help companies that want to be 'cool'. What artists do now is help brands build an identity. They end up styling or set decorating. That's where we're at now".
38 Thompson, C.J. & Tian, K. (2008), "Reconstructing the South: how commercial myths compete for identity value through the ideological shaping of popular memories and counter-memories", *Journal of Consumer Research*, Vol. 34, No. 5., pp. 595-613.
39 See, for example, Fillis, I. (2014), "The artist as marketer and entrepreneur". In D. O'Reilly & F. Kerrigan (Eds.), *The Routledge Companion to Arts Marketing*, pp. 51-58. London: Routledge; Schroeder, J.E. (2010), "The artist in brand culture". In D. O'Reilly & F. Kerrigan (Eds.), *Marketing the Arts: A Fresh Approach*, pp. 18-30. London: Routledge.
40 Muniz, A.M., Norris, T. & Fine, G.A. (2014), "Marketing artistic careers: Pablo Picasso as brand manager", *European Journal of Marketing*, Vol. 48, No. 1/2, pp. 68-88.
41 Crawford, R. (2015), *Young Eliot: From St. Louis to The Waste Land*, London: Jonathan Cape.
42 As I've described in detail elsewhere, marketing's so-called "art or science debate" is a misnomer. There was no debate. Art never got a look in.
43 Sedivy, J. & Carlson, G. (2011), *Sold on Language*, Chichester: Wiley-Blackwell.
44 Stern, B.B. (1998), "Poetry and representation in consumer research: the art of science". In B.B. Stern (Ed.), *Representing Consumers: Voices, Views and Visions*, pp. 290-307. London: Routledge.
45 Richards, op cit., poem quoted on p. 233.
46 Sivulka, J. (2011), *Soap, Sex and Cigarettes: A Cultural History of American Advertising*, Belmont, CA: Wadsworth, advertising jingle quoted on p. 274.
47 Canniford, R. (2012), "Poetic witness: marketplace research through poetic transcription and poetic translation", *Marketing Theory*, Vol. 12, No. 4, pp. 391-409.
48 Sherry, J.F. Jr. & Schouten, J. (2002), "A role for poetry in consumer research", *Journal of Consumer Research*, Vol. 29, No. 2, pp. 218-234.
49 James, C. (2014), "Product placement in modern poetry". In C. James, *Poetry Notebook 2006-2014*, pp. 94-108, London: Picador.
50 Since you ask – no, I'm not the Spartacus responsible for the great Ulster overthrow. I have been known to work under pseudonyms, though! FYI, I checked out the bells while writing this chapter and they have since been moved indoors, for safety's sake presumably. It also turns out that they are a mixture of Chinese and Japanese artefacts, though it's the big Qianlong Emperor bell that sticks in my memory.

3 Value and values of cultural heritage

Marilena Vecco

Introduction

Built cultural heritage can be the subject of different evaluations that are, at times in conflict with one another. The *cultural significance*[1], or rather the multiple values linked to a cultural object – its economic, aesthetic, cultural, political, educational value, etc. – depends on the variety of stakeholders taking part in the heritage conservation process. Establishing these values when it is time to take decisions regarding its conservation and therefore meeting the needs of the numerous stakeholders is no simple task. What should be preserved? How? For whom? For how long? and so on.[2] These questions have to be answered in the context of the different value systems.

This paper explores the concept of values of cultural heritage combining cultural and economic approaches. Its goal is to clarify this concept to be able to identify the appropriate methodologies and tools to assess heritage values as part of an integrated and sustainable conservation process. It is structured as follows: we present a review of the evaluation process of cultural heritage which leads to the identification and attribution of the status of cultural heritage to items within our society. In section 2, we proceed with an analysis of the concept of value within the economic perspective to move later on to the cultural one (section 3), while in section 4 we analyze the typologies of value (cultural and economic) and provide a new taxonomy of these values. In section 5, we analyse two relevant concepts of the total economic value and complex social value within the evaluation process, pinpointing that the latter can capture a comprehensive set of values because it is based on the individual's centrality, without separating them from the community or ecological context. This complex social value reunites the economic and extra-economic evaluations. It makes it possible to preserve the multitude of agents interested in the cultural heritage resource.

The social and cultural process of creating heritage

If we go back to the distinction of the evaluation process – a fundamental part of cultural conservation – an initial division can be made between the economic value system that arises from the actual evaluation (the estimate of its current value), and the system of cultural values that arises from the valorisation process (the creation of value)[3].

Being a product of society that is regarded as "the relative condition of a thing or the consideration in which it is held, depending on its merit, utility or actual or presumed importance", the value of an asset is subject to both temporal and spatial changes[4].

When discussing cultural heritage, reference is made to the judgements of value that have developed over a period in a certain social, cultural and historic context. The creation process of these values depends on a multitude of parameters that are derived from a learning process in society, individual experience and their reactions to specific situations.

The values that are attributed to cultural heritage are contingent and are not objective in nature. They are "produced" by the interaction of the object with its surroundings and are not intrinsic to it. They cannot be understood if no reference is made to the social, historic, political, cultural context, etc.

In the cultural or economic field, the concept of value is the result of an active, dynamic process that can be defined as a concept *in fieri*. If the value is an element that makes it possible to distinguish between the two different fields, it can also be "[...] a starting point in a process of linking the two fields together, that is as a foundation stone upon which a joint consideration of economics and culture can be built"[5].

These values give things meaning, making it possible to isolate the objects in the social context and transform them into heritage. In fact, the ultimate aim of any conservation process is not to preserve the material nature of the objects but rather to defend the inherent values in the heritage.

It is thanks to the values recognized in certain objects that the process of the creation/production of heritage can begin (figure 3.1).

The theory of value from an economic perspective

The concept of value[6] is central to economic analysis and may be regarded as the origin or reason for any kind of economic behaviour.

In economic thinking regarding the concept of value[7], the obligatory starting point is Adam Smith's book *The Wealth of Nations* (1776). Smith was the first to introduce the distinction between the value of the use of an asset, or rather its capacity to satisfy one or

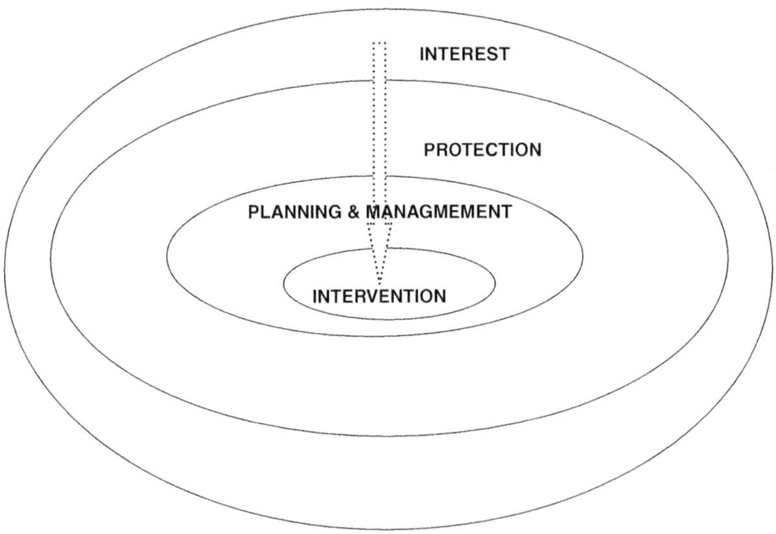

Figure 3.1 The process of the creation/production of heritage.

Source: Avrami E., Mason R., Torre M. de la (edited by, 2000), "Report on Research" in Avrami E., Mason R., Torre M. de la (edited by), *op. cit.*, p. 5.

more human needs, and the value of exchange, understood as the quantity of other goods and/or services that one is willing to offer to acquire a unit of the asset.

Following Smith and the political economists of the nineteenth century, the theories of value were based on the cost of production: The value of a good was the result of the costs of the input used for its production. Smith, followed by Ricardo and Marx developed theories of value, according to which the value of an asset was determined by the quantity of work it contained, or rather how much work was required for its production. According to Marx, any other factors of recompense (such as profits, interest, dividends, revenue) were an added value compared to the work value. His value theory was a distribution theory characterized by the relations in a social field.

During the eighteenth and nineteenth century, the distinction between the actual value and the natural value of the goods established itself: whilst the former was the result of "contingent causes" the second was determined by the production costs of the individual goods[8]. One value that was correlated to the latter was the intrinsic or absolute value; this was a sort of number or measure that could be attributed to a unit of an object regardless of an exchange and that had to remain unchanged in time and space.

Smith's definition of intrinsic value is based on the work theory. Ricardo goes back to this theory, distinguishing between absolute and relative values. The idea that absolute and natural ideas exist, Malthus also shared, was criticized by Samuel Bailey and other theoreticians who denied the existence of such values for goods. Ruskin himself was highly critical of the classic theory of value: Inspired by Carlyle, the idea that the value of an asset/good could be determined by the market processes and monetized was a violation of the principles of intrinsic value, according to which the value of objects can be established in advance. It establishes a connection between the value and work, characterized by the skill of the worker who produces the object to improve his efforts during his life.

At the end of the nineteenth century, the marginalists (Jevons, Menger and Walras) replaced the production cost theories with an economic behaviour model based on individual utility. According to the marginalists, individuals and their preferences comprised the last phase in the exchange and market process. The value was explained in terms of consumer's preferences for goods that could satisfy their needs. The utility theory represents the foundation of the consumer behaviour theory: Individuals have preferences that are ordered according to levels, and the marginal utility gradually decreases as the good consumption increases.

Since the value is a constructed phenomenon in a society, one must bear in mind that its determination and therefore also that of the prices cannot be isolated from the social context in which these processes take place. Veblen and Commons developed the social value theory, attacking the foundations of the marginalist theory of value, or rather, that consumers could formulate ordered preferences based on their needs alone, without being influenced by the institutional context, interactions and the social processes that regulate exchange.

The birth of cultural values[9]

The origins of value in the cultural field vary greatly to those regarding the economic domain. A long tradition of Western thought regards the true value of a work of art as the whole of its aesthetic, artistic and cultural qualities[10]. This position is characterized by extreme relativism, in the sense that the cultural value systems are not universal and can change in space and time: from one society to another, and from one period to another.

Throsby has put forward a set of cultural characteristics[11]:

- *the aesthetic value:* regarding the canons of beauty, harmony and form;
- *the spiritual value:* linked to a religious context, for example, an art work is of great value to the members of a religious community;
- *the social value:* regarding the work as a mirror of society, it can help the understanding of social nature and help create a feeling of identity[12];
- *the historic value:* the work reflects the living conditions of the period in which it was created, and can help an understanding of the present by showing continuity with the past;
- *the symbolic value:* just like any other element of cultural heritage, the work also refers to a certain system of values and symbols that is characteristic of every society;
- *the value of authenticity:* this value refers to the fact that the work is original and usually unique.

The typologies of value

There is a vast number of different types of values and the interactions between them can be highly complex. Any description of the values related to cultural heritage comes up against difficulties of both a conceptual and practical nature that hide the diverse expressions of the values of heritage (cultural, economic, social dimension, etc.). These are expressions of the same qualities recognized in heritage but seen from different perspectives, and incomparable with one another. Furthermore, one must also bear in mind that these values are relative and change in time and space.

The creation of a value typology could facilitate the understanding of the different evaluation processes that are involved in the preservation process of heritage while, at a later stage, allowing a comparative evaluation of the diverse heritage projects (table 3.2).

The different categories of values correspond to the different positions of the stakeholders involved in the process of the decision-making, organisation and conservation of the cultural heritage. These different ways of assessing heritage result in different approaches to conservation.

If one studies table 3.1, which summarises the key systems in the literature of values in reference to heritage, one can observe that the object being described remains the same while basically the way, approach and at times the descriptive levels change. It must be pointed out that several authors, for example, Randall (1987) or Allison et al. (1996), only analysed the purely economic values of heritage. On the other hand, in the Burra Charter the economic values are minimized as they are either regarded as derivations of cultural and historic values, or simply from a historic and artistic perspective (Riegl).

Later, a classification of the values founded on the distinction between the economic and cultural fields was put forward as it is these dimensions that are considered a semiotic asset of cultural heritage (Barrère and Santagata, 1999). Similarly, one must bear in mind that owing to the existence of cultural values and the fact that these goods produce external effects (that usually lead to the market collapsing), the exchange of cultural goods on the market is problematic.

It should be observed that another two categories of values were introduced (table 3.1): the values of communication, which have a cultural matrix, and ecological

Table 3.1 Comparative diagram of the types of values recognized in heritage

A

		Riegl (1902)	*Lipe (1984)*	*Kellert (1986)★*	*Mason (1988)*	*Nijkamp (1988)*
Cultural values	Aesthetic value					
	Artistic value					
	Historic value					
	Antiquity value					
	Commemoration value					
	Novelty value					
	Scientific value					
	Cultural value					
	Universal or global value					
	Social value					
	Moral value					
	Educational or cognitive value					
Economic values	Economic–monetary–market value					
	Urban value					
	Existential or intrinsic value					
	Option value					
	Almost option value					
	Altruism value					
	Resource value					
	Touristic value					
	Use value					
	Value as a public asset					
	Non-use value					
Communication values	Symbolic-associative value					
	Prestige value					
	Information value					
	Recreation value					
	Value for local, national and community identity					
	Utility value for creation of new knowledge					

(continued)

Table 3.1 Continued

B

		Frey Pommerehne (1989)	*Greffe (1990)*	*Pagiola (1996)*	*Powe-Willis (1996)*	*Allison -Ball-Cheshire-Evans-Stabler (1996)*
Cultural values	Aesthetic value					
	Artistic value					
	Historic value					
	Antiquity value					
	Commemoration value					
	Novelty value					
	Scientific value					
	Cultural value					
	Universale or global value					
	Social value					
	Moral value					
	Educational or cognitive value					
Economic values	Economic-monetary or market value					
	Urban value					
	Existential or intrinsic value					
	Option value					
	Almost option value					
	Altruism value					
	Resrouce value					
	Touristic value					
	Use value					
	Value as public asset					
	Non-use value					
Communication values	Symbolic-associative value					
	Prestige value					
	Information value					
	Recreation value					
	Value for local, national and community identity					
	Value useful for creation of new knowledge					

C					
		Burra Charter (1998)	*English Heritage (1997)*	*Klamer-Zuidhof (1999)*	*Moretti (1999)*
Cultural values	Aesthetic value				
	Artistic value				
	Historical value				
	Antiquity value				
	Commemorative value				
	Novelty value				
	Scientific value				
	Cultural value				
	Universal or global value				
	Social value	**			
	Moral value				
	Educational or cognitive value				
Economic values	Economic–monetary–market value				
	Urban value				
	Existential or intrinsic value				
	Option value				
	Almost option value				
	Altruism value				
	Resource value				
	Touristic value				
	Use value				
	Value as a public asset				
	Non-use value				
Communication values	Symbolic-associative value				
	Prestige value				
	Information value				
	Recreation value				
	Value for local, national and community identity				
	Value useful for the creation of new knowledge				

Table 3.2 The typology of values

Cultural values	*Economic values*	*Communication values*	*Ecological values*
Historical Social	Usage	Symbolic	of diversity
	• direct • indirect		
Artistic	of option		
Aesthetic Moral Scientific	• of non-use • of existence • of bequest	of information of recreation of community/ national identity	of ecosystem of durability of integrity
Cultural Spiritual/religious Educational	Intrinsic	Use as knowledge capital	of uniqueness of unreplacability of authenticity

Source: Our elaboration.

values[13]. Given the importance they have acquired in our society since they are an expression of the interest of other stakeholders, it was decided they should be treated as independent categories. In particular, the ecological values that play a role in the definition of the sustainability of cultural heritage can play an important role in conservation decisions and, at times, may actually be in conflict with the economic field.

This classification proposes values that are most often referred to as heritage but it is important to point out that each cultural heritage asset does not necessarily have all the values mentioned above.

These four categories of values represent different ways of defining heritage; what changes is the conceptual context and the methodology used for its expression.

Cultural values

The historic value is the capacity of the heritage asset to represent or stimulate a relation or reaction to the past and it depends "moins en effet de l'état dans lequel il nous a été transmis que de sa capacité à témoigner de manière cohérente le passé"[14]. It is testimony to a period and the stratifications of the traces left by time. This value is founded on the norms of antiquity and authenticity. Heritage reflects the culture of a given society; it is the social expression of a specific period in a specific context. Heritage without cultural or social value cannot exist[15].

The aesthetic value is the result of the pleasure and emotion one feels when looking at a cultural heritage asset; it is a subjective dimension; the artistic value, on the other hand, its contribution to artistic development and the perfection of its fulfilment, its style – is established by norms and it has an objective dimension.

The spiritual value refers to the fact that the heritage asset is associated with spiritual or religious meanings while the cognitive or educational value depends on the fact that heritage can be regarded as a document that can teach us something and that can, therefore, be useful to the development of society.

Economic values

The use value is the value derived from the possible commercial use of the resource, whether present or future. The use values of a constructed heritage asset refer to the goods and services that are derived from its use. Since these goods/services can be exchanged easily on the market, it is easy to give them a price. The non-use value expresses the value linked to the pure and simple existence of a heritage asset. Its existence is known, but it is not used.

The option value is not easy to express in terms of price since it is an economic value that cannot be exchanged on the market. It represents the value it has been given by an individual (that does not benefit from cultural or heritage activities), derived from the possibility (the option) of consuming the heritage asset in the near or distant future, if so desired.

Some of the values we have just classified as cultural values are also non-use values. The values of use usually belong to the category of economic values since individuals are willing to pay to acquire or protect them. The non-use value is usually classified into sub-categories, with the aim of highlighting the characteristic that could motivate the economic decision to conserve the heritage:

- **The existence value** The heritage asset is evaluated for its existence: This is the value that individuals give to a site/heritage asset based on their knowledge of it, even if it is not consumed or if they have not yet decided to visit it;
- **The bequest value:** It expresses the desire to make the heritage asset available to future generations. This value represents the protection of future generations' rights, for whom one must guarantee the possibility of "consuming" heritage assets and services.

The total economic value of the heritage asset

The economic evaluation of the assets and services is a science that is in continuous evolution. For certain goods, such as a kilo of tomatoes or a litre of petrol, the market fixes the price that expresses their economic value. This operation of determining the price of the good on the market is not possible for other categories of assets since this price, if it existed, would only be a partial expression of their total value.

As far as the evaluation of cultural heritage is concerned, the same approach could be used as for natural heritage, recognising its total economic value (TEV). TEV is divided into use value (Uv) and non-use value (NuV). The use value, which regards the effective use of the resource, can be divided into the direct use value (DuV), the indirect use value (IuV) and the option value (Ov). The non use values are the bequest value (Bv) and the existence value (Ev). The bequest value reflects the benefit derived from the knowledge that other people may benefit from the same resource in the future while the existence value studies the benefit derived from the awareness that a resource is protected.

The TEV can be expressed by the following equation:

$$\mathrm{TEV} = \mathrm{UV} + \mathrm{NUV} = (\mathrm{DUV} + \mathrm{IDV} + \mathrm{OV}) + (\mathrm{BV} + \mathrm{EV}) \qquad (1)$$

The TEV is based on the idea that every asset and service is made up of different attributes; some are easy to assess, others less so. Techniques from environmental economics are used to quantify these attributes: the Contingent Valuation Method, the Hedonic Price Method, the Travel Cost Method and the Petition Method[16]. According to Pagiola[17], the TEV is founded on two main categories: the use value and the non-use value; the option value is somewhere between the two.

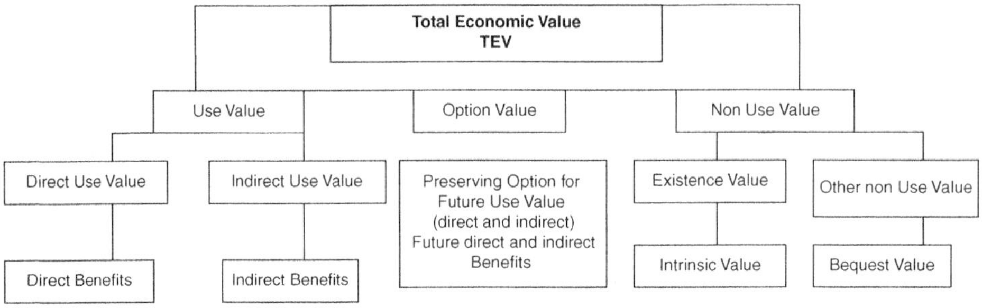

Figure 3.2 The Total Economic Value (TEV).

Source: adapted from Serageldin I. (1999), *Very Special Places: The Architecture and Economics of Intervening in Historic Cities*, Washington DC, The World Bank, and Powe N., Willis K. (1996), "Benefits received by Visitors to Heritage Sites: A Case Study of Warkworth Castle", *Leisure Studies*, n. 15, p. 27.

The use value (figure 3.2) can be either indirect or direct. The latter is differentiated into the extractive use value and non-extractive use value[18]. The extractive use values of an asset are the values that can be derived from a site; Serageldin[19] gives the example of a historic city in which a direct use is made of the buildings such as the houses or commercial premises. On the other hand, the non-extractive-use values are derived from the heritage site services. If we go back to the previous example of the historic city, people can only walk through it and enjoy it, without paying any price; their use of the city is not determined by any economic or financial transaction[20]. Measuring the non-extractive use value is a much more complicated operation than that of determining the mobile use value.

In the category of the non-extractive use values[21], the most important are the aesthetic and recreational values. The indirect use value concerns benefits that an asset may create "unconsciously". For example, the restoration of a monumental complex may improve the quality of life in the district where it is located.

The option value is linked to the willingness to pay for future use, even if not clearly defined from a temporal perspective. For an individual, this benefit is comparable to an "insurance premium" that they are willing to pay to ensure they will have the asset at their disposal in the future. The idea of the existence of an option asset goes back to Weisbrod who, in 1964, suggested the existence of a use value that was unrelated to the number of actual visits made. In 1967, referring to Weisbrod's idea, Krutilla focussed on the idea of a willingness to pay that was unrelated to the use of the resource but instead, to its simple existence (existence value) or the possibility to guarantee its consumption for future generations (bequest value).

Several authors[22] have recently claimed that willingness exists to pay for the anticipation of visiting a specific site as well. This value (Av) expresses the benefit to certain subjects from the anticipation of the visit by purchasing an informative CD-rom, thematic maps or books and magazines.

According to Fusco Girard[23], the TEV still represents an anthropocentric approach that is slightly bio-eco-centric, in the sense that the TEV refers to individual willingness to pay, excluding all those who do not have this willingness: first and foremost, future generations, followed by the more marginalized subjects such as the poor, the natural environment, etc.

The expression of the TEV can, therefore, be written as follows:

$$\mathrm{TEV} = \mathrm{UV} + \mathrm{NUV} + \mathrm{AV} = \left(\mathrm{DUV} + \mathrm{IDV} + \mathrm{OV}\right) + \left(\mathrm{BV} + \mathrm{EV}\right) + \mathrm{AV} \tag{2}$$

The problem is understanding whether the TEV makes it possible to "capture" the entire economic value of an asset. According to Margolis (1982) and Etzioni (1999), the individual has two sources of value: the utility and ethics that are expressed via participation in the *polis*. On the one hand, the subject acts according to their interests and personal profit (they are the real "consumers"); on the other, they seek solutions that can also benefit the others. According to Page (1991), the evaluation of the social foundations, linked to individual behaviour, is of great importance because it is aimed at satisfying not only consumption needs but also social and relational needs, as suggested by Maslow (1970)[24].

As early as 1992, Turner[25] had already spoken of *glue value* as all the values that are not "captured" by the TEV. According to Turner, the autopoïetic system has a primary value because it is the primary foundation that allows the system to distribute services and functions that are useful to people. This is the value of the latent functions underlying the ones that are usually appreciated and they express the system value as a whole. This primary value underlies the heteropoïetical activities that define the total secondary value (TSV). The premise for the distinction between use and non-use values is the existence of an ecosystem that is in good condition and from this perspective they represent secondary values. The TEV includes the differences that make up the total secondary value[26], but not the primary value of the aggregate system.

It is only this total secondary value that can be defined in monetary terms through the total economic value (TEV). A total value (Tv) is recognized in an ecosystem and is represented as follows:

$$\mathrm{TV} = \left(\mathrm{TEV}, i\right) \tag{3}$$

where i represents the intrinsic value. The total value is only annulled if this value equals zero; but if i is different to zero, one gets:

$$\mathrm{TV} = \left(\mathrm{TEV}, i\right) > 0 \tag{4}$$

The TEV is unable to express the global value, it has two limits. The first regards the difficulty in expressing all assets and services in economic terms, the second the structural impossibility of expressing the intrinsic value i in monetary terms.

Similarly, Fusco Girard[27] proposed the concept of complex social value (CSV), or, rather, a broader value than the TEV:

$$\mathrm{CSV} = \left(\mathrm{TEV}, \mathrm{I}\right) \tag{5}$$

where I indicates the intrinsic value of the good/resource.

In the case of cultural heritage, this value can be estimated using procedures of a multicriterial nature that refer to quantitative–qualitative indicators: "the cultural/historic/monumental capital of a city is an element that contributes, albeit indirectly, to the stability and resilience of an urban ecosystem and that, as such, has an intrinsic value (I) in the measure in which it contributes to the production of social capital, or rather the "glue"

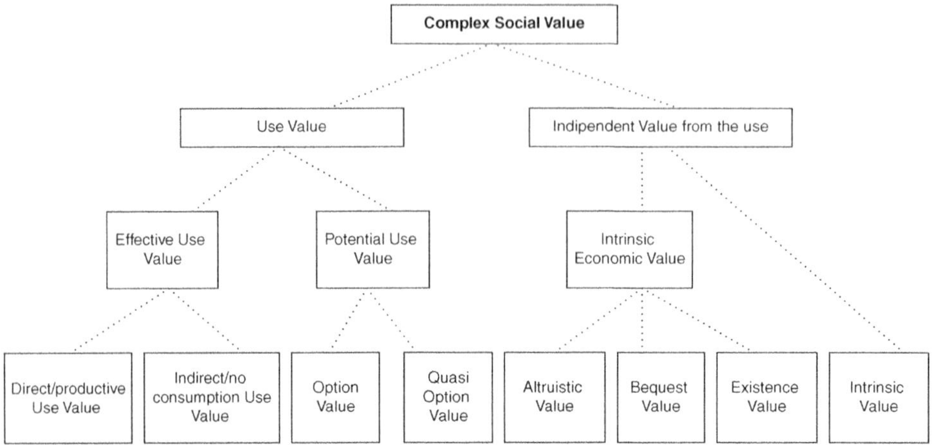

Figure 3.3 The Complex Social Value (CSV) of cultural capital.

Source: Fusco Girard L., Nijkamp P. (1997), *op. cit.*, p. 122.

that makes it possible to unite all the subjects of a community, reflecting common history, a whole of common knowledge, creativity and values"[28].

The complex social value reflects a conception that is based on the individual's centrality, without separating them from the community or ecological context, this is an ecological-community conception of the person. It has nothing to do with either the bio-ecocentric culture or anthropocentric-economic culture but only with the value of existence.

The complex social value reunites the economic and extra-economic evaluations (figure 3.3). It makes it possible to preserve the multitude of agents interested in a resource: direct users, indirect users, potential and future users. It expresses the value for future generations in terms of potential value. In fact, future generations are not interested in the value that a use demand might generate but in the intrinsic value that is independent of the use value. As a result, the criterion for the choice and economic calculation for each conservation project has to be rewritten as follows[29]:

$$\begin{aligned} &V_{present}\left(B_{conserv.(D,I,P,FU)} - C_{conserv.(D,I,P,FU)}\right) \\ &-V_{present}\left(B_{transf(D,I,P,FU)} - C_{trasf(D,I,P,FU)}\right) > 0 \end{aligned} \tag{6}$$

where D, I, P, FU indicate the value of the benefits (B) and costs (C) linked to the conservation of transformation of the heritage for the direct, indirect, potential and future users.

In this fashion, it is possible to take the decision into account over a long period, and the relationships between the different users and the qualitative or intrinsic values. The intrinsic values that the future generations are also interested in, integrate the economic approach of the use values, making an overall evaluation possible from a social perspective.

According to Fusco Girard[30], the decision to transform or conserve a monumental site has to be founded on a comparison between the monetary benefits of the transformation

($B_{transf.} - C_{transf.}$) and the complex social value of the area. Only in those cases in which the net benefits are generally superior to the complex social value CSV of the zone or site, may the transformation take place:

$$V_{present}\left(B_{trasf.} - C_{transf.}\right) > CSV \tag{7}$$

where CSV = (TEV, I)

TEV is the total value in monetary terms,

I is the intrinsic value in non-monetary terms deduced from the information regarding the role of the resources in the social system

> means generally superior so as to make it preferable.

Notes

1 "Cultural significance is the term that the conservation community has used to encapsulate the multiple values ascribed to objects, buildings, or landscapes" (Avrami E., Mason R., Torre M. de la (2000, edited by), *Values and Heritage Conservation*, Los Angeles, The Getty Conservation Institute, p. 7).
2 Throsby D. (1997), "Seven Questions in the Economics of Cultural Heritage" in Hutter M., Rizzo I. (edited by), *Economic Perspectives on Cultural Heritage*, New York, St. Martin Press, pp. 13–30.
3 For a more detailed analysis of this distinction and its implications see: Klamer A., Zuidhof P.-W. (1998), "The Value of Cultural Heritage: Merging Economic and Cultural Appraisals" in Getty Conservation Institute, *Economics and Heritage Conservation*, Los Angeles, The Getty Conservation Institute, pp. 23–61.
4 "Value", *Oxford English Dictionary*, available on www.oed.com.
5 Throsby D. (2001), *Economics and Culture*, Cambridge, Cambridge University Press, p. 20.
6 The value of an asset is formally defined by micro-economics as the variation of the relative utility of the consumption of this asset. This value can be expressed (U1–U0) or dU. A value is therefore defined by two terms that are levels of utility. The first utility level, U0, correspondends to the non consumption of the good, while the second U1to its consumption.
7 Cf. Throsby D. (2001), *Economics and Culture*, Cambridge, Cambridge University Press, pp. 20–23.
8 See: Petty W. (1662), *A Treatise of taxes and contribution*.
9 For a more detailed study on the creation and nature of cultural values see: Benedikt M. (edited by, 1997), *Center 10/Value*, Austin, Centre for Architecture and Design, School of Architecture, University of Texas; Bok S. (1995), *Common Values*, Columbia, University of Missouri Press; Ingarden R. (1983), *Man and Value*, Washington DC, Catholic University of America Press; Johnston Ch. (1992), *What is Social Value? A Discussion Paper*, Camberra, Australian Government Publishing Service; Kermal S., Gaskell I. (1993), *Explanation and Value in the Arts*, Cambridge, Cambridge University Press; Kermode F. (1988), *History and Value*, Oxford, Clarendon Press; Klamer A. (edited by, 1996), *The Value of Culture: On the Relationship between Economics and Arts*, Amsterdam, Amsterdam University Press; Meynell H.A. (1986), *The Nature of Aesthetic Value*, Albany, State University of New York Press; Tighman B. R. (1984), *But is it Art? The Value of Art and the Temptation of Theory*, New York, Basil Blackwell.
10 Throsby D. (2001), *op. cit.*, p. 28.
11 *Ivi*, pp. 28–29.
12 "Heritage objects are a looking glass that reflects the image we hold of ourselves – our values, our beliefs, our understanding of who we are – as products of a common past. As such, cultural heritage transmits an existential quality of human belonging" (Avrami E., Mason R., Torre M. de la (2000), "Overview" in *op. cit.*, p. 16).
13 Carter R.W. and Brambley R. Discussed the characteristics and physical and biological values, abstracting one can talk of ecological values (Carter R. W. and Brambley R (2002). "Defining Heritage Values and Significance for Improved Resource Management: An Application to Australian Tourism. *International Journal of Heritage Studies* (8)3: 175–199).
14 Greffe X. (1999). *op. cit.*, p. 52.
15 One can also consider the social value as the capacity to establish and facilitate social relations, ties and other relations that are not necessarily linked to the historical dimension of the heritage.

16 For more detail about these methods see and Mourato S., Mazzanti M. (2002). Economic Valuation of Cultural Heritage: Evidence and Prospects. In Torre M. della (edited by). *Assessing the Values of Cultural Heritage*, Los Angeles: The Getty Conservation Institute, pp. 51–76; Greffe X. (1999). *La gestion du patrimoine culturel*. Paris: Anthropos, pp. 57–72; Coccossis H., Nijkamp P. (1995). *Planning for our Heritage*. Aldershot/Brookfield/Hong Kong/Sidney: Avebury; Nijkamp P. (1993). "Lo sviluppo sostenibile e la valutazione socio-economica ed ambientale" in Girard L. F. (edited by). *Estimo ed economia ambientale: le nuove frontiere nel campo della valutazione. Studi in onore di Carlo Forte*. Milan: F. Angeli, pp. 281–304; Mitchell R. C., Carson R. T. (1989). *Using Surveys to Value Public Goods: The Contingent Valuation Method*, Washington: Resources for the Future.

17 Pagiola S. (1996). Economic Analysis of Investment in Cultural Heritage: Insights from Environmental Economics, paper, Washington D.C., Environment Departement. Washington: World Bank, p. 2.

18 *Ibidem*.

19 Serageldin I. (1999). *Very Special Places: The Architecture and Economics of Intervening in Historic Cities*. Washington: World Bank, coll. "Culture in Sustainable Development", pp. 25–26.

20 This distinction was also put forward by Tirendi D. as the distinctioin between the consumed direct use value (active) and the non-consumed direct use value (passive) (Tirendi D. (2003), Valutazione di contingenza per la stima delle risorse culturali. *Genio rurale – Estimo e Territorio*, 5: p. 12).

21 Cf. Pagiola S. (1996). *op. cit.*, p. 3.

22 Walsh R. G., Mckean J. R. (1998). Option and Anticipatory Values of US Wilderness, mimeo.

23 Fusco Girard L. (1994). I beni ambientali: valutazioni e strategie di conservazione, tra conflitto e cooperazione. *Genio rurale – Estimo e Territorio*, 5: p. 38; Fusco Girard L., Nijkamp P. (1997). *Le valutazioni per lo sviluppo sostenibile della città e del territorio*. Milan: F. Angeli, p. 105.

24 Fusco Girard L., Nijkamp P. (1997). *op. cit.*, pp. 104–105.

25 Turner R. K., Pearce D. W., Bateman I. (1992). *Economia ambientale. Una introduzione elementare*. Bologna: Il Mulino: 149–152.

26 It must be noted that at times the TEV is unable to capture the total secondary value completely.

27 Fusco Girard L. (1995). *art. cit.*, p. 38; Fusco Girard L., Nijkamp P. (1997). *Le valutazioni per lo sviluppo sostenibile delle città e del territorio*. Milan: F. Angeli, pp. 105–123.

28 *Ivi*, p. 116.

29 Fusco Girard L., Nijkamp P. (1997). *op. cit.*, p. 119.

30 *Ivi*, p. 121.

References

Allison G., Ball S., Cheshire P., Evans A. and Stabler M. (1996). *The Value of Conservation*. London: English Heritage.

Avrami E., Mason R., de la Torre M. (2000). *Values and Heritage Conservation. Research Report*. Los Angeles: The J. Paul Getty Trust.

Barrère C., Santagata W. (1999). Defining Art. From the Brancusi Trial to the Economics of Artistic Semiotic Goods. *International Journal of Arts Management*, (1) 2: 28-38.

Benedikt M. (edited by, 1997). *Center 10/Value*, Austin, Centre for Architecture and Design, School of Architecture, University of Texas.

Bok S. (1995). *Common Values*. Columbia, University of Missouri Press.

Carter R.W. and Brambley R (2002). Defining Heritage Values and Significance for Improved Resource Management: An Application to Australian Tourism. *International Journal of Heritage Studies* (8) 3: 175-199.

Coccossis H., Nijkamp P. (1995). *Planning for our Heritage*, Aldershot: Avebury.

De La Torre M. (edited by, 2002). *Assessing the Values of Cultural Heritage. Research Report* Los Angeles: The Getty Conservation Institute.

Etzioni A. (1999). Voluntary Simplicity: Characterization, Select Psychological Implications, and Societal Consequences. In *Essays in Socio-Economics. Studies in Economic Ethics and Philosophy*. Berlin: Springer, pp. 1–26.

Fladmark J. M. (edited by, 1993). *Heritage. Conservation, Interpretation, Enterprise*. Shaftesbury: Donehead Publishing Ltd.

Fusco Girard L. (1987). *Risorse architettoniche e culturali: valutazioni e strategie di conservazione. Un'analisi introduttiva*. Milan: F. Angeli.

Fusco Girard L. (1994). I beni ambientali: valutazioni e strategie di conservazione, tra conflitto e cooperazione. *Genio rurale – Estimo e Territorio*, 5: 35-44.

Fusco Girard L., Nijkamp P. (2004). *Energia, bellezza, partecipazione: la sfida della sostenibilità*. Milan: F. Angeli.

Greffe X. (1999). *La gestion du patrimoine culturel*. Paris: Anthropos.

Greffe X. (2001). Les activités culturelles: un levier de développent et d'emploi pour les territoires. In *3e Jornadas Iniciativa Privada y Sector Publico en la Gestion de la Cultura, Malatzaren, 23–25 de mayo de 2001* Vitoria Gasteiz, 14 p.

Greffe X. (2003). *La valorisation économique du patrimoine*. Paris: Ministère de la culture et de la communication, Département des études et de la perspective.

Howe C.W. (1993). Le frontiere nella valutazione di risorse prive di mercato: problemi e prospettive. In Girard L.F. (a cura di), *Estimo ed economia ambientale: le nuove frontiere nel campo della valutazione. Studi in onore di Carlo Forte*. Milan: F. Angeli, pp. 57–83.

Hutter M., Rizzo I. (edited by, 1997). *Economic Perspectives on Cultural Heritage*. London: MacMillan Press.

Ingarden R. (1983). *Man and Value*. Washington DC: Catholic University of America Press.

Johnston Ch. (1992). *What is Social Value? A Discussion Paper*. Canberra: Australian Government Publishing Service.

Kermal S., Gaskell I. (1993). *Explanation and Value in the Arts*. Cambridge: Cambridge University Press.

Kermode F. (1988). *History and Value*. Oxford: Clarendon Press.

Klamer A. (edited by, 1996). *The Value of Culture: On the Relationship between Economics and Arts*. Amsterdam: Amsterdam University Press.

Klamer A., Zuidhof P.W. (1998). The Value of Cultural Heritage: Merging Economic and Cultural Appraisals. In Getty Conservation Institute, *Economics and Heritage Conservation*. Los Angeles: The Getty Conservation Institute, pp. 23–61.

Krutilla J. V. (1967). Conservation Reconsidered. *The American Economic Review* (57) 4: 777–786.

Margolis H. (1982). *Selfishness, Altruism, and Rationality*. Cambridge: Cambridge University Press.

Maslow A. H. (1970). *Motivation and Personality*. New York: Harper & Row.

Mason R. (1998). Theoretical and Practical Arguments for Values-centered Preservation. *CRM: The Journal of Heritage Stewardship* (9) 3: 21–48.

Meynell H. A. (1986). *The Nature of Aesthetic Value*. Albany: State University of New York Press.

Mitchell R. C., Carson R. T. (1989). *Using Surveys to Value Public Goods: The Contingent Valuation Method*. Washington: Resources for the Future.

Moretti A. (1999). *La produzione museale*. Turin: Giappichelli.

Mourato S., Mazzanti M. (2002). Economic Valuation of Cultural Heritage: Evidence and Prospects. In Torre M. De la (edited by). *Assessing the Values of Cultural Heritage*. Los Angeles: The Getty Conservation Institute, pp. 51–76.

Nijkamp P. (1993). Lo sviluppo sostenibile e la valutazione socio-economica ed ambientale. In Girard L. F. (a cura di), *Estimo ed economia ambientale: le nuove frontiere nel campo della valutazione. Studi in onore di Carlo Forte*. Milan: F. Angeli, pp. 281–304.

Page T. (1992). Intergenerational Justice as opportunità. In Maclean D., Brown P. (edited by). *Energy and the Future*. Totowa: Rowman and Littlefield, pp. 34–49.

Pagiola S. (1996). Economic Analysis of Investment in Cultural Heritage: Insights from Environmental Economics (paper). Washington D.C: Environment Department, World Bank, 13 p.

Pearce D., Maddison D., Pollicino M. (2001). *Economics and Cultural Heritage. Toward an Economic Approach to Valuing and Conserving Cultural Assets*. London: University College, 22 p.

Riegl A. (1903). *Der moderne Denkmalkultus (Entwurf einer gesetzlichen Organisation der Denkmalpflege in Österreich)*. Wien: Zentral Kommission.

Riegl A., Bacher E. (1995). *Kunstwerk oder Denkmal?*, Wien, Köhl, Weimar: Böhlan Verlag.

Riegl A., Scarrocchia S. (a cura di, 1995). *Alois Riegl: teoria e prassi della conservazione dei monumenti. Antologia di scritti, discorsi, rapporti 1898–1905, con una scelta di saggi critici*. Bologna: CLUEB.

Serageldin I. (1999). *Very Special Places: The Architecture and Economics of Intervening in Historic Cities*, Washington, World Bank, coll. "Culture in Sustainable Development". Washington: The World Bank.

Throsby D. (1995). Culture, Economics, and Sustainability. *Journal of Cultural Economics*, (19) 3: 199–206.

Throsby D. (1997). Seven Questions in the Economics of Cultural Heritage. In Hutter M., Rizzo I. (edited by). *Economic Perspectives of Cultural Heritage*. New York: St. Martin Press.

Throsby D. (1997). Sustainability and Culture: Some Theoretical Issues. *International Journal of Cultural Policy* 4: 7–20.

Throsby D. (1999). Cultural Capital. *Journal of Cultural Economics* (23) 1–2: 3–12.

Throsby D. (2001). *Economics and Culture*. Cambridge: Cambridge University Press.

Tighman B. R. (1984). *But is it Art? The Value of Art and the Temptation of Theory*. New York: Basil Blackwell.

Tirendi D. (2003).Valutazione di contingenza per la stima delle risorse culturali ed ambientali. *Genio rurale – Estimo e territorio, Il Sole 24 Ore*, (LXVI) 5:12–22.

Walsh R. G., Mckean J. R. (1998). Option and Anticipatory Values of US Wilderness, mimeo.

Zuidhofl P.W. (1999). The Values of Cultural Heritage, paper presented at ICARE Summer School, *The Economics of Built Heritage*, July 11–17, 1999, 26 p.

4 Using contestation to elicit values for heritage planning

The case of the urban park at Ekeberg in Oslo, Norway

Torgrim Sneve Guttormsen and Joel Taylor

Introduction

In the heritage literature on contestation, aspects of 'dissonance'[1] or the lack of agreement and consistency in contradictory uses of heritage, and 'authorization'[2] in power relationships, have provided insights on how heritage can embody rival discourses in contemporary communities. Other related concepts are 'processes of heritagization' and 'monumentalization of memorial places'[3] in studies that emphasize disputes or debates and 'winners' striving for hegemonic control in the on-going fabric of creating heritage. In recent literature, a greater emphasis on 'negotiating'[4] the past is also emphasized in order to avoid conflict and legitimizing claims as the only approaches to divisive heritage. In this context, the strategy of 'silencing' would be relevant for understanding how some aspects of heritage become more significant than others and take part in power relationships, for instance when a complex historical reality is framed and reduced into branded stories producing black-and-white notions such as 'us versus them' or 'virtue versus vice'. From a long-term perspective, heritage contestation can be viewed as a valuable resource, creating a living heritage that mediates important social discourses in democratic societies. There are also negative impacts, however, derived from rivalry and contestation, when heritage – due to ideology, gender, class, and ethnic distinctions – becomes the means for exclusion and precipitates cultural battles, or even wartime conflicts. In this context, the concept 'difficult heritage'[5] directs attention to issues dealing with the heritage of assaults and victims of war, racial discrimination, and genocide, to name a few topics where associations lead to a 'dark' history associated with atrocity, pain, and shame.

In other words, divisive aspects of heritage contestations have many concepts and perspectives depending on the situation and discourses at stake. Altogether, the common study of heritage contestation is to gain knowledge about how disagreements act as a creative force, sometimes also in very destructive ways, in the (re-)making of heritage. Heritage meanings are socially constructed, and therefore inherently contestable. The heritage site provides the realm in which this contestation takes place. As such, the complex, multi-layered relationship between site and discourse illustrates a shifting landscape. Considering discourse and conflict, it becomes evident that the communication of heritage sites is a complex matter, which can become more complex over time. This is especially the case when heritage sites have had different uses, including unwanted appropriation or 'dark' uses. Differing interpretations of sites, through the exercising of different discourses, means that divergent interests can become intertwined. Heritage, a complex social concept, involves performing activities that recall the past, which includes staging and displaying the past for present educational, political and/or commercial needs and aims.[6] As Laurajane Smith states:

> [H]eritage is a multi-layered performance – be this a performance of visiting, managing, interpretation or conservation – that embodies acts of remembrance and commemoration while negotiating and constructing a sense of place, belonging and understanding in the present. [7]

This suggests that the question of meaning and significance of a heritage site relies on a number of interrelating factors, whilst the embodiment of cultural memory rests on a number of values that might be represented to quite different degrees. This raises the question of how dynamic a heritage site can be without losing the qualities that identified it as a heritage site in the first place. Characterizing and assessing heritage value is both important and challenging, not least because these values can conflict. "What may be 'comfortable' and 'worthy' to someone will *always* be 'uncomfortable' and 'problematic' to another."[8] This can be lost in the attempt to describe the significance of a place or provide recommendations for management.

In this chapter, we argue that acknowledging contestation elicits values that would be significant for heritage planning. The inclusive approach, where many voices or values are taken into account, is also the focus in heritage policies, like the Burra Charter.[9] We use the urban park at Ekeberg in Oslo, Norway, as a case study[10]. The heritage values defining the park, and the contested discourses related to those heritage values today, characterize a place that has multiple meanings and diverse public uses that appeal to many stakeholders. Building on the Bakhtinian concept of the carnivalesque[11], we argue that heritage contestation represents the polyphonic public voices that define the *multi-vocality of place*, which in turn becomes a valuable resource in planning openly accessible public places. In our analysis of the public park, we use the theory of the carnivalesque as a conceptual tool for exploring 'heritage as multi-layered performance'.

Analytical approach: contestation elicits values

There are a variety of useful methods for analyzing the complexity of social relations and cultural dynamics at play in the planning, design, reconstruction, and management of historic urban parks which, in addition, also are acknowledged heritage sites that undergo heritage preservation activities.[12] In the area of conflict management affected by contested discourses of heritage values, ethnographic knowledge can help heritage managers to identify opportunities for compromise and potential mitigating measures. In this chapter, we discuss a variety of methods for assessing values. The methods discussed embody various qualities found in other methods, such as the Rapid Ethnographic Assessment Procedures (REAP) analysis used by the USA National Park Service (NPS) historical parks. These qualities are: historical and archival document analysis, expert interviews (survey based on workshop participants), and experiences based on our 'situated knowledge' of the park when walking and observing the park design. Some of the methods used to assess public value for heritage management will be discussed later.

We will first analyze the different types of heritage values that are represented in Ekeberg Park, and then analyze the contested discourses which today are related to these values. This will lead to a discussion about how contested heritage could be valued as a societal resource today and the implications for heritage management. We will use a multi-analytical approach to the case study in order to explore the interface of heritage values and public values. One strand is the media debate about Ekeberg Park during the planning process of the establishment of the renewed park that took place between 2011 and 2013.

Results from a survey conducted with workshop participants who visited the Ekeberg Park are included in this paper. The participants were presented with descriptions (for the uninitiated) of three different methods used for assessing heritage value that would be valid for the site. Participants had the opportunity to consider how the park might have been different if the values had been assessed in a different way. This was carried out by heritage experts considering the potential variation that could stem from the three valid methods for assessing value at the site.

As well as considering the history of the park, which has contributed to disparate voices and values being expressed, we will consider how the values have contributed to the public debate and analyze how these values can be assessed in traditional heritage management.

Theoretical approach: heritage contestation as carnival

Low, Taplin, and Scheld[13] believed that urban parks host democratic ideals; they are public places for socially and culturally diverse behavior 'where a wide variety of people of different gender, class, culture, nationality, and ethnicity intermingle peacefully.'[14] When emphasizing urban parks as diverse multi-usable places for public culture, there is good reason to consider a Bakhtinian theoretical approach based on 'multi-vocality'.

For the linguist theorist Mikhail M. Bakhtin (1895–1975), the carnivalesque is defined as 'the language of the marketplace'.[15] With the carnival tradition, the market place becomes a 'multi-voiced' social arena where high and low blend and where the social domains are turned upside-down. It is an arena where public culture is performed from the bottom up and where the staged frivolous emotional outbursts contribute in defining an ecstatic hyperreal liminal place, a distorted sewn reality which also expresses a distortion of the vernacular. The carnivalesque is defined by theatrical, grotesque performances which are perceived from the perspective of the masses.

The carnivalesque refers to a cultural theory that is useful for describing aspects of heritage production. For instance, Tony Bennett highlights the emergence of museums in the 1800s by drawing a historical connection between the carnivalesque and various exhibition traditions such as festivals, department stores, and amusement parks.[16] Carnivals, festivals, funfairs, bazaars, theme parks, tourist sites, and sports venues are carnivalesque because they constitute places that construct an imagined and performed reality in which the fictional and real world are mixed and where the mixed 'dream world' is consumed as entertainment on the basis of popular needs.[17] Added to the list of 'the carnivalesque places' are heritage sites and museum collections where public performances based on satiric political activism (absurd/grotesque examples, vulgar cartoons, etc.) and popular entertainment (historical plays, fun festivals, exhibitions) are performed.[18]

The carnivalesque contains characteristic features – such as multiple interaction, eccentricity, (mis)alliance, outrageousness, and criticism – which are pertinent for analyzing public parks as 'multi-vocal public places'. Using the Bakhtinian concept of the Carnivalesque, this chapter analyzes the public discourses taking place at the Ekeberg Park in Oslo, Norway which has been derived on the basis of private investments behind the renewed design and opening of the park in 2013.

The Ekeberg Park as public value

In 1889, the municipality of Oslo decided to protect parts of the Ekeberg area as a public park out of consideration for the people's physical health.[19] An extended area of the park was bought by the city council from private owners and protected in 1937. Pollution from the factories and atrocious working conditions took their toll on the poor working classes in the east side of the city and there was a need for somewhere nearby with nature and fresh air for recreation. Another motivation was to secure a proper recreational space close to the city for the population, a green space for the population to exercise and for relaxation and exploration, to gain knowledge and reflection. A third aspect of this was the urgent need to protect one of the most attractive natural areas around the city for property development in a rapidly growing city.

Based on the arguments above, the public park at Ekeberg soon became known as 'the beloved Forest of the City'. Officially, it was named the 'Folkepark' – the People's Park. The area was first used as a pavilion for music and dancing and a lookout point for recreational visitors, but the construction of a restaurant in 1915 (figure 4.1), replaced by a monumental restaurant built by Oslo municipality in 1927–1929, attracted even more people to the park (figure 4.2). The restaurant was called the 'Peoples' Restaurant', which in accordance to general ideals on welfare at the time, was to serve a decent meal at a reasonable price so all could afford it when visiting the park. This very basic park ideal during the mid-war period was, in other words, based on facilitating public values as common welfare that benefitted and provided access to all people.

Today, the idea of Ekeberg Park as a public space has been under fierce debate due to the involvement of private investors, that had shown their interest in developing the area. The Ekeberg Restaurant was closed in the late 1990s and deteriorated until the Norwegian

Figure 4.1 View from the Ekeberg restaurant, 1915.

Photo: J.H. Küenholdt. Oslo byarkiv/A-40207/Uaa/0001/095 Creative Commons 3.0 licence. *Kristiania, Ekebergrestauranten*. Oslo byarkiv. Accessed January 18 2016 from: http://www.oslobilder.no/BAR/A-40207/Uaa/0001/095?query=%22K%C3%BCenholdt%22&count=415&search_context=1&pos=15

Figure 4.2 The Ekeberg restaurant from 1927–1929 surrounded by forest, an example of functionalism in a Norwegian context.

Photo: Normanns Kunstforlag A/S. Year: unknown. Oslo byarkiv/A-10001/Ua/0006/006. Licenced under Creative Commons 3.0. Ekebergrestauranten, Oslo. Oslo byarkiv. Accessed January 15 2016 from: http://www.oslobilder.no/BAR/A-10001/Ua/0006/006?query=Ekebergrestauranten&count=175&search_context=1&pos=88

businessman and art collector Mr. Christian Ringnes and his partners bought the restaurant and renovated the building to its 'former glory'. Today, the historical restaurant is faring well and has gained a reputation for its cuisine as well as the fine restoration work. In August 2011, the city council of Oslo voted in favour of a zoning plan for a sculpture park around the restaurant, financed by the C. Ludens Ringnes Foundation, to which Christian Ringnes is the main investor. The aim of the foundation 'is to build a solid capital base and distribute grants for public interest purposes, with a primary focus on the arts, culture, experiences, and environmental protection. The foundation may also itself contribute to the mediation of arts, culture and experiences'.[20] The 'renewed' Ekeberg Park was officially opened 26th of September 2013 under the heading 'ekebergparken.com'.

These interfaces of private–public cooperation have led to extensive public debate about whose interests are represented and who currently benefits in the planning of public parks. An element of those arguments has been about the extent to which the various types of heritage in the park, as well as the dimension of the park's cultural heritage representing the history of welfare ideas, promote public values that could be used as a common good that is accessible to different communities.

Layers of heritage

The layers of heritage at the Ekeberg Park can be summarised into five interrelated categories: natural heritage, archaeological heritage, built heritage, dark heritage, and artistic heritage. It is a set of heritage values that have helped to build up the perception of Ekeberg as a valuable public park.

Firstly, as shown by the arguments used for establishing the area as a Public park in the late 1800s, a weighty argument was the area's importance as healthy nature. The forest at

Ekeberg has become a term that defines the area's importance as a public value. In 2008, parts of Ekeberg Park became protected as a natural reserve, the highest category for landscape protection in the Norwegian Natural Heritage Act.[21]

Heritage values are defined by the many archaeological traces at Ekeberg, protected by the Norwegian Cultural Heritage Act, which are also closely connected to the environment of the Ekeberg forest. The area is scattered with prehistoric sites from 10,000-year-old Stone Age settlements to Bronze Age rock art sites and Iron Age grave mounds. Experiencing the archaeology of Ekeberg requires a degree of expertise in knowing what to look for in the landscape. Since the 1990s and in the planning for a sculpture park from 2011, however, efforts have been made to design heritage trails with signposts and footpaths that enrich the experience of archaeological traces in the area.

A third type of heritage value defining the Ekeberg Park is connected to the Second World War, when the German military forces, who occupied Norway from 1939 to 1945, erected a monumental ceremonial stairway and a cemetery of honours for German soldiers who died during the war (figure 4.3).[22] The place was probably chosen because it is believed that a significant battle between the Swedish and the Norwegian–Danish troops happened at the spot in 1567, which gave the place the name of 'Svenskesletta' ('the Swedish plain'). Today, this part of the Ekeberg Park testifies to how a difficult past has become a dark heritage that is affected with pain and shame. After the war, the corpses at the cemetery were relocated and the cemetery and the stairs were partly destroyed and left to ruin. These processes of 'silencing' are also evident in the renaming of the place after the war. Today, the place is called 'Hundesletta' ('the Dog plain') because so many people walk their dogs there, thus changing the meaning of the place from being synonymous with war and the darker legacy of Nazi history to a more innocent content related to recreation and the harmony between humans and animals.

Figure 4.3 Reichskommissar for Norway during the German occupation of Norway, Josef Antonius Heinrich Terboven, lays a wreath at the German cemetery of honour at Ekeberg March 15th 1942.

Photo: NTB scanpix.

Figure 4.4 From the website *Galleri Brandstrup Oslo*:'2013 was the 150 year anniversary of Edvard Munch, a grand celebration in Norway. In this event Marina Abramovic created her own version of his famous painting 'The Scream', in the exact same spot in Ekeberg Sculpture Park where Munch was inspired to paint 'The Scream'. The result was three interactive works of art; sculpture, performance and video works'.

Photo: Gorm Kallestad/NTB scanpix'

A fourth type of heritage value defining Ekeberg Park is architectural value, the built heritage. Among the protected buildings are the Ekeberg Restaurant erected during 1927–1929, designed by architect Lars Backer (1892–1930), and today considered one of the finest examples of Classical Functionalism in Norway (see figure 4.2).

The Ekeberg Restaurant has one of the most spectacular views in Oslo, which directs attention to a fifth type of heritage value, Ekeberg Park's artistic or scenic value. The outlook from Ekeberg to the Oslo fjord and towards the town has been a viewpoint for many painters and photographers for centuries. For example, 'Der Schrei der Natur' (The Scream of Nature, 1893–1910) by the famous Norwegian painter Edvard Munch (1863–1944) uses the motif from 'Utsikten' ('the View'), a part of Ekeberg. The artistic heritage at Ekeberg became a resource when planning a sculpture park with the installation of 25 sculptures chosen from the private collection of Christian Ringnes. One of these installations was made by the artist Marina Abramovic, who paid homage to Munch with her interactive performance during the opening of the Ekeberg Park in 2013 (figure 4.4).

Conflicts and divergent interests

The debates in the media about what Ekeberg is in terms of a public park have been extensive as a result of the plans to create a sculpture park at Ekeberg. Main questions were for whom the park is designed, who are involved in the designing, and the benefits to people using the park. Is Ekeberg a natural park, an archaeological or cultural heritage park, a tourist park, a city park, or a sculpture park? Whose voices should be strongest in how to define the park? A review of media found that national newspapers (e,g, Aftenposten, Dagbladet), national broadcasts (NRK), and other commentaries of the park on the web indicate that Ekeberg Park is an important place for public attention and interaction. The park and its heritage mediate public opinions, and act as 'a speakers' corner' for questions and topics that occupy people in today's society. Using Bakhtin's terminology, Ekeberg Park functions as a 'language of the Marketplace', giving space for the voices of the People. As such, Ekeberg Park shows how public parks could act as social arenas where democratic ideals can be played out.

An example of the democracy discourse was shown when the local heritage management (Byantikvaren i Oslo) together with the businessman Mr. Ringnes during the planning of a sculpture park at Ekeberg launched the idea to revitalise the steps from the Nazi ceremonial site as part of the experience of the park. A group of 22 professors at the University of Oslo signed a protest document against the plan arguing that any kind of reconstruction of the Nazi ceremonial site would attract unwanted groups to the area. *Byantikvaren i Oslo* replied that part of democracy is to preserve the history of all time, not only the history of the victors or the rich.[23]

The function of the park as 'a Speakers' Corner' is shown by many other examples. Environmental activists have for instance occupied the park and received media attention for their protests against the plans for the development of the sculpture park (figure 4.5). They initiated a campaign called '*People's Action Movement for the Protection of the Ekeberg Forest*'[24] and received attention from the media when they placed knitted scarfs around the trees, symbolising how people were protecting the forest. The nature proponents

Figure 4.5 Environmental activists camping in the Ekeberg Park, early May 2012.

Photo: Bjørn Bratten. Picture from Østkantliv.no May 19 (2012). *Ekebergsaken: Korrupsjons-etterforskning mot kommunen*. Accessed January 19 2016 from: http://ostkantliv.blogspot.no/2012/05/ekebergsaken-korrupsjonsetterforskning.html

argue that the recreational qualities of the park are based on the experience of aesthetic pleasure, purity, and the silence of nature when walking or jogging. This critique takes into consideration that the park was originally planned for people to enjoy nature, therefore, according to the nature activists, protecting nature is to protect the original idea of the public park for everyone.

When referring to Mr. Ringnes' strong influence – both financially and in the planning and design of the sculpture park – these critical voices also asked the rhetorical question: "What happens when a rich businessman can buy the right to do what he wants in a public forest?" Part of the argumentation among the critical public is, therefore, also a consideration for the caretaking of the 'heritage of welfare ideals' and of democratic ideals about public decision making in planning processes.[25] This theme refers to a fundamental welfare issue unique to Norway, called 'Allemannsretten' (the right of public access to outlying areas), which promotes the idea that it is a citizen's right to have access to and be able to use these public areas for hiking and other recreational activities. A significant aspect of this is how heritage is defined as a common good which should be accessible to all citizens.

It is worth noting that Mr. Ringnes could well be considered to be but a member of the public, just as much as the environmental activists. However, compared to the critical public voice expressed by environmentalist activists, Mr. Ringnes has a privileged position as a wealthy patron and urban developer or entrepreneur investing in developing the park for public enjoyment. That leaves the question to which function wealthy patrons (and heritage experts as described below) should have within this diverse context of influencing actors.

The critique has also been directed towards Mr. Ringnes himself, saying that he gives voice to forces of capitalism and the intervention of private interests in public space (figure 4.6).[26] For instance, Ringnes first announced that he would invest a considerable amount of money to make a sculpture park at Ekeberg with sculptures that honoured the female body (figure 4.7). A female sculpture park would, according to Ringnes, attract

Figure 4.6 Picture from the media, titled: 'Ringnes loves women'.

Photo: Andreas Sundby / NRK. NRK Østlandsendingen, May 24 (2011). *Her er kvinnene til Ringnes.* Accessed January 19 2016 from: http://www.nrk.no/ostlandssendingen/her-er-ringnes_-kvinnelager-1.7646485

Figure 4.7 Mr. Ringnes in the public.

Photo: Jacques Hvistendahl.

visitors and make the park different from other sculpture parks like Vigelands Park, also in Oslo. The nudity statement resulted in massive protests where the critics accused the benefactor of being the proponent of sexist opinions. Critics asked rhetorically: Why should the idea of femininity put forward by a rich, elderly man have an impact on how a public park should be designed? The nudity discourse gave an artist the idea to create an app with a virtual 'man park', which according to the artist, is an artistic contribution to the debate about private art in public space.[27] The humorous members of the hard rock band Black Debbath showed their sincere political protest by posing nude in the park.[28] The carnivalesque within this context is shown by the grotesque elements of strange bodily gestures, extravaganza, and frivolous emotional outbursts that allude to popular laughter (figure 4.8).

Mr. Ringnes' initiative also led to a strong local protest movement that used a number of arguments to protect the area from further development. One of the arguments was based on a fear that the area will be destroyed as a result of increased tourism, and they made protest posters that alluded to tourism as synonymous with vulgarity and public decay (figure 4.9). The grotesque elements of the carnivalesque tradition are also evident within this context. The local critique can be viewed as the result of the so-called NIMBY-effect (Not In My Backyard) in planning processes, since the local protesters value and are willing to partake in tourism, but don't want the tourists in their community.

Today, after the opening of the renewed Ekeberg Park in 2013, the discourse of the park has entered into a new phase. Since its opening, the Ekeberg Park has according to a social media source[29] been lauded as one of the world's 10 most beautiful sculpture parks. The protests have died down, and the debate in the media is more focused on the success of the park as a place that attracts many types of visitors that is helping brand Oslo as a cultural capital.[30] The Ringnes Foundation has been clever in including the critique into the project. This is shown, amongst other things, on the web site Ekebergparken.com where Ringnes' subjective motivation for creating a female sculpture park is redressed by including 'art, nature and history' as topics for exploration in the park. The inclusion of

Figure 4.8 Black Debbath's nudity protest. Op.cit.

Figure 4.9 Local protests against tourism – 'Neighbour Warning: New Neighbours'.

the various voices in the debate can be summarized with the heading in the media: 'The Park who parked the critique!'[31] However, criticism quickly flared up again, for example, when the Ringnes foundation proposed the construction of an aerial gondola that would carry even more visitors to the park, which may mean higher costs to get to the park and the park becoming more private rather than public.[32]

All of the previously mentioned debates about Ekeberg Park, which are evident in the media, reflect that the park and its heritage is continuing in the creation of meaning of the place. The debates about the destruction of nature, sense of place lost to vulgar tourism, the sculptural or built environment becoming sexist, lost archaeological heritage, or venerated dark heritage are all part of the ongoing shaping of new layers which is caused by multiple carnivalesque performances at the place. Dynamic layers continue, so it cannot be said that these matters are just about the past, considering how knowledge of the past and interaction with the present can shape future layers. Ekeberg Park has many functions, thus fulfilling multiple interests, and the varied debate about what kind of park it is or should be is rich, but also divisive. A major challenge when planning the sculpture park is how to include this divisive content, which appears in the media debate, in the planning process, and how the experts should be involved in this process.

Imagined futures and the impact of assessing values

A useful consequence of considering the imagined future is the opportunity to elicit the values of the present. The future of the park rests on how it is conceived and understood in the present. This connection between real and imagined worlds has parallels with the carnivalesque. However, assessing the values of a heritage site, is commonly carried out by expert opinion or expert-driven consultation of the public. The range of approaches is diverse and the extent to which the ways heritage values are assessed and prioritised is affected by the actors involved in the process and the nature of the process itself. The potential to influence, or be influenced by, the measurement or prioritisation of value can be highly significant. Defining how a heritage site or item's values are assessed goes a long way towards defining what that heritage is.

However, the process is often controlled by a narrative or mediated towards existing ideas. Perhaps the most profound influence on value assessment is who selects the method. Before an assessment is carried out, the method is chosen which means that there is a subtle, even invisible influence on everything that follows. Different methods emphasize different values of a heritage site – the kinds of value captured, to what extent, and how. Methods can vary in the amount of expertise required, and how the values are expressed (categories, econometric, etc.). Whoever gets to choose the assessment method gets to frame a value system onto the heritage site – a system that will influence its future, and be influenced by different voices and assessors but within the chosen framework. The result of that framing of the situation returns to a common call – whose heritage? 'Heritage is a powerful source of meaning; those who can't see themselves reflected in the mirror are therefore excluded'.[33] The complex relation between kinds of heritage and different communities creates a situation where the future of the park could take a number of directions.

An opportunity to consider the different approaches of value assessment methods arose when cultural heritage experts from a range of disciplines and countries met to discuss heritage value. Having visited the park, they took the opportunity to consider the implications of different approaches to assessing and understanding value on potential futures. Individual responses were compiled together. They were not chosen as identical forms of assessment but all valid approaches that could have been used to consider changes to the park. The value assessments considered were:

- Contingent Valuation methods (CVM)
- Environmental Impact Assessment (EIA)
- Urban Heritage Analysis (DIVE)

As well as exploring the park, each expert was given a short description of the three methods for consistency, clarity and to support any knowledge gaps within the diverse group of individuals (figure 4.10).

There was limited time for background information, but the collective expertise provided some useful insight into how the choice of a value assessment method could impact upon a heritage site that was the focus of so many different perspectives and drivers. The experts' considerations of the methods gave comparative insight into the methods that demonstrates the practical consequences of the assessment method through a case study perspective in a way that is not discussed in heritage literature. Because of the time available, participants' knowledge of the case was limited in the experiment. This experiment was not intended to choose the most effective assessment, but to examine their similarities and differences by using the same case study as the subject of assessment – Ekeberg Park.

Figure 4.10 Posted on Twitter. One of the flipcharts used for collecting data on the delegates' opinions on different assessment methods.

Photo: H@V.

Environmental Impact Assessment

Environmental Impact Assessment (EIA) examines the potential consequences of any planned or expected changes to heritage sites. The version used was 'Handbook 140' (the latest version is called Handbook v712), which measures the impact on natural environments, cultural heritage, and community life. It provides a numerically expressed appraisal of different options for change, utilizing expertise and judgement to provide a qualitative evaluation that can be entered into the framework to rank the different options. The framework charts the overall value of the site against the magnitude of any proposed change to express the degree of impact.[34] The method is applicable to a wide range of sites, but is often criticised as being too rigid. Furthermore, the broad impacts that are assessed overlap to some extent, so the method could lead to systematic errors embedded within its format because assessors will sometimes double-count, i.e., disproportionately weight the same factor.

EIA was considered a practical, holistic way of approaching changes that could incorporate different factors within its design. The preparation for the method makes it a rigorous process. However, there was considerable commentary on the lack of involvement of the local community and the loss of non-expert values (unless specifically built into the design). Comparative weighting was not considered to capture attitudes and correlate secondary impacts, the site's capacity for change, or cost. This practicality missed some nuance, detail, and potential for compromise through communication.

Potential impacts of using this method on the park were the potential to promote broad ideas of public benefit at the possible expense of costs. The different layers of heritage were considered problematic for the methods, as one would dominate over another and the overlap between them could not be addressed as the quantitative method must avoid double-counting. Because the background work and design are based on expert judgment, public values could be submerged in the design as 'low' or 'medium' in the eyes of experts. However, the potential to express funding needs through the ranking of alternative options for the park was a potential positive.

The emphasis on experts over the public, landscape over activity, and rarity over creativity leaned towards a reactive, top-down approach to heritage management that did not facilitate dynamic change. However, the rigour of the process also meant that less visible elements of the park would have attention. A deeper perspective of the past is possible, but at the possible expense of a dynamic future for a multi-layered, evolving landscape.

Contingent valuation methods (CVM)

Contingent valuation is part of a wider group of methods that determine peoples' willingness to accept or pay for a particular situation, often either a change or the avoidance of change.[35] The econometric method goes beyond entrance fees and visitor numbers to consider social impact and benefit, and allows experts to quantify and standardize the extent of a site's significance. CVM is often carried out by asking hypothetical questions about a scenario or set of options in order to gauge the extent of preferences. The method is considered inclusive, in that it engages the wider public, often a randomly selected group of local residents or site visitors. The method has, however, received criticism for being too theoretical and excluding non-use values, as well as the potential problems of how the questions are framed, if they effectively elicit values and also simplifying value to the single scale of money.

CVM methods have an advantage of relating costs to benefits explicitly and justifying funding. As the method directly consults the public, it allows social values and proactive planning to be considered at a specific point in time. Although consulting people is at the heart of this, the questions are designed by experts and asked of randomly selected individuals without background knowledge, so just 'uses' the public. Returning to Bakhtin's carnival, the procession and discussion are still led by a top-down process. However, it was considered realistic in the sense that the survival of heritage requires (future) societal support. The lack of focus on 'soft' or 'secondary' attributes and specific focus was considered to run the risk of not representing the multiple values of the park.

Although it expresses the readiness of people to be involved in the park's future, CVM methods didn't express *why* people value things. The expected impacts on the park included the possibility that people might be engaged but shouldn't have to pay for the park (prompted by the focus on monetary issues), but also increase visitors (and collateral risks). The emphasis on public opinion may miss some less visible aspects, so the acceptance of change may come from the commodification or simplification of values. If contestation about the park is in the media, and has the potential to influence public opinion, there is a chance that the timing of the assessment may result in different outcomes. It was seen by some as a complementary method to assess values, not a stand-alone approach.

DIVE

DIVE (Describe, Interpret, Valuate, and Enable) uses a range of disciplinary methods to examine the site in some depth in qualitative terms. It has been used in a range of urban planning procedures, particularly in Norway. Past, present and future are considered at different scales – area, local and detailed levels – considering various themes including values and significance. The method can comprise other methods, such as historical research, which demonstrates its comprehensiveness, but also the resource and time-intensive nature of the process. Targeting stakeholder groups for consultation in both public and private spheres during several stages is a common feature of DIVE analysis, before the most important points and issues are integrated into ensuing planning processes.[36] Its flexibility means it can be adjusted to suit resources, but has been criticised for its process-heavy approach that still allows the expert to frame any consultation.

DIVE was considered to be the most complete of the methods, and useful for establishing options for discussion because of its potential to involve different parties. However, there was still a danger of expert dominance and the potential for expert judgement, public participation, and politics to be mixed. The complexity and nuance were considered to be double-edged as inclusive but making it difficult to communicate issues. Although rooted in preservation management, it was not clear to everyone how decisions were reached. There was a risk that came from the combination of an inclusive, discursive approach that addresses dissonance that could present complex outcomes that were difficult to define against strong development pressure – that actions involving conservation would become fragmented and not provide clear alternatives to change that might not be desired in the future.

In terms of the impact such a study would have on the future of the park, there was a consideration that DIVE would provide a cross-disciplinary approach in which dissonant heritage was likely to be addressed. However, this method appeared to be the one of the three that might lead to the most change, depending on interpretations. This was in the sense of rapid change or gradual development of the park against the lack of strong alternatives. The method had the greatest potential to facilitate change, not least by identifying ways to valorize the park rather than protect existing values (albeit with a narrow focus).

Overview of the methods

The choice of method for eliciting and considering heritage values can have a huge effect on how a heritage site is understood and managed. How the future of the site is conceived, whether this is explicit or not, rests on assessments such as these, and their qualities can shift from advantage to hindrance by the social context alone. None of the methods offer the perfect perspective, or a 'view from Nowhere'. The potential to stifle positive change, or fail to resist changes, the dependency on opaque expert views or a public without in-depth knowledge, the potential for over-simplification, or lack of clarity creates a difficult balancing act. This is a balance that changes over time in ways that can put a strain on formal structures that do not necessarily reflect the voices of the carnival as multi-layered, mutable and contested. Understanding values over time requires a multi-method approach, and some acceptance of the lack of order when using contestation as a means to understand and engage.

Given the storied history of the park, and the layers of heritage and value that it embodies, resistance to change is not really consistent with the historical narrative of dynamic changes and layers of divergent or dissonant heritage co-existing. However, the success of recent developments in the park could be attributed to the possibility of avoiding change going unchecked. There is always likely to be a degree of dominance of one kind of heritage over another at a given time (the archaeological heritage is currently in the same way as the sculpture, partly submerging that narrative, but the sculptures have moved and will change over time – unlike the archaeology). The 'heritage' of the park is sustained by a discourse that is dynamic and changing, which contributes to, rather than detracts from, its authenticity – lived authenticity as an *authenticating process*. Dialogue becomes an authenticating process, authentic in Spinoza's concept of being true to oneself[37] as the values of the park are expressed and created through the dialogue of the carnivalesque. As Stuart Hall notes, "the question of meaning arises in relation to *all* the different moments or practices in our cultural circuit… However, one of the privileged 'media' through which meaning is produced and circulated is *language*"[38].

In the case of Ekeberg Park, contestation arose organically, and different viewpoints that were not solicited emerged through the process, nor were they acts that could be readily applied to an assessment procedure. Like each of the assessment methods, these criticisms were perspectives; imperfect, and incomplete. Eliciting values through formal structures has the risk of stifling or privileging voices, which are often more mobilized or tempered through interaction and opposition. Affording creativity without losing sight of the benefits of intergenerational transfer of heritage means negotiating a changing context and requires a transparency and openness when making decisions.

By acknowledging, rather than stifling or attempting to bring order to, the Bakhtinian carnival presents a range of qualities that can be instructive to understanding social preferences without categorization, difference without contestation, creativity without privilege, and change without artificiality. Following is a summary of the qualities that can be attributed to this approach.

- *Interaction*: Public spaces bringing together different voices not normally connected in a unified arena for freer expression (heritage and beyond).
- *Eccentricity*: A place where one can express values that do not conform. Instead of framing two opposing sides, a more inclusive environment is fostered.
- *(Mis)alliance*: Different concepts and combinations become possible – balances not choices based on different values and needs.

- *Outrageousness*: Creative, theatrical expressions become an authenticating process for a multi-layered space. As a matter of constructing the unknown from the known.
- *Criticism*: Opportunities for evaluation and engagement ensure that discussion is not a matter of 'anything goes', but a progressive development of identity negotiation.

Expertise and value assessment

Depicting heritage values as a Bakhtinian carnival, raises a pertinent, topical question of the role of the expert. The different uses of expertise and experts' authority in the assessment methods illustrate the variation in approach. This variation is not the presence or absence of an expert, but the role and the points of contact. And the kind of expertise, which is assumed to be the traditional heritage management focus, rather than negotiation. In the carnival, experts might show the consequences, but do not direct the way. With all of the mentioned formal methods, the expert has a central role to play in the most profound decisions, whether this is as an agent that can solicit different viewpoints, as the

Figure 4.11 The carnival laughter is found many places in the Ekeberg Park, for example at the toilet in one of the historic buildings called 'Karlsborg Spiseforretning', which is covered with the media discourse about the park.

Photo: H@V.

informed reviewer who can identify cultural significance beyond the immediate issues, or as the arbiter of divergent views.

The essence of the marketplace is that expertise is neither denied nor overpowering. Authority is accepted, but within the context of how it can contribute to the broader context of social welfare. 'In the matter of boots, I refer to the authority of the bootmaker; concerning houses, canals, or railroads, I consult that of the architect or engineer. ... But I allow neither the bootmaker nor the architect nor the *savant* to impose his authority upon me'.[39] The expert can explain the consequences of different possible futures, but does not necessarily have the expertise to say which of these is the most desirable. The expert is not a final arbiter, but a facilitator. Going beyond the triumph of the 'most significant' heritage over all else, or the changeable aspect of the popular vote requires the chance to see the park in new terms, where new connections, possibilities, and expressions can be expressed, criticized, and cultivated.

This leads to the requirement of new skills for experts involved in evaluating the past history, the present values, and the possible futures of heritage sites. Communication between different heritage professionals as well as different communities using heritage in different ways is required. Considering the carnivalesque in this respect presents the opportunity for a dynamic and nuanced approach to understanding heritage on the terms of the communities that use it than the experts' ideas of significance.

Conclusions

As a public park the Ekeberg Park case aligns with the Bakhtinian idea of the market place as carnivalesque – where low and high culture meets – a public space defined as the language of the people, as opposed to power structures found in more hierarchical parks, such as the symmetrical Vigeland Park in Oslo or the common Vitruvian shapes of royal gardens. The carnivalesque promotes dialogues between people, and democratic ideals.

The carnival can, as shown in this chapter, be a complement to traditional value assessment. It is arguably a way of addressing subtle, but powerful influences on the expression of values such as how values are assessed and the choice of method. Heritage conflicts that increase public dialogue promote the creation of a living heritage which mediates significant societal discourses in democratic societies. The valuation of the Ekeberg Park and the heritage in the park becomes divisive as the result of struggles or degrees of polarization between interests, cultural values, lifestyles, and world views. As such, the public park is a cultural space for communication and dialogues – a speaker's corner – where various societal issues are at stake (see figure 4.11). An innovative scope within the theoretical body of 'divisive heritage' and 'heritage dialogue' is, as stressed in this chapter, to gain knowledge about how disagreement acts as a creative force when it is transformed into carnivalesque culture.

The diverse discourses and uses of the Ekeberg Park exemplify the mixed messages that heritage 'broadcasts'. Although the role played by heritage experts is significant in the renewed planning of the park, the expertise is focused on eliciting, rather than deciding on, the different values embodied by Ekeberg Park that are not all found in archives and journals. Ringnes, working together with heritage experts and urban planning authorities for achieving his goals, was the catalyst (albeit unintentionally) for a carnivalesque discourse that combined top-down and bottom-up approaches. A rigorous planning process took place, but did not dictate what values were important to a passive public. The dynamic vocalization of different values allowed conflict to be constructive. In this process of heritagization, dominant discourses promoted by wealthy patrons and heritage experts faced resistance and challenges through a series of public counter-discourses and multiple performances, which also shows that for a renewed park design to be successful, public interests must be included as part of the authorized domain.

The problems of attempting to weave a single narrative or idea of value through the multi-layered nature of the park are highlighted in the Ekeberg Park case, where the nature of the park itself is dynamically changing with changing public values. The carnivalesque approach recasts the role of the heritage expert from the infallible authority to someone who can convene diverse parties, facilitate constructive, creative dialogue, and examine the consequences of imagined futures.

Notes

1 Tunbridge, J.E. and Ashworth, G.J. (1996), *Dissonant Heritage. The management of the past as a resource in conflict*. Chichester: Wiley.
2 Smith, L. (2006). *Uses of heritage*. London and New York: Routledge.
3 Holtorf, C. (1996). Towards a chronology of megaliths: understanding monumental time and cultural memory. *Journal of European Archaeology*, Vol. 4: pp.119–152.
4 Aronsson, P and Gradén, P. (2013). *Performing Nordic Heritage. Everyday Practices and Institutional Culture*. Farnham: Ashgate.
5 Macdonald, S. (2009). *Difficult heritage. Negotiating the Nazi past in Nuremberg and beyond*. New York: Routledge.
6 Ucko, P. J. (2000). Enlivening a 'dead' past. *Conservation and Management of Archaeological Sites*, Vol.4, no.2, pp. 67–92.
7 Smith, p.3.
8 Smith, L. and Waterton, E. (2009) *Heritage, Communities and Archaeology*. Duckworth Debates in Archaeology. London: Duckworth.
9 *The Burra Charter. The Australia ICOMOS Charter for Places of Cultural Significance* (2013). Burwood, Australia: Australian ICOMOS (International Council on Monuments and Sites),
10 For overview, see newsinenglish.no/Nina Berglund, September 23 (2013). *New landmark opens at Ekeberg*. Accessed January 15 2016 from: http://www.newsinenglish.no/2013/09/25/new-landmark-opens-at-ekeberg/
11 Bachtin, M. (1984). *Rabelais and his world*. Bloomington: Indiana University Press.
12 Low, S.M., D. Taplin, S. Scheld and T. Fisher. (2002). Recapturing Erased Histories: Ethnicity, Design, and Cultural Representation – A case study of Independence National Historical Park. *Journal of Architectural and Planning Research*, Vol. 19, no.4: pp.282–299. For overview, see also Low, S. M. (2002). Anthropological-Ethnographic Methods for the Assessment of Cultural Values in Heritage Conservation. In: *Assessing the Values of Cultural Heritage in Heritage Conservation*, ed. Marta de la Torre, pp. 31–49. Los Angeles, CA: Getty Conservation Institute. On the same case studies, see Low, S.M. (2003). Social Sustainability: People, History and Values. In: *Managing Change: Sustainable Approaches to the Conservation of the Built Environment*, eds. J. M. Teutonico and F. Matero, pp. 47–64. Los Angeles, CA: The Getty Conservation Institute.
13 Low, S.M., D. Taplin, and S. Scheld. (2005). *Rethinking Urban Parks. Public Space and Cultural Diversity*, p.4. Austin: The University of Texas Press.
14 Low, S.M., D. Taplin, and S. Scheld. (2005). *Rethinking Urban Parks. Public Space and Cultural Diversity*, p.4. Austin: The University of Texas Press.
15 See Bachtin 1984, pp. 285–286. See also Bakhtin, M. M. ([1981]2006). *The dialogic imagination. Four essays by M.M. Bakhtin*. Slavic series no. 1, edited by Holquist, M. Austin: University of Texas Press.
16 Bennett, T. ([1995]2009). *The Birth of the Museum. History, theory, politics*. London and New York: Routledge.
17 Featherstone, M. (1991). *Consumer culture and postmodernism*. London: Sage.
18 Gardiner, M. (1992). Bakhtin's Carnival: Utopia as Critique. *Utopian Studies* Vol. 3, Issue 2, pp. 21–29.
19 Thingsrud, L. (1998). *Kommunens skogkjøp. Folkepark eller tømmerskog*? Accessed January 15 2016 from: https://www.oslo.kommune.no/OBA/tobias/tobiasartikler/t3983.htm
20 Ekebergparken.com. Accessed January 15 2016 from: http://ekebergparken.com/en/stiftelsen

21 Røsok, Ø. (2011). Forvaltningsplan for Ekebergskråningen naturreservat, Oslo kommune. Fylkesmannen i Oslo og Akershus, Miljøvernavdelingen – rapport 11 (2011). Oslo. Accessed January 15 2016 from: https://www.fylkesmannen.no/Documents/Dokument%20FMOA/Milj%C3%B8%20og%20klima/Rapporter/Forvaltningsplan%20for%20Ekebergskr%C3%A5ningen%20naturreserva t,%20Oslo%20kommune%20-%20siste%20utkast.pdf

22 Vårt Land, Nordgaard Lorentzen, P. February 21 (2013). *Skal pusse opp nazi-monument*. Accessed January 15 2016 from: http://www.vl.no/2.615/skal-pusse-opp-nazi-monument-1.69583

23 NRK Østlandssendingen, Brattset Drabløs, M., Vestre Haram, I., Mordt, H. and Løken, K.-M. February 21 (2013). *Frykter nazi-monument blir valfartssted for nynazister*. Accessed January 15 2016 from: http://www.nrk.no/ostlandssendingen/klager-pa-oppussing-av-nazi-trapp-1.10921560

24 Folkeaksjonen for bevaring av Ekebergskogen, Accessed January 15 2016 from: https://folkeaksjonen.wordpress.com/author/folkeaksjonen/page/3/

25 Aftemposten, Klungrehaug, A. and Sunde, M., August 23 (2011). *Si nei til skulpturparken!* Accessed January 15 2016 from:http://www.aftenposten.no/meninger/Si-nei-til-skulpturparken-6284555.html

26 Picture from Dagbladet.no., Rammefjell, G. August 10 (2013). *Skriket mot skulpturparken*. Accessed January 19 2016 from: http://www.dagbladet.no/2013/08/10/kultur/meninger/hovedkommentar/skulpturparken/ekebergparken/28628476/

27 Manneparken. En skulpturpark som hyller det maskuline. Accessed January 19 2016 from: https://ma nneparken.wordpress.com/2011/07/03/velkommen-til-manneparken/

28 Dagbladet, Nordseth, P. November 30 (2012). *Her er Black Debbaths nakenstunt*. Accessed January 15 2016 from: http://www.dagbladet.no/2012/11/30/kultur/musikk/rock/black_debbath/ekeberg /24616844/

29 Galeriemagazine.com, Randle, S. August 1 (2017). *The World's 10 Most Beautiful Sculpture Parks*. Accessed September 25 2017 from: http://www.galeriemagazine.com/the-worlds-10-most-beaut iful-sculpture-parks/

30 newsinenglish.no/Nina Berglund, September 23 (2013). *New landmark opens at Ekeberg*. Accessed January 15 2016 from: http://www.newsinenglish.no/2013/09/25/new-landmark-opens-at -ekeberg/

31 Aftenposten, Røed, K. February 9 (2014). *Parken som parkerte kritikken*. Accessed January 15 2016 from: http://www.aftenposten.no/kultur/litteratur/Parken-som-parkerte-kritikken-7462024.html

32 Norgesavisen.no., Vega, R. August 24 (2013). *Oslo får egen gondolbane*. Accessed January 15 2016 from: https://norgesavisen.no/oslo-far-egen-gondolbane/ See also Dagsavisen, Gravklev, B.R., December 8 (2014). *Ringnes vurderer inngangspenger*. Accessed January 19 2016 from: http://www.dagsavisen.no/kultur/ringnes-vurderer-inngangspenger-1.303901

33 Hall, S. (2005). Whose heritage? Un-settling 'The Heritage', Re-imagining the Post-nation. In: J. Littler and R. Naidoo, eds. *The politics of heritage: The legacies of 'Race'*. London: Routledge, p. 24.

34 UNESCO. (2011). Recommendation on the Historic Urban Landscape, including a glossary of definitions. [accessed 18 June 2014] Available at: http://portal.unesco.org/en/ev.phpURL_ID=4885 7&URL_DO=DO_TOPIC&URL_SECTION=201.html

35 Throsby, D. (2002). *Economics and Culture*. Cambridge: Cambridge University Press. Navrud, S. and Ready, R.C. eds. *Valuing cultural heritage: applying environmental valuation techniques to historic buildings*. London: Monuments and Artefacts.

36 Riksantikvaren (2010). *Urban heritage analysis: a handbook about DIVE*. Accessed January 19 2016 from: http://brage.bibsys.no/xmlui/bitstream/handle/11250/176994/1/dive_veileder_engelsk.pdf

37 Spinoza, B. de (1958 [1677]) Tractus Politicus. In: The political works, ed. and transl. A.G. Wernham. Oxford: Clarendon Press.

38 Hall, S. (1997) 'Introduction', In: *Representations: cultural representations and signifying practices*. Ed. S. Hall. London: Sage. pp.3–4.

39 Bakunin, M. (1861). *God and the State by Michael Bakunin [1814-1876]*. First American Edition. Accessed January 17 2016 from: http://dwardmac.pitzer.edu/Anarchist_Archives/bakunin/godand state/godandstate_ch1.html

5 Marketing Australia's cultural heritage

The Sydney Olympic Games Closing Ceremony

Leanne White

Introduction

The Sydney 2000 Olympic Games represented the biggest event ever held in Australia. The Opening and Closing Ceremonies were a prime opportunity to sell Australia and the nation's cultural assets to the world. The ceremonies were an overt celebration and commemoration of Australian popular culture – presented in an original and sometimes highly self-deprecating manner. The specific cultural industries promoted included: music, film, art, literature, and television. The ceremonies both told and sold the story of Australia in all its diversity.

The Closing Ceremony in particular showcased Australian humour, popular culture, and the nation's world-renowned icons. Beach culture, sport, music, and Australia's outdoor lifestyle were promoted in the 'Aussie Icons' segment of the Closing Ceremony. Australia's creativity, irreverence and idiosyncrasies were jubilantly celebrated at this carefully planned event. Australian popular culture was promoted to the world in an overt and proud manner. As they are less elaborate and more informal, Olympic Closing Ceremonies have been largely overlooked in the academic literature despite the significant amount of money and planning that goes into the design and staging of the event.

Exploring official, popular, and commercial nationalism

A wide range of similarities and differences exist between 'official nationalism' which is principally generated from the federal government or government departments via significant public events and advertising campaigns, 'commercial nationalism' – the brand of nationalism generated by private organisations, and 'popular nationalism' – the nationalism portrayed via popular culture outlets such as film and television. Understanding the complex relationships and interconnections between these three discourses of nationalism further develops earlier studies which identified commercial nationalism as a subject worthy of analysis (James, 1983).

A diagram and explanation of the relationship between official nationalism, popular nationalism, and commercial nationalism is outlined below (see Figure 5.1). Firstly, official nationalism is the civic, formal, and ceremonial nationalism such as the Australian Federal Government's planning of the Bicentennial celebrations in 1988 or the Centenary of Federation celebrations in 2001. National anthems, flags, and official symbols are part of official nationalism. Secondly, the theorising of popular nationalism was introduced in Australia by Ward (1966) and can include nationalist messages and images as depicted in popular culture texts such as Australian film, television, popular songs, and sport.

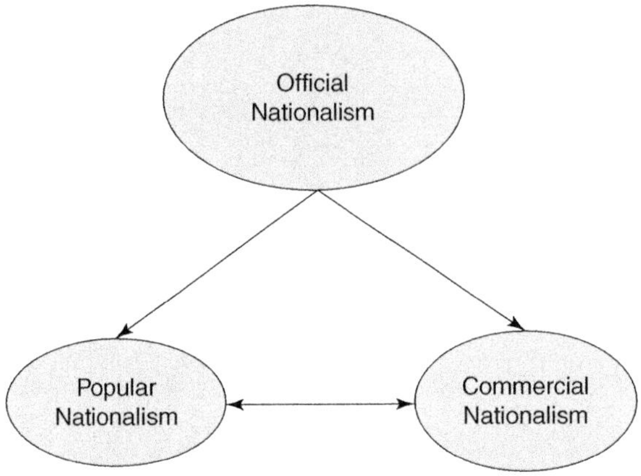

Figure 5.1 Official nationalism is the dominant pool of nationalism that primarily emerges from the nation-state. Both popular and commercial nationalism fall under the larger umbrella of official nationalism. Some popular and commercial images swim to the top while others sink to the bottom and do not develop currency.

Ward's archetypal text *The Australian Legend* attempted to 'trace the historical origins and development of the Australian legend or national mystique' (Ward, 1966, p. v). Thirdly, commercial nationalism refers to consumer-related uses of these national symbols, images, and icons. It is the material, everyday nationalism represented by companies and brands such as Foster's Lager, Qantas, and Vegemite. While popular and commercial nationalism generally play a subservient role to official nationalism, these forms of nationalism occasionally overlap. An example of all three forms of nationalism intersecting in Australian culture would be the kangaroo being displayed on the Australian coat of arms and the one dollar coin, the popular boxing kangaroo flag being flown frequently at sporting events, and the use of the kangaroo as the Qantas airline logo.

While numerous theorists have analysed the term 'nationalism', Benedict Anderson's ground-breaking work *Imagined Communities: Reflections on the Origin and Spread of Nationalism* has reconceptualised the way scholars have come to think about nationalism and related terms such as nation, nation-state, national, and nationalistic. Anderson popularly conceptualised the nation as an 'imagined political community'. He argued, 'It is imagined because members of even the smallest nation will never know most of their fellow-members, meet them, or even hear of them, yet in the minds of each lives the image of their communion' (Anderson, 1991, p. 6).

Of the books produced on theories of nationalism over the past few decades, Anderson is among the most frequently cited (Culler and Cheah, 2003, p. vii). Ozkirimli argues that Anderson's work 'constitutes one of the most original accounts of nationalism to date' (Ozkirimli, 2000, p. 151) while James claims that Anderson's key text 'remains the most insightful book written in the area' (James, 1996, p. ix).

Anderson contends that official nationalism is the 'willed merger of nation and dynastic empire' and argues that the concept came about in response to popular nationalism that emerged in Europe from the 1820s (Anderson, 1991, p. 86). He explains that official nationalism emanates 'from the state' and has as its primary feature a focus on 'serving the interests of the state first and foremost' (Anderson, 1991, p. 159).

Horne provided a significant study of Australia nationalism – particularly as it related to popular nationalism and official nationalism – when he claimed in the late 1960s that a serious discussion was beginning to emerge on the subject of breaking constitutional links with England, changing anthem and flag, and generally re-assessing the images projected in many forms of Australian representation. He asserted that Australia experienced a genuine 'cultural awakening' in the arts and in works produced by public intellectuals. Horne defined 'new nationalism' as an acceptance that there was nothing embarrassing about being Australian and that our nation's stories were as valid as the next country's (Horne, 1981, p. 67). In many respects, Horne's new nationalism displayed some similarities to popular nationalism and (in its more strident manifestation) commercial nationalism.

However, it was White's landmark text *Inventing Australia: Images and Identity 1688–1980,* that broke significant ground on the topic of national imagery, symbols, and icons. White claimed: "There is no 'real' Australia waiting to be uncovered. A national identity is an invention. There is no point asking whether one version of this essential Australia is truer than another because they are all intellectual constructs, neat, tidy, comprehensible – and necessarily false" (White, 1981, p. viii).

White argued that national identity is an invention which is constantly being 'fractured, questioned and redefined' (White, 1981, p. x). He claimed that the question is not whether definitions of Australia are correct, but who is responsible for the production of these definitions and whose interest do they serve? White observed that the continual questioning and search for an Australian identity in this country has become a 'national obsession' (White, 1981, p. viii). He put forward an observation about the commercialisation of nationalism in his argument that dominant economic interests find it advantageous to suggest that they identify with the Australian identity.

As argued above, commercial nationalism describes the style of nationalism promoted by advertisers and advertising agencies as it encompasses the suggestion that commerce and the nation are deliberately constructed entities. The term commercial nationalism alludes to the notion that the once clearer boundaries of the domains of commerce and nation have been virtually eliminated and that the broader concept of nationalism which deals with ideas and beliefs, has combined with the economic forces in the world of commerce which compete for the consumer dollar. Thus, commercial nationalism is essentially a paradox – two potentially conflicting sectors combining their influences and occupying the same space (White, 1994: 1).

In 2004, in a contribution to the book *National Days / National Ways: Historical, Political, and Religious Celebrations around the World*, I also compared commercial nationalism with official nationalism in a chapter focussing on the ways in which Australia celebrates its national day. I argued:

> Commercial nationalism – the adoption of national signifiers in order to generate profit – is a continuation and extension of the overall theme, style and symbols of the official nationalism. Commercial nationalism and official nationalism are directly related, and both contribute to the total discourse on nationalism. The official and commercial strands of nationalism are not binary oppositions; there is a significant degree of overlap between the areas… Commercial nationalism operates like a paradigm; it continues the pattern that has been firmly established by the official body. It is not in the interest of the private company to create conflict between these two types of nationalism; they are merely used for different purposes.
>
> (White, 2004: 28)

Commercial and popular nationalism (often more vociferous manifestations of official nationalism) can become apparent in consumer-related and popular uses of national symbols, images, and icons (signifiers). National signifiers such as the country's flag or landmass are adopted by the worlds of commerce and popular culture for consumption in the market. Images of the nation and types of nationalism intersect and change (depending on the use to which they are put).

This chapter will now explore the various ways in which the nation was imagined by key event planners and then communicated to millions in Australia and billions around the world. The official, popular, and commercial images projected to the world in the 'Aussie Icons' segment of the Sydney Closing Ceremony are examined, along with some discussion of what these images tell us about who we are as a nation, and how we might want to be market ourselves to the world.

Selling Australia's cultural heritage at the Sydney 2000 Closing Ceremony

The Closing Ceremony of the Sydney 2000 Olympic Games, televised on October 1, was the second most-watched event in Australia's history at the time. The overall ratings figure for the Closing Ceremony across Australia was 10,065,000–371,000 fewer than the number for the Opening Ceremony (Warneke, 2000, p. 6). The Closing Ceremony was designed to be a giant party where the less formal side of Australia could be shown to the world. Artistic Director David Atkins explained, 'We're now in kewpie doll land' (Cameron, 2000). Gordon described the event as a 'kaleidoscope of kitsch' in which the 'clichés were rampant' (Gordon, 2003, p. 254). The Games were now almost over and the general consensus was that Sydney had staged a successful Olympics. It was time to show off Australia's popular culture.

The Closing Ceremony generated an entirely different message from that produced in the more formal Opening Ceremony. The party was just about over, the Games had gone remarkably well, and it was time for organisers, participants, and spectators to finally relax and celebrate. Australia's cultural industries continued to be showcased during the event but the festive mood in the stadium became more pronounced when the clichés, symbolic images, and icons were revealed in a carefully directed way.

The Ceremony presented the iconic, the ironic, the internationally successful, and the irreverent. The icons revealed in the Closing Ceremony were recognisably and unmistakably Australian. They were also deliberately ironic, highly irreverent, and inclusive. All icons were internationally successful (particularly in a commercial sense). Being a successful Australian entrepreneur seemed to be one of the key selection criteria for being chosen to participate in the Australian Icons Parade at the Sydney Games.

Australian beach culture

The first Australian icons to be revealed were a colourful collection of Bondi Lifesavers dancing and displaying their red and yellow uniforms which matched the colours of the safety flags on Australia's beaches. The Bondi Surf Lifesaving Club was the first official club of its type in the world. With its kilometre of sand surrounded by headlands, Bondi Beach is instantly familiar to many tourists and locals as one of the best-known beaches in the world (Hutchinson, 2002, p. 70). Bondi, an Aboriginal word for 'the sound of tumbling water', was also the birthplace of the lifesaving reel. The rope on the reel was attached to a lifesaver's belt and allowed the lifesaver to perform a rescue in the surf. The fact that the

Lifesavers emerged dancing rather than marching immediately signalled the ironic nature of the spectacle. The parade signalled a tribute to more than 20,000 volunteers who patrol Australia's beaches as part of the Surf Life Saving Association.

The image of the reliable surf lifesaver has been an enduring part of Australian beach culture for almost a century. Jaggard argues that 'the lifesaver fits the role of the national symbol' due to 'the obvious pride of physique and masculinity, the careless disregard for danger, and their dislike of authority' (Jaggard, 1998, pp. 69–70). Fiske, Hodge, and Turner argue that in Australia the lifesaver is greeted with 'the kind of heroic status accorded the digger' (Fiske et al., 1987, pp. 65–66).

The second important icon or artefact in the Lifesaver segment was the essential footwear item of summer – the ubiquitous thong. While thongs or flip-flops have existed for thousands of years, only in Australia has the cheap and versatile piece of rubber footwear assumed iconic status (*Sydney Morning Herald*, 2003). The nomenclature 'thong' to describe a type of footwear is uniquely Australian. The humble thong has been an essential part of beach culture in Australia since the 1950s but has taken on renewed and redefined status in recent years with ornate versions making their way into the pages of fashion magazines around the world. The organisers of the Closing Ceremony were making a unique statement to the rest of the world by presenting the thong as an Aussie icon. The highly ironic and irreverent statement stressed that Australians have no problem with mocking themselves and the quirky items that form a unique part of their culture. Fiske, Hodge, and Turner argue that the thong speaks of Australia's warm climate, our informality, and its 'cheapness bears our egalitarianism' (Fiske et al., 1987, p. 175).

Australian popular music

Riding on the giant thong as it entered the stadium was Australian pop star Kylie Minogue. Commentator Bruce McAvaney announced, 'Pop Diva taking on surf culture. An icon – Kylie Minogue' (McAvaney, 2000). Alomes also described Minogue, along with Ian Thorpe, Nicole Kidman, and Cate Blanchett as 'almost global icons' (Alomes, 2005, p. 141). Kylie Minogue first came to the public's attention in 1986 when she played the role of motor mechanic Charlene Mitchell on the popular Australian television soap opera *Neighbours*. While Minogue was a promising actor, it was her career as a singer for which she became best known with the cover song *Locomotion* becoming the biggest selling single of the 1980s.

Wearing an identical pink sundress, Minogue was presented as the grown-up version of 'Hero Girl' (Nikki Webster) – the young star of the Opening Ceremony who fell asleep at the beach and entered the ancient world of Australia's dreamtime. Now that the Games were about to conclude, the palpable message presented by the event organisers was that Australia had matured as a nation and had lost its innocence – and so too had the young girl. To accompany the visual metaphor of a matured Australia projected by the young girl who had grown into a woman, commentator Garry Wilkinson explained, 'Any lingering doubts and insecurities Australians might have had about their place in the world ought to be thrown out the window with the success of these Games' (Wilkinson, 2000).

Minogue 'topped and tailed' the Aussie icons section of the Closing Ceremony by commencing with the Abba hit song *Dancing Queen* and concluding with the popular song *On a Night Like This*. References to social inclusiveness, particularly for the world's homosexual community, were reinforced by the choice of Kylie, the choice of the song *Dancing Queen*, the wearing of the colour pink, the style of dancing, and the choice of athletic performers dressed as Bondi Surf Lifesavers to accompany the segment.

Australian sport

Following on from Kylie and the giant thong, and in keeping with the beach theme, a large silver shark emerged accompanied by the theme music from the movie *Jaws*. Commentator Garry Wilkinson explained, 'For many international tourists, this is the first thing they learn or hear or even know about Australia. The alleged shark menace on our beaches in summer' (Wilkinson, 2000). While the mechanised menace was making its way down the athletic track, there were more than a few hints that this float was not simply a shark. A patch of green on top of the shark and accompanying golfers next to the float suggested another meaning – revealed when Australia's 'Great White Shark', champion golfer Greg Norman, made his entrance hitting golf balls into the crowd.

Prior to his retirement in 1998, Greg Norman was regarded as the world's best golfer and won numerous titles during the late 1980s and early 1990s, including two British Opens and five Australian Opens. In 1998 Norman was announced as Australia's Ambassador for Sport (Willox, 1998) and in 2001 was inducted into the 'World Golf Hall of Fame'. Like many well-known sportspeople, Norman put his name behind a sports clothing business and was rarely seen without his signature hat with shark logo.

Something for the children

The next Aussie Icons to be revealed to the stadium and television audiences were the successful children's television export from the government-owned Australian Broadcasting Corporation (ABC) – *Bananas in Pyjamas*. While the television program has been a success for the ABC, it is the associated global merchandising which has proved to be the real revenue generator as the network also controls the licensing agreements for more than 600 *Bananas in Pyjamas* products in 30 countries (Walter, 2003). The *Bananas in Pyjamas* television program was launched in 1992. B1, B2, and their friends Amy, Lulu, Morgan, Rat in a Hat, and others hold the honour of being Australia's most popular children's character exports. The program has enjoyed particular success in the United States, Asia, and South America.

An iconic female ambassador

Following the famous bananas was Australian icon and supermodel Elle Macpherson. Macpherson was born in Sydney in 1963 as Eleanor Gow. Elle (as she is widely known) in some ways represents the natural beauty of Australia and its people. She is tall, healthy, and portrays a particular sun-drenched sex appeal. As one of the most photographed models in recent times, it was appropriate that Macpherson entered the arena aboard a large camera with a telescopic lens. The lens of the camera was extended and Elle walked down the short runway and paraded the asset that she is most famous for. Macpherson was accompanied by 20 female models and 12 photographers who walked alongside her float.

Besides a successful modelling career, Macpherson started the 'Intimates' range of Bendon lingerie. As explored in a paper which examined the underwear advertising imagery generated by Minogue, Macpherson, and others, the feminisation of the Australian image represented a new breed of cosmopolitan Australianness (Buckell, 2003, p. 25). Macpherson was employed as the face of the Western Australia Tourism Commission for a number of years, and when the Queen's Baton Relay for the Melbourne 2006 Commonwealth

Games commenced on the steps of Buckingham Palace, the Queen handed the baton (containing her voice message on a microchip) to Australian icons Cathy Freeman and Elle Macpherson.

An iconic male ambassador

The next Australian icon presented by the event designers was the highly recognisable laconic 'Face of Australia' for many years – Paul Hogan. Hogan secured himself a unique place in Australia's international imagery and identity in the 1980s with an advertising campaign promoting Australia, and the *Crocodile Dundee* movies. As Rivenburgh and colleagues argue, Australia's 'two most influential cultural ambassadors' as far as the United States is concerned 'are, without question, *Crocodile Dundee* (Paul Hogan) and the kangaroo' (Rivenburgh et al., 2004, p. 22).

Paul Hogan's phenomenal movie successes with *Crocodile Dundee* (1986), *Crocodile Dundee II* (1988) and *Crocodile Dundee in Los Angeles* (2001) entrenched his global position as Australia's key ambassador. The first two *Crocodile Dundee* movies made more than $600 million in box-office sales worldwide (Jinman, 2003). The movie scripts were penned by Hogan and his business partner John Cornell, and essentially juxtapose the life of Mick Dundee, an outback larrikin crocodile hunter from Walkabout Creek, against that of Sue Charlton, an outgoing and savvy journalist from New York. Turner describes the *Crocodile Dundee* films as exhibiting the "familiar 'bush myth' nationalism" (Turner, 1993, p. 151). Until his death in 2006, Steve Irwin – *The Crocodile Hunter*, superseded Hogan to become a familiar and exceptionally popular symbol of Australia on a global scale.

While Paul Hogan stood on top of the giant *Crocodile Dundee* hat cracking a stock-whip in the Closing Ceremony, some shrimps (or prawns – as Australians know them) rode nearby on bicycles. Some found it unfortunate that the chief ceremonies organiser Ric Birch and his team decided to parade some of the well-worn stereotypes such as the prawns – even if they were deliberately mocking themselves. Cashman argued:

> While shrimps on the barbie might have impressed many overseas in the 1980s, such images are now dated and hackneyed – they undersell the richness of Australian culture and convey a view of the country which is not comfortable with many Australians.
>
> (Cashman, 1999a, p. 58)

To further emphasise the Australian stereotypes, crocodiles on roller-blades, water buffalo on scooters, and frill-necked lizards on unicycles also accompanied Paul Hogan. The viewer who was well-tuned to irony might have realised that this was another one of Ric Birch's moments of sweet revenge directed at those who mocked his kangaroos on bikes when Australia was briefly promoted as the next Olympic Games venue at the Atlanta Closing Ceremony in 1996.

It was in 1984, when the Australian Tourist Commission (ATC) – now Tourism Australia – employed Hogan to promote holidays, that he became a living national icon. 'Hoges' sold Australia by informing prospective visitors that they should make the trip down under and 'Come and say g'day'. To further entice the traveller he promised to personally 'throw another shrimp on the barbie' for them. Paul Hogan was awarded Australian of the Year at the height of his tourism fame in 1985. Former ATC Managing Director John Morse claimed that when Hogan uttered those famous words '...it was actually one of the first times that the world has taken any sort of notice of Australia' (ABC and Open Learning Australia, 1997).

The relationship between Hogan and the ATC has been ongoing and successful for both parties, particularly in one of the key markets, the United States. John Morse explained, 'The Australian people are a major drawcard for Americans and Paul Hogan is perceived to be the quintessential Aussie – warm, friendly, irreverent and genuine' (Bombara, 2002). Day argues that the *Crocodile Dundee* figure resonates with Australians because it embodies 'echoes of the bushman/digger' stereotype (Day, 1998, p. xi). Understandably, the ATC made the most of the enormous marketing opportunity presented by the Olympics Games and featured Hogan as Mick Dundee and the Qantas mascot Vic the koala in a $7 million advertising campaign. The advertisements were aired in New York and Los Angeles and reveal Hogan telling his target audience to, 'Stop dreaming! C'mon. I've had a lot of fun in your country. How about you come down and have some fun in mine' (Australian Associated Press, 2000, p. 4). Morse also explained that 'Interest and awareness in Australia is at an all-time high in the US and this tactical advertisement will help convert the interest into holiday bookings' (AAP, 2000, p. 4).

Australia: the diverse and tolerant nation

Celebrating another successful Australian export was the next float in the Parade of Icons which paid tribute to the 1993 hit film *The Adventures of Priscilla: Queen of the Desert.* The film was a commercial success grossing $16 million in Australia and $70 million worldwide (ABC, 2000a). The movie traces the journey of three drag queens as they head west across the rugged Australian outback from Sydney to Alice Springs in a pink and silver bus named Priscilla. Adam/Felicia (played by Guy Pearce) and Anthony/Mitzi (Hugo Weaving) are transvestites, while Bernadette (Terence Stamp) is a transsexual. The character played by Weaving was loosely based on Mitzi Macintosh – a popular Sydney drag queen.

The film was partly responsible for the revived interest in Abba and their music in the 1990s as it featured the popular song *Mama Mia*. Another Australian film, *Muriel's Wedding* (1994), also glorified the Swedish band as Muriel Heslop (Toni Collette) played the role of an obsessed Abba fan. The announced inclusion of this particular segment in the Closing Ceremony drew an adverse reaction from church groups and conservative politicians. David Oldfield, then head of the extreme right-wing political party One Nation declared, 'Lifestyle drag queens need psychological help or perhaps gender re-assignment surgery, not public attention or adulation' (British Broadcasting Corporation, 2000).

In an interview for the ABC's *Lateline*, the outspoken Reverend Fred Nile said, 'I say let's take say, *Forty Thousand Horsemen*, something which shows Australians – a true reflection of Australia, its manhood, not a lot of men dressed up as women' (ABC, 2000b). Event designer Ric Birch dismissed the complaints, asserting that the extreme views expressed by right-wing reactionaries were not representative of Australia's open, tolerant, diverse, and accepting society (ABC, 2000b). Birch also said that including the *Priscilla* segment was an acknowledgement of Sydney's popular annual Gay and Lesbian Mardi Gras (BBC, 2000).

The inclusion of *Priscilla* in the Closing Ceremony was an opportunity for an alternative version of Australian masculinity to be projected to the world – a version already internationally famous through the drag performances of Australia's best known Dame – Edna Everage. Birch and Atkins originally conceived the idea of the Closing Ceremony being hosted by Dame Edna. Unfortunately, Barry Humphries turned them down

(Cameron, 2000). Housewife Superstar Dame Edna Everage was however successfully integrated into the Melbourne 2006 Commonwealth Games Closing Ceremony. Dame Edna sang the praises of her city with the tribute *We've Made the Most of Melbourne*.

As mentioned earlier, Australian pop diva Kylie Minogue provided the figurative bookends for the Aussie icons section of the Closing Ceremony by commencing with the Abba song *Dancing Queen* and concluding with *On a Night Like This*. All Australian icons revealed in the Closing Ceremony were ironic, irreverent, inclusive, and internationally successful. References to inclusiveness were evident with female elements (Minogue and Macpherson), male elements (Norman and Hogan), gay elements(*Priscilla*), and elements which appealed to the young (B1 and B2) – thus appealing to men, women, the gay community and children. All the icons that appeared in this segment circled the arena as Kylie Minogue's *On a Night like This* was performed.

Commentator Garry Wilkinson emphasised the distinctively Australian nature of the spectacle by observing that the arena was 'filled with things uniquely Australian and yet instantly recognisable anywhere in the world' (Wilkinson, 2000). The scene was extravagant and vibrant. In another uniquely 'Australian' moment captured by the cameras, one of the Australian athletes had broken away from the enclosed area where the athletes of the world were partying and managed to perch himself on top of the toe-piece of the now 'Kylie-less' giant thong. This brazen Australian athlete in a Mambo shirt relished the attention, waved to the crowd, threw kisses, and pretended to conduct the music. There were no officials or security guards to be found anywhere near the athlete or the thong – an example of unscripted Australian humour playing a unique role in the proceedings.

Conclusions

Australia's popular cultural exports were proudly displayed in the Closing Ceremony of the Sydney 2000 Olympic Games. The Closing Ceremony showcased Australian humour, popular culture, and its world-renowned icons. Australia's irreverence and idiosyncrasies were jubilantly celebrated. While the Opening Ceremony told (and sold) the story of Australia in all its diversity, the Closing Ceremony was an overt celebration, commemoration, and commercialisation of Australia presented in a unique and highly self-deprecating Australian way.

Former Premier of New South Wales, Bob Carr, announced 'Sydney 2000 is one story nobody need fake. This was Australia on show as never before – an intelligent, friendly, contemporary society…' and the Sydney Games were '…the biggest and most exciting thing to happen in this nation during peacetime' (Veal and Lynch, 2001, p. 424). Cashman argued that 'The Olympic Games have become the world's greatest peacetime event because it is an evolving and dynamic festival' (Cashman, 1999b, p. 16). If the Sydney 2000 Games were Australia's greatest story, the Opening and Closing Ceremonies were considered the bookends (Webb, 2001, p. 96).

There has been no better opportunity in Australia's history to showcase the country's popular culture to such a large and attentive audience. The event managers had thought outside the square and presented a uniquely Australian production. The organisers of the London 2012 Olympic Games Closing Ceremony have also admitted to following Australia's eccentric example.

By examining the ways in which event organisers carefully planned the Sydney Olympic Games Closing Ceremony and expanding on the social and cultural meanings attached to the event, this chapter has contributed to cultural heritage, destination marketing, and event management knowledge bases. The Closing Ceremony of the Sydney Games is an incredibly rich text to examine. It is a text which says an enormous amount about the Australian nation-state. Director of Ceremonies Ric Birch said he was surprised to discover 'that academic circles around the world put so much effort and emphasis on the content of ceremonies' (Birch, 1996, p. 289). He should not have been so surprised. These iconic national texts create key archival images that shape the nation and its sense of self into the future.

The Sydney Olympic Games in 2000, particularly the Opening and Closing Ceremonies, were key moments in Australia's history – moments when the eyes of the world were keenly observing Australia. The gaze of the outside world was upon us and we were acutely aware of the stare. The local and national media reported on that mega event in September and October 2000 – and we reported on how the world reported on us. At the beginning of a new millennium, how we chose to present ourselves at the Sydney Games was an important prologue to how the world might perceive the Australian nation-state in future years.

References

Alomes, S. (2005). Conclusion: Pacific Comparison, Global Futures. In S. Alomes (Ed.), *Islands in the Stream: Australia and Japan Face Globalisation* (pp. 139–145). Hawthorn: Maribyrnong Press.

Anderson, B. (1991). *Imagined Communities: Reflections on the Origins and Spread of Nationalism (Second Edition).* London:Verso.

Australian Associated Press (2000, September 26). Dundee and Elle go for Tourism Gold Again. *The Age*, p. 4.

Australian Broadcasting Corporation (2000a, August 23). Glittering Ceremony. Retrieved from http://www.abc.net.au/lateline/s166926.htm

Australian Broadcasting Corporation (2000b, August 23). Closing Ceremony Surprise Sparks Public Outrage. Retrieved from http://www.abc.net.au/worldtoday/s166844.htm

Australian Broadcasting Corporation and Open Learning Australia (1997). Framing Australia, *Wish You Were Here.* Retrieved from http://www.abc.net.au/ola/tourism/transcripts/tran13.htm

Birch, R. (1996). The Sydney 2000 Ceremonies. In M. Moragas, J. MacAloon and M. Llinés (Eds.). *Olympic Ceremonies: Historical Continuity and Cultural Exchange* (pp. 289–294). Lausanne: International Olympic Committee.

Bombara, P. (2002, October 20). The ATC: Maintaining the Olympic Afterglow. *B and T Marketing and Media.* Retrieved from http://wwwbandt.com.au/articles/a1/0c002ba1.asp

British Broadcasting Corporation. (2000, August 24). Olympics to Feature Drag Queens. Retrieved from http://news.bbc.co.uk/1/hi/world/asia-pacific/893299.stm

Buckell, J. (2003, October 8). Identity Rooted in Desire. *The Australian*, p. 25.

Cameron, D. (2000, October 1). A message or two before thank you, and goodnight. *Sydney Morning Herald.* Retrieved from http://www.olympics.smh.com.au/new/2000/10/01/ffxlesvtrdc.html

Cashman, R. (1999a). *Olympic Countdown: Diary of the Sydney Olympics 1998.* Petersham: Walla Walla Press, University of New South Wales.

Cashman, R. (1999b). The Greatest Peacetime Event. In R. Cashman and A. Hughes (Eds.), *Staging the Olympics: The Event and its Impact* (pp. 3–17). Sydney: University of New South Wales Press.

Culler, J. and Cheah, P. (Eds.) 2003. *Grounds of Comparison: Around the Work of Benedict Anderson.* New York: Routledge.

Day, D. (1998). Introduction. In D. Day (Ed.), *Australian Identities* (pp. ix–xv). Melbourne: Australian Scholarly Publishing.

Fiske, J., Hodge, B. and Turner, G. (1987). *Myths of Oz: Reading Australian Popular Culture.* Sydney: Allen and Unwin.

Gordon, H. (2003). *The Time of Our Lives: Inside the Sydney Olympics.* St Lucia: University of Queensland Press.

Horne, D. (1981). National Identity in the Period of the New Nationalism. In *Nationalism and Class in Australia: 1920–1980.* Brisbane: Australian Studies Centre, University of Queensland.

Hutchinson, G. (2002). *True Blue,* Camberwell: Viking.

Jaggard, E. (1998). The Australian Surf Lifesaver as a National Symbol, 1920–60. In D. Day (Ed.), *Australian Identities* (pp. 58–72). Melbourne: Australian Scholarly Publishing.

James, P. (1983). Australia in the Corporate Image: A New Nationalism. *Arena,* No. 63, 65–106.

James, P. (1996). *Nation Formation: Towards a Theory of Abstract Community.* London: Sage.

Jinman, R. (2003, May 15). Hoges Ready to Approach Comeback with Gay Abandon, *Sydney Morning Herald.* Retrieved from http://www.smh.com.au/articles/2003/05/14/1052885295260.html

McAvaney, B. (2000, October 1). *Sydney 2000 Closing Ceremony.* Seven Network.

Ozkirimli, U. (2000). *Theories of Nationalism: A Critical Introduction.* Houndmills: Macmillan.

Rivenburgh, N., Louw, E., Loo, E. and Mersham, G. (2004). *The Sydney Olympics and Foreign Attitudes Towards Australia.* Gold Coast: Cooperative Research Centre for Sustainable Tourism.

Sydney Morning Herald (2003, January 14). Fashion Flips over the Thong. Retrieved from http://www.smh.com.au/1041990233098.htm

Turner, G. (1993). *National Fictions: Literature, Film and the Construction of Australian Narrative (Second Edition).* St Leonards: Allen and Unwin.

Veal, A. J. and Lynch, R. (2001). *Australian Leisure (Second Edition).* Frenchs Forest: Pearson Education Australia.

Walter, B. (2003, April 14). Put those Bananas in a Pair of NRL Pyjamas. *Sydney Morning Herald.* Retrieved from http://www.smh.com.au/cgi-bin/common/popup

Ward, R. (1966). *The Australian Legend.* Melbourne: Oxford University Press.

Warneke, R. (2000, October 5). Games Finale Beats Opening, *The Age* (Green Guide supplement), p. 6.

Webb, T. (2001). *The Collaborative Games: The Story Behind the Spectacle.* Annandale: Pluto Press Australia.

White, L. (1994). Commercial Nationalism: Images of Australia in Television Advertising, Unpublished Master of Arts Research thesis. Footscray: Humanities Department, Victoria University of Technology.

White, L. (2004). The Bicentenary of Australia: Celebration of a Nation. In L. K. Fuller (Ed.), *National Days / National Ways: Historical, Political and Religious Celebrations around the World* (pp. 25–39). Westport: Praeger.

White, R. (1981). *Inventing Australia: Images and Identity 1688–1980.* Sydney: George Allen and Unwin.

Wilkinson, G. (2000, October 1). *Sydney 2000 Closing Ceremony.* Seven Network.

Willox, I. (1998, August 28). Greg Norman Appointed as Ambassador for Sport, Minister for Foreign Affairs (Media Release). Retrieved from http://www.dfat.gov.au/media/releases/foreign/1998/fa118_98.html

6 Managing sustainable consumption of cultural heritage

The key role of existential authenticity

Tomaž Kolar, Mateja Kos Koklič and Vesna Žabkar

Introduction

There is a widespread consensus regarding the importance of sustainability for contemporary tourism, and also that cultural heritage plays an important role in sustainability efforts. According to the European Commission, conserving cultural as well as natural heritage is fundamental to sustainable tourism[1]. Some agendas even consider cultural heritage as the fourth pillar of sustainable development[2], alongside the economic, social, and environmental pillars. In the context of cultural heritage, the sustainability principle implies "ensuring the continuing contribution of heritage to the present through the thoughtful management of change"[3]. It has been debated that cultural heritage as one of the expressions of culture enables and drives sustainable development, and is a key to poverty eradication, quality education, sustainable environmental management, the sustainability of cities, social cohesion, and inclusion[4]. Further, cultural heritage provides a potential source of employment, social capital, cultural diversity, and energy savings, and thus importantly contributes to sustainability[5]. It is, however, less clear how the sustainability *of* cultural heritage can be managed.

In this regard, we posit that authenticity and its relationship with sustainability should play a strategically important role due to their overlapping goals and conceptual synergies. For that purpose, we first comparatively examine sustainability and authenticity in terms of their definition and key ideas, commonalities, and implications. Sustainability has generally been defined either narrowly in terms of environmental stasis and system maintenance or more broadly in terms of balancing economic, ecological, and social goals and consequences[6]. Sustainable consumption encompasses a process of search, use, and disposal of any good or service that has an effect on the environment. Such consumption should minimize environmental effects, consider the needs of future generations, and strive to achieve the satisfaction of needs that produce a better quality of life[7]. According to UNEP and WTO, sustainable tourism "takes full account of its current and future economic, social and environmental impacts, addressing the needs of visitors, the industry, the environment and host communities". Moreover, respect for socio-cultural authenticity is one of the key goals of sustainable tourism[8]. The development of sustainable tourism rests on three features: (1) quality of the visitor experience and life; (2) the continuity of tourism; and (3) sustainable development including a balance of the needs of tourists, operators, host communities, and the environment[9].

While authenticity is also acknowledged as something of a universal value in tourism[10], it is primarily understood as a broad and diffuse "driver" rather than a proactive stance or clear goal. Although various declarations regarding the preservation of cultural heritage state the importance of authenticity[11], it is also clear that the lack of a timely definition and consensus among researchers is hindering the progress of "authenticity management" in tourism[12]. Today, a mere focus on the preservation and curation of heritage objects seems too narrow and obsolete. Authenticity is not relevant as an inherent property of objects, places, or cultural practices, but as a quality which is culturally constructed and dependent upon the observer and the context[13]. Various notions of authenticity evolved into three distinctive types, named objective authenticity (i.e., as an objectively identifiable attribute of objects and cultures), constructive authenticity (i.e., subjective, socially, and individually constructed perception) and existential authenticity (i.e., the state of being, the sense of "real self")[14]. As a result of conceptual evolution, some contemporary definitions have been proposed in the cultural heritage domain which defines authenticity as the "ability of a property to convey its significance over time"[15]. The central meaning of authenticity has thus evolved from emphasizing originality towards "appreciation of the layers of history and cultural diversity" and towards "communication and related socio-culturally sustainable activities"[16].

The core ideas of sustainability and authenticity, therefore, have much more in common than appears at first glance. Both emphasize the appreciation, preservation, and communication of the meaning and significance of cultural heritage, albeit with some distinctive emphases. Sustainability is more explicit with regard to the question of for *whom and what* significance should be preserved and communicated – that is, not only for tourists, but also for the economy, environment, and society in general. On the other hand, authenticity addresses the issue of *why and how* the significance of cultural heritage evolves. It is thus surprising that the relationship between these two concepts has been explicitly addressed in the literature so rarely. Moreover, while some authors do explore and suggest how authenticity can play a role in sustainable development[17], others are critical and suggest that the literature regarding these two concepts is "in hiatus" and that authenticity in some respects endangers sustainability[18]. Based on their indicated compatibility, we assert that their conceptual partnership may be immensely productive. It might inform, inspire, and help researchers and managers set and act upon relevant hypotheses regarding *how* authentication elements and processes might contribute to sustainable consumption. However, the dynamics and managerially accessible mechanisms of the reinforcement of sustainability via authenticity are complex and poorly explored, and therefore represent the primary goal of this chapter. In order to realize this goal, the chapter is structured into three parts. In the first part, the conceptual connectedness and intersections among sustainability and authenticity are explored via the existential self, which is the core underlying sub-concept that links them. Based on the examined mechanisms of self-authentication, various implications for the encouragement of sustainable consumption are discussed. In the second part, an extended logic of the management of sustainable consumption of cultural heritage is suggested, where next to the traditional marketing approach which emphasizes value for money, satisfaction, and loyalty an additional "managerial level" is proposed. It focuses on intrinsic values, cultural motives, existential authenticity, and encourages sustainable consumption as the end goal. The concluding part of the chapter explains the research and methodological implications of the addressed concepts and the integrative model as a whole.

Existential authenticity and sustainable consumption

The existential quest, which drives tourists to connect with the past in order to understand and find their true self, is the core premise of existential authenticity in the cultural heritage domain[19]. While empirical support regarding the impact of existential authenticity on sustainable consumption in the cultural heritage tourism is scarce, some arguments indirectly support this relationship. It has, for instance, been found that the overlap between the self and nature is an important predictor of ecological behavior[20]. In a similar manner, it might be hypothesized that a connection with culture and heritage fosters appreciation and preservation – its sustainable consumption. The relevant question is how might the sense of authentic self and connection to cultural heritage be enhanced and tourists motivated for sustainable consumption? We arranged possible answers and their implications along two dimensions (see Figure 6.1), which are both relevant as mechanisms for strengthening the re-connection with the self, past, and humanity, but also for sustainable consumption. The first is termed self-affirmation and is grounded in the assumption that tourists seek self-coherence and affirmation in the (post)modern era of the lost, fragmented, and insecure self. The second dimension is called self-transcendence and builds on the idea of the dynamic self, which is in constant flux vis-à-vis the improved, ideal self. As the existing self is alienated from nature, past and also future concerns, it needs a re-extension in these direction(s) rather than the reaffirmation of the existing "true and alienated" self.

There are abundant opportunities for self-affirmation in cultural heritage tourism which are grounded on the idea that "getting closer to history" allows for reflection about oneself[21]. For self-authentication, it is, however, important to acknowledge that different types of authenticity are relevant because tourists' perceptions and evaluations of authenticity are interconnected, holistic by nature. Existential authenticity pertains to a sense of being in touch with both the real world and with one's real self[22]. Diverse aspects of the "real world" and their impact on the self-experience of tourists are thus also of key importance. The relationship between authentic objects and identity benefits are, for instance, found to be well supported[23]. Yet existential authenticity is not related to objects, but might also depend on tourists' activities and the context. Participation in traditional local festivities allows for a diverse spectrum of experiences, which were found to be related with a tourist identity quest[24]. In this manner, the authenticity of a certain object (i.e., objective authenticity) and of a particular experience (experiential authenticity) might be seen as a means through which tourists authenticate their self (existential authenticity). Such means–ends relationships and goal hierarchies among consumption and higher (i.e., self) goals are well explored in consumer behavior[25]. Managers in the cultural heritage domain can build on these hierarchies and processes in a pragmatic manner. As a result, diverse

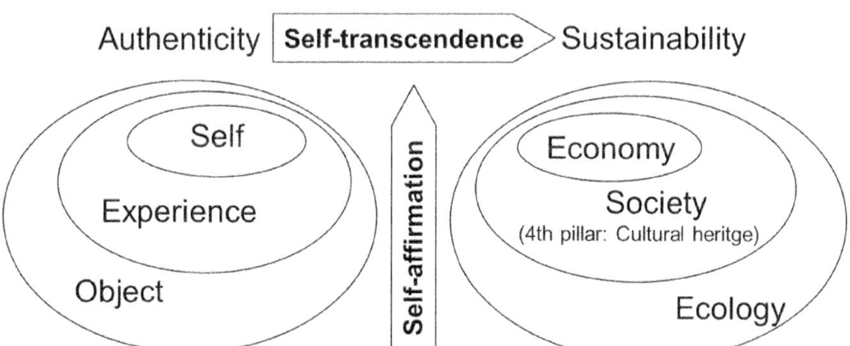

Figure 6.1 Self-authentication as a lever for sustainable consumption.

cultural heritage elements and aspects could become an authentic existential experience if tourists are involved in the authentication process. For this purpose, knowledge of how tourists reflect, affirm, and express their "real self" is valuable. Creative work with objects, for instance, represents such *authenticating acts* of consumers[26] and some forms of creative tourism have already been productively introduced in cultural tourism[27], while others are waiting to do so. The quest for the authentic self might, for example, be manifested as the need for uniqueness, which affects purchasing and/or displaying vintage, antique, or handcrafted goods, as well as purchasing in nontraditional outlets such as antique stores, garage sales, and swap meets[28]. In these ways, the consumption of cultural heritage could become more self-affirmative, but also relevant for the encouragement of sustainable consumption. Similar to the authentic self, sustainability is also a distant and abstract idea and as such requires a more concrete and immediate "construal" of it – by means of specific heritage objects (products), cultural activities, and experiences. Managers need to highlight and ground motivation for sustainable consumption by means of concrete forms, features, and benefits of sustainable options[29]. Sustainability efforts, in addition, require a repositioning (detachment) of the sustainability concept away from the existing notion of threat and catastrophe towards something more familiar, certain, and status-quo-compatible in order to become less absurd and more *existentially bearable*[30]. Sustainability is too often communicated as a cataclysmic idea, which represents a threat to the self. This is counterproductive when a change in existing inappropriate (i.e., un-sustainable) behaviors is warranted. People tend to justify existing behaviors (even unethical ones) by means of various *techniques of neutralization* in order to maintain a positive self[31]. As a result, successful strategies for sustainable consumption require not just a "non-threatening" approach, but need to be aligned with tourist self-affirmation. The encouragement of sustainable consumption might benefit from invoking the sense of social distinctiveness among tourists. Some approaches like that of evolutionary psychology suggest that sustainable consumption should indeed be used as a means to signal superiority to others, implying that sustainable needs to be kept as costly, exclusive, and elitist[32].

While self-affirmation as a mechanism for encouraging sustainable consumption is appealing and sound, there are also some challenges and alternative arguments which support another mechanism termed self-transcendence. Namely, some authors argue that sustainable consumption for the sake of future generations is not evolutionarily logical[33], while others have found that focusing on "I" leads people to feel less connected with nature[34]. As such a quest for an "egoistic and anti-social" self might be antithetical to sustainable consumption, this raises the question of what enables additional avenue(s) of pursuit. Such an avenue is another powerful self-dynamism on which we can build, namely self-transcendence. It implies that tourists need to overcome the disjuncture between the existing self (which is often inauthentic and unsustainable) and the ideal self through the creation of novel (sustainable) identities where the focus is on *becoming rather than on being*[35]. Such self-extension might be grounded in insights from social psychology and consumer behavior which explain the dynamics of the multiple-self and extended-self[36]. According to these concepts and theories, the self is not fixed and given, but dynamic and interdependent. Various social roles played in everyday life (including tourism) are integrated into an extended notion of the self. Such a particularly relevant notion of self is the ecological-self, which needs to be encouraged and stimulated through activities, designated as mindful practices[37].

Extension of the self beyond the individual horizon might also be operationalized via specific models like the social identity model of collective action (SIMCA), which suggests further concepts through which such an extension is possible, such as moral convictions, a sense of efficacy, and socially oriented emotions[38]. Here (again) it seems that cultural heritage as a pillar of sustainability could and should learn from ecology. Following these ideas, managers can pursue opportunities for self-extension that are abundant in cultural heritage tourism. Tourists want to experiment with their identity and explore "who can I be" in other places and times[39]. These self-extension experiences might be grounded on various elements and aspects of cultural heritage. One possibility is interaction with objects and material possessions. Given the natural inclination of modern consumers to identify with products and brands[40], the same mechanisms might be used for tourists' identification with heritage artifacts and symbols, especially those relevant to collective identities. Here symbolic ownership and identification might be simulated in a similar manner as in an ecological context where, for instance, the "adoption" of trees has proven to be an effective means to connect tourists with nature and good causes[41]. In this manner, objects become part of extended selves through processes like resource investment, (more) conscious decision-making, product use/enjoyment, and collections[42]. The same processes might be utilized for the extension of the self with heritage "products" that are both authentic and sustainable. Other possible means of self-transcendence in tourism are *activities*, *experiences*, and *narratives*. According to some studies, tourists are construed as narrators whose identity, stories, and experience of self-change are founded on and *rhetorically validated* by the unique experiences of authenticity and adventure[43]. Here identity quest is situated in a social space and emerges from connections between the individual and the community where, through different types of *authoritative performances,* like festivals and rituals and more specific activities like rehearsals, scripting, ritualization, and stylization, a collective sense of identity is revived[44]. A collective identity, in turn, invokes social emotions like empathy and societal values in tourists, which might serve as a cohesive force among one's various social identities[45], including past and possible (future) identities. In this way, an existential authentication might serve as a powerful conceptual lever for the appreciation, preservation, and communication of the meaning and significance of cultural heritage and its extension from the past to the sustainable future.

Conceptual modeling of authenticity for sustainable consumption

In what follows we provide a relevant conceptual and managerial model for encouraging sustainable consumption in the field of cultural heritage. According to the basic idea of the chapter, we posit that the core lever for maintaining the sustainability of cultural heritage is existential authenticity. For that purpose, we focused on relevant conceptual drivers of authenticity and their expected impact on sustainability. In past studies, authenticity was linked with traditional marketing goals like increased satisfaction and loyalty of visitors[46], but also with other antecedents and consequences (see Table 6.1). Although concepts like satisfaction and loyalty are traditionally considered as important in tourism management and marketing, it is a question of whether they are sufficient in order to effectively contribute to the sustainability imperative.

To make sustainable consumption more manageable, an advanced model of the antecedents and consequences of the existential authenticity of a cultural heritage site is proposed (see Figure 6.2). The model incorporates several key concepts of contemporary destination policy development, namely, the perceived value of destination offerings, visitor satisfaction and their loyalty, which form the first level of the model. Several studies provide support for the chain of effects where perceived value positively affects

Table 6.1 Overview of the antecedents and consequences of authenticity

Author (year)	*Variable*	*Antecedent*	*Consequence*
Bryce et al. (2015)	*Existential authenticity*	Object-based authenticity Cultural motivation Serious leisure Heritage-related behaviors Self-connection	Engagement Loyalty
Chhabra (2001)	*Perceived authenticity*		Levels of visitor spending
Chhabra et al. (2003)	*Perceived authenticity*	Cultural motivations	
Kolar & Žabkar (2010)	*Perceived authenticity*	Cultural motivation	Loyalty
Lin & Wang (2012)	*Authenticity perception*		Perceived value
Meng & Choi (2015)	*Authentic perception*		Behavioral intention to slow travel
Paiva et al. (2013)	*Authenticity*	Place identity Place dependence Place memory Cultural values Cognitive image Affective image	Behavior intentions
Ramkissoon & Uysal (2011)	*Perceived authenticity*		Cultural behavioral intentions of tourists
Ramkisoon (2015)	*Authenticity*		Place satisfaction
Rani et al. (2014)	*Perceived authenticity*		Tourist satisfaction
Shen et al. (2014)	*Existential authenticity*	Attitude to world cultural heritage sites (WCHS) Constructive authenticity	WCHS loyalty
Sie (2011)	*Brand authenticity*		Purchase intention Overall brand rating
Zhou et al. (2013)	*Existential authenticity*	Objective authenticity Attitude to calligraphy (Motivation)	Loyalty

satisfaction, which in turn positively impacts loyalty[47]. However, the existing satisfaction models in tourism suffer from short-sightedness since satisfaction is basically a short-term concept[48]. In order to assure long-term implications that will concur with sustainability endeavors, three additional concepts are included in the second level of the model. The first concept in the second level of the model is *cultural motivation*, which explains tourist motives beyond short-term immediate egoistic gratifications. Instead, cultural motivation is treated as a cluster of intellectually-based interests in culture, history, and heritage[49]. The second and the core concept is *existential authenticity*, which has (already) been defined as the "state of being, sense of real self"[50], and can be manifested as "feelings of enjoyment in and connectedness to human history and civilization"[51]. The third pillar is *sustainable consumption of cultural heritage*, which in our model pertains to ethical and socially responsible tourist attitudes, intentions, and behaviors with regard to cultural heritage that minimize adverse consumption effects on the natural and socio-cultural environment[52].

The model proposes that existential authenticity mediates the relationship between cultural motivation and sustainable consumption of cultural heritage, and that the three constructs interact with perceived value, visitor satisfaction, and destination or site loyalty. The first relationship captured in the chain of core constructs on the second level is between Cultural Motivation and Existential Authenticity (P1). The existing literature suggests that motivations affect perception, tourists' expectations[53], and the cognitive organization of environmental perceptions[54]. Similarly, cultural motivation tends to increase one's perception of existential authenticity. The argument for this proposition rests on previous studies in which various authors found positive impacts of cultural motivation on existential authenticity[55]. Further, the conceptual model proposes a relationship between existential authenticity and sustainable consumption (P2), which was established and extensively debated in the first part of this chapter. Although past studies did not empirically examine the impact of existential authenticity on sustainable consumption, there are some studies which confirm the impact of (product) authenticity on sustainability[56] and a few authors who look into various behavioral intentions[57] or actual relevant behaviors as consequences of perceived authenticity[58]. Hence, we posit that experiencing existential authenticity in the context of cultural heritage leads to sustainable consumption.

P1: Cultural motivation positively influences existential authenticity.
P2: Existential authenticity positively influences sustainable consumption.

As depicted in Figure 6.2, we also propose that constructs from the existing satisfaction models interact with constructs at the second level of the model. In proposition 3, we link cultural motivation to perceived value. A similar relationship has been established in a somewhat different context – the destination experience – where it has been shown that push motivation is a significant antecedent of tourist perceptions of destination value[59]. Interestingly, not all studies find a positive influence of motivation on value. For example, contrary to expectations it was found that novelty as one of the basic motivations driving leisure travelers had a negative instead of a positive impact on perceived overall cruise value[60]. To address this controversy, we propose that cultural motivation positively influences perceived value (P3).

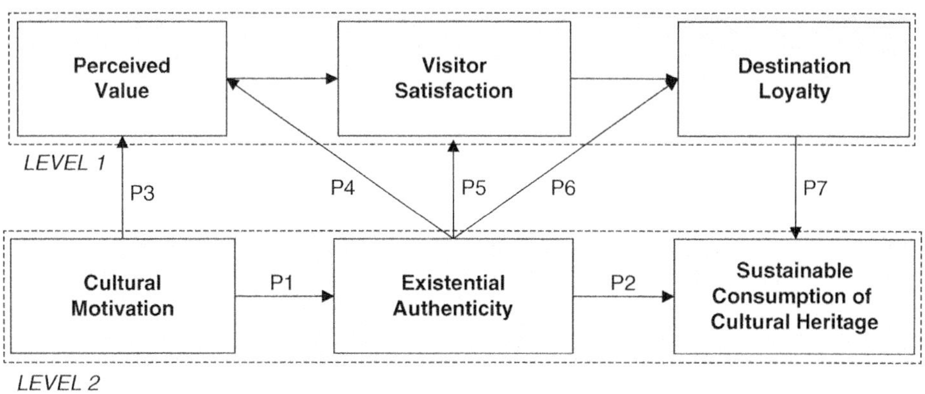

Figure 6.2 Conceptual model of the antecedents and consequences of existential authenticity related to cultural heritage.

P3: Cultural motivation positively influences perceived value.

Along with sustainable consumption, the conceptual model predicts several other consequential factors of existential authenticity: perceived value, visitor satisfaction, and destination loyalty. In previous studies, authenticity was considered an antecedent of the value that consumers place on marketing offerings[61]. This was also empirically demonstrated in the case of purchasing ceramic souvenirs, where a perception of authenticity significantly and positively influenced the perceived value of souvenirs[62]. Hence, we propose that existential authenticity positively influences perceived value (P4). Next, we also propose that existential authenticity increases visitor satisfaction (P5), based on several studies that theoretically and empirically validate this relationship[63]. Another of the proposed consequences of authenticity in the model is tourist loyalty to a destination or site. We propose that existential authenticity positively influences a consumer's loyalty to a specific cultural heritage place (P6). As in the case of the authenticity–satisfaction relationship, limited research efforts have been devoted to the authenticity–loyalty relationship, with those that have been made indicating either an insignificant[64] or a positive impact of authenticity on loyalty[65].

P4: Existential authenticity positively influences perceived value.
P5: Existential authenticity positively influences visitor satisfaction.
P6: Existential authenticity positively influences destination loyalty.

Finally, we infer that loyalty exerts a positive influence on sustainable behavior related to cultural heritage (P7). That is, the more loyal consumers are to a specific cultural heritage site, the more likely they are to exhibit sustainable consumption behavior with respect to that site. This proposition rests on the premise that loyalty implies both favorable (committed) attitudes and repetitive behavior in the future and this behavior is likely sustainable as it is associated with a "pro-orientation"[66].

P7: Destination loyalty positively influences sustainable behavior.

Conclusions and recommendations

By means of the proposed model and corresponding propositions, this chapter aims to contribute to the existing body of knowledge on sustainable consumption of cultural heritage. It does so by means of a two-level structure that provides a conceptual framework for better understanding the role of cultural motivation and existential authenticity in shaping the sustainable consumption of cultural heritage. In addition, the model links these concepts to a well-established chain of value–satisfaction–loyalty constructs. Theoretically and empirically well supported, the conceptual model offers various implications for destination policy and management. It can, for instance, serve as a basis for the *development* and *communication* of cultural heritage "products". Moreover, the proposed concepts might serve as a promising *segmentation* base for targeting various tourist segments based on their level of cultural motivation and other concepts. Levels of perceived existential authenticity might, for example, be considered as a segmentation variable alongside cultural motivation in order to create more clearly profiled groups of consumers. The examined concepts can also be useful for the development of *evaluative measures* that are needed for examining tourists' perceptions, and policy evaluations. The customer-based perspective posits that perceived existential authenticity depends on the effectiveness of various communication and other "interactive" activities. As such, existential authenticity might complement other evaluative measures like quality assurance, satisfaction, and perceived value.

However, the most important potential contribution is the insight into the drivers of sustainability that might result from this model. Namely, further empirical verification of the model would enable testing the assumed relationship between the perception among visitors (e.g., a feeling of being existentially connected to humankind) and their immediate activities and future intentions in terms of the sustainable consumption of cultural heritage sites. With respect to the latter, one additional challenge for consideration in future studies is the operationalization of the sustainable consumption of cultural heritage. In the existing tourism literature, the measurement of sustainability has been addressed in various contexts, for example as measuring sustainable tourism[67], sustainability in tourism development[68], sustainability for tourism destinations[69], sustainability of cultural heritage sites[70], and attitudes to sustainable tourism[71], but rarely in terms of *sustainable consumption behaviors* per se. Given the aforementioned conceptualization of sustainable consumption as tourist attitudes, intentions, and behaviors with regard to cultural heritage, a new scale should reflect this structure.

Another area calling for further attention is a more holistic operationalization of existential authenticity. Namely, as evident from the first part of the chapter, authenticity is a concept "in progress" and, consequently, a lack of proper *existential* authenticity scales is discernible, although a few studies have tackled this challenge by applying a scale of existential authenticity specifically adapted to the cultural heritage context[72]. Existential authenticity should be associated with reflective (effect) indicators, in line with the conventional measurement practice which is based on reflective measurement. Indicators should reflect variation in the construct and co-vary at a high level as good measures of the underlying construct. In developing such a scale it would also make sense to ponder the existing scales of connectedness to nature[73] or nature relatedness[74], and place attachment[75].

Due to the high level of complexity of the sustainable consumption and existential authenticity concepts, a series of exploratory qualitative interviews would be needed to further test conceptual characteristics, explore underlying sources, and provide insights into consequences. The development of the measurement instrument of the construct would follow standard procedures that assure validity and reliability. The first step of such a procedure is a more explicit conceptualization (i.e., defining the nature and domain(s) of a construct), followed by the generation of a larger number of questions (pool of items) that measure the construct of interest. The item pool should be tested in survey interviews with a structured questionnaire. Subsequent exploratory factor analysis should reveal high internal reliability and consistency in different contexts. In the second phase of the research project, several antecedents and consequences of authenticity could be examined and included in a structural equation model (SEM). Confirmatory factor analysis (CFA) would be applied to test the measurement model, item, and construct reliability, as well as discriminant validity. The data gathered would be used to empirically test the proposed model and develop policy implications.

In this manner the presented model could fill the established gap concerning managerial models for sustainable cultural heritage tourism and offer a base for managerially relevant operationalization and management in the area of sustainable consumption and cultural heritage. Two key requirements are needed for the effective assurance of sustainable consumption of cultural heritage. The first one is a valid measurement of sustainable consumption and existential authenticity, including the explicit definition, operative conceptualization, and measurement of the constructs in the model. The second one is the provision of operative implications for policy and strategy in the area of cultural heritage, including an empirical test of the model and the development of policy implications. A set of policy development propositions could serve to underpin the improved performance of cultural heritage in order to preserve its authenticity and promote sustainable consumption initiatives.

Notes

1 EC (European Commission) (2013). *Sustainable tourism based on natural and cultural heritage: Europe's natural & cultural wealth*. Available at: http://ec.europa.eu/enterprise/sectors/tourism/files/studies/using_natural_cultural_heritage/heritage_en.pdf
2 Southeast Europe (2013). *Concept study on the role of Cultural Heritage as the fourth pillar of Sustainable Development*. Available at: http://www.southeast-europe.net/document.cmt?id=614
3 Matero, F. (2001). "Preface", in: *Managing Change: Sustainable Approaches to the Conservation of the Built Environment. Proceedings of the 4th Annual US/ICOMOS international Symposium*, eds. Teutonico, J. M. & Matero, F., Philadelphia, Pennsylvania, April, 2001. Los Angeles: The Getty Conservation Institute.
4 United Nations General Assembly (2014). *Culture and Sustainable Development in the Post-2015 Development Agenda*. Available at: http://www.un.org/en/ga/president/68/pdf/culture_sd/Culture%20and%20SD%20Summary%20of%20Key%20Messages_FINAL%20rev.pdf
5 Southeast Europe, *op. cit.*
6 Schaefer, A., & Crane, A. (2005), "Addressing sustainability and consumption", *Journal of Macromarketing*, Vol. 25, No. 1, pp. 76–92.
7 Kilbourne, W., McDonagh, P., & Prothero, A. (1997), "Sustainable consumption and the quality of life: A macromarketing challenge to the dominant social paradigm", *Journal of Macromarketing*, Vol. 17, No. 1, pp. 4–24.
8 UNEP and WTO (2005), *Making Tourism More Sustainable – A Guide for Policy Makers*. Paris, France: UNEP.
9 Moscardo, G., & Woods, B. (1998), "Managing tourism in the Wet Tropics World Heritage Area: Interpretation and the experience of visitors on Skyrail", in: *Embracing and managing change in tourism: International case studies*, eds. Laws, E., Faulkner, B. & Moscardo, G. London: Routledge, pp. 285–306.
10 MacCannell, D. (1973), "Staged authenticity: arrangements of social space in tourist settings", *American Journal of Sociology*, Vol. 79, No. 3, pp. 589–603; Cohen, E. (1988), "Authenticity and commoditization in tourism", *Annals of Tourism Research*, Vol. 15, No. 3, pp. 371–386; Naoi, T. (2004). Visitors' evaluation of a historical district: the roles of authenticity and manipulation. *Tourism and Hospitality Research*, Vol. 5, No. 1, pp. 45–63.
11 ICOMOS (1964). "International Charter for the Conservation and Restoration of Monuments and Sites", *IInd International Congress of Architects and Technicians of Historic Monuments*, Venice, Italy; Australia ICOMOS (1979, 1981, 1988, 1999). *The Burra Charter: The Australia ICOMOS Charter for the Conservation of Places of Cultural Significance*. Burra, Australia; ICOMOS (1994), "The Nara Document on Authenticity", *Nara Conference on Authenticity in Relation to the World Heritage Convention*, Nara, Japan: ICOMOS.
12 Wang, N. (1999), "Rethinking authenticity in tourism experience", *Annals of Tourism Research*, Vol. 26, No. 2, pp. 349–370; Taylor, 2001, p. 8; Taylor, J. (2001), "Authenticity and sincerity in tourism", *Annals of Tourism Research*, Vol. 28, No. 1, pp. 7–26.
13 Jones, S. (2010), "Negotiating authentic objects and authentic selves: Beyond the deconstruction of authenticity", *Journal of Material Culture*, Vol. 15, No. 2, pp. 181–203.
14 Wang, op.cit
15 Stovel H. (2007), "Effective use of authenticity and integrity as world heritage qualifying conditions", *City & Time*, Vol. 2, No. 3, p. 3.
16 Niskasaari, K. (2008), "Towards a Socio-culturally Sustainable Definition of Authenticity: Re-thinking the Spirit of Place", in: *16th ICOMOS General Assembly and International Symposium: 'Finding the spirit of place – between the tangible and the intangible'*, 29 September – 4 October 2008, Quebec, Canada.
17 Sims, R. (2009). Food, place and authenticity: local food and the sustainable tourism experience, *Journal of Sustainable Tourism*, Vol. 17, No. 3, pp. 321–336.

18 Cohen, E. (2002), "Authenticity, Equity & Sustainability in Tourism", *Journal of Sustainable Tourism*, Vol. 10, No. 4, pp. 267–276.

19 Steiner, C. J., & Reisinger, Y. (2006), "Understanding existential authenticity", *Annals of Tourism Research*, Vol. 33, No. 2, pp. 299–318; Chhabra, D., Healy, R., & Sills, E. (2003), "Staged authenticity and heritage tourism", *Annals of Tourism Research*, Vol. 30, No. 3, pp. 702–719; Goulding, C. (2000), "The commodification of the past, postmodern pastiche, and the search for authentic experiences at contemporary heritage attractions", *European Journal of Marketing*, Vol. 34, No. 7, pp. 835–853; Naoi, *op. cit.*

20 Mayer, F. S., & Frantz, C. M. (2004), "The connectedness to nature scale: a measure of individuals' feeling in community with nature", *Journal of Environmental Psychology*, Vol. 24, No. 4, pp. 503–515.

21 Steiner & Reisinger, *op. cit.*; Chhabra et al., *op. cit.*; Goulding, op.cit.; Naoi, op.cit.

22 Wang, op.cit

23 Beverland, M. B. & Farrelly, F. J. (2010), "The Quest for Authenticity in Consumption: Consumers' Purposive Choice of Authentic Cues to Shape Experienced Outcomes", *Journal of Consumer Research*, Vol. 36, No. 5, pp. 838–856.

24 Kim, H., & Jamal, T. (2007), "Touristic quest for existential authenticity", *Annals of Tourism Research*, Vol. 34, No. 1, pp. 181–201.

25 Huffman, C., Rattneshwar, S. & Mick, D.G. (2000), "Consumer Goal Structures and Goal Determination Processes: An Integrative Framework", in: *The Why of Consumption: Contemporary Perspectives on Consumer Motives*, eds. S. Rattneshwar, Mick, D.G. & Huffman, C., London: Routledge, pp. 9–35.

26 Arnould, E.J. & Price L. (2000), "Authenticating Acts and Authoritative Performances: Questing for Self and Community," in: *The Why of Consumption: Contemporary Perspectives on Consumer Motives, Goals, and Desires*, eds. Ratneshwar, S., Mick, D.G. & Huffman, C., New York: Routledge, pp. 140–163.

27 Richards, G. & Wilson, J. (2006), "Developing Creativity in Tourist Experiences: A Solution to the Serial Reproduction of Culture?", *Tourism Management*, Vol. 27, No. 6, pp. 1209–1223.

28 Tepper, K. (1997), "Categories, contexts, and conflicts of consumers' nonconformity experiences", in: *Research in Consumer Behavior*, ed. Belk, R.W., Greenwich, CT: JAI Press, pp. 209–45.

29 Fujita, K., Clark, S.L. & Freitas, A.L. (2014), "Think globally, act locally: Construal levels and Environmentally relevant decision making", in: *Encouraging sustainable behavior*, ed. van Trijp, H.C.M., New York: Psychology Press, pp. 203–215.

30 Prolux, T. (2014), "Is the sky falling? The notion of the absurd versus the feeling of the absurd", in: *Encouraging sustainable behavior*, ed. van Trijp H.C.M., New York: Psychology Press, pp. 203–215.

31 Costello, B. J. (2000), "Techniques of neutralization and self-esteem: a critical test of social control and neutralization theory", *Deviant Behavior*, Vol. 21, No. 4, pp. 307–329.

32 Miller, G. (2014), "Twenty-seven thoughts about multiple selves, sustainable consumption and human evolution", in: *Encouraging sustainable behavior*, ed. van Trijp, H.C.M., New York: Psychology Press, pp. 203–215.

33 *Ibid.*

34 Frantz, C., Mayer, F.S., Norton, Ch., & Rock, M. (2005), "There is no "I" in nature: The influence of self-awareness on connectedness to nature", *Journal of Environmental Psychology*, Vol. 25, pp. 427–436.

35 Postmes, T., Rabinovich, A., Morton, T. & van Zomeren M. (2014), "Toward sustainable social identites: Including our collective future into hte self-concept", in: *Encouraging sustainable behavior*, ed. van Trijp, H.C.M., New York: Psychology Press, pp. 203–215.

36 Solomon, M. (2015), *Consumer behavior (11th.ed)*. London: Prentice Hall.

37 Koger, S.M. & Winter, D.N. (2010). *The Psychology of Environmental problems*. New York: Psychology press, Taylor & Francis.

38 Postmes et al., op.cit

39 Morgan, N., Pritchard, A., & Piggott, R. (2002), "New Zealand, 100% pure. The creation of a powerful niche destination brand", *Journal of Brand Management*, Vol. 9, No. 4/5, pp. 335–354.

40 Mittal, B. (2006), "I, me, and mine: how products becomes our extended selves", *Journal of Consumer Behaviour*, Vol. 5, No. 6, pp. 550–562.

41 Upadhayaya P.K. (2015), "Sustainability Threats to Mountain Tourism with Tourist Mechanized Mobility Induced Global Warming: A Case Study of Nepal", *Journal of Tourism & Hospitality*, Vol. Vol. 4, No. 3.

42 Mittal, op.cit

43 Noy, C. (2004), "This Trip Really Changed Me. Backpackers' Narratives of Self-Change", *Annals of Tourism Research*, Vol. 31, No. 1, pp. 78–102.
44 Arnould & Price, op.cit.
45 Hitlin, S. (2003), "Values as the Core of Personal Identity: Drawing Links between Two Theories of Self", *Social Psychology Quarterly*, Vol. 66, No. 2, pp. 118–137.
46 Bryce, D., Curran, R., O'Gorman, K., & Taheri, B. (2015), "Visitors' engagement and authenticity: Japanese heritage consumption", *Tourism Management*, Vol. 46, pp. 571–581; Kolar, T., & Žabkar, V. (2010), "A consumer-based model of authenticity: An oxymoron or the foundation of cultural heritage marketing? ", *Tourism Management*, Vol. 31, No. 5, pp. 652–664; Poria Y., Butler R., & Airey, D. (2003), "The core of heritage tourism", *Annals of Tourism Research*, Vol. 30, No. 1, pp. 238–254.
47 Chen, C., & Tsai, D. (2007), "How Destination Image and Evaluative Factors Affect Behavioral Intentions?", *Tourism Management*, Vol. 28, pp. 1115–1122; Gallarza, M. G., & Saura, I. G. (2006), "Value dimensions, perceived value, satisfaction and loyalty: An investigation of university students' travel", *Tourism Management*, Vol. 27, No. 2, pp. 437–452; Lee, C. K., Yoon, Y. S., & Lee, S. K. (2007), "Investigating the relationships among perceived value, satisfaction, and recommendations: The case of the Korean DMZ", *Tourism Management*, Vol. 28, No.1, pp. 204–214; Um, S., Chon, K., & Ro, Y. (2006), "Antecedents of revisit intention", *Annals of tourism research*, Vol. 33, No. 4, pp. 1141–1158.
48 Oliver, R.L. (1997), *Satisfaction: a behavioral perspective on the consumer*. New York: McGraw-Hill.
49 Kolar & Žabkar, *op. cit.*; Middleton V.T.C., & Clarke J. R. (2004), *Marketing in Travel and Tourism*. Oxford: Butterworth-Heinemann.
50 Wang, op.cit
51 Kolar & Žabkar, *op. cit.*; Goulding, *op.cit.*
52 Blackstock K., White, V., McCrum, G., Scott, A., & Hunter, C. (2008), "Measuring Responsibility: An Appraisal of a Scottish National Park's Sustainable Tourism Indicators", *Journal of Sustainable Tourism*, Vol. 16, No. 3, pp. 276–297; Budeanu A. (2007), "Sustainable tourist behaviour – a discussion of opportunities for change", *International Journal of Consumer Studies*, Vol. 31, No. 5, pp. 499–508; Dolnicar S, & Leisch, F. (2008), "Selective marketing for environmentally sustainable tourism", *Tourism Management*, Vol. 29, No. 4, pp. 672–680; Dolnicar S, Crouch G, & Long P. (2008), "Environment-friendly Tourists: What Do We Really Know About Them?", *Journal of Sustainable Tourism*, Vol. 16, No. 2, pp. 197–210; Johnston, R J. (2005), "A Dynamic Model of Sustainable Tourism", *Journal of Travel Research*, Vol. 44, No. 2, pp. 124–134; Lee W H, & Moscardo G. (2005), "Understanding the Impact of Ecotourism Resort Experiences on Tourists' Environmental Attitudes and Behavioural Intentions", *Journal of Sustainable Tourism*, Vol. 13, No. 6, pp. 546–565; Stanford, D. (2008), "'Exceptional Visitors': Dimensions of Tourist Responsibility in the Context of New Zealand", *Journal of Sustainable Tourism*, Vol. 16, No. 3, pp. 258–275; Stone, G., Barnes J.H., & Montgomery, C. (1995), "ECOSCALE: A Scale for the Measurement of Environmentally Responsible Consumers", *Psychology & Marketing*, Vol. 12, No. 7, pp. 595–612.
53 Gnoth, J. (1997), "Tourism motivation and expectation formation", *Annals of Tourism research*, Vol. 24, No. 2, pp. 283–304.
54 Beerli, A., & Martin, J. D. (2004), "Factors influencing destination image", *Annals of tourism research*, Vol. 31, No. 3, pp. 657–681.
55 Bryce et al., *op. cit.*; Chhabra et al., *op. cit.*; Kolar & Žabkar, *op. cit.*
56 Sims, *op.cit.*
57 Meng, B., & Choi, K. (2015), "Extending the theory of planned behaviour: testing the effects of authentic perception and environmental concerns on the slow-tourist decision-making process", *Current Issues in Tourism*, DOI: 10.1080/13683500.2015.1020773; Paiva, O., Seabra, C., Abrantes, J. L., & Cravidão, F. (2013), "Perception of Authenticity in World Heritage Historic Centers-The case of French tourists", *5th Advances in Tourism Marketing (ATMC) Conference*. Faro, Portugal: Universidade do Algarve; Ramkissoon, H., & Uysal, M. S. (2011), "The effects of perceived authenticity, information search behaviour, motivation and destination imagery on cultural behavioural intentions of tourists", *Current Issues in Tourism*, Vol. 14, No. 6, pp. 537–562; Sie, H.G. (2011), *In The Eye Of The Beholder The Effects of Authenticity Cues on Purchase Intention and Overall Brand Rating, depending on Desire for Control*. Master thesis. Enschede, the Netherlands: University of Twente.
58 Brida, J.G., & Tokarchuk, O. (2011), "Perceived Authenticity and Museum Visitors' Behavior: A Case of South Tirol's Museum of Archeology in Bolzano", Available at: http://ssrn.com/abstract=1920743; Chhabra, D. (2001), "An Analysis of Perceived Authenticity and Economic Impact of the Scottish Highland Games in North Carolina", PhD dissertation, North Carolina State University.

59 Prebensen, N. K., Woo, E., Chen, J. S., & Uysal, M. (2012), "Motivation and involvement as antecedents of the perceived value of the destination experience", *Journal of Travel Research*, Vol. 52, No. 2, pp. 253–264.

60 Duman, T., & Mattila, A. S. (2005), "The role of affective factors on perceived cruise vacation value", *Tourism Management*, Vol. 26, No. 3, pp. 311–323.

61 Grayson, K. (2002), "Telling the difference: Consumer evaluations of authentic and inauthentic marketing offerings", *Advances in Consumer Research*, Vol. 29, No. 1, pp. 44–45.

62 Lin, C. H., & Wang, W. C. (2012), "Effects of authenticity perception, hedonics, and perceived value on ceramic souvenir-repurchasing intention. *Journal of Travel & Tourism Marketing*, Vol. 29, No. 8, pp. 779–795.

63 Ramkissoon, H. (2015), "Authenticity, satisfaction, and place attachment: A conceptual framework for cultural tourism in African island economies", *Development Southern Africa*, Vol. 32, No. 3, pp. 292–302; Rani, Z. M., & Ahmad, K. N. (2014), "Perceived Authenticity as a Determinant to Revisit Heritage Tourism Sites in Penang", *Tourism, Leisure and Global Change*, Vol. 1, No. 1; Song, H.J., Moon, J.H., Choi, S.S., & Lee, C.K. (2013), "Estimating the economic impact of Oriental medicine festival: The case of 2011 Jecheon Oriental medicine bio expo", *Korean Academic Society of Hospitality Administration*, Vol. 22, No. 3, pp. 221–233.

64 Zhou, Q. B., Zhang, J., & Edelheim, J. R. (2013), "Rethinking traditional Chinese culture: A consumer-based model regarding the authenticity of Chinese calligraphic landscape", *Tourism Management*, Vol. 36, pp. 99–112.

65 Bryce et al., *op. cit.*; Kolar & Žabkar, *op. cit.*; Shen, S., Guo, J., & Wu, Y. (2014), "Investigating the structural relationships among authenticity, loyalty, involvement, and attitude toward world cultural heritage sites: An empirical study of Nanjing Xiaoling Tomb, China", *Asia Pacific Journal of Tourism Research*, Vol. 19, No. 1, pp. 103–121.

66 Corall-Verdugo, V., Bonnes, M., Tapia-Fonllem, C., Fraijo-Sing, B., Frias-Armenta, M., & Carrus, G. (2009), "Correlates of pro-sustainability orientation: The affinity towards diversity", *Journal of Environmental Psychology*, Vol. 29, pp. 34–43.

67 Lozano-Oyola, M., Blancas, F. J., González, M., & Caballero, R. (2012), "Sustainable tourism indicators as planning tools in cultural destinations", *Ecological Indicators*, Vol. 18, pp. 659–675; Miller, G. (2001), "The development of indicators for sustainable tourism: results of a Delphi survey of tourism researchers", *Tourism management*, Vol. 22, No. 4, pp. 351–362.

68 Choi, H. C., & Sirakaya, E. (2006), "Sustainability indicators for managing community tourism", *Tourism management*, Vol. 27, No. 6, pp. 1274–1289.

69 Schianetz, K., & Kavanagh, L. (2008), "Sustainability indicators for tourism destinations: A complex adaptive systems approach using systemic indicator systems", *Journal of Sustainable Tourism*, Vol. 16, No. 6, pp. 601–628.

70 Liao, D., & Wang, P. (2011), "Sustainable tourism development-how sustainable are China's cultural heritage sites", in *Proceedings of the Northeastern Recreation Research Symposium, University of* Massachusetts Amherst; Ngamsomsuke, W., Hwang, T. C., & Huang, C. J. (2011, March), "Sustainable Cultural Heritage Tourism Indicators", in *International Conference on Social Science and Humanity, Singapore.*

71 Choi, H. S. C., & Sirakaya, E. (2005), "Measuring residents' attitude toward sustainable tourism: Development of sustainable tourism attitude scale", Journal of Travel Research, Vol. 43, No. 4, pp. 380–394.

72 Bryce et al., *op. cit.*; Kolar & Žabkar, *op. cit.*; Poria et al., *op. cit.*

73 Mayer, F. S., & Frantz, C. M. (2004), "The connectedness to nature scale: A measure of individuals' feeling in community with nature", *Journal of environmental psychology*, Vol. 24, No. 4, pp. 503–515.

74 Nisbet, E. K., Zelenski, J. M., & Murphy, S. A. (2008), "The nature relatedness scale: Linking individuals' connection with nature to environmental concern and behavior", *Environment and Behavior*, Vol. 41, No. 5, pp. 715-740.

75 Gross, M. J., & Brown, G. (2008). An empirical structural model of tourists and places: Progressing involvement and place attachment into tourism. *Tourism Management*, 29(6), 1141-1151; Williams, D. R., & Vaske, J. J. (2003), "The measurement of place attachment: Validity and generalizability of a psychometric approach", *Forest science*, Vol. 49, No. 6, pp. 830–840.

7 Heritage as embodied co-creation

'Living the history' of the Titanic in Cobh

Aggelos Panayiotopoulos, Maria Lichrou, Lisa O'Malley and Maurice Patterson

Introduction

Heritage refers to "things of value that are inherited" and to "things we want to keep" (Hall and McArthur 1998, p. 4). Fundamentally heritage indicates an interest in the past (Lowenthal, 1994; Nuryanti, 1996). Since the 1980s concern with heritage is particularly prevalent in Europe and North America, where diverse aspects of history, culture, and everyday life have been turned into marketable commodities through being re-classified as 'heritage' (Hewison, 1987; Prentice, 1993; Ashworth, 1994).

Heritage was traditionally concerned with "the preservation or reconstruction of material objects" through a process which effectively "isolates them from the flux of history" (Meethan, 1996, p.325). Detachment from history is enabled through *re-contextualisation*; a process in which abstract qualities, such as the nation, people, locality, and the past are embodied in "narratives of material culture and localities, narratives that emphasise the continuity of the past in the present" (Meethan, 1996, p. 325). Heritage is understood to include any physical relic that has survived from the past. Besides physical relics, it encompasses all accumulated cultural and artistic productivity, the natural environment as well as non-physical elements including individual and collective memories. Cumulatively, these cohere as the 'heritage industry' and its associated commercial activity (Hall and McArthur, 1998). Given its evolving nature and malleable character, heritage essentially defies definition (Brett, 1996).

> Indeed, the term [heritage] celebrates every conceivable thing and theme: anchorites and anoraks, Berlin and Bengal, conkers and castles, dog breeds and dental fillings, finials and fax machines, gorgonzola and goalposts are topics typical of a thousand recent books entitled Heritage of ______.
>
> (Lowenthal, 1994, p. 42)

This expansion of heritage and intensified concern with the past is theorised as a symptom of the transformation of post-industrial economies into what Lash and Urry (1994) termed *economies of signs*. This transformation is intertwined with a number of related trends: increasing dominance of the consumer and the need for the producer to be more consumer-oriented; greater volatility of consumer preferences; the development of many new products, each of which has a shorter life; increased preferences for non-mass forms of production and consumption; increased aestheticisation of consumption, i.e., consuming products less and less for their functional and increasingly for their aesthetic and symbolic values (Urry, 1995). Information, images, symbols, and desire assume prominence over materials and physical goods.

Also symptomatic of this transformation is an increasing reconceptualisation of places from spaces of production to spaces of consumption; in other words, places are no longer centres for the production of goods, but centres for the consumption of services. This is evident in the increasing promotion of tourism in many post-industrial places across the globe and the expansion of cultural tourism as a tool to attract visitors and investment:

> In order to attract investment capital and the spending power of the middle class, regions now differentiate themselves by emphasising the aesthetic qualities of material commodities and services that represent symbolic capital. Examples of this can be found in the use of museums, monuments and other heritage attractions in regional economic development strategies".
>
> (Richards, 1996, p. 267)

In re-imaging themselves as spaces of consumption (Miles, 2010) places invoke authenticity to create a sense of the past and encourage cultural tourism. What has emerged, then, is a new 'service' class (Bourdieu 1984) to stimulate, attend to, and legitimise this preoccupation with the past. Individuals within this new middle class possess significant cultural capital and express their need for status and social differentiation through different styles of cultural consumption, including tourism (Munt, 1994, Sharpley and Sharpley, 1997). These consumers are interested in the consumption of goods that are perceived to be auratic rather than mass-produced and which provide metaphysical experiences (Holt 1998) and evoke authenticity (Prentice 2001). Museums and heritage attractions offer opportunities for meaningful, 'authentic' experiences because visitors and communities often use them in their construction of individual and social identities (see, for example, Newman and McLean, 2006; Gouthro and Palmer, 2010).

Heritage and the search for authenticity

Concerns about the corrosive nature of modernity (Meethan 2001) are expressed in a nostalgic search for 'authentic' experiences (Goulding 2000) and a re-evaluation of tradition, accompanied by the consumption of products and services associated with heritage and culture (Jenkins 2000). Notions of a vanishing more authentic cultural life that existed outside the market, although contested, are prevalent in western society, which often locates authenticity in the past (Shepherd 2002).

Albeit problematic, authenticity attracts a strong interest in discussions around heritage and cultural attractions. For heritage management, authenticity is a valued concept because it is used to verify the originality of sites, artefacts, and exhibits. Museum curators in particular, rely on authenticity as a measure of museum distinctiveness and a criterion for resource allocation (Chhabra 2008). In addition, marketers employ authenticity as a tool to promote tourism attractions. Prentice (2001) identifies myriad of forms and ways in which authenticity is promoted: authentication by direct experience, objectivist authentication, naturalness, location, associations with famous persons, place-branding or place myth, the offer of origins, extended authenticity through brand extension, celebration, learned authenticity, and constructed authenticity.

In this chapter we use the case of the Titanic Experience in Cobh (pronounced Cove) to explore emerging understandings of heritage and authenticity. More specifically, we consider how heritage is invoked for consumption, and how it is particularly tied to the making of tourist places. Our consideration of the Titanic Experience Cobh is based on our own experience of visiting, as well as by consideration of published material and online visitor reviews. We then revert to the extant literature to explore the multiplicity of claims to authenticity, from authenticity of the object, to opportunities for authentic tourist experiences. Finally, we offer concluding comments regarding the implications for heritage management.

Titanic: the unsinkable ship

The Titanic was heralded as the most impressive and luxurious ship of the early twentieth century. Built in Belfast, her maiden voyage began at Southampton where most of its crew of 900 men were picked up, and her intended destination was New York. Passengers boarded at Southampton, in the South of England, Cherbourg, in France and Queenstown (now Cobh) in the South of Ireland. The ship left Cobh with around 1,300 passengers on board but unfortunately never made it to New York having hit a submerged iceberg en route. The ship sank within three hours on April 14th 1912 with a loss of almost 1,500 lives.

> Within weeks of the sinking, movies, songs, poems, and books about the calamity were in circulation, and macabre memorabilia were on sale, most notably a black teddy bear by Steiff. The shock waves reverberated for decades in cities like Southampton, where most of the crew resided, Belfast, where the allegedly unsinkable ship was built, and New York, which lost numerous eminent citizens, including Astor, Straus, and Guggenheim … All erected Titanic memorials in due course, as did many other places, including Liverpool, Halifax, Queenstown, and Washington, DC. All were determined never to forget that fateful night ….
>
> (Brown et al., 2013, p. 599)

While the sinking of the Titanic was a significant event in 1912, its importance increased exponentially with the passing of time. Since the 1950s interest in the Titanic has been re-kindled by a raft of documentaries, books, and films on the subject. *Titanic*, a fictional romance–disaster big budget movie by James Cameron, was released in December 1997. It was nominated for 14 academy awards in 1998 and won 11 of these including Best Picture and Best Director. While the film broke box office records at the time, its re-release in 3D form on 4th April 2012 was to push it towards breaking new records. As such, it became only the 2nd film ever to gross more than two billion worldwide! While the success of the movie might be attributed to Cameron's abilities as a Director and to the investment by Paramount Pictures, it seems that there is more to the story than this. There is an appetite for understanding what happened or might have happened on board the fateful ship. There is a dedicated website for Titanic memorabilia[1] and in 2017 the last known letter to have been written by a fatality was sold at auction in the UK for £126,000. The letter was written by Alexander Oskar Holvason a first class passenger to his mother, and, according to the auctioneer is "exceptional on several levels including content, historical context and rarity" (Annonymous, 2017).

The story of the Titanic, laden with mythical overtones perpetuated by the media ever since the fateful night of April 14th 1912, is a point of global fascination (Brown et al. 2013). Significantly, to mark one hundred years since the sinking of the ship, in 2012 several Titanic Experiences were launched in commeration. For example, Belfast, the birthplace of the Titanic, erected "a striking, six-story, steel-clad, star-shaped, staggeringly expensive commemorative centre" (Brown et al., 2013, p. 599) beside the original slipway, graving dock and drawing office. Not only has this contributed to the gentrification of the dockland area, it has had a massive impact on tourism in the area. While Belfast pins its authentic link to the Titanic on the basis of its construction, other places claim their links based on other historical facts as well as on the reconstruction of collective and personal memories and stories.

Smaller in size than the attraction in Belfast, Titanic Experience in Cobh is located in the building where the White Star Line Ticket Office stood. Launched in 2012, the building overlooks the original pier, which, on Thursday April 11th 1912, was the last port of call of the Titanic during its maiden trip to New York. Cobh's historical associations extend beyond the Titanic; the town has a strong link to Ireland's colonial past; from 1849 until 1920 the town was named Queenstown in honour of Queen Victoria's visit to the town. More importantly, it had commercial, shipping, and military significance for the British Empire (Neville, 2015). As Ireland's main sea passage to North America and Australia, Cobh is also deeply associated with exile and emigration; from the deportation of nationalist campaigners to Australia to the mass emigration of the Irish during the Great Famine (1845–1849) (Neville, 2005). The Titanic is one of the many ships that left from Queenstown (Cobh). Most of the 4.75 million people that left Ireland for the USA between 1841 and 1925 passed through Queenstown (Neville 2005). Remembering such an association, Cobh already had 'The Queenstown Experience'[2], a long-standing and very successful visitor centre.

In terms of heritage, it seems that what 'we want to keep' (Hall and McArthur, 1998) is not just the memory of a sinking ship, but somehow we wish to *know* what the experience of being on the Titanic might have been. Because Cobh was the last port visited by the Titanic it has certain unassailable claims to authenticity. Some of the passengers who boarded at Cobh perished in the disaster while others were lucky enough to survive. Thus, the Titanic Experience at Cobh is very much part of what Lennon and Foley (2000) refer to as 'dark tourism', a fairly recent manifestation of the heritage industry involving the commodification of occasions and locations associated with death and destruction (Seaton, 1996; Stone and Sharpley, 2008). In total, 123 passengers boarded the ship on that day (of whom only a family of four were travelling first class, fifteen were travelling second class, and the remaining 104 were travelling third class). Cobh offers a 21st century interpretation that uses modern technology to help transform the experience.

Authenticity is established by the nature of its location, and in particular through association with the original White Star Line Ticket Office as well as the pier (also known as heartbreak pier). However, the artefacts exhibited are for the most part replicas and copies rather than originals. This might be considered problematic if we only consider the authenticity of the objects, but less so if we shift focus from the originality of the toured object to the potential for existential authenticity (Wang, 1999) or the realisation of the self through tourist experience. This is particularly true of the Titanic Experience at Cobh where the attraction centres on the experience of the story of the Titanic as narrated with the aid of audio-visual technology: cinematic shows, scene sets, holographic imagery and touch screen technology[3]. Significantly, tourists are offered the opportunity to engage in a really meaningful experience. This is evident in the attraction's motto, which invites visitors to *Live the history – Feel the story*.

The experience consists of 30 minutes guided tour, followed by unguided exploration of the exhibition area. As with many contemporary museums and heritage experiences, visitors are offered the opportunity not only to interact with the space, and the objects, but also to interact with other visitors and staff. In particular, the Titanic experience is a space for multisensory interactivity. Moving away from the concept of object authenticity, the focus is truly placed on the experience. In this sense, space and objects become part of this experience, in an attempt to enhance it. The attraction's motto (Live the history – Feel the story) promotes the multisensory and embodied aspect of the experience. Although the space and objects have their own claims to authenticity, the real opportunity for the visitor is to immerse him or herself in the experience in different ways at the different stages of the attraction. According to the virtual visitor website[4]:

> The visitor experience is presented in two parts. The first is an exciting immersive audio visual tour retracing the steps of the 123 passengers who boarded Titanic from Cobh on April 11th 1912. Importantly, this is the sole exhibition with a focus on the passengers who boarded at Cobh highlighting the intimate Irish connection to this legendary story. The second part of Titanic Experience examines how it all went wrong; the unbelievable and "almost" impossible sequence of events that occurred to cause Titanic to sink. Finally, the Story Room of Touchscreen Computers allows one to look at the personalities on board the ship and in particular to discover the fate of the 123 Queenstown passengers.

Having visited Titanic Experience in the summer of 2017 we understand that 'feeling the story' and 'living the history' results in a truly embodied experience. Below, we try to share our experiences including the very personal nature of the quest, how the experience stimulates the imagination and (re)locates the visitor to the past. Its engagement with personal and collective memories as they are evoked and (re) constructed throughout the tour and how it simultaneously facinates and repulses the visitor creating ambivalent emotions.

Personal quest

Upon admission, the visitor is given a replica of a boarding card as a ticket. The card shows the personal details of one of the 123 passengers who boarded the ship at Queenstown. It is with this boarding pass that the visitor's personal quest begins. As little is known about that passenger beyond their name, age, and class, a sense of curiosity about their fortune emerges. This immerses the visitor into the narrative early on. As you are taking the tour, the personal quest is aided by information about the conditions under which different classes travelled, but also with the shocking details of the sinking of the Titanic through cinematography, visuals, sonic accounts, and holographic audio-visual narratives.

Transference and imagination

> The tour is designed to simulate the boarding of the Titanic. We are now the passengers on our boarding cards. While the tour begins in a lobby where initial information via a guide and audio-visual means is provided, we are briefly taken outdoors to a balcony overlooking the pier before moving to the main attraction. This movement between the lobby, the balcony, and the former first class waiting room is a process that sparks the imagination. The lobby is insipid and dark, with no natural light, which triggers feelings of ambiguity, but also anticipation about the tour. Going outside, we are faced with the natural conditions of the third class

> passengers waiting outside at the pier to board the Titanic. The combination of the stories given by the guide, as well as the conditions – in our case wind and rain – allows you to begin to imagine what it would be like for those passengers. We are in the present, yet imagining the past.
>
> All aboard! The bell on the wall, next to the entrance of the first class waiting lounge is a playful trigger for further immersion. The guide rings the bell once calling you to board the ship. We, along with other passengers, playfully repeat that action, ringing the bell as we go in one by one. Interaction with the object here is encouraged by the interaction with others.
>
> We are now inside again. There is no natural light, as the windows are covered with period photographs of the fist class lounge and passengers. And this is the end of us being in the present. The space, the artefacts, the story is taking us to the past, to the day the Titanic left for it's first and final journey. This movement from indoors to outdoors and then back indoors, creates a sense of discontinuity, both spatial as well as temporal, engendering the transference of the visitor from Cobh to Queenstown, from present to past.

Transference and imagination are aided by audio-visual technology, but also the use of smells. A funnel-shaped artefact hosts 4 lids reading: "Guess the smell? Where is it on titanic? Lift the flap". The lids are placed at children's height level. Families, but also adults interacted with the exhibit, but children played an important role in engendering interaction with these particular objects. Importantly, children's (inter)actions with the exhibit, also triggered interaction amongst the adult visitors themselves. The smells are intended to transfer the visitor to different rooms and functions of the ship.

Personal stories and collective memory

The experience involves the interplay between personal and collective memory. We are given personal accounts of the lives and circumstances of specific people involved, either as passengers or staff or rescuers, including a sailor who failed to report for duty and was thus saved. These stories are enacted through photographs, and exhibits of personal belongings: Family portraits, articles of clothing, letters, etc. These are juxtaposed with general information about the construction and specifications of the ship, the journey, the disaster and the aftermath. Once again, oral accounts, audio-visual presentations, holographs, cinematography, audio recordings, and textual displays guide us through the personal and the collective.

Personal and collective memories are evoked and constructed throughout the tour. The experience taps into the collective memory of emigration to the new world, leaving poverty in hope of a better life, particularly vivid in Ireland, as these narratives are part of the Irish identity. This aspect of the Irish identity is relevant to both domestic and American visitors due to the deep connection between Ireland and the United States. It is important to note, however, that narratives of emigration to the United States are not unique to Ireland, which makes a point of connection for visitors from other places as well. For instance, two of the researchers who visited the attraction, even though coming from Greece, felt part of the experience, as the exhibits and stories also tapped into the collective narrative of Greek migration. Indicative of this was a conversation among the researchers about a Greek film titled *Nyfes* (Brides)(2004), which narrates the story of women that emigrated to the United States aboard the SS King Alexander, in 1922, told through the perspective of a Greek mail-order bride. The collective memory intertwines with the personal.

Personal, more intimate memories from family (hi)stories of emigration are also triggered, depending on each visitor's personal history. An American visitor enthusiastically proclaimed: "my family came from Ireland, I'm here to find out my history!" while buying his ticket at the reception. While a Greek visitor (one of the researchers) remembered her maternal grandfather, born in Chicago in 1910, and family stories about the months-long journey on ship to the States.

Ambivalence

The experience of the tour, the movement through the different rooms and spaces, the interaction with objects and people, induces a range of feelings and emotions. In particular feelings of ambiguity are invoked throughout the tour. The story of the Titanic itself has cultural significance as an ambiguous myth: it is the archetypal disaster story (Brown et al. 2013). This simultaneously fascinates and repulses. From the moment one decides to visit the attraction, this ambivalence kicks in as the experience verges on the edge between celebration and dark tourism. This is further perpetuated upon entrance, when the boarding pass with the passenger's details is handed and the tour begins in the dark, insipid lobby room.

Then there is ambivalence between immersion and detachment. On one hand, this is an intimate experience due to the personal stories and the imagined fortune of the passenger whose boarding pass you are holding. Yet, on the other hand, throughout the tour one also maintains a sense of detachment, as one is aware that this is a construction and is reminded of this fact by the addition of displays with impersonal information as well as children-friendly activity exhibits.

The stimuli also produce ambivalent, even contradictory emotions: apprehension, knowing how the story ends, but also excitement, at embarking into an experience the specifics of which are yet to be discovered; a sense of excitement and amusement in interacting with some of the exhibits, such as the bell at the start of the tour and the guess the smell exhibit later on; sorrow over the tragedy expressed through personal accounts aided by audio-visual technology; shock and tension when witnessing the sinking of the ship and listening to the cries of people running to their rescue; (partial) closure when looking up 'your' destiny (the name on the boarding pass).

Our experience is shared by other visitors as evident from the selection of reviews[5] below:

> This is a very cool piece of history. This is the original location of the White Star Line Ticket Office. This is the location for the final boarding of the RMS Titanic. You get to see what is left of the original pier which is in definite need of repair. It was nice to take a picture by the window that you can see in the movie and in pictures from that time in history. It's a great experience to learn more about the Titanic, Queenstown (Cobh), and the RMS Carpathia. What a tragedy. I like how they give you a ticket of one of the 123 who boarded here and you can see if the person survived. I thought it was a great tour with the guide and clips showing the story. Great experience!
>
> Titanic Experience very dramatically and creatively conveys the 'human' tragedy of the disaster.
>
> We were really impressed by the short time in this experience. The first half an hour we were on a guided tour with a very good guide taking us to the dock where

> the last bunch of unlucky passengers boarded the Titanic before its fateful disaster, and setting the scene well describing how impressive the ship was and giving good historical context. After she finished guiding us, the rest is self-guided, and really captivating. Utilising technology well, it shows staggeringly scary statistics of who perished, has good letters from passengers giving testimonials to the horror, and shows with disturbing clarity what would have happened to the human body upon submerging with the icy waters. Really good hour well spent.

The Titanic Experience Cobh offers a multisensory experiential approach to the consumption of heritage. For the most part, visitors enjoy this opportunity to feel the story and live the history. This allows us to understand that authenticity is not just in the object, but can be found in the story and in the experience. We locate this shift from object authenticity to experiential authenticity in the discussion below and consider the significance of embodied experiences and interactions in the co-creation of meanings in relation to art, heritage, and identity. Finally, we offer some concluding comments.

Authenticity in heritage tourism: from objects to experiences

While many commentators acknowledge authenticity as a marketing tool for museums and heritage attractions (Prentice 2001, Apostolakis 2003, Chhabra 2008), understandings of authenticity can be located on a continuum of theoretical streams from pure *essentialism* to pure *constructivism* (Chhabra 2008). Essentialism tends to reify particular traditions and cultures (especially those that continue from pre-modern times) as authentic, constructivism views culture as dynamic and flexible (Chhabra 2008), thus questioning the existence of an original moment (Shepherd 2002). A middle ground is *negotiation* of essentialism to address the fluidity of authenticity (Chhabra 2008). Negotiation is linked to the concept of emergent authenticity (Cohen 1988), which observes that something initially thought of as inauthentic may become authentic with the passage of time, particularly when a culture is in decline. Hence, while authors in Europe and North America align themselves with one of these stances, discussions are often framed around the existence or impossibility of authenticity.

However, engaging with such dualisms can limit the scope and usefulness of the concept for museum curators and heritage managers. For example, the very process of removing artefacts and placing them in museums, as well as the acts of abstraction and interpretation involved in doing so, render the authenticity of these objects questionable (Prentice 2001), because "[e]vry relic displayed in a museum is a fake in that it has been wrenched out of its original context" (Lowenthal, 1990, cited in Prentice 2001, p.6). While there is no need to dismiss considerations of the authenticity of the object, authenticity can be evoked in other important ways. For example, Wang argues that authenticity is "not a matter of black or white, but rather involves a much wider spectrum, rich in ambiguous colours" (1999: 353). He proposes a different stance, *existential authenticity*, which doesn't necessarily focus on the originality of toured objects but has predominantly to do with the realisation of the self through tourist experiences (Wang 1999). Existential authenticity is therefore activity-related:

> Existential authenticity refers to a potential existential state of Being that is to be activated by tourist activities. Correspondingly, authentic experiences in tourism are to achieve this activated existential state of Being within the liminal process of

tourism. Existential authenticity can have nothing to do with the authenticity of toured objects.

(Wang 1999, p. 352)

Existential authenticity involves *intrapersonal* and *interpersonal* processes. Intrapersonal authenticity relates to bodily feelings and is an important part of tourism as it involves relaxation, rehabilitation, diversion, recreation, entertainment, sensation-seeking, sensual pleasures, excitement, play, etc. This involves body and mind. On the one hand, it involves the sensual, that is, the body as subject/body as feeling, and on the other the symbolic, where the body becomes a display of personal identity (health, naturalness, youth, fitness, movement, beauty, etc.). Intrapersonal authenticity is therefore essentially concerned with 'self-making' (e.g. Kim and Jamal 2007). For example, it provides tourists with opportunities to experience risk, daring, and uncertainty – which their everyday lives do not allow.

Interpersonal authenticity relates to the formation of touristic 'communitas' (Wang 1999). Building on Maffesoli, Wang notes "the toured objects or tourism can be just a means or medium by which tourists are called together, and then, an authentic interpersonal relationship between themselves is experienced subsequently" (1999, p. 364). Tourism can, therefore, involve a search for 'communitas', characterised by 'liminality', that is, "any condition outside of or on the periphery of everyday life" (Turner 1974, cited in Wang 1999, p. 364). Tourist journeys thus afford tourists opportunities to alleviate "the pressures stemming from inauthentic social hierarchy and status distinctions" (Wang 1999, p.365). For example, a study of Renaissance festival reveals tourists' active participation in bonding, friendship, identity seeking, and transcendence (Kim and Jamal 2007). Furthermore, it reveals how participants' experiences of the festival were implicated in self-making, meaning making, and belonging. Such interpersonal experiences play an important role in consumers' re-enchantment with the world (Rojek 2000) and as such are transformative not only for their members, but for business practices and society in general (Cova et al. 2007).

Authenticity, therefore, depends on the tourists' experiences, as these experiences are constructed through sensations, interactions, and in tourists' imagination. Tourist products are reconceptualised as experiences (Prentice 2001). Experience value is gaining renewed interest in the tourism literature (Prebensen et al. 2014). Facilitating a range of embodied and relational experiences, tourism and heritage attractions are contexts in which authenticity is constructed and negotiated. In our case, the Titanic Experience offered opportunities for discovery, excitement, and wonder, as well as personal meaning through connection to intimate and collective stories, as well as opportunities for reflection beyond the remit of our everyday realities.

Multisensory experiences and co-creation of meaning in heritage attractions

Visitor experiences at heritage and cultural attractions are not one-dimensional or passive; they engage body and mind. In the case of the Titanic, as we have seen, this was engendered by the experiential, multisensory design of the attraction. Yet, it is important to note that the consumption of culture and heritage is an embodied experience, rather than a mere cognitive reception of historical facts. Hence, consumption of heritage can be best viewed as a *multisensory, synesthetic experience* (Chronis 2006). Multisensory refers to the involvement of the senses, while experiencing particular attractions, while synesthetic refers to the emotional experience as opposed to impersonal knowledge (Chronis 2006). Thus, the visitor comes to appreciate history and culture in an embodied way. Heritage artefacts should not be simply understood as distant physical objects, but rather as tangible multisensory mnemonic devices, because of the emotions, memories, and meanings they evoke, which produce perceptions of cultural identity (Chronis 2006).

Furthermore, *somatic* experiences (Joy and Sherry 2003) are important, because they inform our thinking about culture and the past. Joy and Sherry demonstrate how museum visitors' reasoning and imagination is shaped through important embodiment processes:

> Perception is both a physiological and intellectual judgment, for perceiving an object requires grasping the object as a whole as well as in terms of its parts. It is also closely linked with imagination for it is through virtual body enactments that creative projections are possible and an individual's skill acquisition improves. Although one acquires knowledge primarily through the eye and the act of seeing, many participants found themselves in situations where seeing allowed them to engage in other sensations – touch, taste, and smell. The order in which these sensations are experienced depends on the stimuli in question.
>
> (2003, p. 278)

In addition, these embodied experiences are relational. Visitors interact with objects, but also with other visitors and staff. In interactions with objects, visitors employ the senses: seeing, listening, touching, smelling, tasting. In interactions with other visitors and staff, visitors influence and learn from each other how to move through space, how to interact with the exhibits, or even which exhibits have more value over others. Visitors make sense of the exhibits "through a range of activities, including walking and looking, glancing and inspecting, pointing and showing, talking and discussing, and so forth" (von Lehn 2006, p. 1353). The multisensory, synesthetic, relational, somatic nature of the experience triggers the fantasy and imagination in a quest for meaning. Museums and heritage attractions as contexts thus become spaces for the social construction of knowledge, collective memory and identity.

Conclusions

In this chapter we used the case of the Titanic Experience in Cobh, to explore emerging understandings of heritage and authenticity. In doing so, we discussed the consumption of heritage as a *multisensory*, *embodied*, and *relational* experience. Appreciation of the combined role of embodiment processes, sensations, and interactions opens up opportunities for heritage managers in the facilitation of meaningful heritage experiences. Furthermore, it opens up possibilities for retaining the integrity of the experience through personal connection even when object authenticity or large-scale spectacle is not feasible. In the case of the Titanic Experience in Cobh, this was achieved in a relatively small-scale attraction, with very few original artefacts.

A concern with heritage and desire for authenticity preoccupy individuals in contemporary society. Although heritage was traditionally concerned with the preservation or reconstruction of material objects, understanding of what heritage is has been dramatically expanded. Understanding of authenticity has also expanded to move beyond the authenticity of the object to appreciating the potentialities of existential authenticity in the context of tourism. Together they open up the possibilities for the production and consumption of heritage. The heritage industry is no longer limited by a preoccupation of material objects that have been authenticated. Rather, claims to authenticity can be made with reference to experience, location, association, or myth. Moreover, freed from the constraints of object authenticity, and bolstered by modern technology, the past can now not only be experienced from the comfort of the present but it can truly be appreciated via more personally meaningful experiences.

Notes

1 http://www.titanicmemorabilia.net
2 http://www.visitcobh.com/index.php/reviews/cobh-the-queenstown-story/ accessed 22 October 2017.
3 http://www.titanicexperiencecobh.ie/
4 http://www.virtualvisittours.com/titanic-experience-cobh/ accessed 22 October 2017.
5 https://www.tripadvisor.ie/ShowUserReviews-g211925-d2718185-r532929975-Titanic_Experience_Cobh-Cobh_County_Cork.html

References

Annonymous (2017) "Letter written on Titanic fetches record £126,000 at auction", The Guardian, https://www.theguardian.com/uk-news/2017/oct/21/letter-written-on-titanic-fetches-record-126000-at-auction

Apostolakis, A. (2003). The convergence process in heritage tourism. *Annals of tourism research*, *30*(4), 795–812.

Ashworth, G. J. (1994). From History to Heritage – from Heritage to Identity: In Search of Concepts and Models. In G. J. Ashworth and P. J. Larkham (Eds.), *Building a New Heritage: Tourism, Culture and Identity in the New Europe*, London; New York: Routledge, 13–30.

Bourdieu, P. (1984). Distinction: *A Social Critique of the Judgment of Taste*. London: Routledge.

Brett, D. (1996), The Construction of Heritage, Cork, Cork University Press.

Brown, S., McDonagh, P., and Shultz, C. J. (2013). Titanic: Consuming the myths and meanings of an ambiguous brand. *Journal of Consumer Research*, *40*(4), 595–614.

Chhabra, D. (2008). Positioning museums on an authenticity continuum. *Annals of Tourism Research*, *35*(2), 427–447.

Chronis, A. (2006). Heritage of the senses: Collective remembering as an embodied praxis. *Tourist Studies*, *6*(3), 267–296.

Cohen, E. (1988). Authenticity and commoditization in tourism. *Annals of tourism research*, *15*(3), 371–386.

Cova, B., Kozinets, R., and Shankar, A. (2012). *Consumer tribes*. London: Routledge.

Goulding, C. (2000). The commodification of the past, postmodern pastiche, and the search for authentic experiences at contemporary heritage attractions. *European Journal of Marketing*, *34*(7), 835–853.

Gouthro, M.B and Palmer, C. (2010). Pilgrimage in Heritage Tourism: Finding Meaning and Identity in the Industrial Past. In Conlin, M.V. and Jolliffe, L. (eds) *Mining Heritage and Tourism: A Global Synthesis*. London: Routledge, pp. 33–43.

Hall, C. M. and McArthur, S. (1998). *Integrated Heritage Management: Principles and Practice*. London: Stationery Office.

Hall, M. C., & McArthur, S. (1998). *Integrated heritage management: Principles and practice*. London: Stationery Office.

Hewison, R. (1987). *The Heritage Industry: Britain in a Climate of Decline*. London: Methuen.

Holt, D. B. (1998). Does cultural capital structure American consumption?. *Journal of consumer research*, *25*(1), 1–25.

Jenkins, T. N. (2000) Putting postmodernity into practice: endogenous development and the role of traditional cultures in the rural development of marginal regions. *Ecological Economics*, 34 (2000): 301–304.

Joy, A., and Sherry Jr, J. F. (2003). Speaking of art as embodied imagination: A multisensory approach to understanding aesthetic experience. *Journal of consumer research, 30*(2), 259–282.

Kim, H., and Jamal, T. (2007). Touristic quest for existential authenticity. *Annals of Tourism Research, 34*(1), 181–201.

Lash, S., & Urry, J. (1993). *Economies of signs and space*(Vol. 26). London: Sage.

Lennon, J. J. and Foley, M. (2000). *Dark tourism*. London: Cengage Learning EMEA.

Lowenthal, D. (1994). Identity, heritage, and history. *Commemorations: The politics of national identity*, 41–57.

Meethan, K. (1996). Consuming (in) the Civilised City. *Annals of Tourism Research*, 23 (2), 322–340.

Meethan, K. (2001). Tourism in Global Society: Place, Culture, Consumption. Hampshire: Palgrave.

Miles, S. (2010). *Spaces for consumption*. London: SAGE.

Munt, I. (1994). The "Other" Postmodern Tourism: Culture Travel and the New Middle Classes. *Theory, Culture & Society*, 11: 101–123.

Neville, P. (2015). Nostalgia and Titanic commemorations in Cobh, Ireland. *Irish Studies Review, 23*(3), 292–309.

Newman, A., and McLean, F. (2006). The impact of museums upon identity. *International Journal of Heritage Studies, 12*(1), 49–68.

Nuryanti, W. (1996). Heritage and postmodern tourism. *Annals of tourism research, 23*(2), 249–260.

Nyfes. Dir. Pantelis Voulgaris. Writ. Ioanna Karystiani. Perfs. Damian Lewis, Victoria Haralabidou. Odeon SA, 2004.

Prentice, R. (1993). *Tourism and Heritage Attractions*. London: Routledge.

Prentice, R. (2001). Experiential cultural tourism: Museums and the marketing of the new romanticism of evoked authenticity. *Museum Management and Curatorship, 19*(1), 5–26.

Richards, G. (1996). Production and consumption of European cultural tourism. *Annals of tourism research, 23*(2), 261–283.

Rojek, C. (2000). Mass tourism or the re-enchantment of the world? Issues and contradictions in the study of travel. *New forms of consumption*, 51–70.

Seaton, A.V. (1996). Guided by the dark: From thanatopsis to thanatourism. *International Journal of Heritage Studies*,2(4), 234–244.

Sharpley, R. and Sharpley, J. (1997). Sustainability and the Consumption of Tourism. In M.J. Stabler (Ed.), *Tourism and Sustainability: Principles and Practice* (231–243), Wallingford: CAB International.

Shepherd, R. (2002). Commoditisation, Culture and Tourism. *Tourism Studies*, 2 (2): 183–201.

Stone, P., and Sharpley, R. (2008). Consuming dark tourism: A thanatological perspective. *Annals of tourism Research, 35*(2), 574–595.

Urry, J. (1995). *Consuming places*. London: Routledge.

Vom Lehn, D. (2006). Embodying experience: A video-based examination of visitors' conduct and interaction in museums. *European Journal of Marketing, 40*(11/12), 1340–1359.

Wang, N. (1999). Rethinking authenticity in tourism experience. *Annals of tourism research, 26*(2), 349–370.

8 The people and processes underscoring authentication of the Blaenavon World Heritage Site

Mediating "hot" and "cool" authentication

Laura Reynolds, Adam Lindgreen and Michael Beverland

Authenticity is central to cultural heritage offerings, because it functions as a signpost of quality and value in this fiercely competitive arena (Cavanaugh and Shankar 2014). The process of authentication is imbued and enacted by multiple stakeholders, such that it entails dynamic social processes that serve to co-create objective, experiential, and existential authenticity (Cohen and Cohen 2012; Mkono 2013; Zhu 2012). The question is no longer what gets classified as authentic; instead, the focus is on the people and processes involved in authenticating assets, rituals, destinations, sites, or places. Accordingly, recent literature highlights stakeholders' influences on augmenting and diminishing authenticity (Cohen and Cohen 2012). The enhanced recognition that stakeholders are integral to the process of authentication has prompted a stream of studies exploring the role of particular actors and groups in constructing authentic experiences (Zhu 2012), such as tourists and tour guides (Chronis et al. 2012), the local community (Aas et al. 2005), management and marketers (Kolar and Žabkar 2010), experts such as curators and critics (Glynn and Lounsbury 2005; Halewood and Hannam 2001), and performers (Zhu 2012).

Yet these studies largely elide the nuances of stakeholder-centered authentication. In response, this chapter addresses four key omissions. Specifically, it offers a novel comparison of stakeholders' operations when they function in the public eye versus behind the scenes. This chapter also explores the collaborative functions adopted by a network of stakeholders who both cooperate and compete. Within this overarching stakeholder network, this chapter addresses the need for individual stakeholders to integrate official and unofficial forms of authentication. Finally, it acknowledges a particularly relevant but omitted stakeholder, namely, host-community volunteers.

In seeking to span these research gaps, this chapter applies and extends Cohen and Cohen's (2012, 2017) theorizing about "hot" and "cool" modes of authentication. It specifies and recognizes the different actors that operate in the foreground and background of cultural heritage efforts. Furthermore, this chapter explores the collaborative stakeholder network who provide hot and cool authentication. By investigating host-community volunteers, it uncovers the influence of an important stakeholder. Overall then, this chapter provides an analysis of functional and symbolic dynamics, operating at the structural and procedural levels of authentication, by highlighting the collaborative nature of authentication and emphasizing stakeholders' positions as partners in this process, rather than passive recipients of its outcomes.

Conceptual framework

Authenticity to authentication

The evolution of the notion of authenticity reveals multiple domains: objective (Leigh et al. 2006), staged (MacCannell 1973), and existential (Wang 1999), as well as their combination through a constructivist approach (Cohen 1988; Olsen 2002). The varied nature of authenticity research has led critics to question the usefulness of the term (Steiner and Reisinger 2006), but these various domains do not contest its definitive meaning. Rather, these conceptualizations operate as analytic tools, facilitating a better understanding of this complex discourse (Belhassen and Caton 2006). The multiple forms of authenticity also can co-exist (Chhabra et al. 2003; Wang 1999), so exploring this notion is best achieved by recognizing the co-existence of diverging discourses to understand how the multiple genres get constructed and enacted.

The rising acceptance of multiple authenticity discourses parallels the growing recognition that these forms are constructed by key players in cultural heritage arenas. Both cultural heritage and authenticity are transitioning toward an "endlessly constructed" (Chhabra 2008, p. 428), stakeholder-centered process. Tangible objects remain important, yet people and intangible performances and processes represent the focus of recent studies. As Jones (2010, p. 182) surmises, authenticity arises from the "networks of relationships between people, places and things that appear to be central, not the things in themselves." Recent literature accordingly notes the role and importance of salient stakeholders in constructing authenticity, such as tour guides (Chronis et al. 2012), the local community (Aas et al. 2005), visitors (Leighton 2007), critics (Glynn and Lounsbury 2005), managers (Kolar and Žabkar 2010), and curators (Halewood and Hannam 2001). The varying input of these stakeholders operates in both the foreground and the background of cultural heritage (Waitt 2000).

Volunteers also are increasingly critical, due to the rising need for voluntary support to cover tasks required by financially strained heritage sites (Leighton 2007). They have become a hot topic in tourism and cultural heritage research (Wearing and McGehee 2013), yet understanding of host-community volunteers remains sparse and mostly presented in relation to some other stakeholder groups. For example, some studies address the effects of volunteers' roles and experience on the experiential value of a tourist experience (Yeoman et al. 2007) or their functions as tour guides (Hede and Thyne 2010). Yet limiting volunteers to their functions for other stakeholder categories omits their role as key stakeholders, whose efforts infuse the dynamic authenticity process. A notable exception highlights the idiosyncratic role of volunteers for destination storytelling (Olsson et al. 2016), such that their personal engagement and enthusiasm define the storytelling process, particularly if the volunteers are from the local community. Thus, a host-community volunteer may intensify the sense of authenticity perceived by visitors. Beyond the benefits when host-community volunteers present intangible stories and interact with visitors, the various roles that volunteers adopt imply that they actually interact with multiple stakeholders in both the foreground and the background.

The backgrounds and foregrounds of cultural heritage

Stakeholder roles differ, depending on whether they take place in the foreground or background of cultural heritage activities. In the foreground, the processes are physically visible, involving interactions with other stakeholders to undertake functional, symbolic, performative acts (Knudsen and Waade 2010). They might include reenactments, storytelling, demonstrations, and front-of-house staffing. For example, a representation of the past offers an ongoing social process of engagement and storytelling, usually shaped by tour guides in the foreground of the consumption exchange (Chronis 2005). The narrative and storytelling can be readjusted constantly, according to the tour guides' and visitors' simultaneous interest and knowledge (Chronis et al. 2012). The dynamic interaction of tour guides and tourists, thus, informs both the narrative and the form of authenticity, such that their multiple interests concurrently shape the stakeholder authentication process.

Stakeholders operating behind the scenes instead discretely authenticate, by structuring and influencing predefined accounts of events that later get showcased in the foreground. For example, critics of art and culture operate as gatekeepers by defining what might be deemed authentic (Glynn and Lounsbury 2005). Authentication results from their credence as certified experts, signaling their ability to resist or spark cultural and institutional change. Other common background tasks that can encourage authentication are curation and archeology (Halewood and Hannam 2001). Curators serve as custodians of heritage, protecting and preserving accepted accounts of events, though it is possible to question their authoritative domination over what may be deemed genuine, under the guise of objective authenticity (Chhabra 2008). That is, curators actually influence the authenticity pursued and enacted, as agents with the ability to promote or stifle change. A similar critique might be leveraged against literary guardians, who advance claims of truth for their own personal betterment, to the exclusion of rival claims (Fawcett and Cormack 2001). Authenticity, as it is pursued and enacted, thus, is not a static or catchall asset; rather, those who possess knowledge and status are better equipped to provide input to authentication processes.

Authentication also can be espoused and enacted through national and international institutional verification, which provides, perhaps, the highest stamp of legitimacy (Cohen and Cohen 2012). For example, a site or activity might be identified as a United Nations Educational Scientific Cultural Organization (UNESCO) World Heritage Site (WHS) (Cohen and Cohen 2012). This status prompts a heightened sense of pride, which may encourage wider participation and support for the cultural heritage, in that it has been deemed officially worth protecting (Poria et al. 2013). However, WHS status also may prompt skepticism, because the powerful few dictate this authenticity to the masses (Elliot and Schmutz 2012). Despite the practicality of this evaluation, WHS status threatens to create a management dystopia, marked by multiple overlapping claims that need to be coordinated (Alberts and Hazen 2010), without providing substantial financial or statutory protection (Rodwell 2014). The institutional stamp of authentication provides objective recognition, but WHS still are evolving, dynamic entities, within local, national, and international networks of stakeholders. The difficulties of coordinating multiple stakeholder views, alongside an institutional stamp, suggests why living heritage sites are so complicated to manage.

"Hot" and "cool" authentication

To address the intricate authentication process, this chapter applies and builds on Cohen and Cohen's (2012, 2017) "hot" (existential) and "cool" (objectivist) modes of authentication. Power dynamics and complexities underlie any authentication process, and they differ according to the stakeholder, time, and place. These authors move beyond singular stakeholders to look at the wider web of stakeholders who collectively and collaboratively authenticate cultural heritage. They define authentication as "a process by which something—a role, product, site, object or event—is confirmed as original, genuine, real or trustworthy" (Cohen and Cohen 2012, p. 1297), then conceptualize different social processes underlying authentication as two interlocking modes: "hot" (existential) and "cool" (objectivist). In so doing, they extend Selwyn's (1996) conceptual development of the use of these terms. That is, Selwyn aligns hot authentication with the notion of an authentic self and an authentic other within an imagined tourist arena, whereas cool authentication refers to more objective, scientific claims to legitimacy. Cohen and Cohen (2012), going beyond a socio-psychological approach, look at the social and political processes aligned with each mode, such that the emphasis shifts "to what authenticity does, rather than what it is" (Cohen and Cohen 2017, p. 12).

In this sense, cool authentication implies a formal process, in which professional, socially accepted agents provide official seals of approval to certify an objectivist claim. They can be affirmed through expertise, claims to knowledge, or scientific evidence. This process tends to foster a formal approach, developed through predefined criteria and procedures. Once cemented as authentic, it becomes difficult to amend this status, unless deauthorized through official channels, as exemplified by the WHS classification of a site as warranting protection (Cohen and Cohen 2012). However, even cool authentication is unlikely to remain static, because stakeholders' roles and power relations are constantly in flux. Arguably though, this narrow view might prevent a clear understanding of the complex nature of competing stakeholders' inputs and the resulting outputs.

In parallel and often in competition, hot authentication occurs when agents iteratively, informally, and creatively co-create authenticity through performative tools. It centers on the user processes that underscore existential and experiential authentication, as well as social actors' performative acts and how they shape implicit beliefs, which makes hot authentication more problematic to analyze, given the intangible nature of the "informal performative process of creating, preserving and reinforcing an object's, site's, or event's authenticity" (Cohen and Cohen 2012, p. 1300). In contrast with cool authentication, which seeks evidence of originality and truthfulness (Cohen and Cohen 2012), hot authentication relies on collective acts of worship and participation to strengthen customs and beliefs (Cohen and Cohen 2012). This intersubjective, experiential authentic experience allows for incremental changes, outside formal or traditional authentication structures.

The two socially constructed processes must be considered in tandem, yet existing research has not explored the implications when multiple stakeholders undertake competing, hot *and* cool performative tasks, nor does it specify how key stakeholders might mediate the tensions of objectivist authentication versus existential authentication. Actors must ensure that sites do not become "frozen in time" (Cohen and Cohen 2012, p. 1304), which implies avoiding the rigidity of official accreditations and verifications. Yet such a recommendation also omits the potential for cool authentication to provide a foundation for flexible applications and interpretations, through performative acts, by visitors and other supplementary stakeholders within the wider network. While acknowledging the underlying dimensions of power and legitimacy, it is necessary to identify mediating alternatives that can relieve some of the strain on contemporary living in operational heritage towns and cities too.

Mkono (2013) builds on Cohen and Cohen's (2012) theoretical grounding, illuminating the contestation and power dynamics inherent to all forms of authentication. For both hot and cool modes, the process is never complete, power imbalances keep emerging, and contestation never ceases. This argument reiterates the need to evaluate networks of stakeholders that shape the dynamic authentication process, rather than investigating official stakeholder pursuits, according to whether they are aligned or in opposition to unofficial claims. This dynamism is particularly pronounced in the interwoven performative roles that stakeholders take, in the foreground or background of cultural heritage.

Methodology and context

To explore the network of stakeholders that shapes hot and cool authentication, this chapter presents an in-depth case study of Blaenavon WHS over a six-month period prior to October 2014. This single, intensive case study supports detailed exploration of this underresearched area (Eriksson and Kovalainen 2008), and the clear focus provides context-specific understanding (Flyvberg 2011), benefiting theory generation (Järvensivu and Törnroos 2010). The case study comprises 15 semi-structured interviews, one focus group, unstructured onsite observations, and supportive secondary data analysis (Table 8.1). The interviews and focus group all lasted approximately 60 minutes. The 21 stakeholders exhibit power, urgency, and legitimacy in relation to the authentication process (Mitchell et al. 1997); they were selected according to their roles and interest in the processes in the foreground and background of Blaenavon's WHS. The sample, thus, includes stakeholders from Blaenavon's heritage sites, WHS management and marketers, volunteer project coordinators, volunteers, local residents, and national heritage representatives. The interviews and focus groups were transcribed per dictum.

This research uses grounded theory principles to guide the data collection and analysis, as well as the abductive development of emergent theory. This approach combines the procedural Gioia methodology, which recognizes the pivotal influence of

Table 8.1 Case study data collection tools

Data Collection Tool	*Number of Items*	*Selection Criteria*
In-depth interviews, single informant	13	Salient stakeholders were selected from the visitor economy, local community, voluntary sector, local authority, and visitors. Interviews were tailored to the specific participant. Visual and verbal cues of the site illustrated aspects of the discussion.
In-depth interviews, pairs of informants	2	Same salient stakeholders as above, pairing volunteers and visitors. The dual interviews focus on the joint enterprise of volunteers and visitors.
Focus group	1 (with 4 participants)	Group's participation enhanced knowledge and meaning through social interaction. All participants volunteered in the community and voluntarily led heritage attraction events.
Onsite observations	8	Supporting evidence for interviews and focus groups. Eight central sites around the WHS: Blaenavon World Heritage Centre, Blaenavon town center, Big Pit National Coal Museum, Blaenavon Ironworks, Blaenavon Community Heritage and Cordell Museum, Keeper's Pond, and the Pontypool and Blaenavon Heritage Railway.
Secondary data	20 sources	Breadth of secondary sources, compiled to develop initial theoretical insights. Key documents in the collection and analysis include The Blaenavon World Heritage Environmental Group (BWHEG) Volunteer Ranger Handbook and the Blaenavon WHS Management Plan 2011–2016.

researchers in the research process, while mapping the process of theory construction in an abductive, strategic, and innovative manner (Charmaz 2006; Gioia *et al.* 2012). The three-stage data analysis started with the open coding of processes, then clustered these processes into collective incidents, and finally analyzed the incidents, with reference to existing literature, to develop and extend extant theory (Charmaz 2006; Gioia et al. 2012). This approach ensures flexibility, integrity, and depth in the emergent theoretical and empirical findings.

The initial focus of the data exploration was a multi-stakeholder approach to authentication, together with an individual analysis of potential mediating actors. These foci were refined through the data collection process, which guided future interview questions and allowed for more nuanced investigation. Following the data collection, the authors thematically analyzed the transcripts and devised codes for two interconnected areas. Comparisons across their codes helped ensure the validity and reliability of the results.

Blaenavon is located in the South Wales Valley; it received WHS status in 2000 (UNESCO 2014), following the recognition that the region possesses "one of the few authentic examples of an area shaped by coal and iron-making development during the eighteenth and nineteenth centuries" (Jones and Munday 2001, p. 585). Its outstanding universal value is typified in the following statement:

> The area around Blaenavon is evidence of pre-eminence of South Wales as the world's major producer of iron and coal in the 19th century. All the necessary elements can still be seen—coal and ore mines, quarries, a primitive railway system, furnaces, workers' homes, and the social infrastructure of their community.
>
> (UNESCO 2014, para. 1)

The site is marked by a rich industrial landscape, embellished by a unique tangible and intangible heritage and enriched by a local community that can recount tales of the town's industrial legacy. Within Blaenavon's industrial landscape, multiple attractions employ a variety of interpretive techniques to present the town's industrial past (Table 8.2). These diverse offerings ensure that varied stakeholders participate in the background and foreground of the industrial heritage presentation, providing idiosyncratic influences on the process by which authenticity gets constructed.

The emphasis on collaboration and partnerships among stakeholder groups in Blaenavon was invigorated by the establishment of the Blaenavon Partnership in 1997 (Visit Blaenavon 2014a). This partnership is pivotal for aligning stakeholders' interests around the protection and promotion of the Blaenavon industrial landscape, as well as managing a consistent presentation of the site (Torfaen County Borough Council 2011). The need to present and protect the industrial legacy collaboratively was of paramount importance to the Forgotten Landscape Project (FLP), funded by the Heritage Lottery Fund and the Welsh Government (Visit Blaenavon, 2014b), for which the key focus was ensuring a sustainable heritage, coordinated by a motivated, engaged volunteer base. The FLP heightened public awareness of an industrial landscape "pitted with mines and quarries, blackened by the tips of colliery spoil, and dissected by tram roads and railways" (Visit Blaenavon 2014c). It relied on collaboration, partnerships, and volunteers to remind the public of the industrial legacy left behind, such that Blaenavon still possesses its distinctive combination of tangible and intangible heritage, a medley of stakeholders, and an overarching structure of coordination and collaboration.

Table 8.2 Selection of Blaenavon attractions, based on onsite observations (July 2014)

Attraction	*Overview*	*Interpretive Techniques*
Big Pit	The Big Pit National Coal Museum is situated at a former working coal mine that closed in 1980. Entrance is free, and the site is open daily from 9:30 am to 5:00 pm; the last mine tour runs at 3:30 pm. While operational, the mine was the oldest working mine in Wales, providing railway coal to Britain, France, and South America.	An underground tour of the mine with a pre-existing miner guide; digital interactive gallery; audio simulation of life in mine; tram circuit; sawmill; winding house; fan house, pithead baths; exhibitions, blacksmith's shop; conservation workshop; and viewpoints.
Blaenavon Ironworks	The Blaenavon Ironworks is managed by Cadw Welsh Historic Monuments. The site has been recently restored and enhanced, helping increase visitor numbers. It highlights the industrial and social heritage, with a combination of furnaces, cast houses, and towers, alongside examples of dwellings and local shops.	Six viewing platforms, each containing boards and audio describing the tangible structure through intangible reencounters; well-preserved blast furnaces, cast houses, and a restored Water Balance Tower; refurbished company shop and workers' cottages that vary, depending on the period they represent.
Blaenavon Community and Cornell Museum	The Blaenavon Community Heritage Museum is positioned in the town center, next to the Blaenavon Library. Entrance requires a donation of £1.50. The Museum is run entirely by volunteers and remains independent of any governing body. It features three main exhibition rooms, which present artifacts from Blaenavon's history.	Two main exhibitions; donated social and industrial artifacts from a prolonged period; area focusing on Alexander Cordell (one of Wales's most prolific writers); guided tours by volunteers; reenactments of events associated with Blaenavon.
Blaenavon and Pontypool Railway	The Pontypool and Blaenavon Railway was established after the line closed in 1980, starting operations in 1983. It is entirely led and operated by volunteers, who sign up for annual memberships. The organization consists of two components: a society that raises funds to support the railway, and a Board of Directors who discuss the running and operation of the site. The Railway is open to visitors on Saturdays and Sundays, and also Wednesdays during summer months; an adult ticket costs £7.	Series of special events held at the site throughout the year, including a 1940s day and vintage days; recently restored station; rail running through Blaenavon landscape (three lines); museums; onsite interactions with volunteers; railway maintenance and protection.

Themes and discussion

Two key themes emerge from the application of Cohen and Cohen's (2012) hot and cool authentication concept to the Blaenavon WHS. First, the multiplicity of stakeholder involvement reveals how stakeholders' hot and cool authentication acts interact. Partnership, collaboration, and the world heritage designation provide the basis for cool authentication; the intertwining use of hot forms of authentication support variation in actions, processes, and stakeholder roles. With this flexibility, stakeholders can alter and augment their representations and achieve diversity, in response to the power dynamics leveraged by cool authentication. Second, the findings indicate the importance of individual stakeholders who operate as mediators of the problems associated with authentication. Host-community volunteers, in particular, are fundamental, because they can mediate tensions between hot and cool authentication, providing a crucial function in the authentication of fragmented, complex heritage sites.

Negotiating hot and cool authentication across a network of stakeholders

Previous research tends to highlight how a single stakeholder group functions in the authentication process, which ignores the interconnectedness of stakeholders operating in both the foreground and background of cultural heritage sites. In a living WHS in particular, stakeholders juggle an array of official and unofficial demands to represent and protect the site's functional and symbolic assets. The extremely complex process of authentication, thus, involves interlocking people, places, and processes. By incorporating a wider array of stakeholders, the current case study analysis is able to highlight the importance of partnership and collaboration to coordinate multiple, competing stakeholder roles. The strength of the partnership allows it to span the foreground and background, providing direction and strategy for salient stakeholders. Specifically, the Blaenavon Partnership works with the coordinating vision of the UNESCO WHS designation to provide cool authentication that directs the stakeholders toward a common vision, as noted in the following quote:

> The granting of outstanding universal value by UNESCO is the reason we're a World Heritage Site. So obviously all the partners are aware, and it's quite useful in a nutshell really why we're a World Heritage Site.
>
> (Torfaen County Council, WHS coordinator)

According to Cohen and Cohen (2012), official verification of authenticity, as afforded by the UNESCO seal, establishes predefined acceptance by a few power players. This cool authentication aligns with official certification or accreditation. Despite the need for some caution, because of the underlying power connotations involved when official versions threaten to stifle competing claims (Waitt 2000), the benefit of this central coordination is clear for the Blaenavon WHS. Along with providing a source of pride and passion for stakeholders emotively invested in the town, the UNESCO guidelines provide a point of unison that helps multifaceted partners work toward a central vision, because it outlines expectations and responsibilities applicable across the stakeholder network.

This unison is strengthened by the Blaenavon Partnership structure, designed to be a precursor for coordination efforts in the lead-up to the WHS designation (Blaenavon World Heritage Site Management Plan 2011). The partnership combines stakeholders from the visitor economy, business community, voluntary sector, and local authority, in an attempt to ensure clear understanding and parallel decisions:

> The vision has to be a complete and accurate story of everything really that happened within the World Heritage Site. I think certainly the partnership, the Blaenavon WHS, ensures that.
>
> (Torfaen County Council, WHS coordinator)

The Management Plan attached to the partnership addresses "how the partners can work together to promote a common message about the site and its offerings" (Torfaen County Council, WHS marketing executive). The partnership also provides benefits beyond the structural level, by bringing together key stakeholders to deal with a specific issue or development. For example, in the FLP, stakeholders work collectively to map a coordinated plan to link the town's cultural heritage attractions with the promotion of its rich, diverse industrial landscape (Figure 8.1). Thus, partnerships can promote collaboration, ongoing relationships (Aas et al. 2005), and consistent plans, in contrast with fragmented approaches across the WHS site.

The cool authentication manifested in the UNESCO designation and partnership structure largely operates in the background, as exemplified by the official guidelines for Blaenavon WHS branding and the policies in place to direct actors and guides at sites across the WHS, in line with the accepted legacy of Blaenavon's industrial heritage. These forms of authentication strengthen and legitimize the site's claims to authenticity, without being directly visible to stakeholders removed from the partnership structure. The overarching processes also help coordinate cool authentication occurring at the attraction level, such as curating exhibitions or scripting guided tours.

Yet these partnerships and the top-down coordination in cool authentication processes do not always respond to the needs of the array of stakeholders operating at the WHS site. Instead, they require some flexibility and diversity in authentication processes, as bolstered by hot authentication that encourages stakeholders to "embrace" (Torfaen County Council, WHS coordinator) authenticity through active participation and (re)

Figure 8.1 Keeper's Pond, Blaenavon, August 2015 (authors' photo)

interpretation. The forms of hot authentication evident at the Blaenavon WHS include storytelling, reenactments, events, tours, and trails. These performances mainly occur in the foreground, operating across Blaenavon and the framework of multiple attractions and subsidiaries. The benefits of this performativity and connectivity of stakeholders are pronounced, as one participant notes:

> One of our guides grew up in this area. When he does the walk, he tells stories of how it was, which really adds something extra. So, when passing some cottages, he'll be able to recount stories of when the residents used to shout out and wave to those passing by, and personal accounts like that, adding even more to the experience.
>
> (Blaenavon volunteer, environment and heritage protection and preservation)

Although the tour of the Blaenavon landscape is commissioned and planned by stakeholders within the Blaenavon Partnership, its authentication gets enhanced by the connectivity and recollections provided through hot authentication. This finding resonates with the imagined mode of authentication described by Bryce et al. (2017), who note how ancestral connectivity to a home can carve out a niche of authentication. Cohen and Cohen (2012) are skeptical of cool modes of authentication being disguised as hot, but some degree of flexibility allows for a fusion across modes. Managers operating strategically plan the structure and content; the tour guide demonstrates a symbolic and indexical connection to the heritage, which augments and alters the experience. The unofficial version builds incrementally on the official version, and the reenactments and storytelling foster a stronger connection, based on the people connected to the place. Similarly, the high acclaim awarded to the Big Pit coalmine and museum stems from its incorporation of ex-miners as tour guides, who recount anecdotes, tribulations, and the everyday working conditions they experienced before the closure of the mine. Underlying these tales are curated narratives though, which recommend key points to disclose, even while allowing the tour guides some discretion to diverge to meet the needs of the audience. As a representative of the attraction explains:

> When a new guide starts they are given, well a script if you like, but just more information they need to tell people as they go along. Like certain stopping points that they would show, that this is like whatever, or where the horses were. So, there are specific points that are scripted to say. But we don't tell them how to say it, they can say it in their own way. That's what's nice about it.
>
> (Big Pit, communications)

Thus, a visitor notes,

> I think it's really good that they were miners and you know that they were actually people who have done this as a job. They're not just somebody who comes along and offers their time ... this is somebody who actually worked down there and knows what it was like to work down there.

As this finding indicates, hot and cool modes of authentication often are not discrete but rather co-constitutive (Cohen and Cohen 2012). This co-construction exists both across stakeholder groups and in the dichotomy between the foreground and background. Both forms of authentication serve to strengthen the legitimacy and acceptance of stakeholder claims and actions. The visibility of performances bolsters the value of the official stamp of authenticity, by creating an authentic experience for stakeholders. As a stakeholder involved in promoting the industrial landscape exclaimed, the "most powerful interpretive tools occur when there is face-to-face engagement and interpretation" (Brecon Beacons National Park, support and trails).

By detailing the network of stakeholders operating in the Blaenavon WHS, this research uncovers interactions of hot and cool authentication at the site, attraction, and individual levels. In turn, it pinpoints some mechanisms for overcoming conflicts and contestations, which are nested within "balances of power" (Blaenavon Ironworks, interpretation and representation) that often make coordinated presentations burdensome. The flexibility of hot authentication provides a starting point for identifying mechanisms that might mitigate competition and conflict, but it cannot offer a complete resolution to the underlying power dynamics. A dichotomy persists for various attractions; for example, the strength of the Big Pit's tangible and intangible offerings is matched by its performative and interactive mechanisms, such that stakeholders of Big Pit have a powerful impact on the wider partnership structure. Discontent arises in turn, related to uneven power distributions among competing stakeholder groups. The prevalence of official stamps of authentication also endures, met with episodes of disdain and apathy from the local community and smaller enterprises. Although it is critical to consider the wider structure that enables and impedes authentication, it also is important to note how core stakeholders might function to mediate the discontent and contradictions that arise between hot and cool authentication.

The individual as essential for manufacturing authenticity: host-community volunteers

Stakeholders are crucial to authentication processes, particularly in cultural heritage arenas. Even while acknowledging the connections among stakeholder groups though, it remains pertinent to identify the idiosyncratic roles of each stakeholder, especially as they relate to the uneven power distribution between official and unofficial authentication (Waitt 2000). Both individuals and specific stakeholder groups influence the authentication of cultural heritage sites, events, and actions, and they also can mediate certain tensions and power dynamics that emerge between hot and cool authentication. A particularly pervasive group is host-community volunteers, who respond to the need for connectivity even in financially strained settings (Leighton 2007).

Host-community volunteers undertake various roles, related to the presentation, restoration, and protection of the authenticity of the Blaenavon WHS. Some groups operate largely in support of cool authentication tasks and responsibilities; others perform and enact the heritage and thus spark hot authentication. Together, the volunteers act as guardians and ambassadors of the town's industrial legacy. Their ambassador status fosters strong connections, such that these volunteers shape Blaenavon's future authentic experience:

> When volunteers are out on the landscape doing work, they know they have an ambassadorial role. They'd be helpful and explain what they're doing. They'll offer guidance, and help out and whatever they can.
>
> (FLP, coordination and management)

That is, host-community volunteers operate in both the foreground and background of this cultural heritage site, engaging in a multiplicity of activities such as guided walks, reenactments, ongoing guest interaction, curatorial planning, preservation, promotion, maintenance, and active engagement in town and local meetings. Their background functions predominately support cool authentication, by undertaking vital guardianship roles associated with conservation, restoration, and protection of the tangible heritage and assets. These activities are pivotal to the sustainable maintenance and protection of the physical assets:

> To get volunteers proactively out there, helping us maintain the landscape as they do. They take walks out themselves. You know that is sustainability in action.
>
> (Torfaen County Council, WHS marketing executive)

These practical, maintenance tasks are critical but often overlooked in authentication processes. Similarly, volunteers' participation in the planning and execution of policies pertaining to the site remains insufficiently explored, as expressed by one participant:

> That's a new thing that has come with the Forgotten Landscapes Partnership, the fact that the volunteers and commoners are now being invited to join in these working groups. So, their wisdom and their input is allowed to influence the thinking and recommendations of those groups.
>
> (FLP, coordination and management)

Volunteers also operate in the foreground and engage in hot authentication. They participate directly in the re-creation and interpretation of intangible stories associated with the artifacts, and they share their own lived experiences. The benefits of volunteers interacting directly with the public mainly entail the "personal experience that sells the place and differentiates the place" (independent volunteer-led museum, volunteer). Further legitimacy might be sought through specialist training, such that volunteers take training courses and then can provide expert advice:

> What we've done then for those people that are becoming specialists, like the archaeologists for instance. They've been on quite a few training courses, or we've brought in specialist archaeologists to train them in certain techniques.
>
> (FLP, coordination and management)

Volunteers thus operate at the crossroads of the two modes of authentication, undertaking processes associated with planning, protecting, and executing representations of cultural heritage. For example, the Pontypool and Blaenavon Railway volunteers engage in restoring and presenting carriages, locomotives, and railway track from Blaenavon's past, but they also reenact events, interact with the public, and lead journeys through Blaenavon's industrial landscape on a functioning steam train (Figure 8.2). Another group with multiple roles is the independent volunteer-led group established on the basis of FLP's legacy. Their independence allows members of this group to adopt a partnership model, "looking at their own activities, in consultation with other partners" (FLP, coordination and management). The group undertakes tasks associated with the protection and promotion of the landscape and tangible assets. In addition, it provides supplementary representations and ongoing interactions with the public, to enhance user experiences. For example, in the annual Walking Festival, the trails through the industrial landscape are staffed by local, expert guides. Often, the same people perform hot and cool authentication tasks in tandem.

Figure 8.2 Pontypool and Blaenavon Steam Railway (authors' photo)

The discussion surrounding volunteers is not always positive though. Some skepticism arises regarding their ambassadorial and untrained status, as well as the potential threat that volunteers might replace paid staff. This distinction is noteworthy, because replacing paid staff with volunteers would heighten the contestation, reduce collaboration opportunities, and diminish the potential contributions of volunteers to the construction of authenticity. Thus, there is a need to balance the visibility requirements at the attractions and in the industrial landscape, without merely replacing paid employment with a free alternative. As a participant reflects,

> We have to be careful because we cannot really employ someone as a volunteer to do something that someone should be paid to be doing. It's a tricky one.
>
> (Big Pit, communications)

In their supplementary and mediating role, host-community volunteers also manifest a clear connection with the site, in that many volunteers live in close proximity to the Blaenavon WHS. This position reiterates the important link between local people and the heritage they are protecting and presenting. The findings affirm and extend previous research, such that they promote the benefits of including the local community in authentication efforts at heritage sites (Aas et al. 2005). A consensus among participants is that "you can't beat local knowledge" (independent volunteer-led museum, volunteer), such that participants demonstrate the crucial benefit of combining volunteer and local status.

Another important point of unison is the pride, enthusiasm, and passion demonstrated by volunteers. Their dual position, as volunteer and resident, bolsters their sense of pride and passion for the Blaenavon industrial landscape, which helps ease the tensions of juggling multiple stakeholder interests across hot and cool authentication domains. These findings build on Olsson et al.'s (2016) investigation of volunteers engaged in storytelling, whose personal involvement and interest enhance connectivity with the heritage. Moreover, the voluntary nature of the work speaks to the enthusiasm and passion required to devote time voluntarily (Smith and Holmes 2012), which also might help overcome feelings of commodification and profiteering associated with (re)packaging the past, as noted by one volunteer:

> People are volunteering. They're doing guided walks. They're volunteering in museums. They're doing the dry stonewalling. So, I think there's a lot of enthusiasm for that heritage, and pride now I think.
>
> (independent volunteer-led museum, volunteer)

Thus, volunteers perform pivotal roles in the authentication of the Blaenavon WHS. Despite the potential ability of the group to spark pride, passion, and unison across hot and cool authentication processes, host-community volunteers remain underinvestigated in studies of stakeholder-infused authentication. This research pinpoints the potential mediating role of host-community volunteers as guardians and ambassadors in the complex, fragmented authentication process. The volunteers perform essential tasks behind the scenes, encouraging sustainable protection, maintenance, and enhancement of the rich industrial landscape. Alongside this guardianship role, they are ambassadors of the Blaenavon WHS, representing local community interests at the town and local level. Their prominence in the Blaenavon WHS, due to their storytelling, reenactments, and interactions with the public, bolsters the offering. Thus, volunteers undertake core processes assigned to hot and cool authentication, acting as guardians and ambassadors of the cultural heritage.

Conclusions

Authenticity has long been considered "the philosopher's stone" (Taylor 2001, p. 8) of cultural heritage. Its importance remains evident, despite the transition from a focus on outputs to an investigation of the underlying social and political processes shaping the authentication of sites, events, people, and places (Cohen and Cohen 2012; Zhu 2012). This transition also puts the network of stakeholders at the heart of the authentication process. The current research leverages this transition to explore the multifaceted processes undertaken by multiple stakeholders. It applies and extends Cohen and Cohen's (2012, 2017) hot and cool modes of authentication, revealing the importance of the network of stakeholders, as well as individuals and groups that operate as mediators of the tensions underlying authentication.

This study expands on the preoccupation in previous research with specific stakeholders and demonstrates the multilayered role of stakeholders in the foreground and background of cultural heritage sites. It emphasizes the importance of coordination, in the form of partnerships and collaborations, to enable multiple parties to partake in the construction and reconstruction of cultural heritage. The overarching vision is augmented by the WHS status granted by UNESCO. The international status and corresponding inscription details provide a point of unison, as well as enhancing the pride and passion among Blaenavon's stakeholders. Such cool authentication legitimizes stakeholders' interest in representing the WHS and provides a central point of reference for otherwise competing claims.

Partnerships provide an important starting point, yet the inclusion of visible stakeholders and symbolic connectivity also enhances the authentication process. Physical presence and connectivity are required to manifest detached, official claims, as result of processes related to hot authentication, including storytelling, reenactments, guided tours, and ongoing interactions with stakeholders who are connected to the site. These efforts are not required to be show-stopping, overt actions; the processes can align with everyday tasks and ongoing interactions. This finding highlights the importance of intangible assets, driven by multiple people, not merely tangible structures and official accreditations.

The potential for collaboration and coordination extends across hot and cool modes of authentication, such that stakeholders perform hot authentication that incrementally builds on the scripted, official version of events, devised in the background. The structural makeup of the Blaenavon WHS helps reveal how partnerships and networks foster the representation of the past, but tensions and contradictions remain, so it also is important to consider the individual agency of select stakeholders and groups that operate within the wider network. In particular, host-community volunteers effectively mediate the tensions that arise in the Blaenavon WHS, due to their connectivity to the site, community, and partnership structures. Their pride and passion, as manifested in their voluntary dedication of time, energy, and resources to the WHS, also solidifies the host-community volunteers' positions as guardians and ambassadors. The resulting processes transcend the background and foreground of this cultural heritage site, providing visibility, connectivity, and sustainability in the pursuit of authentication.

This research, thus, adds nuance to Cohen and Cohen's (2012, 2017) view of hot and cool authentication. First, it highlights the need to consider multiple parties that operate both in the foreground and in the background. Second, it identifies both structure and agency as essential components of authentication. Third, this study illuminates the importance of host-community volunteers as mediators of the tensions that arise in this convoluted process. Cohen and Cohen (2012) provide a critical lens for exploring authentication; this chapter applies that lens to reveal the positive advancements that occur when stakeholders work collaboratively and allow for multiple interpretations of cultural heritage.

Further research and limitations

This chapter provides an initial investigation of the multiplicity of people and processes engaged in authentication, based on a small-scale case study of one industrial WHS. Further research is needed to extend and advance these preliminary findings to a wider scale, across multiple sites, as well as to explore their applicability to other sites with WHS status. Moreover, this chapter relies predominately on qualitative, exploratory data; continued research could extend the findings by applying quantitative or statistical analyses. These findings represent a starting point and ideally should spark follow-up research on these overlooked concepts. In particular, more research is needed to advance a theoretical framework for managing authentication at cultural heritage sites.

References

Aas, C. et al. 2005. Stakeholder collaboration and heritage management. *Annals of Tourism Research*, 32(1), 28–48.

Alberts, H.C. and Hazen, H.D. 2010. Maintaining authenticity and integrity at cultural World Heritage Sites. *The Geography Review*, 100(1), pp.56–73.

Belhassen, Y. and Caton, K. 2006. Authenticity matters. *Annals of Tourism Research*, 33(3), pp.853–856.

Bryce, D. et al. 2017. Diaspora, authenticity and the imagined past. *Annals of Tourism Research, 66*, pp.49–60.

Cavanaugh, J.R. and Shankar, S., 2014. Producing authenticity in global capitalism: Language, materiality, and value. *American Anthropologist, 116*(1), pp.51–64.

Charmaz, K. 2006. *Constructing grounded theory: A practical guide through qualitative analysis*. London: Sage.

Chhabra, D. 2008. Positioning museums on an authenticity continuum. *Annals of Tourism Research*, 35(2), pp.427–447.

Chhabra, D. et al. 2003. Staged authenticity and heritage tourism. *Annals of Tourism Research*, 30(3), pp.702–719.

Chronis, A. 2005. Coconstructing heritage at the Gettysburg storyscape. *Annals of Tourism Research, 32*(2), pp.386–406.

Chronis, A. et al. 2012. Gettysburg re-imagined: the role of narrative imagination in consumption experience. *Consumption Markets and Culture*, 15(3), pp.261–286.

Cohen, E. 1988. Authenticity and commoditization in tourism. *Annals of Tourism Research*, 15(3), pp.371–386.

Cohen, E. and Cohen, S.A. 2012. Authentication: hot and cool. *Annals of Tourism Research*, 39(3), pp.1295–1314.

Cohen, S.A and Cohen, E. 2017. New directions in the sociology of tourism, *Current Issues in Tourism*, DOI:10.1080/13683500.2017.1347151

Elliot, M.A. and Schmutz, V. 2012. World heritage: constructing a universal cultural order. *Poetics*, 40, pp.256–277.

Eriksson, P. and Kovalainen, A. eds. 2008. *Qualitative Methods in Business Research*. Thousand Oaks, CA: Sage Publications.

Gioia, D.A. *et al.*,2012. Seeking qualitative rigor in inductive research: Notes on the Gioia methodology. *Organizational Research Methods*, 16(1) pp.15–31.

Glynn, M.A. and Lounsbury, M., 2005. From the critics' corner: Logic blending, discursive change and authenticity in a cultural production system. *Journal of Management Studies*, 42(5), pp.1031–1055.

Fawcett, C. and Cormack, P. 2001. Guarding authenticity at literary tourism sites. *Annals of Tourism Research*, 28(3), pp.686–704.

Flyvberg, B. 2011. Case study. In: Denzin, N.K. and Lincoln, Y.S. eds. *The Sage Handbook of Qualitative Research*. 4th ed. Thousand Oaks, CA: Sage, pp.301–316.

Halewood, C. and Hannam, K. 2001. Viking heritage tourism: authenticity and commodification. *Annals of Tourism Research*, 28, pp.565–580.

Hede, A.M. and Thyne, M. 2010. A journey to the authentic: museum visitors and their negotiation of the inauthentic. *Journal of Marketing Management*, 26(7–8), pp.686–705.

Järvensivu, T. and Törnroos, J.Å. 2010. Case study research with moderate constructionism: Conceptualization and practical illustration. *Industrial Marketing Management*, 39(1), pp.100–108.

Jones, C. and Munday, M. 2001. Blaenavon and United Nations World Heritage Site status: Is conservation of industrial heritage a road to local economic development. *Regional Studies*, 35(6), pp.585–590.

Jones, S. 2010. Negotiating authentic objects and authentic selves: beyond the deconstruction of authenticity. *Journal of Material Culture*, 15(2), pp.181–203.

Knudsen, B.T. and Waade, A.M. 2010. Performative authenticity in tourism and spatial experience: rethinking the relationship between travel, place and emotion. In: Knudsen, B.T. and Waade, A.M. eds. *Re-investing Authenticity: Tourism, Place and Emotions*. Bristol: Channel View Publications, pp.1–19.

Kolar, T. and Žabkar, V. 2010. A consumer-based model of authenticity: An oxymoron or the foundation of cultural heritage marketing? *Tourism Management*, 31, pp.652–664.

Leigh, T.W. et al. 2006. The consumer quest for authenticity: the multiplicity of meanings within the MG subculture of consumption. *Journal of the Academy of Marketing Science*, 34(4), p.481–493.

Leighton, D. 2007. Step back in time and live the legend: experiential marketing and the heritage sector. *International Journal of Nonprofit and Voluntary Sector Marketing*, 12, pp.117–125.

MacCannell, D. 1973. Staged authenticity: arrangements of social space in tourist settings. *An American Journal of Sociology*, 79(3), pp.589–603.

Mitchell, R.K. et al. 1997. Toward a theory of stakeholder identification and salience: Defining the principle of who and what really counts. *Academy of Management Review*, 22(4), pp.853–886.

Mkono, M. 2013. Hot and cool authentication: A netnographic illustration. *Annals of Tourism Research*, 41, pp.215–218.

Olsen, K.H. 2002. Authenticity as a concept in tourism research: The social organization of the experience of authenticity. *Tourist Studies*, 2(2), p.159–182.

Olsson, A.K. et al. 2016. Making an effort for free–volunteers' roles in destination-based storytelling. *Current Issues in Tourism*, 19(7), pp.659–679.

Poria, Y. et al. 2013. Tourists' perceptions of World Heritage Site and its designation. *Tourism Management*, 35, pp.272–274.

Rodwell, D. 2014. The World Heritage Convention and the exemplary management of complex heritage sites. *Journal of Architectural Conservation*, 8(3), pp.40–60.

Selwyn, T. 1996. Introduction. In: Selwyn, T. ed. *The tourist image: myth and mythmaking in tourism*. Chichester: Wiley, pp.1–32.

Smith, K.A. and Holmes, K. 2012. Visitor centre staffing: involving volunteers. *Tourism Management*, 33, pp.562–568.

Steiner, C.J. and Reisinger, Y. 2006. Understanding existential authenticity. *Annals of Tourism Research*, 33(2), pp.299–318.

Taylor, J.P. 2001. Authenticity and sincerity in tourism. *Annals of Tourism Research*, *28*(1), pp.7–26.

Torfaen County Borough Council. 2011. *Blaenavon World Heritage Site Management Plan 2011–2016*. Visit Blaenavon [online]. Available at: http://www.visitblaenavon.co.uk/en/WorldHeritageSite/WorldHeritageSite/Publications/BlaenavonWHSDraftManagementPlan(2011).pdf [Accessed 1 August 2014].

UNESCO. 2014. *Blaenavon industrial landscape*. WHC UNESCO [online]. Available at: http://whc.unesco.org/en/list/984 [Accessed 1 July 2014].

Visit Blaenavon. 2014a. *Look after Blaenavon*. Visit Blaenavon [online]. Available at: http://www.visitblaenavon.co.uk/en/WorldHeritageSite/WorldHeritageSite/LookAfterBlaenavon.aspx [Accessed 1 July 2014].

Visit Blaenavon. 2014b. *The project*. Visit Blaenavon [online]. Available at: http://www.visitblaenavon.co.uk/en/ForgottenLandscapes/Project/Project- Information.aspx [Accessed 17 June 2014].

Visit Blaenavon. 2014c. *Forgotten Landscapes*. Visit Blaenavon [online]. Available at: http://www.visitblaenavon.co.uk/en/WorldHeritageSite/ForgottenLandscapes/ForgottenLandcapes.aspx [Accessed 17 June 2014].

Waitt, G. 2000. Consuming heritage: perceived heritage authenticity. *Annals of Tourism Research*, 27(4), pp.835–862.

Wang, N. 1999. Rethinking authenticity in tourism experience. *Annals of Tourism Research*, 26(2), pp.349–370.

Wearing, S. and McGehee, N.G. 2013. Volunteer tourism: A review. *Tourism Management*, 38, pp.120–130.

Yeoman, I. et al. 2007. Current issues in tourism: the authentic tourist. *Tourism Management*, 28, pp.1128–1138.

Zhu, Y. 2012. Performing heritage: rethinking authenticity in tourism. *Annals of Tourism Research*, 39(3), pp.1495–1513.

9 Cultural heritage as a blessing and curse for branding urban destinations

Sebastian Zenker and Erik Braun

Introduction

In response to the increasing competition for tourists, investments, companies, and well-educated residents, cities, regions, and nations are increasingly turning to place branding as a way to become more efficient in their marketing and branding strategies (Braun, 2012; Hanna and Rowley, 2015). The resulting surge of interest in this research domain (Gertner, 2011) has helped place marketers focus on building strong, favorable place brands that can be communicated to diverse target audiences and stakeholders (Merrilees et al., 2012). However, there is an ongoing concern about the conflation of place branding with destination branding (Park and Petrick, 2006; Qu et al., 2011). Conceptually, destination branding solely targets tourists, while place branding describes the general branding of places for all target groups, which encompasses tourists, residents, and companies (Kerr, 2006). Recently, though, destination branding has widened its focus to include these other target groups (Hanna and Rowley, 2015; Palmer et al., 2013). The convergence in focus between destination and place branding has raised meaningful concerns over whether simplified messages (e.g., focusing solely on a place's cultural heritage) constitute an effective strategy for complex brands, like city brands. Indeed, a singular focus on a place's few strengths and attractions (e.g., cultural heritage) may disregard the needs of the diverse target groups that comprise a place (Zenker and Beckmann, 2013; Zenker et al., 2017).

Given the close relationship of both branding concepts, researchers have suggested a framework whereby place branding is understood as the family tree and destination branding is one of the branches (Zenker and Braun, 2010; 2017). However, it is unclear whether, in practice, destination branding can really be separated from the residential part of the place brand. Indeed, residents and industry are important to destination branding (Freire, 2009), and their perceptions are simultaneously affected by destination branding. Likewise, the issue of cultural heritage can be an important part of a place's identity that attracts tourists, but it can also run counter to the needs of residents and companies, who may want to focus on different (i.e., modern and day-to-day) aspects of the place in the place communication.

Consequently, this chapter challenges the use of 'a one size fits all' city brand, which is still considered common sense in many places/destinations. In the following, we will highlight the often-overlooked complexity of place branding, which calls for a more advanced brand management strategy, including sub-brands that are specific to various target groups. Building on the *City Branded House Strategy* proposed by Zenker and Braun (2017), we aim to help tourism experts, urban policymakers, marketing researchers, and place marketers better deal with place branding in general, and better integrate cultural heritage in specific.

Theoretical background

Focus on destination branding and residents

Destination branding is a well-established concept in both academia and practice (Park and Petrick, 2006; Qu et al., 2011), defined as a marketing tool intended to communicate a destination's unique identity and distinguish it from other destinations (Cai, 2002). By definition, destination branding solely targets tourists, while *place branding* describes the general branding of places for all target groups (Kerr, 2006; Zenker and Braun, 2010, 2017). That said, other researchers have expanded the concept of destination branding into a more comprehensive strategy for not only targeting tourists, but also attracting and retaining residents (Hanna and Rowley, 2015).

The 'blurring' of both concepts – destination and place branding – is essentially derived from the important role that residents play in the tourism business. Indeed, residents constitute an important part of the place and, by extension, visitors' experiences (Freire, 2009): They directly benefit from positive developments, as well as perceive the negative social and environmental effects of tourism (Sharpley, 2014). Moreover, citizens play an important role in the general legitimization of place planning and development (Braun et al., 2013), and their satisfaction with such efforts can compel them to function as place ambassadors (Palmer et al., 2013). However, tourism research has devoted considerably more attention to residents' attitudes towards tourists (as individuals) and tourism planning (Sharpley, 2014; Wang and Xu, 2015) than their perceptions of a place and how these might affect touristic goals.

Granted, there have been a few notable attempts at exploring this issue: Zenker and Beckmann (2013) showed that residents and tourists harbor fundamentally different perceptions of a place, with tourists focusing mostly on stereotypical place associations (such as cultural heritage). Later, Palmer et al. (2013) focused on residents' personal identity and identification with the place, and the influence of such identification on advocacy, showing that only cognitive components of identity had an effect on advocacy. In the same area, Zenker et al. (2017) showed that brand complexity is a key factor in place identification, especially for internal place customers (i.e., residents). Recently, Hanna and Rowley (2015) made a first conceptual attempt at developing a model for a more comprehensive strategy that encompasses tourists and residents. These few studies make it generally clear that "residents (…) should be in the central interest of urban tourism planners and managers to ensure that residents are proud and satisfied with the city" (Wang and Xu, 2015, p. 248). A more complete understanding of residents' perceptions would thus be useful for tourism practice (Sharpley, 2014)—not to mention relevant to the wider context of place marketing, where place identification (Zenker and Petersen, 2014), place attachment (Altman and Low, 1992; Lewicka, 2011), and place satisfaction (Fleury-Bahi et al., 2008) are popular concepts.

As it stands, the field is slowly realizing the need to research place brands for all target groups and uncover potential synergies between the different place brands for the specific target groups (Hanna and Rowley, 2015; Zenker and Beckmann, 2013; Zenker and Braun, 2010, 2017). However, accomplishing this goal may require abandoning the disciplinary demarcation between tourism and place marketing, which seems outdated in the face of practitioners' increasingly common use of a joint approach (i.e., either adding the target group of (potential) residents to the tourism brand or incorporating the tourism organization into greater place marketing units).

Focus on destination branding and companies

While the place branding literature explicitly discusses destination branding and its additional resident focus (e.g., Freire, 2009; Hanna and Rowley, 2015; Zenker et al., 2017), scholars have rarely focused on the link between a destination's brand and attracting companies/investors. In the academic literature, the role of companies in destination branding is mostly limited to the impact of hospitality industries on the destination brand (e.g., Blain et al., 2005; Morgan et al., 2003) or business-related factors as part of the destination brand (e.g., tax, staff costs, or shopping facilities; Enright and Newton, 2004). Companies are largely seen as stakeholders that influence the place's image (Blain et al., 2005), or create touristic offerings (and experiences) and generally promoting the place (e.g., Morgan et al., 2003).

However, there are a few other ways of envisioning this relationship: For instance, some researchers link the destination brand to the country-of-origin effect (Balakrishnan, 2008), arguing that the former impacts the perception of local products (Gnoth, 2002). Additionally, many places market themselves as business destinations (e.g., for industry fairs and conferences; Maclaurin and Leong, 2000), which is a way of targeting business professionals (e.g., Hankinson, 2005). Other studies in the tourism literature have focused on how to attract the hospitality industry itself, such as hotels, (e.g., Skokic et al., 2016), small hospitality, and tourism firms (SHTF; e.g., Thomas et al., 2011). To the authors' knowledge, these latter studies have yet to explicitly address destination branding, but they have noted a need for more research and conceptualization regarding destination marketing and the place factors that attract small firms in tourism (Thomas et al., 2011).

Nevertheless, to make a clear distinction for this chapter, we keep the definition of destination branding as an activity that solely targets tourists, while place branding includes all activities that target all potential place target groups, (making destination branding a component of place branding).

Destination branding and cultural heritage

In general, "the use of culture and heritage for tourism and its consequences, have (...) become a major subject area in social sciences research on tourism" (Michelson and Paadam, 2016, p. 141). Heritage tourism (e.g., Apostolakis, 2003; Dallen and Boyd, 2006; Yeoman et al., 2007) focuses on all aspects of place heritage and the history of places—one major part of which is culture. However, the concept of 'cultural heritage' encompasses many aspects and is thus often treated vaguely, as this book shows.

Heritage is mostly defined as something from the past that is maintained in the present. While "initially the historic and artistic values were the only parameters, other additional ones have now been added: the cultural value, its value of identity and the capacity of the object to interact with memory" (Vecco, 2010, p. 324). As Blake (2000, p. 61) states, cultural heritage was "first addressed in international law in 1907 and a body of international treaties and texts for its protection has been developed by UNESCO and other intergovernmental organisations." As a result, much of the cultural heritage research focuses on UNESCO World Heritage Sites (WHS; e.g., Morgan et al., 2003; Ryan and Silvanto, 2009). In relation to the branding of places, Ryan and Silvanto (2009, p. 292) note that the "WHS designation has, in effect, become a brand, an endorsement and a certification of quality" for destinations. It is, therefore, a very important part of the destination brand (Ryan and Silvanto, 2009). However, destination brands that include heritage sites face particular branding challenges since there are many influential stakeholders involved (i.e., UNESCO) but the destination's management exert limited control over the destination brand (Morgan et al., 2003)—another issue discussed in relation to cultural heritage and destination branding.

Other researchers focus more on a broader definition of cultural heritage: Namely, the cultural history of places – regardless of whether they are part of the UNESCO World Heritage Sites – (e.g., Chhabra, 2017; Herrero et al., 2016; Kolar and Žabkar, 2010; Michelson and Paadam, 2016). In the branding of places the relevance of history as part of the place is often highlighted (e.g., Braun, 2008; Rothschild et al., 2012). Some researchers simply include cultural heritage as one aspect of the destination image (e.g., Herrero et al., 2016). Another aspect of the discussion is the issue of authenticity and how cultural heritage delivers authenticity to places (e.g., Kolar and Žabkar, 2010; McIntosh and Prentice, 1999). We also find similarities in relation to company brand heritage (often using the cultural heritage of the place as their brand story) (e.g., Hakala et al., 2011): Here, *heritage brands* are "are about history and history in the making" (Urde et al., 2007, p. 7), which is parallel to the concept of heritage in destination branding.

In this chapter, we concentrate on the cultural heritage (defined in the broader sense of cultural history) of an urban environment, since it best demonstrates the challenges of incorporating a place's history into the place brand. This emphasis serves to address the fact "that tourism-related urban and spatial issues remain theoretically and empirically relatively underexplored" (Michelson and Paadam, 2016, p. 141). In short, we focus on historic cities (like Rome, Vienna, etc.) in their 'living' sense: Namely, how they contend with urban (cultural) heritage in their place branding activities.

Place branding and places as brands

Place branding (and by this destination branding as part of place branding) is located in the broader field of place marketing. In this regard, we understand *place marketing* as "the coordinated use of marketing tools supported by a shared customer-oriented philosophy, for creating, communicating, delivering, and exchanging urban offerings that have value for the city's customers and the city's community at large" (Braun, 2008, p. 43); it follows that place branding is one such marketing tool. Ashworth and Voogd (1990) argue that the objective of place marketing is to contribute to the efficient economic and social functioning of a place in ways that are consistent with its wider goals. These authors' insights have led to two very important arguments: First, although place marketing involves an economic intention, it also centrally aims to increase the place's social functions, like identification or satisfaction. Second, place marketing relies on a customer-focused approach that tries to address the needs of *all* a place's customers (e.g., residents of different socio-economic groups, subcultures, political orientations, and visitors or companies). The first step in this process is to create a shared mental representation of the place—what marketers call the place brand.

According to research, place brands (including destination brands) are multidimensional (Kaplan et al., 2010; Zenker, 2011): They comprise a large variety of variables, such as a place's history, buildings, economical and geographical aspects, and demographic characteristics. Place brands can also encompass more evaluative variables – such as 'modern,' 'successful,' 'old fashioned', or 'central' – that are stored as associations in consumers' minds. Consequently, place brands are understood as complex constructs, i.e., defined by "a set of elements involving relationships among them" (Rapoport and Hawkes, 1970, p. 108). In this regard, Zenker and Petersen (2014) treat place complexity as "a quantitative measure and [...] a construct with different qualities" (pp. 718-719). Specifically, they divide complexity into 'quantity' (i.e., how many different elements are included) and its related 'qualities': namely, 'ambiguity' (having e.g., poor and wealthy residents in the same district) or the 'degrees of entropy' (i.e., the level of organization inherent to the complexity).

Cultural heritage is one important element of a place's complexity, especially because its influence is persistent and pervasive. Place brands are rooted in a place's history, for better or worse: Hence our proposition that, outside of rapid and radical change spurred by some significant event, place brands are generally path dependent. In other words, the events of the past continue to reflect on the present, which means that changes in the place brand are predominantly incremental. Additionally, different target groups possess different levels of awareness of a place's history and thus respond to place change in different ways. This aligns with Zenker and Braun's (2017) definition of a place brand, which is informed by Keller's (1993) concept of brand knowledge: Namely, the place brand is "a network of associations in the place consumers' mind based on the visual, verbal, and behavioral expression of a place and its' stakeholders. These associations differ in their influence within the network and in importance for the place consumers' attitude and behavior" (p. 275). Although scholars have developed many definitions of place brands, we rely on this one because it encompasses the inherent complexity in designing a brand that appeals to disparate target groups (e.g., residents vs. tourists vs. companies) and is a commonly accepted definition in the field (Boisen et al., 2018).

Both practice and academia struggle with this complexity because it runs counter to the general approach to branding products, which often entails selecting a small number of core associations (Anholt, 2009; Keller, 2003). In this view, complexity may be understood as an unclear brand concept, meaning that the brand is fuzzy and incoherently positioned. Indeed, brand managers fear that consumers will become overloaded by information that is too complex (Zenker et al., 2017). For example, Bettman et al. (1998) showed that, in cases of high product complexity, customers apply simpler heuristics and selective information processing, even though this reduces the effectiveness of their decisions. At the same time, in the case of a simple brand, consumers with little information can more accurately identify it, but they may also show more dissatisfaction with the brand and a higher need for more information (Scammon, 1977). However, both situations may be at play in place marketing. For instance, Zenker et al. (2017) showed that residents' identification with and commitment to a place brand are positively influenced by brand complexity, while tourists respond better to a simpler brand.

Although destination branding is conceptually invested in attracting tourists, a successful place brand also requires to be appealing to residents, who are part of a place's identity and more sensitive to a place's heritage. As voters and citizens, residents initiate and legitimate place branding activities, as well as become place ambassadors through (positive) word-of-mouth communication (Braun et al., 2013). Thus, residents and other stakeholders play a central role in the branding process, and their identification with their place of living can be regarded as both an aim and facilitator of place branding (including destination branding as part of branding places).

A more complex management of place brands

Place brand communication

To influence those networks of associations, places try to communicate with their customers. In his place brand communication model, Kavaratzis (2008) included three types of place brand communication. The first, primary communication, includes the architecture, urban design, infrastructure, museums, and other real place offerings, but also the behavior exhibited by residents and other stakeholder groups. The second is the secondary communication, which includes the formal and intended communication through all forms of advertising, public relations, graphic design, and the use of logos and slogans (promotion). Finally, the tertiary communication refers to word-of-mouth reinforced by the wide variety of city users and media, which is usually beyond the control of place marketers. Braun et al. (2014) adopted this content, putting the focus even more on the communicational part and empirically testing these three types of place brand communication:

1 The *physical place*. These are the 'real' place offerings that could be of value for the target groups. This could, on one hand, include buildings, infrastructure, the design of public spaces, and amenities (e.g., shops, theaters, museums, restaurants, sports facilities, schools, and universities). This type of communication is mostly visual (physical buildings) and primarily influenced by the city's politicians, urban planners and urban policymakers, property owners, and private developers. City branding professionals do communicate about these changes (intended communication), but they have little or no influence over investment decisions regarding place physics. On the other hand, this type also encompasses the behavior of the local people and other relevant experiences with the place, including the (unintended) communication that occurs within the place that is outside of officials' control.
2 The *traditional*. This concerns all forms of advertising or public relations via official channels. This is usually undertaken by communication professionals working in the city administration or by specialized marketing organizations operating within arm's length of the city administration. It, therefore, comprises mostly visual (e.g., logos, advertisement) and/or verbal communication (slogans).
3 The *place word-of-mouth*. This 'informal talk' between place stakeholders (e.g., between a tourist and a resident, or within the group) concerning the place is reinforced foremost by the media, residents, and visitors. This type of communication is mostly verbal and behavioral, but also increasingly visual (e.g., sharing pictures on social media platforms). Similar to the physical place communication, this type can be differentiated into intended and unintended communication. As Braun et al. (2014) have shown, word-of-mouth is one of the strongest communication tools, but also hard for place marketers to influence.

The City Branded House Strategy

In the *City Branded House Strategy*, proposed by Zenker and Braun (2017), the authors differentiate between the place brand in general (the network of all associations in the mind of the consumer) and the communicated place brand (referring to those associations with high importance). The former encompasses all of a place's aspects (including negative or less relevant aspects), while the latter reflects a narrow managerial account of the place's positive and influential aspects, which serve as the basis for official communication (and the subsequent misunderstandings about the place brand; see Figure 9.1).

This differentiation is important because target groups only demonstrate so-called brand effects (attitude and behavior) in response to their overall place perceptions (in terms of brand knowledge); neither a logo or slogan (Govers, 2013), nor the (official) place brand communication, carry the same weight. For instance, researchers have empirically

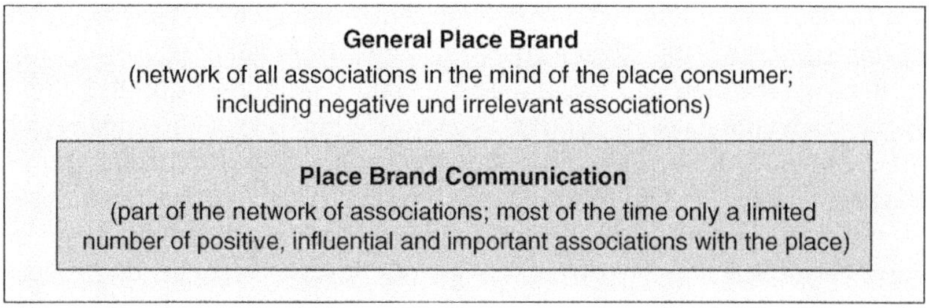

Figure 9.1 Difference between place brand and place brand communication (Zenker and Braun, 2017, p. 277)

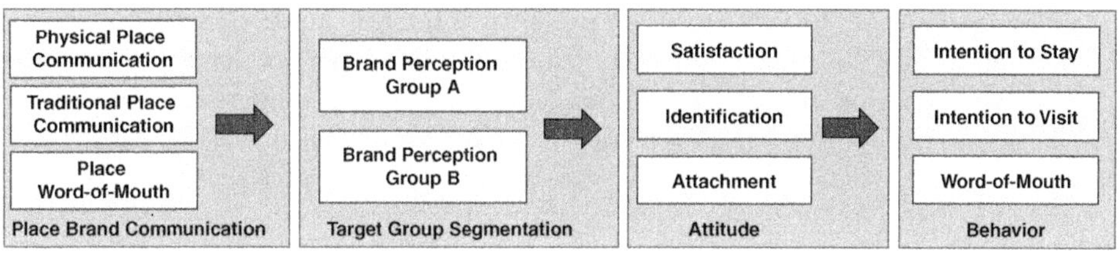

Figure 9.2 The concept of place brand perception (Zenker and Braun, 2017, p. 277)

shown that a more positive evaluation of a place (brand) leads to a higher general satisfaction (Zenker et al., 2013), identification with the place (Fleury-Bahi et al., 2008; Zenker et al., 2017), place attachment (Hernández et al., 2007), intention to stay at a place of living (Zenker and Gollan, 2010), and/or interest in (re-) visiting a place (Zenker et al., 2017)—see Figure 9.2.

However, place brand management mainly tries to influence this (general) place brand knowledge via *place brand communication*—focusing, for instance, on a number of positive aspects that carry importance for certain target audiences. Granted, targets groups possess varying levels of brand knowledge and different demands for a place, so their sensitivity to this influence and subsequent evaluations of city brand aspects will differ. Research indicates that these differences are most striking between internal and external target groups: Zenker and Beckmann (2013) showed that external target groups' (e.g., tourists) city perceptions are much more stereotypical, while those of internal target groups are more diverse and authentic. The issue of cultural heritage is relevant here, as external target groups might be attracted to the stereotypical or prototypical idea of a place's history, while internal target audiences may want to focus on more modern themes.

This is why a 'one size fits all' *place brand communication* for all target groups would probably fail: It would disregard the complexity of a city, especially for target audiences with a profound place knowledge (Zenker et al., 2017). This issue could be overcome with a more customer-focused view, although this is not common in the public sector (Buurma, 2001), or in place marketing practice. In fairness, a stronger customer focus is more difficult to achieve, requiring a differentiated brand architecture that matches specific subbrands to particular target groups. However, place marketers and other urban policymakers who are interested in dealing with the complexity of multiple target groups could find parallels in the marketing and branding of diversified companies. For instance, companies with a complex brand management model often rely on a hierarchical brand architecture (Aaker, 2004): This *Branded House* approach involves creating more focused sub-brands for each product and aligning them with a strong corporate umbrella brand (e.g., 'Nivea' as an umbrella brand and 'Nivea for men' as a target group-specific sub-brand focus; Petromilli et al., 2002). This approach could also be extended to create a link between company and place brands (Uggla, 2006), or fully to the place branding context, with different special levels in mind (Iversen and Hem, 2008; Kotler and Gertner, 2002). In contrast to other researchers, Zenker and Braun (2017) do not use the brand architecture in the sense of an umbrella country brand and regional or city sub-brands. Instead, as suggested by Kerr (2006), cities should develop a brand structure with a city umbrella brand and target group sub-brands. Very much like the modern organizational structures of corporate marketing departments (Homburg et al., 2000) the marketing structure of cities should be organized by their target groups (Braun, 2008). In sum, the *City Branded House Strategy* features target group-specific sub-brands and a city umbrella brand that represents the overall city brand perception that the majority of target groups share (Zenker and Braun, 2017). This strategy has been developed with cities in mind, but it is also applicable to different spatial scales, such as districts, regions, and even countries (Kotler and Gertner, 2002; Zenker and Braun, 2017).

For the *City Branded House Strategy* (see Figure 9.3), a city must be aware of the general city brand (the network of associations in the minds of all place consumers) and the specific place perceptions of the specific target audiences (including the varying importance of place aspects). Official place brand communication should focus on developing target group-specific sub-brands (e.g., for tourists, residents, businesses, and investors), which can better concentrate on the particular needs and wants of different city stakeholders. This allows marketers to foster differentiated perceptions among target audiences, while

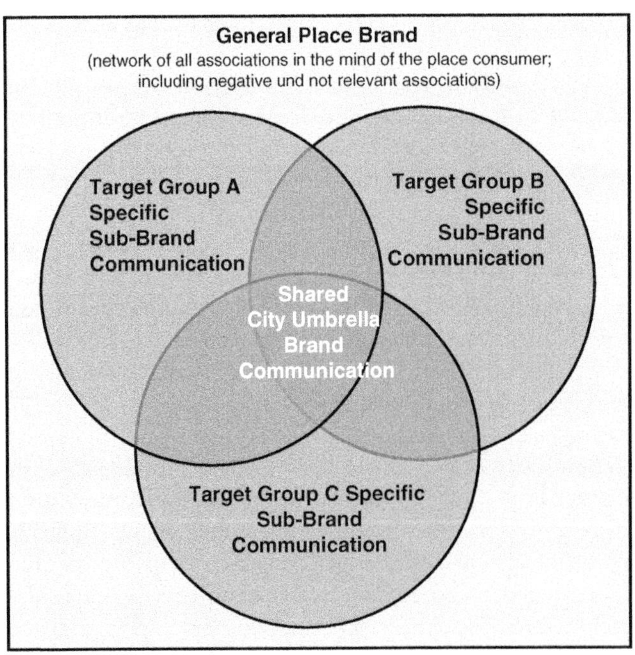

Figure 9.3 The City Branded House Strategy (Zenker and Braun, 2017, p. 278)

still highlighting the most important and central aspects via a shared city umbrella brand (Zenker and Braun, 2017).

Traditional place brand communication and other forms of city communication (i.e., physical place communication and place word-of-mouth) are central to this strategy, as they jointly build the perceptions about the city brand in the minds of the city's customers. Granted, there are some challenges. First, and as outlined before, such communication can have unintended effects. For instance, a city's residents will, to some extent, be affected by the city's communication with tourists (so-called *waste circulation*). Additionally, city customers sometimes fulfill different roles at the same time (e.g., being a resident and an investor), which entails that different sub-brands could overlap, contradict, or otherwise influence each other through waste circulation (Zenker and Braun, 2017).

The *physical place brand communication* is also relevant in terms of influencing people's perceptions, but there is a natural limit to how much city marketers and urban policymakers can control this factor (since place marketers rarely dictate product development). For instance, the presence of cultural heritage sites (Ryan and Silvanto, 2009), flagship buildings (Butler, 2007), or re-development projects (Paddison, 1993) can support the idea of a high-culture tourist brand. However, officials cannot totally ensure that customers perceived the intended message (e.g., making a place more green) in the way that they want (e.g., they might view it as one form of gentrification; Butler, 2007). Moreover, it is very difficult to manage local residents' behavior (Freire, 2009) as part of this communication. Nonetheless, it is vitally important that the urban development department be involved with city branding attempts, since the physical place is one of the most powerful communication tools in the urban-policy context (Braun et al., 2014).

Finally, we want to acknowledge the influential nature of *place word-of-mouth*—a process that city officials cannot truly control, despite their intense efforts (e.g., spreading a positive image via the media). Perceptions about a place are significantly shaped by the contact that target groups have with each other. As such, residents are not only important for initiating and legitimizing the branding process (Braun et al., 2013; Eshuis et al., 2014), but they also generate place word-of-mouth (WOM) that is essential to place brand communication. Thus, stimulating positive place word-of-mouth, for example, through sub-brand creation and stakeholder management, is crucial on a managerial level (Zenker and Erfgen, 2014).

Fortunately, the organizational structure of city governments may already lend itself to developing target group sub-brands (e.g., the separation of the tourism office and business development). In order to mitigate conflicts and foster synergies between those units, cities could designate specialized agents to oversee branding policies. For instance, cities could establish a general place brand manager within a cooperative unit that works to balance and improve the sub-brand communication of the specific units by aligning them with the general city brand.

The role of cultural heritage in the City Branded House Strategy

As we wrote before, place history is highly relevant to place branding (e.g., Braun, 2008; Rothschild et al., 2012) and often uncontrollably linked to the place brand (in the form of associations with the place) and, by extension, the destination image (Herrero et al., 2016). In the case of World Heritage Sites (WHS), the historic sites can be seen as a brand in itself that transfers associations and meaning to the host place (Hanna and Rowley, 2015;

Ryan and Silvanto, 2009). In general, cultural heritage informs people's perception of a place and can imbue the place brand with a kind of authenticity (Kolar and Žabkar, 2010; McIntosh and Prentice, 1999). In the same vein, it can serve to attract tourists (e.g., Herrero et al., 2016; Kolar and Žabkar, 2010) and foster a sense of identity among locals (Gonzáles, 2008).

That said, there is controversy in the literature about using cultural heritage when marketing places (Evans, 2003; Philo and Kearns, 1993). Branding typically involves a selection process that prioritizes some themes above others, and applying this process to place branding (Boisen et al., 2011) could be problematic if other target groups and place stakeholders want a different focus. Some aspects of cultural heritage could also damage the place reputation by attracting the 'wrong' kind of tourists (i.e., dark tourism; Light, 2017) or harming the other place associations that are relevant for other target groups. Meanwhile, in thinking of place brands as *networks* of associations (Zenker and Braun, 2017), cultural heritage associations (even if they would be attractive in the abstract) may be connected to associations that are unfavorable for the place. After all, emphasizing the historical aspects of a place may clash with associations like 'modern', 'innovative', 'young', and 'creative', which are often employed in place brand management. A *City Branded House Strategy* grants officials the opportunity to separate these sub-brands from each other (Zenker and Braun, 2017).

However, the potential collision of the sub-brands remains a challenge. By definition, the sub-brands cannot be seen as independent from each other and may inadvertently influence each other. This isn't necessarily a problem with non-conflicting sub-brands, but it could be an issue when there is high contrast, or even contradictions, in the content of the communications (e.g., historical vs. modern). Target audiences might react with confusion or mistrust, which could lower their identification with the place brand. In this case, the place brand manager must carefully monitor and mediate in order to reduce conflicts. Still, there are currently no other management models (e.g., a 'one size fits all' brand) that have offered solutions to that issue, and we believe that the benefits of the proposed strategy exceed its potential risks.

Conclusions

This chapter contributes to a broader understanding of how the branding of cities affects all place customers, such as residents, companies, and tourists—and what role cultural heritage plays in this. Destination brands (which focus solely on tourists) cannot be seen as separate from other place brand elements (i.e., which focus on residents and companies). Likewise, the simplified messages (e.g., focusing only on the cultural heritage) that typically accompany branding efforts are not effective for complex brands, like city brands. Internal target groups are especially likely to have a nuanced understanding of the place and could disagree with a simplified, tourist-oriented destination brand.

At the same time, place brands are path dependent. Important developments in the past are still relevant for place branding today. In other words, there is no 'clean sheet' for the development of city brands—their perception, whether among residents or tourists, will undoubtedly be affected by the cultural heritage of the place. Ideally, the heritage can be leveraged to foster a sense of identity among locals while attracting tourists and companies. However, in practice, we often see a conflict between the selective focus on cultural heritage for the sake of tourists and the desire for more modern and future-oriented themes from other, more internal stakeholders.

Given this issue, this chapter challenged the use of 'a one size fits all' city brand and suggested a more complex brand management model—namely, the *City Branded House Strategy*). By adopting sub-brands, cities can appeal to different target groups while still maintaining a cohesive identity via the umbrella brand. However, success in this regard requires that place managers carefully monitor their sub-brands for potential overlap and cross-influence, and mediate conflict as needed.

References

Aaker, D.A. (2004), *Brand Portfolio Management*, the Free Press, New York.

Apostolakis, A. (2003), "The convergence process in heritage tourism", *Annals of Tourism Research*, Vol. 30, No. 4, pp. 795–812.

Altman, I. and Low, S. M. (1992), *Place Attachment*, Plenum, New York, NY.

Anholt, S. (2009), "Should place brands be simple?", *Place Branding and Public Diplomacy*, Vol. 5 No. 2, pp. 91–96.

Ashworth, G. J. and Voogd, H. (1990), *Selling the City: Marketing Approaches in Public Sector Urban Planning*, Belhaven, London.

Balakrishnan, M. S. (2008), "Dubai – a star in the east: A case study in strategic destination branding", *Journal of Place Management and Development*, Vol. 1, No. 1, pp. 62–91.

Bettman, J., Frances, L. M., and Payne, J. W. (1998), "Constructive consumer choice processes", *Journal of Consumer Research*, Vol. 25 No. 3, pp. 187–217.

Blain, C., Levy, S. E., and Ritchie J. R. B. (2005), "Destination branding: insights and practices from destination management organizations", *Journal of Travel Research*, Vol. 43, No. 4, pp. 328–338.

Blake, J. (2000), "On defining the cultural heritage", *The International and Comparative Law Quarterly*, Vol. 49, No. 1, pp. 61–85.

Boisen, M., Terlouw, K., Groote, P., and Couwenberg, O. (2018). "Reframing Place promotion, place marketing and place branding – moving beyond conceptual confusion". *Cities*, Vol. 80, October, pp. 4–11..

Boisen, M., Terlouw, K., and van Gorp, B. (2011), "The selective nature of place branding and the layering of spatial identities", *Journal of Place Management and Development*, Vol. 4 No. 2, pp. 135–147.

Braun, E. (2008), *City Marketing: Towards an Integrated Approach*, PhD diss., Erasmus University Rotterdam, Rotterdam.

Braun, E. (2012), "Putting city branding into practice", *Journal of Brand Management*, Vol. 19 No. 4, pp. 257–267.

Braun, E., Eshuis, J. and Klijn, E.-H. (2014), "The effectiveness of place brand communication", *Cities*, Vol. 41 No. 1, pp. 64–70.

Braun, E., Kavaratzis, M. and Zenker, S. (2013), "My city – my brand: the different roles of residents in place branding", *Journal of Place Management and Development*, Vol. 6 No. 1, pp. 18–28.

Butler, T. (2007), "Re-urbanizing London Docklands: gentrification, suburbanization or new urbanism?", *International Journal of Urban and Regional Research*, Vol. 31 No. 4, pp. 759–781.

Buurma, H. (2001), "Public policy marketing: marketing exchange in the public sector", *European Journal of Marketing*, Vol. 35 No. 11/12, pp. 1287–1300.

Cai, L. A. (2002), "Cooperative branding for rural destinations", *Annals of Tourism Research*, Vol. 29, No. 3, pp. 720–742.

Chhabra, D. (2016), "Heritage branding of India: A Gandhi tourism perspective", *Annals of Tourism Research*, Vol. 62, pp. 110–116.

Dallen J. T. and Boyd, S. W. (2006), "Heritage tourism in the 21st century: valued traditions and new perspectives", *Journal of Heritage Tourism*, Vol. 1 No. 1, pp. 1–16.

Enright, M. J. and Newton, J. (2004), "Tourism destination competitiveness: a quantitative approach", *Tourism Management*, Vol. 25, No. 6, pp. 777–788.

Eshuis, J., Klijn, E.-H., and Braun, E. (2014), "Place marketing and citizen participation: branding as strategy to address the emotional dimension of policy making?", *International Review of Administrative Sciences*, Vol. 80 No. 1, pp. 151–171.

Evans, G. (2003), "Hard-branding the cultural city – from Prado to Prada", *International Journal of Urban and Regional Research*, Vol. 27 No. 2, pp. 417–440.

Fleury-Bahi, G., Félonneau, M.-L., and Marchand, D. (2008), "Processes of place identification and residential satisfaction", *Environment and Behavior*, Vol. 40 No. 5, pp. 669–682.

Freire, J. R. (2009), "'Local People' a critical dimension for place brands", *Journal of Brand Management*, Vol. 16, pp. 420–438.

Gertner, D. (2011), "A (tentative) meta-analysis of the 'place marketing' and 'place branding' literature", *Journal of Brand Management*, Vol. 19 No. 2, pp. 112–131.

Gnoth, J. (2002), "Leveraging export brands through a tourism destination brand", *Journal of Brand Management*, Vol. 9, No. 4, pp. 262–280.

González, M.V. (2008), "Intangible heritage tourism and identity", *Tourism Management*, Vol. 29, No. 4, pp. 807–810.

Govers, R. (2013), "Why place branding is not about logos and slogans", *Place Branding and Public Diplomacy*, Vol. 9 No. 2, pp. 71–75.

Hakala, U., Lätti, S., and Sandberg, B. (2011), "Operationalising brand heritage and cultural heritage", *Journal of Product & Brand Management*, Vol. 20, No 6, pp. 447–456.

Hankinson, G. (2005), "Destination brand images: a business tourism perspective", *Journal of Services Marketing*, Vol. 19, No. 1, pp. 24–32.

Hanna, S. and Rowley, J. (2015), "Towards a model of the Place Brand Web", *Tourism Management*, Vol. 48, pp. 100–112.

Hernández, B., Hidalgo, M. C., Salazar-Laplace, M. E., and Hess, S. (2007), "Place attachment and place identity in natives and non-natives", *Journal of Environmental Psychology*, Vol. 27 No. 4, pp. 310–319.

Herrero, A., San Martín, H., del Mar Garcia de los Salmones, M., and Collado, J. (2016), "Examining the hierarchy of destination brands and the chain of effects between brand equity dimensions", *Journal of Destination Marketing & Management*, online first, DOI:https://doi.org/10.1016/j.jdmm.2016.05.001.

Homburg, C., Workman, J. P., Jr., and Jensen, O. (2000), "Fundamental changes in marketing organization: The movement toward a customer-focused organizational structure", *Journal of the Academy of Marketing Science*, Vol. 28 No. 4, pp. 459–478.

Iversen, N. M. and Hem, L. E. (2008), "Provenance associations as core values of place umbrella brands", *European Journal of Marketing*, Vol. 42 No. 5/6, pp. 603–626.

Kaplan, M. D., Yurt, O., Guneri, B., and Kurtulus, K. (2010), "Branding places: applying brand personality concept to cities", *European Journal of Marketing*, Vol. 44 No. 9/10, pp. 1286–1304.

Kavaratzis, M. (2008), *From City Marketing to City Branding: An Interdisciplinary Analysis with Reference to Amsterdam, Budapest and Athens*, PhD diss., Rijksuniversiteit Groningen, Groningen.

Keller, K. L. (1993), "Conceptualizing, measuring, and managing customer-based brand equity", *Journal of Marketing*, Vol. 57 No. January, pp. 1–22.

Keller, K. L. (2003), "Brand synthesis: The multidimensionality of brand knowledge", *Journal of Consumer Research*, Vol. 29 No. 4, pp. 595–600.

Kerr, G. (2006), "From destination brand to location brand", *Journal of Brand Management*, Vol. 13 No. 4/5, pp. 276–283.

Kolar, T. and Žabkar, V. (2010), "A consumer-based model of authenticity: An oxymoron or the foundation of cultural heritage marketing?", *Tourism Management*, Vol. 31, No. 5, pp. 652–664.

Kotler, P. and Gertner, D. (2002), "Country as brand, product, and beyond: A place marketing and brand management perspective", *Journal of Brand Management*, Vol. 9 No. 4/5, pp. 249–261.

Lewicka, M. (2011), "Place attachment: how far have we come in the last 40 years?", *Journal of Environmental Psychology*, Vol. 31 No. 3, pp. 207–230.

Light, D. (2017), "Progress in dark tourism and thanatourism research: an uneasy relationship with heritage tourism", *Tourism Management*, Vol. 61, August, pp. 275–301.

Maclaurin, D. J. and Leong, K. (2000), "Strategies for Success: How Singapore Attracts and Retains the Convention and Trade Show Industry", *Event Management*, Vol. 6, No. 2, pp. 93–103.

McIntosh, A. J. and Prentice, R. C. (1999), "Affirming authenticity: consuming cultural heritage", *Annals of Tourism Research*, Vol. 26, No. 3, pp. 589–612.

Merrilees, B., Miller, D., and Herington, C. (2012), "Multiple stakeholders and multiple city brand meanings", *European Journal of Marketing*, Vol. 46 No. 7/8, pp. 362–367.

Michelson, A. and Paadam, K. (2016), "Destination branding and reconstructing symbolic capital of urban heritage: A spatially informed observational analysis in medieval towns", *Journal of Destination Marketing & Management*, Vol. 5, No. 2, pp. 141–153.

Morgan, N. J., Pritchard, A., and Piggott, R. (2003), "Destination branding and the role of the stakeholders: The case of New Zealand", *Journal of Vacation Marketing*, Vol. 9, No. 3, pp. 285–299.

Paddison, R (1993), "City marketing, image reconstruction, and urban regeneration", *Urban Studies*, Vol. 30 No. 2, pp. 339–350.

Palmer, A., Koenig-Lewis, N., and Jones, L. E. M. (2013), "The effects of residents' social identity and involvement on their advocacy of incoming tourism", *Tourism Management*, Vol. 38, pp. 142–151.

Park, S.-Y. and Petrick, J. F. (2006), "Destinations' perspectives of branding", *Annals of Tourism Research*, Vol. 33, No. 1, pp. 262–265.

Petromilli, M., Morrison, D., and Million, M. (2002), "Brand architecture: building brand portfolio value", *Strategy & Leadership*, Vol. 30 No. 5, pp. 22–28.

Philo, C. and Kearns, G. (1993), "Culture, history, capital: A critical introduction to the selling of places," in Kearns, G. and Philo, C. (Eds.), *Selling Places*, Pergamon Press, Oxford, pp. 1–32.

Qu, H., Kim, L. H., and Im, H. H. (2011), "A model of destination branding: Integrating the concepts of the branding and destination image", *Tourism Management*, Vol. 32, pp. 465–476.

Rapoport, A. and Hawkes, R. (1970), "The perception of urban complexity", *Journal of the American Institute of Planners*, Vol. 36 No. 2, pp. 106–111.

Rothschild, N. H., Alon, I., and Fetscherin, M. (2012), "The importance of historical Tang dynasty for place branding the contemporary city Xi'an", *Journal of Management History*, Vol. 18, No. 1, pp. 96–104.

Ryan, J. and Silvanto, S. (2009), "The World Heritage List: the making and management of a brand", *Place Branding and Public Diplomacy*, Vo. 5, No. 4, pp. 290–300.

Scammon, D. L. (1977), "Information load and consumers", *Journal of Consumer Research*, Vol. 4, No. 3, pp. 148–155.

Sharpley, R. (2014), "Host perceptions of tourism: A review of the research", *Tourism Management*, Vol. 42, pp. 37–49.

Skokic, V., Lynch, P., and Morrison, A. (2016), "Hotel entrepreneurship in a turbulent environment", *International Journal of Hospitality Management*, Vol. 53, February, pp. 1–11.

Thomas, R., Shaw, G., and Page, S. J. (2011), "Understanding small firms in tourism: a perspective on research trends and challenges", *Tourism Management*, Vol. 32, No. 5, pp. 963–976.

Uggla, H. (2006), "The corporate brand association base – a conceptual model for the creation of inclusive brand architecture", *European Journal of Marketing*, Vol. 40, No. 7/8, pp. 785–802.

Urde, M., Greyser, S. A., and Balmer, J. M. T. (2007), "Corporate brands with a heritage", *The Journal of Brand Management*, Vol. 15, No. 1, pp. 4–19.

Vecco, M. (2010), "A definition of cultural heritage: from the tangible to the intangible", *Journal of Cultural Heritage*, Vol. 11, No. 3, pp. 321–324.

Wang, S. and Xu, H. (2015), "Influence of place-based senses of distinctiveness, continuity, self-esteem and self-efficacy on residents' attitude towards tourism", *Tourism Management*, Vol. 47, pp. 241–250.

Yeoman, I. S., Brass, D., and Mcmahon-Beattie, U. (2007), "Current issue in tourism: the authentic tourist", *Tourism Management*, Vol. 28, No. 4, pp. 1128–1138.

Zenker, S. (2011), "How to catch a city? The concept and measurement of place brands", *Journal of Place Management and Development*, Vol. 4, No. 1, pp. 40–52.

Zenker, S. and Beckmann, S. C. (2013), "My place is not your place – different place brand knowledge by different target groups", *Journal of Place Management and Development*, Vol. 6, No. 1, pp. 6–17.

Zenker, S. and Braun, E. (2010), "Branding a city – a conceptual approach for place branding and place brand management", in *Proceedings of the 39th European Marketing Academy Conference*, Copenhagen, Denmark, available at: www.placebrand.eu/publications/ (accessed 26 November 2016).

Zenker, S. and Braun, E. (2017), "Questioning a 'one size fits all' city brand: developing a branded house strategy for place brand management", *Journal of Place Management and Development*, Vol. 10, No. 3, pp. 270–287.

Zenker, S., Braun, E., and Petersen, S. (2017), "Branding the destination versus the place: The effects of brand complexity and identification for residents and visitors", *Tourism Management*, Vol. 58, No. 1, pp. 15–27.

Zenker, S. and Erfgen, C. (2014), "Let them do the work: a participatory place branding approach", *Journal of Place Management and Development*, Vol. 7, No. 3, pp. 225–234.

Zenker, S. and Petersen, S. (2014), "An integrative theoretical model for improving resident-city identification", *Environment and Planning A*, Vol. 46, No. 3, pp. 715–729.

Zenker, S., Petersen, S., and Aholt, A. (2013), "The Citizen Satisfaction Index (CSI): Evidence for a four basic factor model in a German sample", *Cities*, Vol. 31, No. 1, pp. 156–164.

Zenker, S. and Gollan, T. (2010), "Development and implementation of the resident migration scale (ReMiS): measuring success in place marketing", in Witte, E. H. and Gollan, T. (Eds.), *Sozialpsychologie und Ökonomie*, Pabst Verlag, Lengerich, pp. 156–172.

10 Immaterial heritage and sense of place

Adriana Campelo

Sensing places and feeling heritage

Friday is the day to wear white clothes in Salvador. Walking along the streets at sunset, one can smell palm-oil burning. It is the lovely smell of acaraje – the yellow fried bean cake – an African Brazilian delicacy. Together with the natural light and sea views, it provides a sense of Salvador. The repertoire of senses connects people with places. Sensorial perceptions are prime signs one can capture from a place. It is through our senses that we grasp the place, experience it, and create memories that will last. Places have tastes and colours that may not be directly connected with the natural environment. If the sky in Lima is always grey, the incredible colour of Inca clothing, textiles, and tapestries would be the strongest image from Peru. Wearing white clothes on Friday in Salvador, the colourful fabrics of Peru, and African Brazilian food have immaterial heritage in common.

My work in place branding always brings me back to the question of how a collective sense of place is constructed and how a sense of place creates some sort of knowledge about places. To my understanding, sense of place is influenced by tangible and intangible attributes such as history, culture, landscape, social, political, and public affairs. Sensory knowledge plays an important role in the formulation of a sense of place. The sense of place stands for how we sensorily perceive, understand, and share ideas and feelings of a place (Campelo 2017).

This chapter connects immaterial heritage with sensory experiences. It discusses how sensorial knowledge is able to build up an asset (or a lived archive) of taste, sounds, smells, visions, and touch particular to each place. It discusses accounts of how senses, sensorial insights, and experiences can develop knowledge about places (Casey 1996) and includes an argument on how cultural aspects become part of the sense of place.

Many senses for sense of place

Although one's engagement with a place goes beyond a multisensory experience, it is facilitated by the senses as the first way to perceive the atmosphere of a place (Tuan 1975, 2001; Casey 1996). Our senses give us a comprehensive perception of the surrounding world, and help to create links between places and our memories of the place. The importance of these senses is highlighted by Cosgrove and Daniels (1988), Bender (2002), Terkenli (2002), and Medway (2015) who relate senses to visual impressions of landscapes and cities. Feld and Basso (1996) go further to assert that "as place is sensed, senses are placed; as places make sense, senses make place" (p. 91). On a similar note, Tuan (1975) argues that to experience a place we need to construct it with the use of all our senses. He explains that there are passive and active modes of a sensory experience:

> Some sensory modes are more passive or direct than others. With taste, smell, and touch we feel as though we are simply registering sensations provoked by external stimuli. With hearing, and particularly with seeing, we seem to be actively exploring the world beyond us and getting to know it objectively. Seeing is thinking, in the sense that it is a discriminating and constructive activity; it creates patterns of reality adapted for human purposes. Even taste, smell, and touch are affected by thought in the above sense: they discriminate among stimuli and are able to articulate gustatory, olfactory, and tactual worlds.
>
> (Tuan 1975, p. 151)

The author links the passive mode to intimate and individual sensations, whereas the active mode is more likely to be public, communal, and shared. He illustrates his argument with an example of the shared experience of a holiday, "we can articulate visual experience with coloured slides and incidents with words, but the exhilarating olfactory and tactile experiences remain buried in our private selves"(p. 151). In fact, the primacy of some senses (e.g., sight and hearing) contrasts with other senses which are difficult to share, express, represent, and reproduce (e.g., taste, smell, and touch) (Tilley 2006b). However, all of our senses are mixed together in a sort of sensorial entanglement that links our senses with social and cultural aspects of places (Mason and Davis 2009).

This knowledge (that comes from our senses) is part of our understanding of the world, how we see it and how we feel it, which makes difficult, if not impossible, to separate our senses from our everyday experiences. Whereas to take account of our senses is important in our perception of places; it also helps us to understand social and cultural characteristics of places (Tilley 2002). In this regard, Classen (1997) argues that each culture has a particular sensory model and the meanings associated with sensory faculties inform how members of that society "make sense of the world, or translate sensory perceptions and concepts into a particular worldview" (p. 402).

The discussion about the importance of the senses might seem ethereal to understand a place and a sense of place; however, Tuan (1975) provides a more tangible and concrete explanation of how our experience constructs place at different levels. While in a small village it might be possible to create shared and communal sensory perceptions, in big cities, regions, and countries it might only take account of individual encounters. Nevertheless, the shared sensations of seasons (cold and warm) and light, for example, create and define what geographers call the 'boundaries of formal regions', and they are perceived and shared by the people who are experiencing the place. This links back to how our perceptions influence the creation of a sense of place.

Sensory and heritage knowledge

The emergent field of sensory research started in anthropology during the 1990s, and was called the sensorial revolution by Howes (2006a,b). The author emphasised that "the study of the senses is based on the premise that the sensorium is a social construction, [...] lived and understood differently in different cultures and historical periods" (2006a, 114). Scholarship to develop an emphasis on sensory knowledge is growing across many fields of social sciences (Adams and Guy 2007; Classen 1990, 1997; Lindstrom 2005; Middleton

2010; Stroller 1997) concerned with understanding how senses are "enacted in specific cultural contexts" and "how the members of a given culture distinguish, value, relate and combine the senses in everyday life" (Howes 2006a, p.122). We are unable to grasp the surrounding reality in one dimension, one sense connects to another, and our five senses are connected together with social and cultural aspects of a place.

Unsurprisingly, researching the nature of sensory knowledge in the emerging field of "sensescapes" (see Middleton 2010) requires addressing the need for appropriate methodologies. For example, in sensory studies there is a predominance of visual methodologies that do not take into account the dimensions that engage other senses (Mason and Davies 2009; Pink 2006, 2009). More recently, sensory ethnographers have discussed approaches which incorporate the other senses such as: smell (Classen 1990, 1997) and touch (Stroller 1997). The development of sensory knowledge includes not only emic and etic concerns, but also those related to the representation and communication of the senses. In this regard, language is of central importance (Stokowski 2002) with sensory narratives making it possible to share their sensory experiences and the meanings, significance, and influence of them with others. Such narratives represent and reinforce the sensory nature of our perceptions and the way that we create, understand, and share ideas, feelings, and experiences.

Hirschman and Holbrook (1982) explored the idea of sensory marketing and the use of the senses in their research on hedonic consumption. This work relates consumer behaviour to the multisensory and emotive aspects of consumers' experience with products. The experiences are assumed to provide consumers with inputs that contribute to creating a multisensory image either of associative experiences or of products. Joy and Sherry (2003) highlighted the importance of sensory data to "elucidate the contours of the aesthetic experience' in consumer experiences. By investigating consumers" experiences in art museums and galleries, the authors demonstrated "how research on the sensual creation of meaning can add dimensionality to existing research on the mere recovery of meaning" (p. 280), and help to understand the human or "carnal" aspects that constitute consumption and consumer behaviour. Krishna (2009, p. 2) advocates the importance of sensorial studies for marketing in general, and consumer behaviour in particular, as "sensory perceptions affect what we like and what we buy". Research to understand the influence of sensory perceptions on people' attitudes towards buying and consuming products focus on haptic effects and touch (Krishna and Morrin 2008; Peck and Childers 2003), visual (Chandon and Wansink 2002; Wansink and van Ittersum 2003), hearing (Lindstrom 2005; MacInnis and Park 1991), smell (Aggleton and Waskett 1999; Bagozzi 2008; Morrin and Ratneshwar 2003), as well as research considering their integration (Elder and Krishna 2010; Krishna 2006; Peck and Childers 2008).

In branding, Hultén (2011, p. 755) suggests the development of a multisensory brand–experience concept, which "supports their purchase and consumption processes through the involvement of the five human senses in generating customer value, experiences, and brand as image". Despite these appeals to incorporate sensory data and knowledge in consumer and marketing research, it seems that very little research has used multisensory data to investigate how sense of place is related to place branding or to consider the role of senses outside of their use as tactical inducements to purchase products. The exceptions are Henshaw (2014) and Medway (2015). The importance of smells in cities is the legacy of Henshaw who explored the olfactory impact in urban design. In place branding, Medway (2015) has championed this discussion by relating each sense with place branding, especially the non-seeing senses. Medway argues how the leverage between senses and places can create a set of representations for place branding and for promoting places. He provides us with an example of the Italian city of Parma, "which uses the scent of Parma violets in a whole range of souvenir products, including the perfume Aqua di Parma" (p. 196). The idea of connecting senses to places for promotional purposes requires, firstly, an acknowledgement of a particular sense as characteristic of a place. Second, this acknowledgement should be public (as Tuan taught us above) and shared. It also requires some sort of archive and records which can be positively activated to become an asset.

Graham (2002) sees heritage as knowledge that may change through time. The knowledge of how to do things is passed on to generations and becomes ingrained in places habitus and culture. Smells and tastes of places are formed by centuries of heritage, culture, and history. Culinary elements and cusines are closely related to culture and heritage. Choosing ingredients, preparing recipes, and preserving food are daily activities related to a place's heritage (Askegaard, Kjeldgaard, and Arnould 2017). The tastes of Greenland today still have strong memories and deep knowledge from the past. The typical food of Salvador is African food and tells the history of slavery and religion in Brazil during the Portuguese colonial times. The acaraje has been recognised by UNESCO as an object of intangible cultural heritage to be safeguarded. Despite the importance of immaterial heritage as knowledge, it is also important to realise how both intangible culture and immaterial heritage influences the sensory knowledge of places.

Senses make assets

It is well known that assets are resources owned by someone. Whether tangible, intangible, or a combination of both, assets should be able to produce positive economic value. Brands, for example, are intangible assets. In social sciences, Pierre Bourdieu introduced an idea of capital to deal with a sum of shared and communal resources – even intangible. It derives from Marx's theoretical analysis and is intrinsically linked to accumulation and the capacity to produce a surplus. In this regard, both capital and assets keep the meaning of a set of resources. Bourdieu (1986) took the concept of capital to analyse the sum of resources and their impacts on and relationships with social and cultural purposes. He worked with concepts of economic capital, cultural capital, symbolic capital, and social capital, although he agreed that the types of capital "can be derived from economic capital, but only at the cost of a more or less great effort of transformation, which is needed to produce the type of power effective in the field in question" (Bourdieu 1986, p. 252).

In doing so, Bourdieu approached the formation of capital from an ontological perspective. He combined the other forms of capital (cultural, social, and symbolic) with economic capital to explain how it creates and reproduces inequality, "as inequality was to be explained by the production and reproduction of capital" (Field 2003, p.15). Field also suggested that to see capital as a form of accumulation in an economic context is sufficient to understand its implications in a social one (Field 2003). These forms were related to immaterial exchanges and related to culture and relationships. The nature of these exchanges would determine the field of these accumulated assets and how they would work. As a consequence, it reveals the kind of capital these assets constitute, which is extremely relevant to our discussion on sensory experiences as an asset.

Bourdieu (1986) defined social capital as the "aggregation of resources (actual or potential) which are linked to the possession of a durable network of more or less institutionalized relationships of mutual acquaintance and recognition, which provides each of its members with the backing of the collectively-owned capital, a 'credential' which entitles them to credit, in the various senses of the word" (p. 249). Later, he explained social capital as "the sum of resources, actual or virtual, that accrue to an individual or a group by virtue of possessing a durable network of more or less institutionalised relationships of mutual acquaintance and recognition"(Bourdieu and Wacquant 1992, p. 119). Social capital is, by nature, a resource derived from a collective phenomenon linked to a certain group (Siisiäinen 2000), likewise to a certain place, and related to symbolic capital. The social capital "acquires a symbolic character, and is transformed into symbolic capital" (Siisiäinen 2000, p.10) based on mutual cognition and recognition.

The attributes of social capital are accessible through symbolic capital, achieved through the "alchemy of consecration" (Bourdieu 1986, p.250). Recognition and reproduction are possible because of the constitution of symbolism or symbolic content that is produced through exchanges. According to Bourdieu (1986), the practice of exchange transforms "the things exchanged into signs of recognition, and through the mutual recognition and recognition of group membership which it implies, re-produces the group" (p. 250). The processes of cognition, recognition, and reproduction depend to a large measure on the effectiveness of the practices of communication. As explained by Siisiäinen (2000, p.12), "the economic, cultural, and social capital becomes meaningful and socially effective only through the process of symbolic translation", i.e., the content itself is merely a sign, the symbolism arises from what is signified (Saussure 1983).

Social capital is translatable, touchable, and even created through the lens of symbolic capital. It is not always seen, but also sensed. The symbolic feature is the way humans form, organise, and talk about concepts. The symbols help humans to order their experiences, to talk about them, and to refine their behaviour (Weiman and Walter 1957). The symbolic representation of social capital encompasses the perception of the social world via symbols of representations and by actions of representations, individual or collective (Bourdieu 1989).

Indeed, symbolic capital as a path to understanding social capital is a powerful tool for place branding strategies. It is through the symbolic capital that unconscious attributes existing amid a community are revealed. The symbolic resources help reveal social capital and identify its elements and constituents that reproduce and enhance these resources. Seen in this way, the place brand is a semiotic channel to represent cultural values and social capital that should reflect and be part of the symbolic capital of the place. How sensory can symbolic capital be? Senses seem to be part of symbolic capital as well.

Although Bourdieu gave importance to the ties between social capital and symbolic capital, and this relationship matters for the discussion about place branding, he also emphasised the perspective of a resource belonging to a network. Other theorists in social capital, such as Coleman (1988) and Putnam (1993) give more attention to the function of networks, their benefits and the profitable use of social capital theory in many fields of knowledge related to economic development and industry. Coleman (1988) defined social capital as a variety of entities, rather than a single one, that share some aspects of social structures, which facilitate certain actions of actors within the structure. The author argues the productiveness of social capital as it makes possible the achievement of certain ends. The absence of social capital could make certain aims impossible to reach or could make their achievement much more difficult. Coleman (1988) argues that other types of capital, such as economic and social capital have their own structures, but social capital "inheres in the structure of relations between actors and among actors"(p. 98). All these theorists recognize the need for interaction and shared ideas, concepts, values, and so on.

How are sensory impressions connected to places? The sensory experiences are not detached symbolic and cultural resources of places. On the contrary, sensory engagements enable us to delineate the place. Sensory experiences are the realm of ordinary life dealing with everyday objects, symbolisms beauties, tastes, and feelings (Venkatesh and Meamber 2008).

Salvador: feast of senses

Salvador's place branding is based on the argument that the senses experienced in the city make the place different and unique. A film, accessible via Youtube (www.youtube.com/watch?v=UyMeV_C-5E4), presents how one feels the city using the five senses. The taste is related to African–Brazilian recipes, the smell and touch are connected to the sea, the hearing is linked to the rhythm of drums, and the visuals related with symbols and culture. The transcription of the film says:

> "Places are like people. There are those who just go through our lives and those who leave their mark. There are those without grace and those thoughtful. Places are like people has a place that has incredible power to click on our soul and when you realise... they are already in our heart. So, it is Salvador: it's a feast for the senses. The taste of palm oil is in the mouth like a tattoo on the palate. The scent of the sea is not content to be a smell, the salt in the body mix with our sweat. The images are so full of symbols that they always seem to have something new to show you, even though you have already seen dozens of times.
>
> The rhythm happens to have the same name of what in the chest makes people feel alive. It is a city divided into two parts and linked by an elevator. [...] Salvador has a Candomblé Saint for every day of the week and a church for every day of the year."
>
> Salvador: você sente que é diferente

The senses, as presented for Salvador, are related to aspects of immaterial heritage of the city and its culture. It displays the influence of Portuguese culture in the architecture of the city as it shows how African heritage is part of the local music, food, and beliefs. The unique value proposition of Salvador's place branding is the combination of senses and sensory experiences and engagement. Such sensory engagement provides a way of connecting people to the spirit of the place.

Getting senses

It is through symbolic forms that "people communicate, perpetuate, and develop their knowledge about and attitudes toward life" (Geertz 1973, p.89). A sense of place implies sensory, emotional, cognitive, and subjective experiences that represent such knowledge. Being in a place requires a sensory embodiment that mediates the perception of the surrounding environment. It is fundamental to our human experience that we use our senses to understand the world around us and define our place in it.

According to Sparkes (2009, p. 26) "all the senses deserve serious attention in ethnographic work if we are to better understand the life world of others". The narratives involving sensorial perceptions are in large measure multi-sensory. However, despite some narratives clearly favouring one or two senses, they are interlocked and interconnected in the sensory experiences that comprise the perceptions.

Understanding places requires an understanding of the collection of images that comprise meaningful representations of the actions and symbols developed by the people who experience the place in their everyday lives. These representations are not detached from the sensory perceptions existing in the experience of places but are connected to and are part of the representations of the place and its aesthetics. The development of a place brand requires knowledge not only of the symbols that stand for brand values and associations, but also requires an understanding of how a collection of images interact to create an authentic place image. The exercise of representing symbols, associations, and values is largely based on vivid description, rich in sensory words and images able to create meanings that encourage brand 'readers' to use one or more of their senses to engage with the place brand. Our senses connect us to the world around us and mediate the perception of our sense of place. To understand this perception it is necessary to understand the sensory experiences that comprise it. Considering the influence of sensory perceptions on places and its significance in perceiving the social world, at least related to places, I acknowledge sensory perception as one more dimension to be considered when researching places.

The sensory dimension, following Bourdieu, has its own profile in terms of resources, cognitive abilities and capacities, and emotional connections that provide a deeper understanding of the concept of place. The development of the notion of capital in social sciences is based on the understanding of capital as a process rather than a simple materiality. Bourdieu acknowledged society as a plurality of social fields, where each field has a profile of its own, in terms of forms of capital (economic, cultural, social, and symbolic), and explains that "capital – in whatever form – insofar as it is represented, i.e., apprehended symbolically, in a relationship of knowledge or, more precisely, of misrecognition and recognition, presupposes the intervention of the habitus, as a socially constituted cognitive capacity" (1986, p.56). Moreover, the author explains the perception of the social world as a result of a double structure that embraces objectivity and subjectivity. He suggests 'the social world can be perceived and expressed in a variety of ways, since they always include a degree of indeterminacy and vagueness, and, thereby, a certain degree of semantic elasticity' (Bourdieu 1989, p. 20).

Drawing from Bourdieu's concept of capital, I suggest to include the idea of sensory capital as a basis for future research in place branding (Campelo 2017). Along with symbolic capital, the development of a framework to investigate sensory capital might help to elicit the aesthetics of places. Furthermore, to better understand how people and communities recognize, value, interact and experience places.

Sense of place implies sensorial, aesthetic, emotional, cognitive, objective, and subjective experiences. Characteristics of the environment such as contour and shape, colour and quality of light, texture, wind, sounds, and scents, affect our senses and the way we give meaning to our experiences and interactions (Ryden 1993). Sensory perceptions, and the resulting sensory knowledge, form a significant part of place imagery. Given their importance in perceiving the social and natural world, sensory elements should feature more highly on the research agenda for place branding. While sensory knowledge is not a new concept (Adams and Guy 2007; Classen 1990, 1997; Howes 2006a, b; Middleton 2010; Lindstrom 2005; Stroller 1997), it remains incipient in place marketing and branding scholarship.

Conclusions

This chapter discussed how sensory knowledge contributes to a multi-dimensional perspective on place branding and a sense of place. Research on place brands should address the role of the senses and its links with heritage to better understand the sensory experiences that constitute a sense of place.

References

Askegaard, S., D. Kjeldgaard, and E. Arnould (2017), Programmatic authenticity: Culinary place branding in Greenland.In *Handbook on Place Branding and Marketing*. Edward Elgar Publishing, Incorporated, 108–23.

Adams, M., and S. Guy (2007), Editorial: Senses and the city. *Senses & Society* 2 (2), 133–6.

Aggleton, J. P., and L. Waskett (1999), The ability of odours to serve as state dependent cues for real-world memories: Can Viking smells aid the recall of Viking experiences? *British Journal of Psychology* 90 (1), 1–7.

Bagozzi, R. P. (2008), Some insights on visual and verbal processing strategies. *Journal of Consumer Psychology* 18 (4), 258–63.

Bender, B. (2002), Time and landscape. *Current Anthropology*, 43 (s4), S103–12.

Bourdieu, P. (1986), The forms of capital. In *Handbook of Theory and Research for the Sociology of* Education, ed. J. Richardson, 241–58. New York: Greenwood Press.

Bourdieu, P. (1989), Social space and symbolic power. *Sociological Theory* 7 (1), 14–25.

Bourdieu, P., and L.J. Wacquant (1992), *An invitation to reflexive sociology*. University of Chicago press.

Braun, V. and V. Clarke (2006), Using thematic analysis in psychology. *Qualitative Research in Psychology*, 3 (2), 77–101.

Campelo, A. (2017), Smell it, taste it, hear it, touch it and see it to make sense of this place. In *Handbook on Place Branding and Marketing*, 124–246.

Casey, E. (1996), How to get from space to place in a fairly short stretch of time: Phenomenological prolegomena. In *Senses of Place*, eds. S. Feld and K. Basso, 13–52. Santa Fe: School of American Research Press.

Chandon, P. and B. Wansink (2002), When are stockpiled products consumed faster? a convenience–salience framework of post purchase consumption incidence and quantity. *Journal of Marketing Research* 39 (3), 321–35.

Classen, C. (1990), Sweet colors, fragrant songs: sensory models of the Andes and the Amazon. *American Ethnologist* 17 (4), 722–35.

Classen, C. (1997), Foundations for an anthropology of senses. *International Social Science Journal* XLIX (153), 401–12.

Coleman, J. S. (1988), Social capital in the creation of human capital. *American Journal of Sociology*, S95–S120.

Cosgrove, D., and S. Daniels (1988), *The iconography of landscape: essays on the symbolic representation, design and use of past environments* (Vol. 9). Cambridge University Press.

Davies, C. A. (2008), *Reflexive ethnography: A guide to researching selves and others*. London and New York: Routledge.

Denzin, N. K. (1997), *Interpretative ethnography, ethnographic practices for the 21st century*. Thousand Oaks, London and New Delhi: Sage.

Elder, R. and A. Krishna (2010), The effect of advertising copy on sensory thoughts and perceived taste. *Journal of Consumer Research* 36 (5), 748–56.

Elliott, R. and N. Jankel-Elliot (2003), Using ethnography in strategic consumer research. *Qualitative market research: An international journal*, (6), 215–23.

Feld, S. and K. H. Basso (1996), *Senses of place*. Santa Fe: School of American Research.

Field, J. (2003), *Social capital*. London and New York: Routledge.

Geertz, C. (1973), *Interpretation of cultures: Selected essays*. New York: Basic Books.

Graham, B. (2002), Heritage as knowledge: capital or culture?. *Urban studies*, 39 (5–6), 1003–17.

Hackley, C. (2003), *Doing research projects in marketing, management and consumer research*, London and New York: Routledge.

Henshaw, V. (2014), *Urban smellscapes*. Routledge.

Hirschman, E. C., and M. B. Holbrook (1982), Hedonic consumption: Emerging concepts, methods and propositions. *The Journal of Marketing* 46 (3), 92–101

Howes, D. (2006a), Charting the sensorial revolution. *The Senses and Society* 1 (1), 113–29.

Howes, D. (2006b), Cross-Talk between the senses. *The Senses and Society* 1 (3), 381–91.

Hultén, B. (2011), Sensory marketing: The multi-sensory brand experience Concept. *European Business Review* 3.

Joy, A. and J. F. Sherry, Jr. (2003), Speaking of art as embodied imagination: A Multisensory approach to understanding aesthetic experience. *Journal of Consumer Research* 30 (2), 259–82.

Krishna, A. (2006), The interaction of senses: The effect of vision and touch on the elongation bias. *Journal of Consumer Research* 32 (4), 557–66.

Krishna, A. (2009), Introduction to sensory marketing. In *Sensory Marketing: Research on the Sensuality of Consumers*, ed. A. Krishna. Routledge: NYC.

Krishna, A., and M. Morrin (2008), Does Touch affect taste? the perceptual transfer of product container haptic cues. *Journal of Consumer Research* (34), 807–18.

Lindstrom, M. (2005), Broad sensory branding. *The Journal of Product and Brand Management* 14 (2/3), 84–88.

MacInnis, D. J., and C. W. Park (1991), The differential role of characteristics of music on high- and low-involvement consumers' processing of ads. *Journal of Consumer Research* 18 (2), 161–73.

Mason, J., and K. Davies (2009), Coming to our senses? a critical approach to sensory methodology. *Qualitative Research* (9), 587–603.

Medway, D. (2015), Rethinking place branding and the 'other' senses. In *Rethinking place branding*. Springer International Publishing, 191–209.

Merleau-Ponty, M. (2002), Phenomenology of perception.

Middleton, J. (2010), Sense and the city: Exploring the embodied geographies of urban walking. *Social& Cultural Geography* 11 (6), 575–96.

Morrin, M., and S. Ratneshwar (2003), Does it make sense to use scents to enhance brand memory? *Journal of Marketing Research* 40 (1), 10–25.

Nadin, S. and C Cassel (2006), The use of research diary as a tool for reflexive practice some reflections from management research. *Qualitative research in accounting and management* 3 (3), 208–17.

Peck, J., and T. L. Childers (2003), Individual differences in haptic information processing: On the development, validation, and use of the 'Need for Touch' scale. *Journal of Consumer Research* 30 (3), 430–42.

Peck, J., and T. L. Childers (2008), If it tastes, smells, sounds, and feels like a duck, then it must be a... : Effects of sensory factors on consumer behaviors. In *Handbook of consumer psychology*, eds. C. Haugtvedt, P. Herrand and F. Kardes, 193–219.Psychology: New York.

Pink, S. (2006), *The future of visual anthropology: Engaging the senses*, Oxon: Routledge.

Pink, S. (2007), Walking with video. *Visual Studies* 22 (3), 240–52.

Pink, S. (2009), *Doing sensory ethnography*. London: Sage.

Putnam, R. D. (1993), The prosperous community. *The American Prospect*, 4 (13), 35–42.

Ryden, K. C. (1993), *Mapping the invisible landscape: Folklore, writing, and the sense of place*. Iowa City: University of Iowa Press.

Saussure, F. D. (1983), Course in general linguistics, trans. R. Harris, London: Duckworth.

Siisiäinen, M. (2000), Social capital, power and the third sector. *The third sector in Finland: Review to research of the Finnish third sector.* Finnish Federation for Social Welfare and Health. Helsinki, 7–35.

Sparkes, A. C. (2009), Ethnography and the senses: challenges and possibilities. *Qualitative Research in Sport and Exercise* 1 (1), 21–35.

Stedman, R. C. (2003), Is it really just a social construction? The contribution of the physical environment to sense of place. *Society & Natural Resources* 16 (8), 671.

Stokowski, P. A. (2002), Languages of place and discourses of power: constructing new senses of place. *Journal of Leisure Research* 34 (4), 368.

Stroller, P. (1997), *Sensuous scholarship*. Philadelphia: University of Pennsylvania Press.

Terkenli, T. S. (2002), Landscapes of tourism: Towards a global cultural economy of space? *Tourism Geographies* 4 (3), 227-54.

Tilley, C. (2002), Metaphor, materiality and interpretation, in V. Buchli (ed.), *The material culture reader*. Oxford: Berg, 23–56.

Tilley, C. (2006a), Introduction: identity, place, landscape and heritage. *Journal of Material Culture* 11 (1–2), 7–32.

Tilley, C. (2006b), The sensory dimensions of gardening. *The Senses and Society* 1 (3), 311–31.

Tuan, Y.F. (1975), Place: An experiential perspective. *Geographical Review* 65 (2):151–65.

Tuan, Y. F. (2001), *Space and place: The perspective of experience*. Minneapolis: University of Minnesota Press.

Venkatesh, A., and L.A. Meamber. (2008), The aesthetics of consumption and the consumer as an aesthetic subject. *Consumption, Markets & Culture* 11 (1), 45–70.

Wansink, B., and K. van Ittersum. (2003), Bottoms up! The influence of elongation on pouring and consumption volume. *Journal of Consumer Research* 30 (3), 455–63.

11 The economic calculation of conservation

Marilena Vecco

Introduction

This chapter aims to contribute to the theoretical debates in the study of the economics of cultural heritage conservation, in particular, in the context of built cultural heritage by providing a detailed economic analysis of the different meanings of conservations with their economic implications. As has been pointed out by Mason, the economic valuation and heritage conservation – mainly based on economic values, the former, cultural values, the latter – narratives seem to be two disconnected worlds.[1] Their dialogue and interaction appear to be an *anathema* according to the traditional discourse of heritage, in which both the economic and the management dimensions are perceived as secondary and functional to the transmission of the past legacy.

This chapter deals with the economic analysis of the decisions regarding the conservation of artistic and historical heritage in particular in the context of heritage situations where conservation objectives may compete with other market interests and more valuable options of utilizing the cultural heritage. We argue that to be sustainable in the medium and long term, this economic analysis must be integrated within the heritage conservation discourse and narratives and answer the following logical questions:

- why preserve?
- for how long?
- what are the different meanings of preservation?
- what to preserve and for whom?

This chapter is organized as follows. A review of the reasons for conserving everything is proposed. In section 2, we explain the economic calculation of cultural heritage conservation, while in section 3 we analyse the paradoxes embedded in the conservation process and their social and economic implications. In section 4, we propose the possibility to regenerate a cultural good/a cultural heritage asset while section 5 proposes the different concepts of conservation (re-use, restoration, preservation), which are discussed from an economic and historical perspective, while section 6 wraps up some conclusions.

What to preserve: the reason for preserving everything

"Preserving everything"[2] is a characteristic of many countries' contemporary preservation policies. Besides the trivial truism that something is better than nothing (and everything is better than something), there are also economic reasons for this.

The first and maybe, most important, is the preservers' strategy of maximizing their field of intervention. The larger the domain to be preserved, the larger the transfer from consumers. The more extensive the definition of the stock to be preserved as an "aesthetic" or "cultural" asset, the larger the monopolistic power of "preservation" of the cultural establishment.

This reason, however, can be mentioned for the past as well as for the present consideration of the problem, while the "urgency for preservation" is typical of our days, and more generally, of the twentieth century. In the eighteenth century, the ruins of ancient Rome were contemplated without any concern about how to preserve them. Papal Rome transformed Teatro Marcello into a prince's palace and swallowed up Pompey's theatre in a slum in a sixteenth-century version of real-estate speculation.

Renaissance towns were built upon their medieval forerunners and were in turn, devoured by Baroque construction, and successively demolished by twentieth-century "vanguards". Only communist regimes allowed Prague and Cracow to remain untouched in the last fifty years and not to suffer the evolutions of Paris, London and Rome. Prague, however, is a unique and fascinating open-air museum precisely because of the huge transformations it suffered in the past. Nobody, however, is shocked by this. Why then should the residents of Paris scream against the destruction of the "Marché aux Halles", or the Romans strongly defend Vittorio Emanuele II's Memorial, both being rather modest examples of questionable architecture?

Two economic answers can be given: either nineteenth-century cultural production seems less important in terms of quality and quantity to our contemporaries than that of their times to the decision-makers of the past, or the net destruction rate of the culture of the past has been increasing. Both arguments are historically grounded.

Benedictine monks copied Classical works to preserve them, but, at the same time, they invented the great Gothic cathedrals with a concern for permanence shared only by the great architects of the past. Contemporary re-examination of the cultural themes of the past is not linked to any permanent innovation. This is not because any innovation is present, but rather because, nowadays innovation is the behavioural rule in the arts.

The "vanguard" is now the "post-vanguard" of the "vanguard", as it is expressly and conceptually intended to be consumed and destroyed. Modern and contemporary art is conceptual and, as such, it is structurally ephemeral over time. Technology is also responsible for the increase in the destruction rate in art and culture. Conserving a movie is different from conserving a literary work. Modern and contemporary art is multimedial and, therefore, is technologically ephemeral. Economic growth has supplied several good arguments for the urgency of preservation, too. It has created an unprecedented increase in the industrialization of negative externalities, with similar destructive effects on environmental and artistic resources. For example, water pollution in the Venetian lagoon had also had unprecedented negative effects on its artistic heritage.

On the other hand, economic growth, with the related market expansion has caused a decline in quality due both to economic reasons (an ugly thing is often cheaper than a beautiful one) and to the previously mentioned strategic behaviour of certifiers. All the arguments discussed, however, besides the latter, refer to contemporary art (what has been produced today), not to the art of the past. From that point of view, the only difference between us and a citizen in the sixteenth century is the level of pollution and its effects on the artistic heritage. This is a good reason for intensifying preservation initiatives, not for preserving everything, stopping any transformation of the heritage.

Contemporary attitudes toward freezing the past are more likely to result from a negative judgement of contemporary artistic and cultural production. If culture is a different way of using the same resources, it is evident that our contemporaries' opinion of their own way is worse than that of their grandparents. Why should the re-use of the Venice Arsenal give aesthetically worse results than sixteenth-century restoration?

The truth is that this negative judgement is mainly grounded on negative empirical administrative evidence. What is considered worse is the decision-making attitude of those who should "interpret" the heritage in order to preserve it.

Why should Venetian public officials make worse decisions than their sixteenth-century predecessors? As well as all ideological arguments, there is also an economic reason for this.

Their decisions are worse because they do not pay for them. *Ceteris paribus*, that is assuming for decision-makers of all times the same level of interpretation and social welfare maximization capability, contemporaries decide on a heritage they perceive as being a public good subject to their free-riding behaviour, while decision-makers in the past mainly owned it personally or as a part of a collectively-shared wealth, the accumulation and maintenance of which they paid for.

A bureaucratic behaviour may be developed on these grounds, aimed at non-Pareto optimum solutions for society. This has nothing to do with the aesthetic process, which cannot, therefore, be considered a reason for "heritage freezing" in itself.

Preservation decisions go through an interpretation process which helps in defining aesthetic priorities but which also gives non-consequentiality to these choices they can also be influenced on economic and political grounds. This can lead to the refusal of the present as well as of the past. "What to preserve?" is a question that must be analysed on this basis.

The economic calculation of conservation

The cultural heritage conservation process (as a whole of the diagnostic and restoration activities) must not be an end in itself but must be followed by a stage of the actual productive use of the asset in question. The conservation process is made up of two, distinct interdependent stages: assessment, or rather an estimate of the existing value, and valorization[3], understood as the creation of added value. These two different stages generate values of a different nature: the assessment creates the value of an economic nature while valorization, alongside the asset's existing economic value, which is often regenerated, produces the value of a cultural nature. The heritage good becomes the object of restoration, conservation and then reuse; this last stage is aimed at its revalorization, which is achieved thanks to the attribution of a new social function for the existing structure and the space it is part of. The restoration process is, therefore, not regarded from just a conservative perspective but from one that is more reassessable, treating the heritage asset as an economic and productive resource.

The use of the term "resource" when talking about heritage is more than justified since in economic terms, this concept indicates a productive factor, often scarce, that becomes the fundamental input for an economic process aimed at achieving utility in terms of investment or consumption.

Heritage conservation has a clear economic impact, in particular in what we could call the passive phase, during restoration when the heritage good undergoes intervention; this is also the case in the active production phase when it is given a new functional destination that sees the heritage as an agent object in the economic-productive context. In the sixties, Jacobs argued for the utility of old buildings in the urban economy.[4] Later on, in the eighties, other authors put emphasis on the economic effects of the conservation and rehabilitation process.[5] Over time, the conservation process becomes complementary to the physical regeneration and economic development of a place/ area/context.

The need for this operation is justified by three different motives. First of all, the unique nature of the historic and artistic heritage (as is the case for all natural and environmental heritage; its actual use, which is often released from a predominantly economic use; and finally, its future productivity, or rather the heritage asset as a deposit, that although it is not currently being used, could be so and then become productive in the true sense of the word for all future generations. This means that the economy of the heritage has to include:

- *Maintenance*, aimed at the maintenance of the existing, avoiding further deterioration;
- *Depreciation* that, in the specific case of artistic and historic heritage, as a result of the unique nature of the existing resources, is translated into a regeneration process that is carried out following a regenerative model of the natural heritage (regeneration of the water, ground, air, etc.).

Business economy refers to replaceable objects; in the medium-long term they have to be replaced owing to wear and tear and obsolescence; the economy of art, on the other hand, deals with objects that appear to be irreplaceable.

Any decision of a conservative nature is subjected to the following logic:

$$Vc > Vnc \quad \text{or} \tag{1}$$

After conservation, the value of the asset (Vc) must be greater than the sum of its previous value (Vnc) with the cost of conservation (Cc).

$$Vc \geq Vnc + Cc \tag{2}$$

In this manner one calculates the induced added value of the conservative choice (Vac), which is the result of an appreciative analysis of the historic value of the conserved good[6]:

$$Vac \rightarrow Vc \geq Vnc + Cc \tag{3}$$

The paradoxes of conservation

> "La conservation patrimoniale se charge du dépôt des souvenirs et nous délivre du poids des responsabilités infligées à la mémoire."[7]
>
> Henri-Pierre Jeudy

When dealing with the problem of the conservation process, one inevitably comes up against four paradoxes that restrict the extent of its action, very often making the actual conservation intervention problematic.

The first conservation paradox

The economic capacity of conservation decreases with an increase in conservation commitment, owing to the growing scarcity of the resources destined for conservation.

This first paradox is linked to the conceptual changes of the word conservation: conservation as re-use, "re-doing" (*reficere*), restoration, and philological preservation.

These diverse meanings emphasize the importance given to the weight of historical and artistic judgement in the field of deciding on the quantification in economic terms of the conservation intervention whilst also increasing the marginal cost of the actual conservation.

The current period stands out from all earlier ones with its sort of "obsession" with cultural conservation[8], going beyond the mere and justified worry with conserving the cultural heritage that has accumulated in the history of mankind. Furthermore, one must also remember that during the twentieth century, heritage that was subjected to protection, and, therefore, conservation, expanded as much as the total cost of conservation. This situation was the result of three different elements. First of all, the extensive use of the conceptual definition of the term "culture" (up to that of "material culture"); a re-definition of the temporal obligation establishing when one can carry out conservation (the tendency being to conserve anything that is older than fifty, while in the past the obligation was at a hundred); finally, an explosion of manufactured products during this century, which is considerable when compared to centuries past.

The first paradox comes from the paradox called the "dying-art problem"[9]: How can we evaluate the cost-opportunity of the investment of resources for the conservation of an artistic form that is destined to die? This question does not just regard the quantity of the resources available but its actual survival.

The second conservation paradox

Considered as the maximization of the choice capacities of future generations, conservation involves the minimization of the consumption choices of the present generations[10], an impasse that can be put down to the intergenerational scarcity of resources.

Conservation policies are basically founded on protecting the interests of those who today are unable to decide whether people should be able to enjoy cultural heritage produced in the previous centuries in the future or not. Without knowing the preferences of the future generations, the tendency is to conserve the entire heritage of the past so that the future offers the greatest choice possible.

This is an extension of the conservation principle devised by Krutilla and Fisher in reference to environmental assets: Although there is no actual demand, society is supposed to have to be able to foresee the needs of future generations.[11] The principle of sustainable development – or the principle of constant capital – foresees the adoption of a specific position regarding the equity of the transfer of goods between people over time. The ethical reasoning is that future generations have the right to a heritage that guarantees them a level of well-being that is no less than that of the present generation. An intergenerational social contract is required that is founded on the premise of "justice as an opportunity", able to guarantee in the future the same opportunities that are available in the present.

This reasoning can only stand if one assumes that the conservation of cultural heritage is a value that is felt by all generations and does not change over time; likewise, in conditions of uncertainty, the present generation decides their own options, between conservation and the other uses of cultural heritage, are less important than the possibility of the option transmitted to future generations. If these two suppositions are removed, conservation could paradoxically be a cost for the current generation that sacrifices alternative uses of public resources, as it deems preferable, without producing the expected benefits for future generations.

The principle of intra-generational equity has been discussed in terms of the influence of public policy,[12] economic valuation of heritage[13], and sustainability.[14] Throsby[15] defines it as follows: "The intra-generational equity dilemma is a classic inter-temporal allocation problem – that is, a choice between present and future consumption." Both present and future consumption entail costs with respect to preservation and maintenance, but is it possible to define the first or second best option within this scenario? The point is to decide how far the principle of intra-generational equity and its authority should be applied, and what the impact is on the present generation exactly. As Taylor[16] points out, the problem that arises in any intra-generational consideration is whether an action or resource will be valued in the future. Is it possible to understand the needs of future generations that are not concurrent with our own? And should we accept that intergenerational equity should be limited by the intra-generational one?

There is one more matter to be dealt with: how important is cultural heritage compared to the satisfaction of a society's basic needs, or compared to any financial operation on this heritage? What could the substitution terms of an investment between the protection and destruction of heritage be?

The fact that an individual generally tends to prefer well-being in the present to in the future is rational, but it might prove unequal on the basis of the principle of equal treatment that imposes an "agent-neutral behaviour" that is impartial between the diverse figures who benefit. In a cooperative scheme, nobody has the right to act so that they themselves are advantaged, whilst damaging others: "The futures of our selves are something similar to those of future generations. We can make damage their destiny and as they do not yet exist, they are unable to defend themselves. Just like the future generations, the futures of ourselves have no right to vote and their future interests need to be protected".[17] Intergenerational and intra-generational equity must be established[18].

According to Jonas, one must not only consider the immediate consequences of our actions on our contemporaries, but also the more distant ones, beyond any possibility of reparation, taking into account the irreversibility of acts, behaviour, and ecological practices: "But the new imperative states that yes we can put our lives in danger but not that of humanity; [. . .] but that we do not have the right to choose or even risk the non-being of future generations in view of the being of the ones present now".[19] People must be guided by the ethical category of responsibility, they must "leave future generations a legacy of a land that is fit for humans to live in and not change the biological conditions of humanity; without this supposition, the generations would not be assuming their own responsibility".[20] This results in a pragmatic version of Kant's imperative: "Act in such a way that the consequences of your action are compatible with the permanence of authentic human life on earth, [...], act in such a way that the consequences of your action do not destroy the future possibility of such life; [...] include man's future integrity in your current choice as an object of your desire".[21]

According to Robinson, the broader protection of heritage has an economic yield known as the "recompense of waiting" or the "recompense of abstinence".[22] Rather than spending or consuming and, therefore, destroying cultural heritage, its owner (whether public or private) decides to conserve it. This decision could be taken in return in the form of the possibility of a very high yield linked to a real estate or financial project. Since cultural heritage is not an abundant resource (being unique and irreplaceable, a particular economic value is attributed to these assets), and since it does not meet a growing demand, an appropriate way to use it must be found.

The third conservation paradox

In view of the limited nature of the total resources available in a certain period, any marginal quantity that is destined to conserve X is subtracted from the conservation of Y (that represents a relative alternative). The alternative may be absolute: "Save X or save Y?" A decision that is extreme in relation to the absolute scantiness of relevant alternatives. It implies that in a time of scarce resources for cultural heritage, the decisions to save one building or cultural site almost invariably means that some other cultural buildings or sites cannot be saved. These decisions require difficult choices, based on a trade-off of interests among different stakeholders involved in the conservation and valorization process. In reaching these decisions, experts need to define and keep the rationale behind their approach and the detail of its implementation are clearly delineated and publicly available in the policies documents. This understanding and sharing of the cultural heritage sacrifice rationale is a fundamental requirement to maintain the existing and create new significance of the cultural heritage. Only in this way may the choices of the present generations be accepted by the future ones who will understand the sacrifices behind them that led to the present cultural heritage. This is an essential step in constructing both the cultural heritage process and heritage values. Being the one of the future, our generation is challenged by the need to make decisions regarding the significance of cultural heritage.

The fourth conservation paradox

The fourth conservation paradox is closely linked to the second: our society is conserving more and more heritage but is creating less and less. This desire to conserve everything so the heritage can be handed down to future generations implies that all resources are destined to this "investment in memory of handing down", without being able to support new creativity. Our age will, therefore, reach the point of transmitting the past (utopian hypothesis: it is impossible to conserve everything; conserving everything means not conserving anything), but it will be unable to transmit its own testimonies to future generations. A sedimentation process typical of the creation of heritage might be missing: every age leaves behind testimonies to the societies that follow, testimonies that, having acquired the status of cultural heritage, increasing the overall heritage that is to protected and passed on to future generations.

Taking no decision, or, rather, not deciding what should or should not be protected as heritage, leaving the task to future generations corresponds on the one hand to a titanic desire to conserve absolutely everything and on the other to a lack of confidence in one's own creative abilities. One is incapable of making a decision, doubting the validity of one's own artistic creations. To avoid this paradox a trade-off has to be defined between the handing down of memory and current creation, otherwise, the heritage being handed down would be static in nature, unable to operate the intergenerational exchange of creativity.

Being able to create in continuity is very important to escape the inevitable immobility that comes from the desire to want to conserve and classify everything. A sort of "capitalization of heritage" over time has to be asserted: on the one hand, intergenerational capitalization has to be established to valorise it economically, ensuring it does not disappear; on the other, long-term intergenerational capitalization that is able to distribute its benefits over a long term period is necessary.

The successive stage of conservation is represented by its reuse since the conservation intervention creates an added value, which is necessary to cover the growing costs of conservation and overcome its paradoxes. The act of conservation lays down the conditions for later interventions of an economic nature: In fact, the creation of added value implies the re-use of conserved heritage and this, in turn, implies the need for regeneration.

Can a cultural asset be regenerated?

The expression regeneration must be understood in the meaning of change, that is, the regeneration of a resource means modifying how it is used and its destination (and not just its temporary non-use to allow its renewal).[23] In the same way that land is regenerated by crop rotation (artificial cycle), woods by rational felling (artificial cycle), and the water and air by different (natural) cycles of hydrogen and oxygen, the regeneration of cultural heritage consists of intervening in the production or consumption processes it is an integral part of.

This intervention is basically carried out by paying particular attention to their destination and utilization standards. From this perspective regeneration can be interpreted as a historical destruction–reconstruction process (conservation as the 'hijacking of history by the ruling classes'), that makes regeneration seem like an arbitrary act.

First of all, we considered the logic that guides any conservation intervention. We then identified the added value induced by the conservation decision, which goes beyond any quantitative–objective evaluation, resulting from an appreciation–recognition of the historical value of the asset in question. Now comes the problem of identifying the agent that is to decide whether the proposal is valid.

$$\text{Vac} \rightarrow \text{Vc} - \text{Vnc} \geq \text{Cc} \quad (4)$$

This is no easy problem to solve because although it is possible to identify more than one agent (the market, the "mandarins", the rulers), this certification operation cannot be attributed to just one of them. While in the past conservation was regarded as an arbitrary act, now the non-intervention, the non-regeneration can be considered as follows:

non regeneration = lack of confidence in today's creative abilities

Let us now go on to apply what has been said so far on the regeneration process to a concrete case represented by a highly unique example of cultural heritage, Venice. In this case, regeneration is actually carried out with a change in how it is used, one that is necessary to break out of the vicious circle:[24]

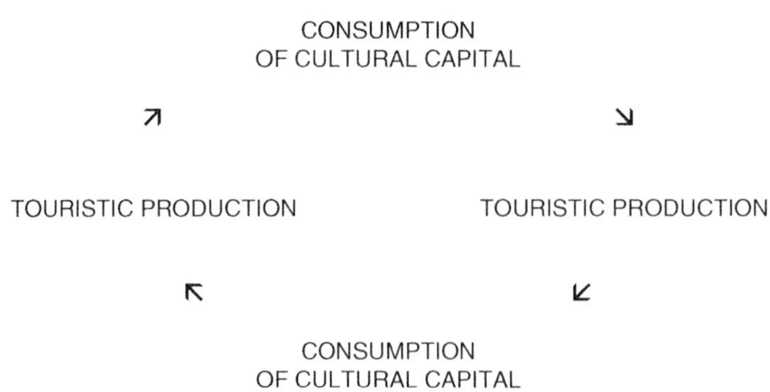

Culture becomes an input of the economic process; it is consumed in the city's productive process without any new forms being produced. The existing cultural capital is usually used until there is none left, and tourism, which can also be considered cultural and non, never takes any part in cultural production, only in its destruction.

Changing how it is used is the indispensable premise to break the vicious circle:

CONSUMPTION
OF CULTURAL CAPITAL

↗ ↘

NEW TOURISTIC OFFER NEW CULTURAL OFFER

↖ ↙

REGENERATION OF
CULTURAL CAPITAL

The vicious circle links economic growth, investments in art and culture and their external effects. Culture represents an instrument, a productive growth factor; in fact, its consumption implies the formulation of a new cultural offer, an increase in conservation investments that, in turn, create a new tourism offer.

This could be achieved by using specific political instruments. In particular, restoration investments aimed at the buildings' re-use, at its image and communicative activities, play an essential role here (Guggenheim paradox): the museum is not represented by its collection but by the building housing it). Another useful intervention is that of a decongestion investment, namely, that set of investments aimed at modifying and rationalizing the seasonal affluence of visits.

It is not the restoration that is fundamental but its re-use; in other words, restoration must not be an end in itself, but has to be part of the cultural heritage asset's restoration and re-insertion project in the socio-economic context, affirming *in toto* the nature of the cultural heritage as an asset that is really an economic-productive one.

Different concepts of conservation

Preservation in history or some history of conservation

Any economic treatment of the process of preserving the cultural and artistic heritage of the past and of the related decision-making processes must necessarily start from a very accurate definition of conservation itself.

This is not because of the usual fussy economists' attitude towards definitions but because the subject risks otherwise being strongly undetermined. The meaning of conservation has changed over time and its current cultural and technical significance is substantially different from that in the Middle-Ages or even in the eighteenth century.

The ancient way of thinking about conservation is linked with an effective re-use of the good to be conserved: *reficere* in Latin. The head of a statue of the Roman Empress Livia used in the eleventh century as the face of Christ in the Herimankreuz, conserved in Cologne, is a good example of this approach which originated in pre-Medieval times and prevailed throughout Europe until the late seventeenth century. The re-make of ancient paintings (*ridipintura*) as regards their iconographic content but also with relevant integrations, is the rule followed in many famous cases like Ambrogio Lorenzetti's Buongoverno and Simone Martini's Guidoriccio da Fogliano 14th century "rifacimenti" in Siena.[25] Restoration in the sense of restoring original works of art to their previous state belongs to the seventeenth century, the first relevant case probably being that of the "pubbliche pitture" in Palazzo Ducale in Venice, by Giambattista Rossi, Sebastiano Ricci, and later on, Pietro Edwards, the first of the great restorers of our times.[26]

It was only during the nineteenth century, however, that the current conservative goals grounding our concept of preservation were progressively adopted by states like France, aiming effectively to preserve the heritage of the past in its integrity, mainly for educational purposes as it was to succeed in doing by founding the Louvre.[27]

The philological unearthing of the past and the extension of the domain to be protected to all the existing heritage which characterize present operations, dates only from the late nineteenth century.

Different economic concepts of conservation

These different definitions of conservation have different economic consequences not only for the utilization of the good they refer to but, more generally, for the way in which the value of the good is determined, and, therefore, for the answer to the crucial questions raised by any conservation process: what to preserve, at what price, for whom?

Conservation as reficere

If Hale and Gold's approach[28] is adopted regarding conservation, namely, that conservation is a *reficere*, a reworking or reutilization of the existing heritage, as a result the effectiveness of the intervention or, on the contrary, the use of the resources (financial, physical) available for other uses can be evaluated on the basis of a simple equation[29]:

$$Vn - Cn \geq Vo + Do \tag{5}$$

where

Vn = market value of the good in the new use
Cn = production cost of the new use
Vo = market value of the good in the previous destination
Do = destruction cost of the previous destination.

From this equation, which defines the value of the good subjected to conservation in the form of reworking, we have the logical justification that must characterize any conservation choice, that the worth of the restored good (market value of the good according to its new destination, net of the production costs required to achieve its new destination) must be greater or equal to the sum of the market value of the good (Vo) and the destruction cost of the good in its previous destination (Do). The first expression has to be greater than the second otherwise this conservation intervention is unacceptable for the perspective of economic rationality. If the market trend of the new structures (defined on the basis of the destruction–restoration cost) is greater than the current market value, it must be destroyed; should the contrary be the case, the existing structure must be protected. In this case, the social cost is insignificant as is the redivision of the rights over the good because it is the market that takes care of the effective definition of the best solutions (this is the market situation for a private good). In the presence of perfectly competitive markets, the market distributes the available resources rationally and efficiently. It indicates what the good should be used for, how the resources should be "directed" towards different sectors and activities where the most profitable investments are to be seen. The market determines the optimal level of the production and price of the good and services exchanged on the basis of the offer–demand interaction. From this perspective, any intervention by the State to modify how the market is functioning would be totally ineffective.

The destruction of the good is, therefore, based on a decision of market price and the consumers are indifferent to whether the original good exists or not.

Conservation as restoration

Compared to the previous case, in this definition, the possibility of destroying the good that is to be destroyed is not taken into consideration and the consumers are not indifferent to whether the original good exists or not, unlike in the previous situation in which the decision to destroy the good depended on the market price alone. No destruction of the previous destination of the good is included in this definition, while the good is still conceived as strictly private in the economic sense, as far as its excludability and rivalry of consumption are concerned.

In this case, the other consumers are not indifferent to the existence or inexistence of the original good as they were in the former where its destruction was decided simply on a market price basis. While the previous concept excluded any external positive effect caused by the existence of the original good, this one specifically includes the presence of an excludable externality, to be eventually appropriated by the agents. As the externality is excludable, the market price will include its value and no free-riding will be possible; that is, it will be the case of a willingness-to-pay-based optimum solution. In ancient Venice the cost of restoring the paintings in Palazzo Ducale was shared by those who benefited from it (the members of the noble families who met there and held ceremonies and received ambassadors there, to develop Venetian trade and economic influence; they were also the main tax-payers of the Republic). More generally, Maecenas in those times were essentially interested in the enhancement of their economic or political image deriving from the investment in art or its restoration. Restoration could, therefore, be seen an investment, with its own costs and returns. The main objective of this conservation was clearly of an economic nature[30].

In this case, the value of the restored good may, therefore, be defined as:

$$Vn - Cn \geq Vo \tag{6}$$

where

Vn = market value of the restored good (including its external excludable effect);

Cn = cost of restoration,

Vo = market value of the good before restoration (including its external excludable effect).

The market does, in principle, assure the social optimum here, too.

Conservation as preservation

The economic significance of this last definition of conservation is somewhat different. The way in which the good is economically conceived has changed. It is no longer a strictly private good. It becomes a semi-public one, whose nature is affected by partial non-excludability and non-rivalry of consumption. Public interest comes into account together with the information asymmetry typical of artistic goods, causing strategic anomalies like free-riding consumer behaviour and information-based rent-seeking.

The appreciation of the artistic quality of a good is conditioned by the ability of the producer to "create" or of the consumer to "interpret" it, which is not distributed homogeneously among the agents. A specific case of market failure can occur when one of them (the supplier/demander) is endowed with it, while the other (the demander/supplier) is not.[31] Someone certifying the good as "artistic" (critics, art historians, merchants, etc.) is needed to determine social optima on the market (as well as out of it).

The value of the preserved good, under these assumptions, is, therefore, the following:

$$Vn - Cn + An \geq Vo + Ao \tag{7}$$

where

Vn = is the market value of the preserved good (which also includes its external excludability or divisibility effect);

Cn = the preservation cost;

An = the historical and aesthetical value of the good after preservation;

Vo = the market value of the good before preservation (which includes its excludability or divisibility effect);

Ao = the historical and aesthetical value of the good before preservation.

Social costs are relevant here as is the distribution of decision-making rights, as they are decisive in defining the value of An and Ao. The market does not supply optimum solutions by itself.

If we suppose that that market is to effectively determine Vn, Cn e Vo, we have to define An and Ao. If Ao = 0, then:

$$Vn - Cn + An \geq Vo \tag{8}$$

In this case, the heritage good will be preserved if the condition An > 0 is met.

Preservation, therefore, implies the attribution of an added value of an aesthetical and historical nature to a specific heritage good that implies an increase in social wellbeing.

The seventh expression can also be written differently:

$$(Vn - Vo) + (An - Ao) \geq Cn \tag{9}$$

if Ao = 0

and Vn = Vo

then, we will find ourselves in a situation in which:

$$An \geq Cn \tag{10}$$

The fundamental condition for any preservation choice is, therefore: The difference between the preservation costs, determined by the market, and the historical and artistic value of the preserved good, the definition of which is extraneous to the market.

Conclusions

The purpose of this chapter is not to propose concrete solutions but rather to encourage discussion and debate regarding the paradoxes that the conservation process may imply and the economic calculation of cultural heritage conservation on a number of levels. Firstly, we have critically analysed the paradoxes raised by the conservation process that may sometimes restrict the extent of its action, very often making the actual conservation intervention problematic. Secondly, we have demonstrated that it is possible to regenerate cultural heritage by activating and increasing the cultural capital. Thirdly, we have identified the different economic meanings of the conservation concept, taking into account the values and interests of different stakeholders involved in the conservation process.

A better understanding of the economic implications and relationship between the economic valuation and the heritage conservation narratives is expected to imply more rational uses of resources, making clear the need to keep the already existing significance and producing new significance within the cultural heritage to make valuable and productive the transfer of knowledge and memory from the past to the present and future generations.

Notes

1 Mason, R. (2008), "Be interested and beware: joining economic valuation and heritage conservation", *International Journal for Heritage Studies*, Vol. 14, No. 4, pp. 303–318.

2 Peacock, A. (1994), "A future for the past: The political economy of heritage. Lecture at the British Academy, 27th October 1994", *Proceedings of the British Academy*, Vol. 87, pp. 189–243; Mossetto, G. & Vecco, M. (2001), *Economia del patrimonio monumentale*. Milan: F. Angeli; Vecco, M. (2005), *L'évolution économique du concept de conservation*. Thèse pour obtenir le grade de Docteur de l'Université Paris 1, Panthéon-Sorbonne, U.F.R. Science économiques, 26 Novembre 2005. Paris: l'Université Paris; Mossetto, G. & Vecco, M. (2006), *Some Economics of Conservation of Cultural Heritage*. Conference proceeding International Art Symposium, 30th November – 2nd December 2006. Canakkale: Canakkale Onsekiz Mart University; Vecco, M. (2007). *Economie du patrimoine monumental*. Paris: Economica.

3 The valorization of heritage can be regarded as a construction process and not just a legacy of history. According to Alain Rallet, the heritage good is initially an immaterial construction, a set of representations that can be inherited or not from the past; it is up to the community in question to animate it and valorise it correctly: "un patrimoine inventé vaut mieux qu'un héritage non exploité. Un certain nombre de territoires ont manifesté sur ce plan un dynamisme remarquable en faisant apparaître comme des traditions ancestrales des phénomènes qui ont tout au plus trente ou quarante ans d'âge ou en faisant surgir de rien des festivals qui comptent aujourd'hui" (Rallet A. (1995), "Le patrimoine et l'économie" in Délégation à l'aménagement du territoire et à l'action régionale, *Les pôles d'économie du patrimoine: définitions et orientations métho-dologiques*, Paris, DATAR, p. 58).

4 Jacobs, J. (1961), *The death and life of great American cities*, New York: Random House.

5 Vaughan, D. (1984), "The cultural heritage: An approach to analyse income and employment effects", *Journal of Cultural Economics*, Vol. 8, No. 1, pp. 1–36; Nijkamp, P. (1988), "Cultural and region: A multidimensional evaluation of monuments", *Environmental & planning: Planning and design*, Vol. 15, pp. 5–14; Lichfield, N. (1988), *Economics in urban conservation*. Cambridge: Cambridge University Press.

6 The same concept was expressed by Fusco Girard and Nijkamp using the total economic value (Fusco Girard L., Nijkamp P. (1997). *Le valutazioni per lo sviluppo sostenibile del territorio*. Milan: F.

Angeli, p. 104). According to the two authors the TEV represents the "measure" of the economic benefits that could be lost when one decides to transform a specific zone, in other words, cost-opportunity. Formally, a transformation hypothesis can only be accepted if the net benefits are positive, after having also considered the cost-opportunity:
if $V_{present} (B_{trans} - C_{trans} - VET) > 0$ the project is acceptable,
if $V_{present} (B_{trans} - C_{trans} - VET) < 0$ the project is unacceptable.

7 Jeudy, H.P. (2001), *La Machinerie patrimoniale*. Paris: Sens & Tonka.

8 Buchanan, C. (1975), "Cities in crisis", *The Planner,* Vol. 61, No.7, pp. 264. As regards the extremism of conservation, we can mention Buchanan's observations: "What happens when everything is conserved? When conservation is expanded to such an extent that one can no longer walk without tripping over some object of veneration, what happens then? Does the danger exist one will become a prisoner of the past, being trapped in a network of bureaucratic paperwork in an uncreative world?" (Buchanan, C., 1975).

9 Mossetto, G. (1994), "The economic dilemma of heritage preservation". In A. Peacock and I. Rizzo (Ed.). *Cultural economics and cultural policies*. Dordrecht: Kluwer Academic Publishers; Mossetto, G. (1993), *Aesthetics and economics*. Dordrecht: Kluwer Academic Publishers. ("How can we judge the opportunity cost of investing resources in preservation of an art form which is otherwise bound to die, the issue being not only the available quantity of the resource but its survival. [...] As resources are scarce, how can we decide which art has to die and which has to survive?"). Another two paradoxes are linked to this one: the paradox of the future generations and that of the optional consumer: on the one hand, since the future generations do not yet exist it is difficult to foresee how they will view the conserved heritage; on the other, the optional consumer does not immediately express his/her intention to consume the heritage and therefore its utility level, but could do so later. See also Peacock, A. (1978), "Preserving the past: An international economic dilemma", *Journal of Cultural Economics*, Vol. 2, No.2, pp. 1–12 and Peacock, A. (1994), "A future for the past: The political economy of heritage. Lecture at the British Academy, 27th October 1994", *Proceedings of the British Academy*, Vol. 87, pp. 189–243.

10 The slogan of this approach could be Jacques Duhamel's formula: "Mieux vaut mille monuments pour cinquante ans que cinquante monuments pour mille ans" (*Discours de Jacques Duhamel devant l'Assemblée nationale, 28 mai 1971*, éd. dans J. Duhamel (1973), *Discours et écrits* (1971–1973). Paris : La Documentation française/Comité d'histoire du Ministère de la culture, p. 52, quoted by Laurent X. (2003), *Grandeur et misère du patrimoine. D'André Malraux à Jacques Duhamel, 1959–1973*, 87, Paris/Chartres, Comité d'histoire du Ministère de la culture et de la communication/École nationale de Chartres).

11 Krutilla J.V. and A. C. Fisher (1985), *The economics of natural environments*, Baltimore, MD: John Hopkins Press.

12 Baer, N.S., and Snickars, F. (2001), *Rational decision-making in the preservation of cultural property*. Berlin: Dahlem University Press.

13 Throsby, D. (2002), Cultural capital and sustainability concepts in the economics of cultural heritage. In M. de la Torre (Ed.). *Assessing the value of cultural heritage*, 101–117. Los Angeles, CA: Getty Conservation Institute.

14 Cassar, M. (2003), Places and stuff: Is it only the language of conservation that is changing? In D. Watt and B. Colston (Ed.), *Conservation of historic buildings and their contents: Addressing the conflicts*, 41–51. Shaftesbury: Don Head Publishing and De Montfort University.

15 Throsby, *op.cit.*

16 Taylor, J. (2013), "Intergenerational justice: A useful perspective for heritage conservation". In *CeROArt: Conservation, Exposition, Restauration d'Objets d'Art*. Accessed July 14, 2014, from: http://ceroart.revues.org/3510.

17 Parfit D. (1984), *Reasons and persons*, p. 45, Oxford: Claredon Press.

18 "[...] the intergenerational equity principle requires the interests of future generations in the project outcomes to be acknowledged. This might to be pursued in several different ways. In quantitative terms, respect for intergenerational concerns might suggest adoption of a lower discount rate than might be otherwise accepted on time-preference or opportunity-cost grounds in the process of reducing both economic and cultural benefits streams to present value terms. In qualitative terms, the issue of fairness itself should be explicitly considered in terms of the ethical or moral dimensions of taking account of the likely effect of the project on future generations. [...], the principle of intra-generational equity would recognize the welfare effects of the heritage project on the present

generation. Consideration might be given to the distributional impacts of the capital costs of the investment project under study, to identify whether any regressive effects might be present" (Throsby, D. (2001), *Economics and culture*. Cambridge: Cambridge University Press, p. 87). See also: Turner, R.K., Pearce, D.W., and Bateman, I.J. (1994), *Environmental economics: An elementary introduction*. Baltimore: Harvester Wheatsheaf and John Hopkins University: pp. 47–48.

19 Jonas, H. (1985), *The imperative of responsibility: in search of an ethics for the technological age*, p. 17, Chicago and London: The Chicago University Press.

20 *Ibid*.

21 *Ibid*.

22 Robinson, J. (1959, 1969). *The accumulation of capital*. New York: Palgrave McMillan.

23 Vecco, M. (2007), *Economie du patrimoine monumental*. Paris: Economica.

24 Mossetto, G. (1992), *L'economia delle città d'arte*: Milan: Etaslibri; Mossetto, G. & M. Vecco (2001), *op. cit*.

25 Conti, A. (1988), *Storia del restauro e della conservazione delle opere d'arte*. Milan: Electa.

26 *Ibid*.

27 *Ibid*.

28 Gold, A. (1975), "Welfare economics of historical preservation", *Connecticut Law Review*, Vol. 8, pp. 348–369; Hale, R. D. (1978), "Economics aspects of historic preservation", *Journal of Cultural Economics*, Vol. 2, No. 2, pp. 43–53.

29 The value of the conserved good can be expressed in the same way.

30 Analysing the case of ancient Venice, Mossetto states that this is a "dependent economy" model in which culture was an instrument of the economy: investment and culture consumption were the instruments used to accelerate economic growth. Investments in art/culture were a display of the city's power and economic success. Mossetto (1992), *op. cit.*; Mossetto G. & M. Vecco (2001), *op. cit.*; Vecco (2007), *op. cit*.

31 Mossetto (1993), *op.cit*.

12 Information and communication technologies in cultural heritage management

Turgay Kerem Koramaz

Introduction

Information and communication technologies (ICT) have brought many challenges and opportunities in cultural heritage management, which requires accurate and reliable documentation abilities and procedures, possibly more than any other discipline. While sustaining this ability, tools of ICT can be classified under three titles in terms of their abilities (or functions), that is, data acquisition and documentation, communication and interaction, comprehensive and analytic evaluations. Through the use of ICT, cultural heritage can be documented, classified, and surveyed in automated systems with high accuracy and reliable data acquisition methods like photogrammetry, laser scanning, and remote sensing. The second function of ICT, in that context, is its communication and interaction ability, which refers to the sharing of information among users with web-based and/or user-oriented dynamic recovery, by increasing public awareness and involvement in cultural heritage management. Since cultural heritage (particularly immovable cultural heritage) needs comprehensive and analytical evaluations in its spatial, topological, locational contexts, ICT also responds to these investigations, as named here as the third function.

This chapter discusses the role and contributions of ICT in cultural heritage management while seeking to respond to two major questions. The first one is "to what extent can the fundamental contributions of ICT be integrated into the enrichment of cultural heritage management?" When responding to this question in various dimensions, conservation challenges are described within the cultural heritage management concept. The era of the information age, with its new communication channels such as the internet, mobile communication, and social media, also corresponds to the semantic extension of cultural heritage. Such an extension of the meaning causes a mandatory paradigm shift in professional, social, and political expressions, associated with emerging contexts such as knowledge economies, information law, and policies . In spite of the challenges of becoming widespread, geographic information systems (GIS) can be commemorated as a revolution in cultural heritage management, which is also triggered by this paradigm shift, especially in the fields of archaeology, restoration, and urban conservation.

The second question that this chapter tries to answer is "to what extent can new forms of ICT increase immersive senses for cultural heritage and communication among cultural stakeholders?" Recent studies related to the conservation of cultural heritage indicated that ICT tools, such as multimedia interfaces, virtual and augmented reality applications, and three-dimensional (3D) visualization techniques, provide different spatial and visual content and increase the level of interaction and communication among various user groups more than conventional documentation and visualization techniques.

After this brief introduction, the chapter continues with an evolution of ICT in chronological perspective in the second section. The next sections provide some information to answer the aforementioned questions in a literature review approach. Literature will be reviewed theoretically in the centre line of Arnold and Geser [1], Silberman [2], and Veltman's [3] key literature that discuss the contribution of ICT to the enrichment of cultural heritage management. Additionally, the article presents the fundamental remarks of empirical studies [4–7] that evaluate the progressive cases, in other words, new forms of ICT tools that increase the immersive senses for cultural heritage and communication among stakeholders. The conclusion section will highlight the facilities of these technologies with both operational and participatory functions in the conservation of cultural heritage. The chapter finalizes the argument of ICT use in cultural heritage management with its attitudes of transitioning a community into an information society.

Brief evolution of ICT

The emergence and rise of the internet can be seen as the first paradigm shift in terms of the evolution of ICT, but the first computer microprocessor, produced by Intel in 1971, has been interpreted as the emergence of the age of information and telecommunication [8]. The internet that we use today dates back to the period of 1985–1995, when NSFNET (the emergence of entire internet structure) was initiated as a program in order to support and promote networking among U.S. research and education institutions (website of NSFNET celebration event [the partnership that changed the World], 2007; http://www.nsfnet-legacy.org/about.php). Internet technology is the major component of the information age, which alters the interaction between the state and society [9] and carries a strong belief in the power of democratic transition in the existing political systems [10].

After the 1990s, information technology has been regarded as a strong means for economic growth especially for liberal economies, following the European Union (EU) decisions and, especially, the Bangemann Report [11], which recommends a common regulatory to construct a Europe-wide market for information services. This entrepreneurial mentality has been fostered by a harsh liberalization of national telecommunication companies in the member countries as the first permanent step of this shift of the economic system. On the other side of the Atlantic, in 1993, the U.S. Clinton–Gore administration, founded the National Information Infrastructure Act [12], which proposes information superhighways across the country, and even the world. As a reflection of the emerging policy, quoted from Gore, "a global information marketplace where consumers can buy and sell" [13:17], e-commerce was promoted across the world, where $55 billion-retail sale in 2004 (which counts for 1.6% of the total sale) were held with e-commerce but the annual growth rate of online shopping was 26% in the same year [14].

At the Marrakesh Summit of the World Trade Organization in 1994 [15], telecommunication was regarded as a service and subject to progressive liberalization of the trade framework. Turkey approved this agreement in 1996. Since the agreement offers regulations for the privatization of telecommunication services, as another international document, the UN World Summits on the Information Society, in Geneva [16] and Tunis [17], designated communication as a human right. These summits were the first international events bringing global multi-stakeholders together in order to frame the principles of a people-centred information society and the notions of culture, identity, and citizenship. After this era, accessibility to ICT has been regarded as a social right.

The 21st century is mainly characterized by a knowledge economy, where significant structural and institutional changes have occurred and the value of knowledge depends on how it is spread through society and institutions. Information has been interpreted as an economic resource and a product, exchanged in the market, primarily the internet and other ICT applications have succeeded in reducing transaction costs, to increasing skilled labour and changing the institutional structures and professions[18], as well as cultural heritage management.

From the very beginning of the 2000s, the EU attempted to create action and strategic documents, to construct a dynamic knowledge-based European market with a skilled and flexible workforce; competitive market; and the promotion of innovation in the ICT sector. Documents signed in 2005, as part of the i2010 strategy, highlighted policies about media literacy; ICT access for rural; digital integration; ICT workforce, established e-government action plans; and digital libraries [19].

ICT tools in cultural heritage management

In cultural heritage management, inventory, documentation, analytical evaluation, and implementation of restoration proposals, the use of ICT has been vitally important to improve the capacity of work and decrease the time spent. Innovative ICT tools such as digital information storing and software tools [20] could also add significance to the evaluation of the value of cultural heritage. Some of the most common ICT tools were CAD-generated visualization and documentation techniques that enable volumetric and manual measurement of cultural heritage with high geometric content, in its earlier applications. For instance, analyzing and representing the visual details could be achieved with low cost, time, and good performance [21], encouraging communication in the cultural heritage management process.

ICT tools are applied in cultural heritage management in three ways. First, 3D models apply architectural photogrammetry to delineate and archive the physical characteristics of the cultural heritage. These models can be constructed for an urban settlement [22] or even a sculpture [23]. The main purpose of these applications in photogrammetry is documenting and surveying the cultural heritage using automated systems with high accuracy. The second is virtual reality (VR) and augmented reality (AR) applications that offer an interactive database in the cultural heritage management processes. VR applications can be used in urban models [24] or most commonly in museums and digital collections. Although conventional types of digital archiving can be used with online collections like the British Museum and Vatican Museum, there are virtual museums, which are better to sustain the web-based and user-oriented dynamic recovery of museum information in an immersive digital environment (like the Smithsonian National Museum of Natural History and Oriental Institute Museum). Besides online digital collections, museums can also benefit from the installation of VR platforms, where assets of cultural heritage can be experienced in an immersive environment next to conventionally exhibited materials. A recent and successfully applied VR platform is from "The Curious Case of Çatalhöyük" exhibition, held in Istanbul – ANAMED, Koc University, Research Center for Anatolian Civilizations (for detailed information: https://anamed.ku.edu.tr/en/curious-case-catalhoyuk; https://www.upf.edu/web/leap/resum-projecte). The collection, which integrates different ICT tools, such as laser-scanned and 3D-printed materials from the archaeological excavations and immersive VR environment enhance the experiment-based display features for its visitors. In addition to VR technology, AR applications enhanced virtuality functions, through overlapped virtual objects in the real environment, so that the users can perceive virtual content merged with reality. AR tools are a recent innovation in cultural heritage management, which can enrich the perceived enjoyment and usefulness for the users [25]. The third and the last set of these applications are ICT tools that are built for the purpose of comprehensive analytical evaluation. Especially in the conservation of archaeological sites and urban historic sites, spatial analyses based on GIS [26] are useful for the purposes of client-based information integration in the areas of media, urban, and tourism services, real estate, and other economic activities.

Accuracy, realism, and abstraction are identified as the main indicators for the efficiency of the aforementioned ICT tools. High-profile realistic models of cultural heritage sites or civil architecture examples may be digitally produced with a perfect consideration of accuracy, which also may generate a "dizziness of technological success" [27]. Especially in architectural representations, material, texture, and light and shadow effects in computer-generated renderings and images can manipulate viewers' perception of visual content in the favour of what the designers may desire to express. Conversely, there should be computer-generated models which represent the visual content with a high level of reality, for the documentation and surveying of historic monuments and unique heritage that are lost or in danger of being lost. But in the cases of conservation, site modelling, and visualization, where the size and mass of the structures are subject to evaluation, abstract models with less realistic effects are preferable in order to respond to prior design feedback from different stakeholders in the participation process [28].

Investigation of the effectiveness of ICT tools in the cultural management process is vital to conservation and restoration studies devoted to sustaining communication and collaboration among different actors, such as professionals and non-professionals. There have been many different evaluation methodologies to investigate user responses for ICT tools, such as cognitive evaluation, comparative experiments, and observational studies to compare the efficiency levels of challenging tools and techniques [29]. The efficiency levels of changing ICT tools in terms of users and/or viewers comprehension and appraisal for cultural heritage, may correspond to abilities to improve learning skills [30] and cognition processes with preferences of users [31–33].

The contribution of ICT to the enrichment of cultural heritage management

The contribution of ICT is basically described by the standardizing processes for data capture, networking, and interoperability as primary strategies in cultural heritage management [1]. However, Silberman [2] advocates that ICT use in cultural heritage has emerged a new multidisciplinary form of historiography with its broader context. Technological advances and facilities brought to cultural heritage management should not only be linked with entire contributions but the encouragement of a transition of cultural heritage meaning and content toward a more inclusive, supportable, meaningful activity. Although many scholars employed in cultural heritage management may restrict themselves only to the improvement of digital recording, data processing, and communication technologies, the recent agenda related to this profession has addressed the widening of the meaning of cultural heritage and strategies for management activities. Consequently, the contribution of ICT for cultural heritage management should be questioned not only in relation to technological advances but also the requirements and needs of the information age [2].

In accordance with the social and economic objectives of the established network in the Sixth Framework Programme of European Commission, EPOCH (European Network of Excellence in Open Cultural Heritage), a clear organizational and disciplinary framework is necessary to increase the effectiveness of work at the interface between technology and the cultural heritage and the human of monuments, sites, and museums. Within the consideration of the EPOCH framework, Silberman [2] described the challenges of ICT for cultural heritage resources which are listed as conservation, intellectual, socio-economic, and cultural challenges.

Many scholars may address the conservation challenges, defined by the technological advances in terms of the creation of reliable, permanent, and distributed repositories [3]. Cultural heritage management should, thus, not be just linked with conventional restoration and consolidation works. A cultural "biosphere," can be offered not only with best practices of conservation, but also through the enrichment of the public sense related to the perception of time and historical orientation [34]. For instance, the photogrammetric studies for the virtual reconstruction of the demolished Great Buddha of Bamiyan in Afghanistan [35] is so significant in the sense of time and historical orientation as the heritage site will not be restored due to political reasons.

The second challenge, refers to intellectual challenges and fragmentation of historical scholarship. Cultural heritage research paradigms may vary with approaches that scholars and professionals interpret. Since academic institutions seek to put forward research and examinations in hypothetical considerations, their approaches can be seen as *analytical*; institutions, in charge of exhibiting and archiving the cultural heritage, mostly deal with the *communicative* function of collected, exhibited, and conveyed heritage [2]. The task of governmental institutions, which differs from the aforementioned stakeholders, is *administrative* and mainly involves the regulation of moveable and immovable heritage resources, through legislation related to documentation, conservation, and enforcement. There is another aspect of this challenge which can be described by anti-technology arguments among these scholars [3]. Some may perceive innovative ICT as a threat to be opposed instead of interpreting them as a human-originated tool to facilitate evaluation and assessment [36].

The third challenge of ICT for cultural heritage resources, socio-economic challenges, refers, primarily, to the issue of marketization of cultural heritage [2]. In the early international charters for conservation and restoration, documentation and archiving of cultural heritage were mentioned as a public responsibility (International Council on Monuments and Sites, ICOMOS, Venice Charter in 1964). Then cultural heritage gained a broader status as a "moral obligation upon all human beings", which transformed governmental responsibilities in relation to the conservation of cultural heritage into a "collective public responsibility" (ICOMOS, Charter for the Protection and Management of the Archaeological Heritage, 1990). Thanks to the following charter of ICOMOS, the conservation of cultural heritage was progressively related with cooperation with governmental authorities, private firms, and non-profit associations (ICOMOS, 1998), due to the efficiency and economic performance, and distinctive skills that these firms and associations offered in cultural heritage management. On the contrary, this neo-liberalization approach may be criticized with the argument that the packaging and promotion of cultural heritage can make them structured and marketed as income generating "attractions", in the cultural agenda [37] and then they can even be subject to transformation into consumption places with the loss of cultural identity, called Disneyfication or Sonyconstruction [38].

The fourth challenge, which is related to the discussion of heritage and identity issues comprising ethnic and cultural diversity, is the cultural challenge [2]. The social function of ICT tools in cultural heritage management is mainly described as the enhanced access to cultural heritage and related activities. From this concept emerges an important issue in terms of the information society, which is called the digital divide. Within the establishment of e-heritage, ICT can overcome the digital divide [39], which means economic and social convergence among different classes in their access to, use of, or knowledge of ICT [40]. The most common e-heritage applications, web and mobile technologies for cultural heritage information, may enhance the relationship between public and cultural heritage institutions, in other words, contributing to democratization. Empirical studies, concerning the contribution of web and mobile technologies to cultural memory, indicated the importance of new forms of participation and public involvement in cultural heritage management, which highlight a bottom-up information share approach (e.g., blogs, forums, and social media), rather than a top-down approach (e.g., official websites) to the presentation of heritage material [41].

New forms of ICT to increase immersive senses for cultural heritage and communication among stakeholders

New forms of ICT tools and virtual reality are essential to transfer and share information and achieve communication in cultural heritage management. In parallel with the advances in ICT, after the 1990s, many scholars employed discussions of information and communication theory via ICT applications in urban planning, design, and architecture, as well as in subjects concerned with immovable cultural assets. Public involvement, participation, and collaboration among different actors (professionals, decision makers, and public entities) can be enhanced with ICT in interaction functions [42], and with VR applications enriched with immersive senses [20]. VR, referred to as immersive multimedia, is not only a computer-simulated environment which simulates (or imitates) physical presence in places in the real world, but it is a strong means, in order to provide communication in planning and design [43]. When considering cultural heritage management, virtual modelling of cultural heritage sites and monuments, or virtual museums, may respond to this function and serve as a tool for communication.

As previously mentioned, the bottom-up information share approach cannot be achieved unless professionals and non-professionals are involved together in different stages of cultural heritage management. If the sharing of information is originated in one direction without any interaction (as the flow is supposed to be from professionals to non-professionals; from innovators to laggards) the role of the stakeholders cannot be enriched in efficient collaboration processes [44]. Blogs, forums, and social and crowdsourcing media can be classified in response to the enrichment of ICT tools, providing efficient collaboration processes of cultural heritage management. (NextIstanbul can be given as an example of inventory by crowdsourcing; the project has one online mapping tool, titled as preservation and change map, where users locate the cultural heritage spots whether they would prefer to preserve or change that certain point. For further information: www.nextistanbul.org/preservation-map/.)

Emerging ICT tools for conveying heritage content to different stakeholders can also enhance the possibilities to promote an effective market for cultural heritage [6]. 3D realistic visualization and VR, multimedia, wireless PDA (personal digital assistant) visitor guides, and AR applications are the most commonly utilized tools which increase communication and immersive senses of the users and provide a powerful perception of cultural heritage. Since the latest technologies need more budgets in cultural heritage management, expensive ICT-based heritage projects should be carefully accomplished considering possible irremediable failures and inadequacies [45].

In the conservation of cultural heritage sites and monuments, restaurateurs, architects, designers, and planners still use Computer-aided Design (CAD) software mostly in mapping purposes for both depicting the actual state or planning and design alternatives [7] rather than Geographic Information System (GIS) [4]. CAD, assembling an exact mathematical input of object and environment geometry, creates a 2D visualization construction document and 3D physical models to visualize and interpret data as a presentation tool with powerful visual simulation [46]. On the other hand, GIS is a software system which can gather, query, manage, store, analyze, interpret, and visualize all types of spatial or geographical data [47]. Although this system is not common in cultural heritage management except archaeology, as the main functions of GIS such as knowledge acquisition processes, exploratory spatial data analysis, decision-making process, implementation, and monitoring can be delivered into the related cultural heritage studies, which may have spatial, topological or geographical contexts.

In the conservation of cultural heritage sites, urban planning and urban design are key subjects; and urban planners and architects are authorized professions in heritage site management. Planners and architects should employ ICT tools in the heritage site management processes, and should establish policies and strategies highlighting the importance of the information society and the new meaning of heritage, transferred with the advances in technology. As a critical example, the Istanbul Historic Peninsula Site Management Plan has a significant strategy under the title of realization and financial resources that includes knowledge, human resources, and technology in the realization of entire actions in the plan [48]. Then planners' and architects' preferences and appraisals based on ICT and computer-based visualization tools are significant in not only planning procedures but also in the measurement of the performance of these technologies. Despite the changing level of prioritization of the responses by professionals of urban planning, design, conservation, and architecture and non-professionals [49], the most important features of ICT and computer-based visualization tools can be classified as below:

- "Explanation ability of conservation project and interventions to structural and visual quality of urban historic environments,
- Representation ability of change in the historic townscape of urban environments,
- Improvement of the cognition and perception levels of urban historic environments with the creation of spatial unity, enclosedness and affection sense" [50:41].

Conclusions

This chapter, titled "Information and Communication Technologies in Cultural Heritage Management", established a brief framework which defines the abilities and functions of ICT in different stages of cultural heritage management process such as inventory, data acquisition, documentation, analytic evaluations, and communication. This chapter discusses the role and contributions of ICT in cultural heritage management while seeking to respond to two major questions of how "contributions of ICT can be integrated into the enrichment of cultural heritage management" and how "new forms of ICT increase immersive senses for cultural heritage". The chapter gives a summarized literature review on chronological, theoretical, and empirical perspectives.

Since the meaning of cultural heritage has been widened toward a more inclusive, supportable activity, ICT plays a critical role in the enrichment of public sense related to the perception of time and historical orientation. Another role of ICT can be defined with the claim of the elimination of the digital divide that briefly referred to economic and social convergence among different classes in terms of use and access to technology. A bottom-up information share approach, where users participate in all stages of cultural heritage management without bureaucratic procedures may overcome the digital divide challenges. In other words, the establishment of official websites (referred to as a top-down approach, here) with limited and strict content in online cultural heritage material is not adequate for the sharing of information and communication. Involvement of different stakeholders like professionals, decision-makers, and the public is necessary in different stages, for instance, the knowledge acquisition process and decision-making process can be combined in a circular feed-back with the participation of non-professionals. With the rise of the "e-Heritage" concept, technology (such as digital museums, interactive platforms for digital documentation and archival, internet and mobile applications, crowdsourcing communication channels and social media, smart city applications, VR and AR tools) will eventually form part of the transformative attitudes of the information society through all segments of the community, encouraging participation and collaboration in the cultural heritage management processes [51]. In relation to technical procedures in cultural heritage management, further research includes exploratory spatial data analysis of cultural heritage in a broader context and ICT-oriented implementation and monitoring mechanisms for the use of representatives of governmental and non-governmental bodies.

ICT tools should be employed and enhanced in cultural heritage management, with related policies and strategies that highlight the fact of being part of an information society. The changing and widening meaning of heritage as a shared common [52] of societies and civilizations in a universal and ubiquitous frame can be maintained and supported by ICT use with operational functions and attitudes of transformation into an information society

Acknowledgement

This chapter is based on the paper, presented and published in the proceedings of the "University and Research Librarians' Association, URLA2014, International Congress on Management of Cultural Heritage and Cultural Memory Institutions", held 17–20 September 2014, Istanbul, Turkey.

References

1. Arnold, D. B., and Geser, G. (2007). Research agenda for the applications of ICT to cultural heritage. Jan. 17, 2007. IST-2002- 507382 [http://eprints.vcc-3d.eu/1/1/research_agenda.pdf]
2. Silberman, N. (2007). Cultural heritage and the information technologies, *Digital Applications for Tangible Cultural Heritage*, 95.
3. Veltman, K. H. (2005). Challenges for ICT/UCT applications in Cultural Heritage. E-Journal of the Humanities and Philology Studies of the UOC, 7.
4. Appleton, K., and Lovett, A. (2005). GIS-based visualization of development proposals: reactions from planning and related professionals. Computers, *Environment and Urban Systems*, 29(3), 321–339.

5. Koramaz, T.K. (2009). Investigation of User's Perception Regarding the Efficiency of Visualization Techniques in Urban Conservation Process (PhD Dissertation), ITU, Institute of Science and Technology, Urban and Regional Planning PhD Program, Istanbul, Turkey.
6. Owen, R., Buhalis, D., and Pletinckx, D. (2004, December). Developing the tourism aspects of a cultural route. In *Proceedings of the 5th International conference on Virtual Reality, Archaeology and Intelligent Cultural Heritage* (pp. 75–84). Eurographics Association.
7. Paar, P. (2006). Landscape visualizations: Applications and requirements of 3D visualization software for environmental planning, *Computers, environment and urban systems*, 30(6), 815–839.
8. Perez, C. (2002). *Technological revolutions and financial capital: The dynamics of bubbles and golden ages.* Edward Elgar Publishing.
9. Fountain, J. E. (2004). *Building the virtual state: Information technology and institutional change.* Brookings Institution Press.
10. Couldry, N. (2007). Communicative Entitlements and Democracy: The future of the Digital Divide Debate. In Mansell, R., Avgerou, C., Quah, D. and Silverstone, R. (eds) *The Oxford Handbook of Information and Communication Technologies.* pp. 383–403, Oxford University Press, New York.
11. Bangemann Report (1994). Bangemnn report: Europe and the global information society [http://cordis.europa.eu/news/rcn/2730_en.html]
12. Federal Standard 1037C, Glossary of Telecommunication Terms, 1996, [http://www.its.bldrdoc.gov/fs-1037/fs-1037c.htm]
13. Schiller, H. (1995). The Global Information Highway: Project for an Ungovernable World. In Brook, J. and Boal, I. (eds) *Resisting the Virtual Life.* City Lights Books, San Francisco, CA.
14. Markillie, P. (2004). A perfect market, *The Economist*, 371(8375), 3–6.
15. Uruguay Round decision on negotiations on basic telecommunications, World Trade Organization, Apr. 15, 1994, [http://www.wto.org/english/tratop_e/serv_e/telecom_e/tel22_e.htm]
16. Geneva Declaration of Principles, United Nations (UN), Dec. 10–12, 2003, WSIS-03/GENEVA/DOC/0004 [http://www.itu.int/wsis/documents/doc_multi.asp?lang=en&id=1161|1160]
17. Final Report of the Tunis Phase of the WSIS, United Nations (UN), Nov. 16–18, 2005, WSIS-05/TUNIS/DOC/9 (rev. 1) [http://www.itu.int/wsis/documents/listing-all.asp?lang=en&c_event=s|2&c_type=all||]
18. Melody, W.H. (2007). Markets and Policies in New Knowledge Economies. In Mansell, R., Avgerou, C., Quah, D. and Silverstone, R. (eds) *The Oxford Handbook of Information and Communication Technologies*, pp. 55–74, Oxford University Press, New York.
19. i2010: A European Information Society for growth and employment, European Union (EU), Jun. 1, 2005, COM (2005) 229 final, [http://europa.eu/legislation_summaries/information_society/strategies/c11328_en.htm]
20. Batty, M., Chapman, D., Evans, S., Haklay, H., Kueppers, M., Shiode, N., Smith, A., and Torrens, P.M. (2000). *Visualizing the City: Communicating Urban Design to Planners and Decision-Makers.*
21. Levy, R. (1995). Visualization of urban alternatives, *Environment and Planning B: Planning and Design*, 22(3), 343–358.
22. Grün, A. and Wang, X. (1998). CC-Modeler: A topology generator for 3-D city models, ISPRS *Journal of Photogrammetry & Remote Sensing*, 53(5), 286–295.
23. Pavlidis, G., Koutsoudis, A., Arnaoutoglou, F., Tsioukas, V., and Chamzas, C. (2007). Methods for 3D digitization of cultural heritage, *Journal of Cultural Heritage*, 8(1), 93–98.
24. Peng, C., and Blundell, J. P. (2004). reconstructing urban contexts online for interactive urban designs, *Design Studies*, 25(2), 175–192.
25. Haugstvedt, A. C., and Krogstie, J. (2012). Mobile augmented reality for cultural heritage: A technology acceptance study. In *IEEE International Symposium on Mixed and Augmented Reality (ISMAR)* 2012, IEEE, 247–255.
26. Wheatley, D., and Gillings, M. (2003). *Spatial Technology and Archaeology: The Archaeological Applications of GIS.* CRC Press.
27. Salzano, E. (1999). Future of town planning, *Computers, Environment and Urban Systems*, 23(3), 187–192.

28. Day, A. (2002). Urban visualization and public inquiries: the case of the Heron Tower, London, *Architectural Research Quarterly*, 6(4), 363–372.
29. Kerren, A., Stasko, J.T., Fekete, J.D., and North C. (2007). Workshop report: information visualization – human-centered issues in visual representation, interaction, and evaluation, *Information Visualization*, 6(3), 189–196.
30. Hamilton, A., Trodd, N., Zhang, X., Fernando, T., and Watson, K. (2001). Learning through visual systems to enhance the urban planning process, *Environment and Planning B: Planning and Design*, 28(6), 833–845.
31. Bates-Brkljac, N. (2007). Investigating perceptual responses and shared understanding of architectural design ideas when communicated through different forms of visual representations. In *Information Visualization*, 2007. IV'07. 11th International Conference, IEEE, 348–353.
32. Houtkamp, J., and Van Oostendorp, H. (2007). Virtual Vandalism: The Effect of Physical Incivilities on the Affective Appraisal of 3D Urban Models. In *Information Visualization*, 2007. IV'07. 11th International Conference, IEEE, 559–566.
33. Neto, P.L. (2001). Evaluation of an urban design project: imagery and realistic computer models, *Environment and Planning B: Planning and Design*, 28(5), 671–686.
34. Zerubavel, E. (2012). *Time Maps: Collective Memory and the Social Shape of the Past*. University of Chicago Press.
35. Grün, A., Remondino, F., and Zhang, L. (2004). Photogrammetric reconstruction of the great Buddha of Bamiyan, Afghanistan, *The Photogrammetric Record*, 19(107), 177–199.
36. McLuhan, M. (1994). *Understanding Media: The Extensions of Man*. MIT Press.
37. Hewison, R. (1987). *The Heritage Industry: Britain in a Climate of Decline*. Methuen, London.
38. Zukin, S. (1997). Cultural Strategies and Urban Identities: Remaking Public Space in New York. In O. Källtorp, I. Elander, O. Ericson, O. and M. Franzén (eds), *Cities in Transformation–Transformation in Cities. Social and Symbolic Change of Urban Space*, pp. 205–217, Avebury, Hampshire.
39. Go, F. M., Lee, R. M., and Russo, A. P. (2003). E-heritage in the globalizing society: enabling cross-cultural engagement through ICT, *Information Technology & Tourism*, 6(1), 55–68.
40. Greenstein, S. and Prince, J. (2007). Internet Diffusion and the Geography of the Digital Divide in the United States. In Mansell, R., Avgerou, C., Quah, D. and Silverstone, R. (eds) *The Oxford Handbook of Information and Communication Technologies*, pp. 168–195, Oxford University Press, New York.
41. Giaccardi, E. (2006). Collective storytelling and social creativity in the virtual museum: a case study, *Design Issues*, 22(3), 29–41.
42. Hall, P. (1999). The Future of Cities. Computers, *Environment and Urban Systems*, 23(3), 173–185.
43. Bourdakis, V. (1997). *Virtual reality: A communication tool for urban planning. CAAD – Towards New Design Conventions*. Technical University of Bialystok, Poland, 45–59.
44. Innes, J. E., and Booher, D. E. (2004). Reframing public participation: strategies for the 21st century, *Planning Theory & Practice*, 5(4), 419–436.
45. Rizzo, I., and Throsby, D. (2006). Cultural heritage: economic analysis and public policy, *Handbook of the Economics of Art and Culture*, 1, 983–1016.
46. Bertol, D. (1997). *Designing Digital Space: An Architect's Guide to Virtual Reality*, John Wiley & Sons Inc., New York.
47. Longley, P. A., Goodchild, M. F., Maguire, D. J., and Rhind, D. W. (2005). *Geographic information systems and science*, John Wiley & Sons, England.
48. Istanbul Metropolitan Municipality and Ministry of Culture and Tourism, Republic of Turkey (2011) Istanbul Historic Peninsula Site Management Plan, http://www.alanbaskanligi.gov.tr/files/Management_Plan_090312_TUM.pdf
49. Koramaz, T. K., and Gulersoy-Zeren, N. (2010). 3D Visualization of Transformation in Historic Townscape: Case of Zeyrek Urban Site. In *Proceedings of the 14th IPHS Conference, Urban Transformation: Controversies, Contrasts and Challenges*, Vol. 2, 360–371.
50. Koramaz, T. K., and Gulersoy-Zeren, N. (2011). Indagine sull'utilizzo delle tecniche di visualizzazione 2D e 3D che rappresentano il cambiamento del paesaggio urbano storico, *Disegnarecon*, 4(7), 30–41.

51. Koramaz, T. K. (2017). Information – Communication Technologies and Management Plans for Heritage Sites. In the Abstract Book of AESOP Annual Congress '17, Spaces of Dialog for Places of Dignity – Fostering the European Dimension of Planning, AESOP, 599–600.
52. Silverman, H., and Ruggles, D. F. (2007). Cultural Heritage and Human Rights, In Silverman, H., and Ruggles, D. F. (eds) *Cultural Heritage and Human Rights*, pp. 3–22, New York: Springer.

13 Visitor segments for the Alto Douro Wine Region cultural heritage site

A multivariate approach[1]

João Rebelo, Lina Lourenço-Gomes and Cristina Ribeiro

Introduction

World cultural heritage sites are potential tourist attractions. In this sense, they are subject to competition with other similar sites, having to meet the needs of a more selective demand. To solve these challenges and to provide relevant information supporting managerial decisions and policies, further studies on demand are required based on an approach that is more active and especially more segmented for the different types of visitors. Landscape managers and public authorities have much to benefit from knowing and understanding visitors' preferences and the related determinants of their cultural behaviour.

The Alto Douro Wine Region (ADWR) located in the northeast of Portugal was classified as a world heritage site, specifically as a cultural landscape, by UNESCO, in 2001. The main inclusion criteria related to the outstanding value of the ADWR as a traditional winemaking region, where the earliest viticulture techniques coexist alongside modern ones. This activity also shaped the lifestyle of the local population (the villages and traditional settlements). The small size of the vineyard plots and the coexistence of other Mediterranean crops transformed the landscape into a mosaic of unique beauty.

The main concern underlying this study is to detect the differences between the Portuguese visitors of the ADWR and, consequently, to identify homogeneous groups in terms of socioeconomic characteristics, cultural consumer experience and travel/visit behaviour (length of stay, average expenditure, accommodation and transport). To achieve this goal sample data are collected and univariate and multivariate (Categorical Principal Component Analysis and Cluster Analysis) statistical data analysis is used. The paper also includes a literature review on the non-market valuation of cultural goods, a description of the study object, the ADWR, the analysis of data and results, concluding with final remarks.

Valuing cultural goods: an overview of stated preferences

The issue of attributing value to public cultural amenities, which net benefits of conservation or preservation that are not totally reflected by the market, has sparked growing research interest in the last decades. Indeed, the estimation of the total economic value (in monetary terms) of the cultural heritage[2] provision is crucial to justify public funding or expenditure decisions in terms of generated wellbeing to consumers.

The total economic value is commonly defined by two components: the use value and non-use value. The first comprises the benefits related to the use of a good/service, while the non-use value includes the benefits of its simple provision or availability, not involving any type of use. The non-use value[3] comes in the form of option value, existence and legacy.[4] Examples of types of coexisting values from a cultural heritage that hinders the process valuation are: aesthetic (beauty and relevant environmental qualities), social (contribution to stability and community cohesion), spiritual (connecting link between people), symbolic (interpretation identity), history (revealing the origins) and authenticity (uniqueness of the site).[5] Although these have been shown to be a significant part of the total economic value of cultural heritage[6], the non-use values are not captured in the marketplace, constituting a source of market failure.

When the cultural heritage amenities exhibit public good features of no rivalry and no exclusiveness the market solution will be sub-optimal leading to under-provision of the good or a market failure ([7]presents a recent discussion about the public nature of cultural goods). Heritage sites, building facades or monuments cannot be apportioned (no competition in consumption) to the extent that their provision (for example, in the form of preservation, conservation or restoration) makes the good available to all in the same amount (except for congestion, they admit the inclusion of additional consumers for a zero marginal cost). Additionally, it is very difficult to exclude anyone from enjoying the benefits or consumption of these goods or services, giving the possibility of enjoying the good without contributing to its provision (free-riding behaviour and the failure of the mechanisms to accurately reveal preferences). In addition, the provision of cultural heritage goods or services generates external benefits (not traded in the market) that extend over the general population.

These market failures (notably because of the public good characteristics, externalities and component independent of use) justify the use of non-market valuation techniques to assess the benefits for changes in non-market goods, with special emphasis on stated preferences technique[8], as the contingent valuation method (CVM) and the family of choice modelling techniques[9]. These techniques assume a hypothetical market for the good or amenity in order to mimic the transactions in real markets. The information about value and preferences is obtained through the administration of questionnaires to users of the good.

The CVM is a well-established method to measure the non-market demand for cultural goods and services[10] and, since the pioneer studies[11], has been applied to cultural goods, assuming primacy in the non-market valuation of cultural heritage.[12] The CVM provides information on the maximum willingness to pay (minimum to accept) to ensure (to abdicate) a hypothetical change in the availability of a non-market amenity[13].

Examples of CVM applications in the cultural sphere include diverse items, namely, *buildings and monuments*[14]; *heritage sites*[15] and *arts and cultural institutions*[16]. The CVM has been applied to goods at varying scales, ranging from the local to worldwide features. Moreover, it has been used to value both funding specific cultural institutions and the composite fine "arts". The estimated benefits are also diverse and are related to capturing the value of preservation and /or restoration (usually monuments and buildings); the value to access (heritage sites and cities); the maintenance of the provision at the present level (arts and cultural institutions).

In the context of multidimensional or multi-attribute valuation the discrete choice experiments technique (DCE) has been suggested as an alternative tool to the CVM and has generated a growing body of both theoretical and applied research.[17] Theoretically, it is based on the assumption that an individual derives utility from the attributes/characteristics of a good[18] and is grounded in the random utility model.[19] Generically, the conception of DCE encompasses the following phases: 1) selection of the relevant attributes and levels; 2) experimental design to combine the attribute levels into a number of alternatives to be allocated in choice sets. In a survey instrument, the respondents are asked to choose their preferred alternative in each sequential choice set; 3) data collection (choices made) and data analysis through discrete choice models, assessing the part worth utilities of each attribute and, if an attribute price (monetary cost) is included, the willingness-to-pay (WTP) estimates for changes in the attribute levels.

Since the pioneering studies[20], DCEs have been applied widely in distinct research fields. An overview of recent theoretical and applied progress of choice modelling is presented in [21].[22] presents a state of the art of environmental valuation using the DCE approach and[23] presents some examples in cultural economics (cultural events; heritage and urban sites; archaeological sites; museums and monuments; broadcast and broadband).[24] reviews DCE applications on cultural goods, detailing the experimental design strategies implemented.

In the cultural economics field, DCEs have been applied in relation to cultural institutions[25], monuments or groups of monuments[26] and sites[27].

Demand for a cultural heritage site

Top heritage sites compete with each other in their attractiveness to visitors increasing demanding and informed. To meet their needs and expectations, public authorities have much to profit from knowing the visitors and understanding their preferences and the related determinants of cultural behaviour. In this context, this study presents the results of a multivariate approach to segment the visitors of the Alto Douro Wine Region (ADWR) into homogeneous groups, allowing the identification of specific measures and policies to increase utility, value and the attraction of this heritage site. Additionally, the evidence of the preceding statistical analysis are complemented with the previously published results of the DCE to assess the preferences of ADWR visitors for alternative scenarios of preservation.

Alto Douro Wine Region (ADWR)

Since 2001, the ADWR has been designated a UNESCO World Heritage Site as an evolving and cultural landscape. The area of the ADWR (24,600 ha) represents only about 10% of the Demarcated Douro Region (DDR), where viticulture (43,805 ha of vineyards in 2014) is the core activity and the mainstay of the region's economy and also of the excellence of its cultural landscape. The ADWR is supposed to be the most representative territory of the DDR, concentrating all the elements, functions and most representative landscape composition of authenticity and integrity of the site according to UNESCO criteria.

The criteria of inscription[28] refer to the centrality of viticulture in adapting and transforming a harsh environment (steep and rocky soils, reduced rainfall and rigorous weather) into a unique landscape reflecting the way of living and the historical evolution of cultivating vines and producing internationally recognized wines, such as the Porto wine and other high quality still wines. Shaped by technical, economic and social factors, diverse vineyard cultivation techniques coexist in the ADWR, testimony to their historical development for 2,000 years ranging from the schist walled terraces in the pre-phylloxera period (until 1860) and post-phylloxera period (end of 19th century until late 1930s) to the most modern techniques such as land walled terraces, vertical planting and no land organization.[29] Beyond the vineyard, other Mediterranean crops are visible in the landscape (e.g., olive, almond, orange grove, apple) and thickets and woods. The co-evolution of human occupancy and landscape is also present in the organization of human settlements, characterized by concentrations of small-scale buildings and adjacent constructions to the viticulture activity. The *Quintas* and *Casais* are emblematic examples of the ADWR regional organization, providing important resources for cultural tourism activities.

The maintenance in the same space of diverse vineyard cultivation systems, Mediterranean crops, natural vegetation and components of human settlements in the region, gives the landscape a mosaic appearance, as Figure 13.1 illustrates.

The living and evolving nature of the cultural landscape imply that preservation efforts should be reconciled with development in the region and the wellbeing of residents, who are the main stakeholders of the ADWR. In this regard, the ADWR as a worldwide heritage site competes with other sites to attract visitors and consequently creates added value which, in turn, will ensure conditions for the site's preservation. For the ADWR to be internationally competitive, management authorities should have knowledge of the actual demand and understand its motivations.

The Douro region is not a massive touristic site. From 2002 to 2013 the number of guests in tourism accommodation establishments in the Douro region, increased by 12% (from 154,874 to 173,178) and the number of nights increased by 16.6%. Despite this behaviour, the Douro region has a very low weight in relation to Portugal's tourism indicators (in 2013, the number of guests in the Douro region represented around 1.2% of the national total and 6.3% of the number of overnight stays; the average stay was 1.6, whereas the reference national was set to 2.9). Even so, the fluvial tourism around the Douro river has shown greater dynamism. From 2007 to 2013, the number of passengers of the boat hotel increased around 122% (from 17,724 to 39,352), which signals the growing attractiveness of and demand for cultural purposes.

Applying multivariate analysis methods, the present study intends to improve knowledge about Portuguese visitors to the ADWR, through the definition of homogeneous groups.

Figure 13.1 Landscape of Casais do Douro village.

Visitor segments for the Alto Douro Wine Region cultural heritage site

A random sample of 249 Portuguese visitors to the ADWR was collected between March and October 2013, at some of the most attractive locations. The survey instrument comprises questions about socio-economic characteristics, consumption and cultural interest, familiarity and experience relating to the ADWR and specific trip data (e.g., accommodation, length of stay, expenditure, transportation). Table 13.1 presents the variables used (nominal qualitative, ordinal and quantitative variables) and the descriptive statistics that summarize the data collected.

Respondents are on average 41 years old, approximately 53% are male and 81% are employed. More than half of the respondents (51%) had completed post-secondary education and for nearly 70% the net average income/household was less than 2000€/month. The average household consists of 2.56 people and an average distance between the ADWR and the place of residence is 149 km.

Around 85% were repeat visitors (only 15% of the respondents were visiting the ADWR for the first time) and the most significant visit purpose (for nearly 49%) was to discover the landscape and cultural heritage. The world heritage status influenced the decision to visit the ADWR for 18.6% of respondents. Most visitors (80%) claimed to have knowledge about the more emblematic ADWR attributes and nearly half (49%) about the criteria for inclusion on the UNESCO list. Regarding the consumers' cultural habits, on average, the respondents attested that they had attended 15 cultural activities during the previous year and 12% are members of a cultural association.

On average each visitor spent 69€ per day and the length of stay was three days. During the visit, 39% of respondents did not use any type of accommodation, 28% stayed overnight in a hotel establishment and for 27% accommodation was provided by friends or relatives. Driving a private car was the main means of transport (92.4%), with others (e.g., bus, boat or train) being far less important.

Multivariate analysis

To reduce the number of original variables and to obtain homogeneous groups of visitors, we applied two multivariate (multiple variable) analysis techniques, namely, Categorical Principal Components Analysis (CATPCA) and Cluster Analysis.

CATPCA can deal simultaneously with categorical variables and quantitative variables, respecting the nature of the variables through differentiated transformation and the dimensionality of the data. CATPCA simultaneously quantifies categorical variables and reduces the dimensionality of the data. As a data reduction technique, it reduces the number of original variables into a smaller set of variables, the uncorrelated principal components, which retain as much as possible the variation present in the data set (representing the most information of the original variables). Simultaneously the CATPCA transforms the categories of the variables into numerical values through *optimal scaling levels*, maintaining the order and/or the distance of the original variables.[30] The principal components have the metric properties of quantitative variables that enable the use of Cluster Analysis, which is used to form homogeneous segments or visitor groups that share common characteristics.

To extract the principal components from the 19 original variables described in Table 13.1 the retention criteria adopted are Kaiser's eigenvalue-greater-than-one rule[31] and the Scree plot.[32] Additionally, the internal consistency of each component is measured by Cronbach's alpha. The application of these criteria leads to four orthogonal components

Table 13.1 Descriptive statistics.

Variable	*Acronym*	*Codification*	*Sample Average*	*Standard Deviation*	*Proportion of 1*
Socioeconomic characteristics					
Gender	GE	1-Male; 0-Female			0.526
Age	AGE	18–70	40.8	12.3	
Education level	EDU	1-Basic; 2-Secondary; 3-Post-Secondary	2.38	-	
Monthly household Income	INCOME	1 <1000€ 2 1000–2000€ 3 2001–3000€ 4 >3000€	2.18	-	
Household size	SIZE		2.56	1.06	
Distance between home and the ADWR	KM	0-1556	148.7	152.1	
Employment status	JOB	1-Employed 0-Other (unemployed, student, retired)			0.807
ADWR familiarity and cultural consumption					
Visiting the ADWR for the first time	FIRST	1-Yes; 0-No			0.15
Purpose of visit	PURPOSE	1-To know the ADWR cultural heritage; 0-others	-	-	0.48
Influence of the world heritage classification on visiting decision	LIST	1-Yes; 0-No	-	-	0.186
Knows the reasons for ADWR inclusion in UNESCO list	KNOW	1-Yes; 0-No	-	-	0.49
Identifies the more traditional attributes	IDENT	1-Yes; 0-No	-	-	0.8
Consumption of cultural activities (no. last year)	CCULT	0-160	14.88	16.7	
Member of a cultural association	MEMBER	1-Yes; 0-No			0.12
ADWR trip					
Length of stay (no. of days)	DAYS	1-120	3.25	10.7	
Persons (no.)	PERSON	1-30	4.2	3.96	
Expenditure €/day (spending)	EXPEND	0-450	68.5	72.2	
Accommodation (housing)	ACCOM	1-hotel or similar establishment; 2- home of friends or family; 3-None; 4-Other	3.35	1.53	
Transportation	TRANSP	1-Own car 0-Public (Bus; Boat; Train; Other)		0.87	0.924

whose relational information between them accounts together for almost 43% of the total variance accounted for (VAF) of the original variables, as can be seen in Table 13.2. The internal consistency of each component is moderate (Cronbach's alpha), being lower in the last component.

Based on the component loadings, the Principal Components are nominated as:

- *ADWR Familiarity (Component 1).* With high negative loadings on DAYS (-0.529), EXPEND (-0.44), KM (-0.419), JOB (-0.447), AGE (-0.621), INCOME (-0.78) and a high positive loading on ACCOM (0.588).
- *Cultural Interest (Component 2).* With heavy positive loadings on EDU (0.491), CCULT (0.417), EXPEND (0.595) and KNOW (0.478) and negative loadings on AGE (-0.491) and JOB (0.453).
- *ADWR knowledge (Component 3).* With heavy positive loadings on INCOME (0.538), EDU (0.553) and IDENT (0.528) and negative loadings on FIRST (-0.415) and KM (-0.540).
- *Visit Purposes (Component 4).* With high positive loadings on PURPOSE (0.515), LIST (0.551) and negative loading on SIZE (-0.646).

Taking the four Components and applying the Cluster Analysis, three homogeneous groups are formed (Table 13.3), with 108, 89 and 49 visitors, respectively. The one-way

Table 13.2 Component loadings*, total variance accounted for (VAF) and eigenvalue for CATPCA with four principal components

Variables	*Components*			
	1	*2*	*3*	*4*
KM	**-0.419**	0.124	**-0.540**	-0.130
JOB	**-0.447**	**-0.453**	0.119	0.370
SIZE	-0.064	0.033	0.041	**-0.646**
GE	-0.124	0.013	0.226	-0.155
EDU	-0.006	**0.491**	**0.553**	0.165
AGE	**-0.621**	**-0.439**	0.151	0.157
INCOME	**-0.478**	-0.035	**0.538**	-0.011
CCULT	-0.136	**0.417**	0.315	0.370
MEMBER	-0.209	-0.317	0.225	-0.117
FIRST	-0.154	0.306	**-0.415**	0.203
PURPOSE	-0.385	0.039	-0.211	**0.515**
LIST	0.256	-0.055	-0.017	**0.551**
KNOW	-0.370	**0.478**	0.374	-0.263
IDENT	-0.086	-0.200	**0.493**	-0.186
DAYS	**-0.529**	-0.085	-0.318	-0.274
PERSON	-0.353	-0.502	0.073	-0.001
EXPEND	**-0.440**	**0.595**	0.055	0.105
ACCOM	**0.588**	-0.278	0.352	0.180
TRANSP	-0.256	0.014	-0.063	0.236
Eigenvalue	***2.462***	***1.990***	***1.963***	***1.686***
VAF(%)	***13.0***	***10.5***	***10.3***	***8.9***
Cronbach's alpha	***0.627***	***0.525***	***0.518***	***0.43***

* Correlation between the principal component and the original variable (the variance explained by each component is equal to the sum of squared loadings across variables)

Table 13.3 Average scores of the components retained in the clusters and ***ANOVA F-test*** statistic*

	Cluster 1 (108 visitors)	*Cluster 2 (89 visitors)*	*Cluster 3 (49 visitors)*	$F = \frac{QMC}{QME}$
ADWR Familiarity (component 1)	0.73	-0.31	-1.05	113.201
Cultural Interest (component 2)	-0.03	0.72	-1.26	121.321
ADWR Knowledge (component 3)	0.48	-0.68	0.21	45.778
Visit Purposes (component 4)	-0.29	0.21	0.23	7.863

* ANOVA: One-Way Analysis of Variance (used to compare means from the three groups from each variable or component); F-test statistic = Cluster Mean Square (QMC) divided by the Error Mean Square (QME).

Table 13.4 Description of each cluster according to the original variables

Original variables	*Clusters*		
	1	*2*	*3*
KM	81	**204**	164
JOB	Employed (82%)	Employed (96%)	**Employed (49%)**
SIZE	4 (31%)	3 (31%)	**2 (61%)**
GE	Male (58%)	Female (56%)	Male (55%)
EDU	Superior (56%)	Superior (46%)	Superior (46%)
AGE	36	37	**57**
INCOME	1000€–2000€ (58%)	1000€–2000€ (61%)	**2001€–3000€ (41%)**
CCULT	14	**18**	12
MEMBER	No (92%)	No (97%)	No (65%)
FIRST	No (99%)	No (63%)	No (94%)
PURPOSE	**Other (79%)**	Landscape and Heritage (71%)	Landscape and Heritage (69%)
LIST	No (79%)	No (81%)	No (88%)
KNOW	No (53%)	**Yes (57%)**	No (57%)
IDENT	Yes (91%)	Yes (57%)	Yes (92%)
DAYS	**1**	3	3
PERSON	3	4	**7**
EXPEND	45	**110**	46
ACCOM	**None (68%)**	Hotel establishment (54%)	Relatives or friends (48%)
TRANSP	Own car (95%)	Own car (89%)	Own car (86%)
DESIGNATION OF GROUPS	***Same-Day visitors***	***Cultural visitors***	***Individual Mass visitors***

ANOVA[33], using the average scores of the components and the clusters determined by K-means, showed that the components 1 and 2 promote greater discrimination in the formation of groups in which the familiarity with the ADWR is more important in cluster 1 (higher mean of 0.73) and the cultural interest predominates in cluster 2 (mean of 0.72).

To improve the interpretation of each group, the original variables are crossed with the variable that identifies the belonging to each cluster (Table 13.4).

According to the more discriminating variables among the three clusters (bold letters in Table 13.4) the visitor groups are nominated as: *Same-day visitors*, *Cultural visitors* and *Individual mass visitors*.

The *Same-day visitors* (cluster 1) live closer to the ADWR, most of them are employed (even though 92% of the students in the sample fall within this cluster). They have higher qualifications (only 6% finished their education after primary school), are middle-income earners (19% earn less than 1,000€/month and 7% more than 3,000€) and their average age is 36 years old. These visitors have a close relationship with the ADWR, almost all (99%) have visited the ADWR more than once, mostly for other purposes beyond the cultural heritage and landscape (visiting family, walking, leisure or professional reasons). The UNESCO status does not determine the decision to visit, 53% do not know the criteria of ADWR inclusion on the UNESCO list, but 91% state that they distinguish the distinctive attributes of the landscape. The visit is short (on average one day) and, therefore, these visitors don't spend a night in collective or private accommodation in the ADWR (68%). On average, the number of persons on the trip/visit is three and the daily expenditure per person is 45€.

The Cultural visitors (cluster 2) have the highest attendance at cultural activities (18 times/ last year) include the majority (89%) of first-time visitors of the sample and the visiting purpose is to know the cultural heritage. Most know the listing criteria and the main attributes of the ADWR. Nevertheless, for the majority (81%) the ADWR status as world cultural heritage site did not influence the decision to visit. On average the visit is made by a group of 4 persons, during 3 days. The visitors stay overnight in a hotel establishment and the daily expenditure per person is 110€. Mostly they travel in their own car; however, from the sample, 48% of visitors who have travelled on public transport (boat, train or bus) belong to this cluster. These visitors live farther away from the ADWR (204 km, on average) and most are employed. The income, educational level and age are identical to the previous group.

The *Individual mass visitors* (cluster 3) visit the ADWR in larger groups (7 persons on average), are older (57 years on average) and those who earn higher income levels (57% earn more than 2,000 €/month). All the retirees of the sample belong to this cluster, but the employment status is divided into employees (49%) and retirees (43%). Although most have higher education, one third only completed primary school. These visitors are the lowest attendees of cultural activities, but have the highest rate of cultural association membership of the three groups. They are repeat visitors with the purpose of discovering the cultural heritage. Although the majority state that they know the ADWR attributes, they are unaware of the inclusion criteria and the UNESCO status does not influence the decision to visit. The daily expenditure per person is 46€.

Based on the above categories some policy implications emerge:

- A transversal evidence for the 3 groups is the absence of a causal linkage between the ADWR's UNESCO status and the decision to visit. This result is in line with the evidence of some unfamiliarity about the inclusion criteria (same-day visitors and mass visitors). There is a clear basis for reinforcing the role of the UNESCO designation to signal value, enhance knowledge and information regarding the good.
- Efforts should be made to extend the length of stay in the ADWR (namely to same-day visitors), through inter-related activities dispersed by the 13 municipalities represented in the ADWR territory.
- To convert first-time visitors (namely cultural visitors) into repeat visitors, by supplying heritage and history, presenting new interpretations, new experiences and new narratives.
- To implement initiatives to expand the attraction of cultural visitors (with the longer duration of stay and higher daily expenditure).
- To consolidate the infrastructure conditions and activities over the year to appeal to the needs of older and retired visitors (individual mass visitors).

ADWR visitors' preferences using DCE

Based on the same sample used in this study, the results of a DCE to elicit the visitors' preferences over preservation plans regarding the ADWR,[34]show that visitors assign positive utility to the preservation of three landscape attributes, namely the vineyards with schist walls, the traditional settlements and the mosaic landscape, demonstrating consensus on the maintenance of these elements in the cultural landscape.

In addition to socioeconomic factors (educational level, income and employee status) the respondents' knowledge about the ADWR characteristics, the influence of the UNESCO status in the decision to visit and the length of stay are significant (and positive) determinants of visitors' utility for contributing to a preservation programme to safeguard the ADWR. This evidence suggests some policy measures: i) based on education, information and interpretation of the meaning of the cultural value intrinsic to the ADWR; ii) to increase the length of stay, for example, by presenting routes and interconnected activities in the ADWR; to explore the potentialities of the UNESCO landmark to attract visitors.

The opposite effect is exhibited by the older, first-time visitors and those belonging to larger households. The results suggest the design and implementation of specific programmes/attractions to the older segments and to improve visitor loyalty, since experience and exposure to the good increase the associated value on its preservation.

Conclusions

The economic valuation of cultural heritage has become a fruitful area of research in the last three decades. Demand side approaches have assumed a relevant role in determining the optimal level of provision of cultural heritage goods, leading to market studies providing a better understanding of the demand, to identify the visitors, to attract new visitors and to promote repeat visits.

In this study, the use of multivariate analysis techniques (CATPCA and Cluster Analysis) identified three segments or homogeneous groups of visitors to the Alto Douro Wine Region world heritage site, specifically: *Same-day visitors, Cultural visitors* and *Individual mass visitors.* From the main characteristics of each group, policy and entrepreneurial implications emerge related to the expansion of the stay length (*Same-day visitors*), the improvement of visitor loyalty through repeat visitation (*Cultural visitors*) and the heritage offered over the year to older visitors (*Individual mass visitors*). The importance of educational and promotional measures is transversal for the sample.

This evidence is corroborated and complemented by the results of a previous application of the discrete choice experiments technique applied to the same respondents, giving robustness to the results.

Notes

1 This work is financed by the project NORTE-01-0145-FEDER-000038 (INNOVINE & WINE – Innovation Platform of Vine & Wine) and by European and Structural and Investment Funds in the FEDER component, and supported through the Operational Competitiveness and Internationalization Programme (COMPETE 2020) [Project No 006971 (UIC/SOC/04011)]; and national funds, through the FCT – Portuguese Foundation for Science and Technology under the UID/SOC/04011/2013.

2 According to the Convention Concerning the Protection of the World Cultural and Natural Heritage (UNESCO, 1972, http://whc.unesco.org/world_he.htm), the definition of cultural heritage should

include monuments, groups of buildings and sites. In 1992, the UNESCO World Heritage list included the possibility of cultural landscapes being included in the Convention (Article 1). Cultural landscape is defined as an illustrative of the evolution of man over time, under the influence of the natural environment and of social, economic and cultural, external and internal constraints (UNESCO, 2008, http://whc.unesco.org/archive/opguide08-en.pdf#annex3).

3 The option value is related to the satisfaction of ensuring the possibility of using the amenity in the future. The existence value arises from the knowledge that the cultural heritage exists, even though it does not represent current or future use. The legacy value or altruism value accrues from ensuring the availability of a good or resource for future generations.

4 Frey, B. (1997), "The Evaluation of Cultural Heritage: Some Critical Issues". In Hutter, M. and Rizzo, I. (eds.). *Economic Perspectives on Cultural Heritage*. New York: St. Martin's Press; Santagata, W. & Signorello, G. (2000), "Contingent Valuation of a Cultural Public Good and Policy Design: The Case of Napoli Musei Aperti", *Journal of Cultural Economics*, Vol. 24, pp.181–204; Throsby, D. (1997), "Seven Questions in the Economics of Cultural Heritage". In Hutter, M. and Rizzo, I. (eds). *Economic Perspectives on Cultural Heritage*. New York: St. Martin's Press.

5 Throsby, D. (2001), *Economics and Culture*. Cambridge, UK: University Press.

6 Carson, R., Conaway, M., & Navrud, S. (2013), "Preliminary valuation of a cultural heritage site of global significance: A Delphi contingent valuation study". In Rizzo, I. and Mignosa, A. (eds.). *Handbook on the Economics of Cultural Heritage.* Cheltenham, UK: Edward Elgar.

7 Towse, R. (2014), *Advanced Introduction to Cultural economics*. Cheltenham, UK: Edward Elgar.

8 The non-market valuation techniques include revealed and stated preferences methods. The Revealed Preference Techniques (e.g., Hedonic Price method, Travel Cost method) assess the value of a non-market good from the observation of consumer behaviour in an actual market for a complementary good or service. Although revealed preference techniques can be used to value cultural heritage, stated preference methods "seem to be most appropriate in terms of their capability of capturing the potentially largest benefit component; the non-use values" (Carson et al., 2013: pp 586, *op. cit.*) For this reason, the focus of this chapter is the stated preferences methods.

9 Including contingent ranking, contingent rating, paired comparisons and discrete choice experiments.

10 Throsby, D. (2003), "Determining the Value of Cultural Goods: How Much (Or How Little) Does Contingent Valuation Tell Us?", *Journal of Cultural Economics*, Vol.27, pp. 275–285.

11 Throsby, D. & Withers, G. (1984), "What Price Culture? Australia Council, Sydney". Reprinted in Towse, R. (ed.) (1997). *Cultural Economics, The Arts, the Heritage and the Media Industries, Vol. II.*, pp. 577–610. Edward Elgar: Cheltenham. Throsby, D. & Withers, G. (1983), "Measuring the Demand for the Arts as a Public Good: Theory and Empirical Results". In Hendon, W.S. and Shanahan, J.L. (eds.). *Economics of Cultural Decisions*. Cambridge: Abt Books.

12 Navrud, S. & Ready, R. (*eds.*), (2002). *Valuing Cultural Heritage. Applying Environmental Valuation Techniques to Historic Buildings, Monuments and Artifacts.* Cheltenham, UK: Edward Elgar; Tuan, T. & Navrud, S. (2007), "Valuing Cultural Heritage in Developing Countries: Comparing and Pooling Contingent Valuation and Choice Modelling Estimates". *Environmental Resource Economics*, Vol. 38 (1), pp. 51–69; Kaminski, J., McLoughlin, J., Sodagar, B. (2007), "Economic Methods for Valuing European Cultural Heritage Sites (1994–2006)". In McLoughlin, J., Kaminsky, J. and Sodagar, B (eds.). *Perspectives on Impact, Technology and Strategic Management. Heritage Management Series,* Vol. 1. Budapest: EPOCH publication.

13 Using the open ended format, an example of a valuation question is "what is the maximum amount you would be willing to pay for an increase in the quality level of the amenity x?" Using the referendum format (single bounded question), the respondent is asked to indicate whether he/she is willing to pay, or not, a specific monetary amount for a proposal. The gathered information is the yes/no answers to the price vector presented to each respondent.

14 Navrud, S. & Strand, J. (2002), "Social Costs and Benefits of Preserving and Restoring the Nidaros Cathedral". In Navrud S. and Ready R. (eds.). *Valuing Cultural Heritage. Applying Environmental Valuation Techniques to Historic Buildings, Monuments and Artifacts.* Cheltenham: Edward Elgar; Pollicino, M. & Maddison, D. (2002), "Valuing the Impacts of Air Pollution on Lincoln Cathedral". In Navrud S. and Ready R. (eds.). *Valuing Cultural Heritage. Applying Environmental Valuation Techniques to Historic Buildings, Monuments and Artifacts.* Cheltenham: Edward Elgar; Whitehead, J. & Finney, S. (2003), "Willingness to Pay for Submerged Maritime Cultural Resources", *Journal of Cultural Economics*, Vol.27, pp. 231–240; Kling, R., Revier, C. & Sable, K. (2004), "Estimating the Public Good Value of Preserving a Local Historic Landmark: The Role of Non-Substitutability and Citizen Information", *Urban Studies*, Vol. 41(10), pp. 2025–2041; Salazar, S. & Marques J. (2005), "Valuing Cultural Heritage:

the Social Benefits of Restoring and Old Arab Tower", *Journal of Cultural Heritage*, Vol. 6, pp. 69–77; Kim, S., Wong, K. & Cho, M. (2007), "Assessing the economic value of a World Heritage site and willingness-to-pay determinants: A case of Changdeok Palace", *Tourism Management*, Vol. 28(1), pp. 317–322.

15 Carson, R., Mitchell, R. & Conaway, M. (2002), "Economic Benefits to Foreigners Visiting Morocco Accruing from the Rehabilitation of the Fes Medina". In Navrud S. and Ready R. (*eds*). *Valuing Cultural Heritage. Applying Environmental Valuation Techniques to Historic Buildings, Monuments and Artifacts*. Cheltenham: Edward Elgar; Willis, K.G. (2002), "Iterative Bid Design in Contingent Valuation and the Estimation of the Revenue Maximising Price for a Cultural Good", *Journal of Cultural Economics*, Vol.26, pp. 307–324; Tuan, T. & Navrud, S. (2007), "Valuing Cultural Heritage in Developing Countries: Comparing and Pooling Contingent Valuation and Choice Modelling Estimates", *Environmental Resource Economics*, Vol.38 (1), pp. 51–69.

16 Hansen, T. (1997), "The Willingness to pay for the Royal Theatre in Copenhagen as a Public Good", *Journal of Cultural Economics*, Vol.21, pp.1–28; Santagata, W. & Signorello, G. (2000), "Contingent Valuation of a Cultural Public Good and Policy Design: The Case of Napoli Musei Aperti", *Journal of Cultural Economics*, Vol.24, pp. 181–204; Thompson, E., Berger, M., Blomquist, G. & Allen, S. (2002), "Valuing the Arts: A Contingent Valuation Approach", *Journal of Cultural Economics*, Vol.26, pp. 87–113.

17 Mazzanti, M. (2003), "Discrete Choice Models and Valuation Experiments", *Journal of Economic Studies*, Vol. 30 (6), pp. 584–604.

18 Lancaster, K. (1966), "A New Approach to Consumer Theory", *Journal of Political Economy*, Vol.74, pp. 132–157.

19 Manski, C. (1977), "The structure of random utility models", *Theory and Decision*, Vol. 8(3), pp. 229–254.

20 Louviere, J. & Hensher, D. (1982), "On the Design and Analysis of Simulated Choice or Allocattion Experiments in Travel Choice Modelling", *Transportation Research Record*, Vol. 890, pp. 11–17; Louviere, J. & Woodworth, G. (1983), "Design and Analysis of Simulated Consumer Choice or Allocattion Experiments: An Approach Based on Aggregate Data", *Journal of Marketing Research*, Vol. 20, pp. 350–367.

21 Hess, S., & Daly, A. (2013), *Choice Modelling. The State of the Art and the State of Practice*. Cheltenham: Edward Elgar.

22 Hoyos, D. (2010), "The state of the art of environmental valuation with discrete choice experiments", *Ecological Economics*, Vol.69 (8), pp. 1595–1603.

23 Snowball, J. (2008), *Measuring the Value of Culture*. Verlag Berlin Heidelberg: Springer.

24 Lourenço-Gomes, L., Pinto, L.C., & Rebelo, J. (2013a), "Using choice experiments to value a world cultural heritage site: Reflections on the experimental design", *Journal of Applied Economics*, Vol. 16(2), pp. 303–332.

25 Maddison, D., & Foster, T. (2003), "Valuing congestion costs in the British Museum", *Oxford Economic Papers*, Vol.55, pp. 173–190; Mazzanti, M. (2003), "Discrete choice models and valuation experiments", *Journal of Economic Studies*, Vol. 30(6), pp. 584–604; Apostolakis, A., & Jaffry, S. (2005), "A choice modeling application for Greek heritage attractions", *Journal of Travel Research*, Vol.43, pp. 309–318; Snowball, J.D., & Willis, K.G. (2006), "Estimating the marginal utility of different sections of an arts festival: the case of visitors to the South African National Arts Festival", *Leisure Studies*, Vol. 25(1), pp.43–56; Willis, K., & Snowball, J. (2009), "Investigating how the attributes of live theatre productions influence consumption choices using conjoint analysis: The example of the National Arts Festival South Africa", *Journal of Cultural Economics*, Vol. 33, pp.167–183; Choi, A., Ritchie, B., Papandrea, F., & Bennett, J. (2010), "Economic valuation of cultural heritage sites: A choice modeling approach", *Tourism Management*, Vol.31, pp. 213–220; Jaffry, S., & Apostolokis, A. (2011), "Evaluating individual preferences for the British Museum", *Journal of Cultural Economics*, Vol. 35, pp. 49–75.

26 Morey, E., Rossmann, K., Chestnut, L., & Ragland, S. (2002), "Modeling and estimating E[WTP] for reducing acid deposition injuries to cultural resources: Using choice experiments in a group setting to estimate passive-use values". In S. Navrud and R. Ready (eds.), *Valuing Cultural Resources*. Cheltenham: Edward Elgar Publishing.

27 Alberini, A., Riganti, P., & Longo, A. (2003), "Can people value the aesthetic and use services of urban sites? Evidence from a survey of Belfast residents", *Journal of Cultural Economics*, Vol.27, pp. 193–213; Tuan, T., & Navrud, S. (2007), "Valuing cultural heritage in developing countries: Comparing and pooling contingent valuation and choice modelling estimates", *Environmental and Resource Economics*, Vol. 38(1), pp. 51–69; Lourenço-Gomes, L., Pinto, L.C., & Rebelo, J. (2013b), "Preservation of a

rural and cultural landscape. Insights from the multinomial and error components logit model", *New Medit*, Vol. 12(2), pp. 65–72; Lourenço-Gomes, L., Pinto, L.C., & Rebelo, J. (2013a), "Using choice experiments to value a world cultural heritage site: Reflections on the experimental design", *Journal of Applied Economics*, Vol.16 (2), pp. 303–332; Lourenço-Gomes, L., Pinto, L.C., & Rebelo, J. (2014), "Visitors' preferences for preserving the attributes of a world heritage site", *Journal of Cultural Heritage*, Vol.15, pp. 64–67; Lourenço-Gomes, L., Pinto, L.C. & Rebelo, J. (2015), "Wine and cultural heritage. The experience of the Alto Douro Wine Region", *Wine Economics and Policy*, Vol. 4, pp. 78–87.

28 Criterion (iii) The Alto Douro Region has been producing wine for nearly two thousand years and its landscape has been molded by human activities; Criterion (iv) The components of the Alto Douro landscape are representative of the full range of activities associated with winemaking – terraces, quintas (wine-producing farm complexes), villages, chapels, and roads; Criterion (v) The cultural landscape of the Alto Douro is an outstanding example of a traditional European wine-producing region, reflecting the evolution of this human activity over time (UNESCO, 2001; http://whc.unesco.org/sites/1046.htm).

29 The Appendix illustrates the different land organization systems of the vineyards in the ADWR.

30 Meulman J., Heiser W. & Kooij A. (2004), "Principal Components Analysis With Nonlinear Optimal Scaling Transformations for Ordinal and Nominal Data". In Kaplan, D. (ed.), *The SAGE Handbook of Quantitative Methods in the Social Sciences*. Madison: Sage Publications, pp. 49–70.

31 Each eigenvalue represents the amount of variance that has been captured by one component. When the CATPCA uses standardized variables (each of the *original* variable's variance is standardized to one, as is the case), the rule is to retain only components with eigenvalues greater than 1. The goal is that each principal component retained explains more variance than the original variable (that is equal to 1 in standardized variables).

32 Linting M., Meulman J., Groenen P. & Kooij A. (2007). "Nonlinear Principal Components Analysis: Introduction and Application", *Psychological Methods*, Vol. 12, No. 3. Leiden, p. 336–358.

33 To identify the most important variables in the formation of the groups in the Cluster analysis, Marôco (2011) recommends the use of the F-test statistic value (test statistic used for ANOVA). High statistic values indicate the variables more important to the group definitions, presenting high variability *between* groups (QMC) and low *within* the groups (QME). If this ratio (QMC/QME) is large, it produces a statistically significant result (i.e., rejection of the null hypothesis of that *all* population *means* are *equal*).

34 Lourenço-Gomes, L., Pinto, L.C. & Rebelo, J. (2015), "Wine and cultural heritage. The experience of the Alto Douro Wine Region", *Wine Economics and Policy*, Vol. 4, pp. 78–87.

Appendix – Vineyard cultivation systems (from the most ancient to the more recent)

Source: Magalhães N., Magalhães M., & Sousa V. (2013), "Alterações ao Uso do Solo ». In *Avaliação do Estado de Conservação do Bem Alto Douro Vinhateiro – Paisagem Cultural Evolutiva Viva*, Volume 2 – Estudos de Base. Porto: CIBIO UP/UTAD: A1.01-A1.31.

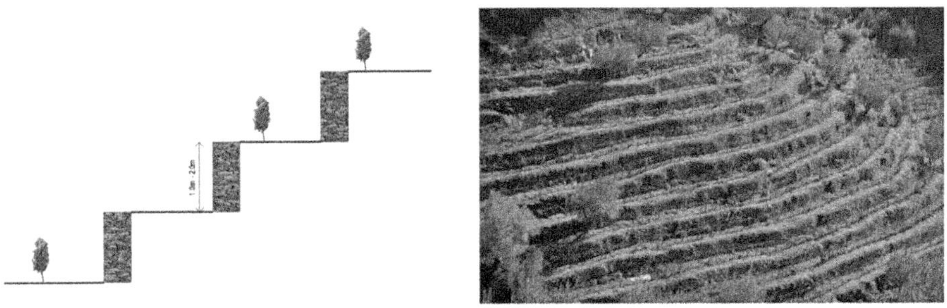

Figure 13.2 Pre-phylloxera walled terraces (*socalcos*).

Figure 13.3 Post-phylloxera schist walled terraces socalcos.

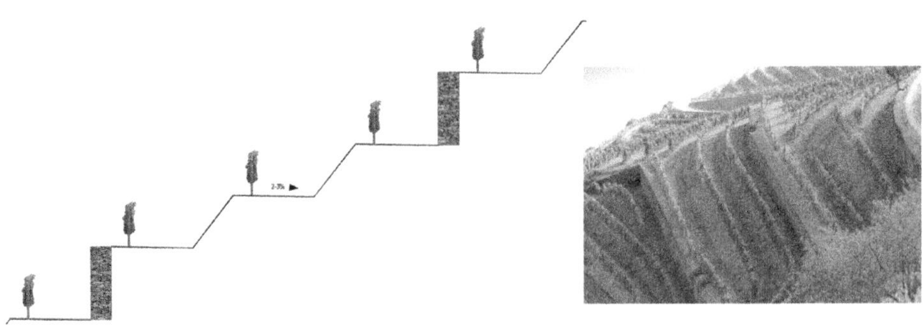

Figure 13.4 Walled terraces with land platforms.

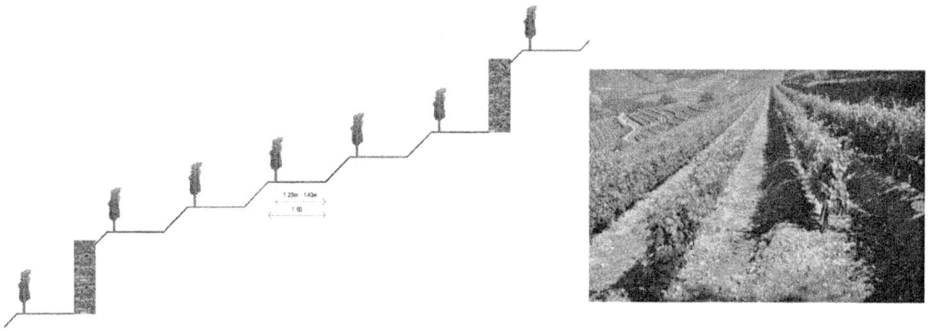

Figure 13.5 Land walled terraces with narrow platforms.

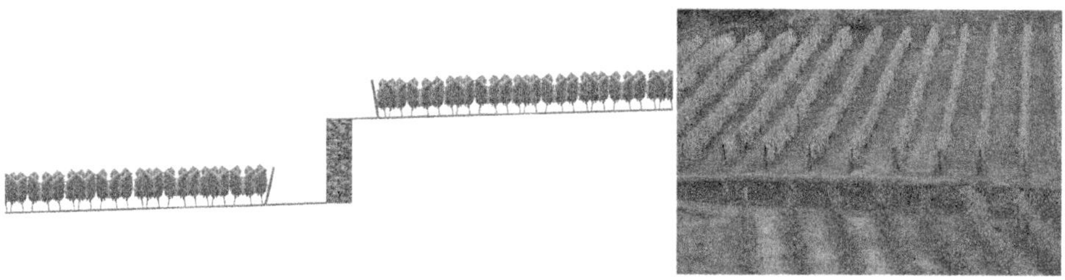

Figure 13.6 Vertical planting.

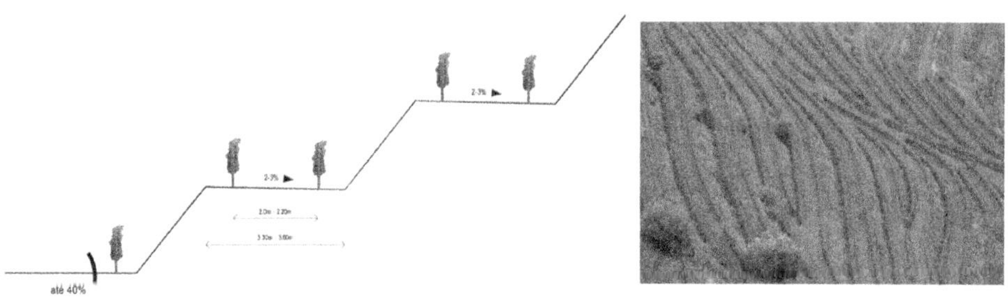

Figure 13.7 Wide platforms.

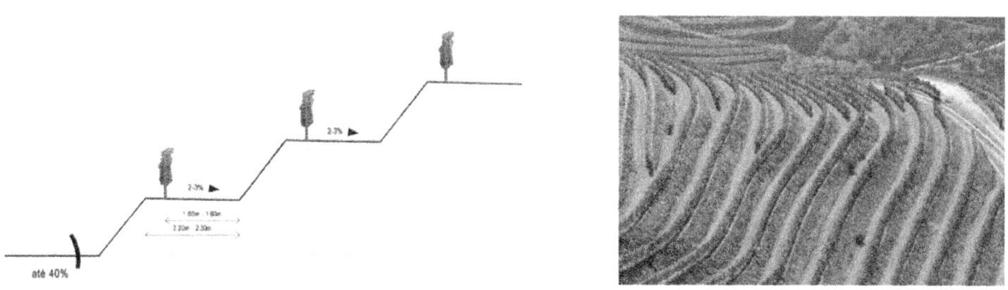

Figure 13.8 Narrow platforms.

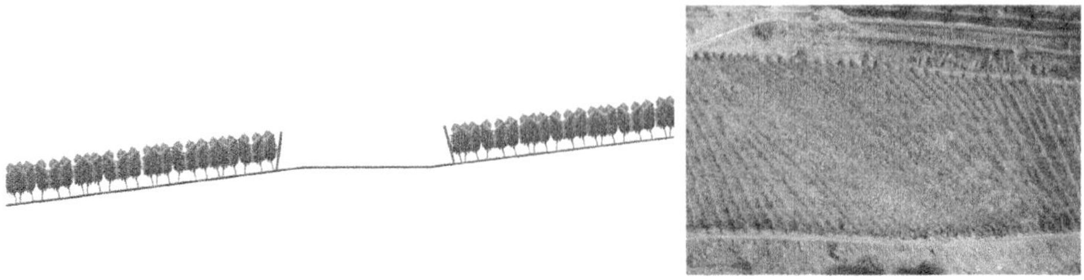

Figure 13.9 Vertical planting.

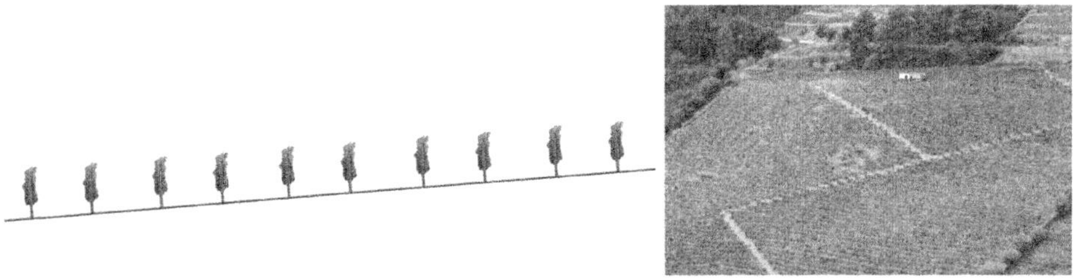

Figure 13.10 No land organization.

14 Consuming our national parks

Cultural heritage in a consumer culture

Stephen Wearing, Stephen Schweinsberg and Simon Darcy

Introduction

Over the course of the 150-year history of the national park movement, we have seen dramatic changes in humankind's relationship to the natural world based around the evolving interaction of two contradictory and also mutually reinforcing forces; environmental preservation and the altruistic motives of human society and industry. In the chapter we will suggest that landscapes such as national parks are best seen as "symbolic environments created by human acts of conferring meaning to nature and the environment, of giving the environment definition and form from a particular angle of vision and through a special filter of values and beliefs" (Greider & Garkovich, 1994, p. 1). In short, they are cultural spaces as much as physical spaces. What constitutes a person's perspective of a national park is a series of public benefits, social beliefs and values that are in a constant state of becoming. As Denzin (2005, 2007, 2008) has noted in the context of the historically formulated position of Native Americans in the landscape of Yellowstone National Park, it is through the quoting of history with all of its inbuilt societal and cultural discourses that we are able to "expose those contradictions and ruptures that brought science, art, capitalism, railroads and tourism together" (2008, p. 453) in the production of national park space.

Historically, the rise of neoliberalism across western governments has seen an increasing emphasis on developing user-fee systems in areas that have traditionally been regarded as "public goods" (Veal, 2002). As national park environments have come under greater pressure commercially and recreationally, the governments charged with the upkeep and management of the terrestrial and maritime areas have been required to provide higher levels of service for stakeholder groups and to manage user conflicts. The user conflicts are brought about by competing uses for the same areas that are either under pressure from their spatial location to population centres or through having competing uses within the same spatial context. The user-pays approach is now well-established in protected areas worldwide to provide and maintain visitor facilities, and for the conservation and management of park estate (Steckenreuter & Wolf, 2013). We see that user fees can contribute to the financial sustainability of national parks (Thur, 2010; Uyarra, Gill, & Ct, 2010)

Any level of management requires resources for the increased level of service provision. With an underlying philosophical dislike of larger government, neoliberalism seeks to reduce the size of government through cutting costs and at the same time recoup costs from those who benefit commercially from the public good. National park environments are a classic example where user fees have been developed based on a series of "private use" rights as a way of avoiding the "tragedy of the commons" (Hardin, 1968). Private use rights can be assigned through a variety of mechanisms over space and time (Lindberg, 2001). Private use rights are based on the following conceptual approaches: exclusivity where other potential uses are excluded; the disability where national park sites can be divided over space or time; duration where use can be provided for investments to be made by commercial operators, for example, a 99-year lease; rights have a transfer ability that, from a market perspective, allow efficient operators to purchase from less efficient operators; and there is a quality of title where, if there is a breach of the use right, it can be enforceable due to some form of policing and legal definition. In the most extreme cases, private use rights deny public access to the national park environments (e.g. private beaches in the USA). The Great Barrier Reef Marine Park Authority (2002) recognised the importance of generating its own funds but decided that its user-pays fees would be generated from stakeholders who are commercial operators. This allowed independent recreational and tourism users access to the Great Barrier Reef without incurring charges. However, those users accessing the Great Barrier Reef through commercially provided services pay a predetermined and annually reviewed fee, currently $6 per ticket sold, collected by the service provider who then passes this on to the authority as part of their licensing agreement. The determination of any user-fee system is based on the level of service to be provided, the extent to which the resource should be rationed and whether it is effective to collect charges (Van Sickle & Eagles, 1998). User fees also act as a regulatory mechanism to manage visitor numbers in national park environments where resources have been provided to management to enforce entry cf. Bonaire and Buraker (Dharmaratnea, Yee Sang, & Walling, 2000). This aspect of (albeit hypothetical) user fees is the basis of contingent valuation methods where recreationists and tourists make visitation decisions based on the relative cost of access to national park environments (Tongson & Dygico, 2004). However, as this chapter will argue with the march of neoliberalism, the recuperation of user charges has been overshadowed by a targeted consumerism of our national parks from both a recreational, tourist and industrial mechanism. In particular, we have seen the rise of the marketing of national parks to all manner of visitors in the same way that all tourist attractions have been marketed.

In the present chapter we will focus on the manner in which the evolution of neoliberalist-based cultures in national parks (see Sellars, 2009) has led to a reappraisal of humankind's relationship to our natural cultural heritage. Focussing in on the issue of tourism marketing, we will show how capitalist-based agendas have often sat uneasily with those aspects of the park space that sit outside of the expected tourist experiences. As Runte (1997) noted in his influential work *National Parks: The American Experience*, cultural nationalism is best pursued through the dramatisation of what society may expect to lose through indifference and apathy. With tourism marketing often having been predicated first and foremost on tapping into the innate wants and desires of travellers, such altruistic concerns have often meant that as the power of the environmental movement has grown, tourism marketing has often come to be somewhat unfairly situated as one of the primary architects of capitalist consumption (Sharpley & Pearce, 2007). Denzin (2008, p. 453) has eloquently noted that it is:

> "Capitalists who build hotels and railroads pay artists to paint pictures of exotic settings. These paintings are turned into advertisement, and used to entice tourists … Soon the economic and cultural geographies of tourism take over. Pristine wilderness and the wilderness experience are quickly commodified … If tourism is a devil's bargain, then paintings … are part of the devil's toolkit".

In this chapter we will explore whether it is necessarily fair to accept Denzin's analogy of the marketing industry as the devil's instrument. We will seek to achieve this aim with respect to a short case study of aspects of the representation of the Quarantine Station [hereafter Q Station] located in the North Head National Park, Sydney, Australia. Bashford (1998) has described the quarantine line as a mechanism for the creation of national identity through the demarcation spaces as variously self and other. Over the course of nearly two hundred years of history, the Q Station line has been owned and disowned by generations of users. Whilst it was only in recent years with the arrival of Mawland's Pty Ltd. and the establishment of a formal boutique resort that the area has taken on an overt industrialised tourism focus, the long history of often forced human engagement with the site has left generations of imprints on the natural environment. In the present chapter we will explore some aspects of the historical formulation of the Q Station as a consumptive space, situated as it is within a range of wider cultural and environmental preservation forces.

National parks, the Q Station and cultural heritage: the natural as sacred

In 1921 former Park Service Director Stephen Mather noted that "national parks are stabilizing and inspiring influences in times of national restlessness ... And there is no finer opportunity in the Americanisation movement than to spread the gospel of the parks far and wide" (Ross-Bryant, 2005, p. 31). Like America, Australia is also a former convict colony. Settled a little over 200 years ago as an outpost of the United Kingdom; Australia has since the earliest years of its European occupation viewed the environment as a buttress of its cultural legitimacy. For instance, the site of the earliest permanent European settlement in Australia, Sydney Harbour, has variously served as the site for early agriculture and industrial endeavour (Beasley, 1996; Edwards, Griffin, & Hayllar, 2010; Endersby, 2000; Proudfoot, 1996), as a front line for national defence (Hoskins, 2009; Karskens, 2009) and as the backdrop for major sporting and cultural events. Covering an area of 392 hectares, the Sydney Harbour Foreshore National Park has been created progressively since 1975 with the aim of preserving the natural and cultural history of the region. Managed variously by the Sydney Harbour Foreshore Authority, the Sydney Harbour Federation Trust, the Royal Botanic Gardens and Domain Trust and the NSW National Parks and Wildlife Service, the region includes some of the most iconic tourism and cultural sites in Australia including Fort Dennison, Camp Cove, Bradley's Head, Mrs Macquarie's Chair, Goat Island and the North Head National Park. Over the course of its history, the North Head National Park region has served as the home for the Australian Defence Force's School of Artillery and from 1828 until the 1980s the region was also the site for the North Head Quarantine Station.

The North Head Quarantine station site covers 31 hectares and includes 67 heritage buildings on the north head of Sydney Harbour and only a few kilometres from Manly, which was Australia's first tourism precinct (see Butler & McDonnell, 2011). The first use of the North Head site for the detaining of people suspected or confirmed as being infected with communicable diseases occurred in 1828 with the detaining of the convict ship *Bussorah Merchant* (Darcy & Wearing, 2009). Permanent facilities including hospital and accommodation blocks, processing facilities and administration centres were established progressively from the mid-nineteenth century with the area forming the backdrop to Australia's historical bid to combat the effects of a range of medical crises including the 1830s European cholera epidemic and later the 1957 Asian Flu Epidemic. A less positive aspect of the site's history relates to its use as a location for the forced detaining of Asian and other migrants (Bashford, 1998; Bashford & Strange, 2002). Some of the last recorded arrivals at the site were Vietnamese refugees and Cyclone Tracy survivors in the 1970s (Department of the Environment, ND). When the area was finally closed in the 1980s, more than 13,000 people from over 580 ships had been detained at the facility. From the time that the Q Station ceased to perform its historical disease preservation function and control of the site was ceded to the National Parks and Wildlife Service, there has been consternation in the community over its sustainable usage.

Scholarship by Darcy and Wearing (2009) and Wilson et al. (2009) have discussed recent stakeholder conflict over the use of the North Head Quarantine Station site in the context of moves by the National Parks and Wildlife Service to establish public–private partnerships. Recognising their responsibilities to maintain the site's cultural and environmental significance, the NPWS have, since the mid-1980s, sought to encourage small-scale commercial utilisation in the form of conferences, interpretive tours, etc. (Wearing & Darcy, 1999). Wearing et al. (2016) have noted that, due to limitations imposed by current state government funding arrangements, the NSW Government in the early 2000s put the site out to commercial tender, a process that led to the awarding of a 21-year-lease to the group Mawland Hotel Management Pty Ltd. in 2006. Darcy and Wearing (2009) have noted that the Mawlands proposal for the Quarantine Station site was the only proposal that did not include provisions for a major hotel development. Preferring instead to pursue a future of adaptive reuse and restoration, Mawlands have sought to restore a number of historical buildings and to develop the site as a cultural tourism precinct with facilities developed to allow for the running of guided tours, boutique restaurants and conference accommodation (Brown & Weber, 2011). Redevelopment of the site as a commercial resort was essentially finalised by 2008 with the new operators subject to some of the most stringent operating regulations in Australia (see Wilson et al. 2009).

Wearing et al. (2016, p. 63) have noted that "for all its potential as a site of conservation/tourism partnership, for years the Quarantine station redevelopment has been clouded by stakeholder contestation over its future" making it a wicked problem for tourism policy makers. Over 1,340 written submissions were received in a public inquiry in the late 1990s (Darcy and Wearing, 2009). Today a range of stakeholder groups can be identified for the Quarantine Station including the self-entitled Friends of the Quarantine Station (FOQS), the Manly Greens, Friends and Residents of Manly and the National Parks Association of NSW (see Darcy and Wearing, 2009). The mission statement of the FOQS is:

> To raise public awareness of the rich heritage that exists at Manly Quarantine Station, to campaign to reverse the current privatisation plans of the National Parks and Wildlife Service and to work towards a sustainable management structure for the Manly Quarantine Station which would preserve the station intact for this and future generations. (Friends of the Quarantine Station, 1999)

From its earliest days, the North Head Quarantine Station site has been characterised by consumptive patterns that are reflective of their time. Similar trends are observable in the broader scholarship on national parks (Goldstein, 1979; PBS, 2009; Runte, 1977, 1997; Runte, 2002; Sax, 1980). National parks are, at their core, "environmental management instruments created … to ensure that natural or near natural areas are set aside for to protect large scale ecological processes, along with the complement of species and ecosystems characteristic of the area" (International Union for the Conservation of Nature

2014 in Wearing, McDonald, Ankor, & Schweinsberg, 2015, p. 225). Notwithstanding the continued legislative responsibility of park managers to protect the natural world, national parks the world over have for many years now been characterised by evolving societal expectations of what our connection to the natural world should be. Much of the complexity in this area derives from the evolution of the sacred and cultural elements of national parks (see Ramakrisha, 2003). National Parks in the US have been described as nothing less than 'America's cathedrals' (Feinstein, 2006). Cronon (1996) has written on the overt religious imagery in the early environment writers including Muir and Thoreau. While the sacred imagery of the national park is often set apart from human reality, as something we can come back to – unchanging, Ross-Bryant (2005) has noted that increasingly the multiplicity of types of stakeholder engagement with parks means that it cannot simply be treated as abstract and separate from its reality. The sacred wilderness is inherently subject to change. As Klingle (2003) notes, consumption is spatial and historical in the sense that how we relate to the environment around us, such as, a national park, is dictated by the historical evolution of what is deemed to be acceptable over time.

Consumer culture and the North Head National Park: a match made in heaven or a devil's bargain

Over the course of the 150-year history of the North Head Quarantine Station, there is a dramatic shift observable in the way in which humankind has reacted to the same physical space. At a time in the early nineteenth century when steam ferries were first starting to traverse the seven mile sea crossing from Sydney Cove to Manly pier, ferrying tourists to what was to become Australia's first ever tourism resort, a mile or so further around the headland, other visitors to Sydney were facing a different kind of reality (Clarke, Frederick, & Williams, 2010, p. 80):

> Sky … Ocean
> I am very frightened of having the disease.
> Moreover the doctor is helpless to control the sickness.
> Feeling pessimistic and despondent
> I am not used to maintaining hygiene yet.
> If you asked me the feeling about the voyage
> I shall persuade you never to come here for pleasure.
> Wish you good health and a long life.
>
> Xie Ping De, a resident of HE Country
> Early summer, Ding Ji Year

People quarantined at the North Head Quarantine Station faced an uncertain future and a reality far removed from the opportunities afforded to contemporary visitors. The following quote is taken from the current Q Station website:

> Leave the hectic world behind and experience the magic of Sydney Harbour from the privacy of your own room. Wake up to the tranquil and wild beauty of Sydney Harbour National Park. Visualise a rich past while enjoying the comfort of contemporary conveniences. Q Station Sydney Harbour National Park Manly

> (Q Station) is one of Australia's significant heritage and environmental landmarks preserved within 30 stunning hectares of Sydney Harbour National Park.
>
> It is the ultimate way to experience the unique grounds of Sydney Harbour National Park, with everything you could want in a getaway.
>
> From swimming, snorkelling and kayaking to bush walking or simply just relaxing, you can experience the invigorating, restorative beauty of the Australian bush and the salt sea air. End the day by dining on the edge of Sydney's amazing Harbour at the Boiler house Harbourside Restaurant & Bar.
>
> Powerfully inspiring and truly unique, Q Station is located at the historic site of the former Quarantine Station at North Head. There's nothing like feeling history's power with Q Station's expansive and historic surrounds. Host a meeting or a conference; celebrate a birthday or an anniversary; or just get away for the weekend.
>
> (Q Station, 2015)

Clarke et al. (2010) characterise early visitors to the Q Station as travellers; travellers that made the most perilous of journeys before seeking to leave messages for others who would follow. The rock art that can be found throughout the Q Station site today, and which forms an important part of the modern tourism experience, is a form of tourism marketing (Clarke et al., 2010). Much as Australian Aborigines used rock engravings as a form of cultural expression, so too did early visitors to the Q Station seek to leave their mark on the environment in which they travelled. In doing so they were essentially helping to define personally negative aspects of cultural heritage that paradoxically are so prized by consumers today. In the rest of this section we will consider the implications of this historically informed evolution of the national park cultural space for the marketing of culture in national parks.

In its most basic form the role of tourism marketing and the strategies that surround it are predicated on an "internally integrated but externally focussed set of choices about how a firm addresses its customers in the context of a competitive environment" (Clegg, Carter, Kornberger, & Schweitzer, 2011, p. 150). Mainstream tourism industry interests have historically placed the tourist at the centre of marketing endeavours. Whilst understandable in the sense that supporting the attainment of a desired tourism experience is central to all tourism industries throughout the world, the corresponding tendency for tourism marketing to thus be seen as the instrument of an inherently evil neoliberal and capitalist marketing system has, we would suggest, created barriers for the active integration of tourism into broader national park land use planning (see arguements in S. Wearing et al., 2016). Donohoe (2012) has suggested in the context of a discussion of World Heritage areas that the power of the heritage brand is not defined on the basis of whether site x or site y makes a particular preservation list. Instead, its power is derived from the way it is marketed and the ability of the marketer to tap into historically formulated links that a society sees in an area's preservation.

What value is there in the Q Station on Sydney's North Head National Park? Previous scholarship has answered this question by seeking to apply stakeholder theory to the study of public–private partnerships in a contested cultural space. Darcy and Wearing (2009) established that as much as stakeholder collaboration is key to sustainable development, so to do all stakeholders have immense pride in the formative effects of historical cultural institutions. Whether one sees the modern Q Station as an example of poor planning or as a sustainable and responsible adaptive reuse of a cultural tourism site, is in many respects irrelevant; there will always be ideological debates over the sale of public land to commercial tourism interests. As to whether such sales or leases are good or bad depends, we would suggest, on the ability of tourism industry interests to promote the recognition of an all-encompassing and respectful notion of culture. Engelstad (2009) has argued that legitimacy is central to any individual or group being able to lay claim to a culturally accepted position of power. The processes whereby cultural-based tourism industries can claim cultural legitimacy is contentious and is dependent on the ability of tourism managers to merge cultural preservation interests with product development interests (McKercher, Ho, & du Cros, 2005). In national parks, managers have often resorted to demarketing and other strategies designed to drive down tourism visitation numbers in an attempt to almost by default limit tourism's impact by limiting its size (Armstrong & Kern, 2011; Beeton, 2001; Beeton & Benfield, 2002; Kern, 2006; Kotler & Levy, 1971; McKercher, Weber, & du Cros, 2008).

Tools including demarketing have their place in an expanding lexicon of marketing methods that are available to park managers. Armstrong and Kern (2011, p. 34) noted in the context of future research directions that "diverse cultural and political contexts will have an effect on the use of demarketing". Such contexts have been evident in the work of Darcy and Wearing (2009). In this paper it was identified that the community action group Friends of the Quarantine Station were concerned about the potential loss of control of important parts of one's cultural heritage that may result from privatisation. At the time of writing, it has been ten years since Mawlands first signed the lease for the Quarantine Station site and people must evaluate on its merits whether Mawlands has been successful in achieving the sustainable management conditions it was prescribed by the government. As such, the question of whether consumer culture at the North Head National Park is a match made in heaven or a devil's bargain is still an open question.

Hall and Tucker (2004) noted that it is only through human valuing and interpretation that sites become significant. Over the last few decades a substantial body of literature has been published over the authenticity of tourism (Cohen, 1988; Gilmore & Pine, 2007; Hillman, 2007; Hughes, 1995; Johnson, 2009; MacCannell, 1973; Pearce & Moscardo, 1986; Reisinger & Steiner, 2006; Steiner & Reisinger, 2006; Wang, 1999), authenticity being important to the present discussion in the sense that what is valued by tourists may not necessarily be a true reflection of history. But what of the aforementioned situation where it is the constituent parts of the living history of the site (specifically the early migrants and other residents of the Q Station) that have laid the groundwork for defining the cultural significance of the site through their engravings and other historical remains? To quote Stewart (1993, p. 50 in Clarke et al. 2010, p. 82):

> "The inscriptions become souvenirs of these events by capturing the viewer into a reverie that restores a sense of the contexts and times of their creation".

By opening ourselves up to the possibility that tourists can in some circumstances be the creators of authenticity for future generations, we are left with the prospect that consumer culture and heritage need not always be mutually exclusive and opposing forces. Instead, there is the possibility that tourism and consumer culture can create and support the maintenance of cultural heritage, a point that the United Nations World Tourism Organisation (2015) recently made in the course of advertising 2017 as the International Year of Sustainable Tourism for Development, where they recognised:

"the importance of international tourism, and particularly of the designation of an international year of sustainable tourism for development, in fostering better understanding among peoples everywhere, in leading to a greater awareness of the rich heritage of various civilizations and in bringing about a better appreciation of the inherent values of different cultures, thereby contributing to the strengthening of peace in the world".

Conclusions

There is no doubt that our natural cultural heritage is being consumed by our neo-liberalist treatment of nature. In the present chapter we have examined the case of our national parks where the commercialisation of recreation and travel experiences has become a central tenant of management and income generation. We have demonstrated the complexities of this relationship and find that, as a result of this commodification of nature, the tourism industries need the national park environment in its various physical, socio/cultural, economic and other forms as much as said environments need tourism to add value to their long-term sustainable development. By encouraging visitors to enjoy and value the environment and culture of the area they are entering and at the same time pay for their usage, it becomes possible for tourism services to make positive contributions to the local communities and others who inhabit a park locale.

We have asked what activities "are truly green enough to serve the long term interests of the environment and its inhabitants" (Shultz and Holbrook, 1999, p. 218) and suggest this is an evolving question for national parks in contemporary society. The answer, we would argue, comes from our ability to reconcile the commodification process. In this chapter we have demonstrated how the commodification of park environments and our cultural heritage are a part of the way neo-liberalist societies work and in this socially constructed environment in which national parks have developed, this has offered both opportunities and costs.

References

Armstrong, E., & Kern, C. (2011). Demarketing manages visitor demand in the Blue Mountains National Park. *Journal of Ecotourism, 10*(1), 21–37.

Bashford, A. (1998). Quarantine and the imagining of the Australian nation. *Health, 2*(4), 387–402.

Bashford, A., & Strange, C. (2002). Asylum-seekers and national histories of detention. *Australian Journal of Politics & History, 48*(4), 509–527.

Beasley, M. (1996). *Wharfies: A history of the Waterside Workers' Federation of Australia*. Rushcutters Bay, Australia: Halsted Press.

Beeton, S. (2001). *Cyclops and sirens - Demarketing as a proactive response to negative consequences of one-eyed competitive marketing.* Paper presented at the Travel and Tourism Research Association 32nd Annual Conference Proceedings, Fort Myers, FL.

Beeton, S., & Benfield, R. (2002). Demand control: The case for demarketing as a visitor and environmental management tool. *Journal of Sustainable Tourism, 10*(6), 497–513.

Brown, G., & Weber, D. (2011). Public participation GIS: A new method for national park planning. *Landscape and Urban Planning, 102*(1), 1–15.

Butler, R., & McDonnell, I. (2011). One man and his boat (and hotel and pier…): Henry Gilbert Smith and the establishment of Manly, Australia. *Tourism Geographies, 13*(3), 343–359.

Clarke, A., Frederick, U., & Williams, A. (2010). Wish you were here: Historic inscriptions from the North Head Quarantine Station, Manly, NSW. *Australian Historical Archaeology.*

Clegg, S. R., Carter, C., Kornberger, M., & Schweitzer, J. (2011). *Strategy: Theory and practice*. London: Sage.

Cohen, E. (1988). Authenticity and commoditization in tourism. *Annals of Tourism Research, 15*(3), 371–386.

Cronon, W. (1996). The trouble with wilderness: Or, getting back to the wrong nature. *Environmental History, 1*(1), 7–28.

Darcy, S., & Wearing, S. (2009). Public–private partnerships and contested cultural heritage tourism in national parks: A case study of the stakeholder views of the North Head Quarantine Station (Sydney, Australia). *Journal of Heritage Tourism, 4*(3), 181–199.

Denzin, N. K. (2005). Indians in the park. *Qualitative Research, 5*(1), 9–33.

Denzin, N. K. (2007). Indians in the park: Part II. *Studies in Symbolic Interaction, 24*(1), 33–44.

Denzin, N. K. (2008). Drawn to Yellowstone. *Qualitative Research, 8*(4), 451–472.

Department of the Environment. (ND). National Heritage Places – North Head, Sydney. from https://www.environment.gov.au/heritage/places/national/north-head

Dharmaratnea, G. S., Yee Sang, F., & Walling, L. J. (2000). Tourism potentials for financing protected areas. *Annals of Tourism Research, 27*(3), 590–610.

Donohoe, H. M. (2012). Sustainable heritage tourism marketing and Canada's Rideau Canal world heritage site. *Journal of Sustainable Tourism, 20*(1), 121–142.

Edwards, D., Griffin, T., & Hayllar, B. (2010). Darling Harbour: Looking back and moving forward. In B. Hayllar, T. Griffin, & D. Edwards (Eds.), *City Spaces – Tourist Places* (pp. 275–294). Oxford: Butterworth-Heinmann.

Endersby, J. (2000). A garden enclosed: Botanical barter in Sydney, 1818–39. *The British Journal for the History of Science, 33*(3), 313–334.

Engelstad, F. (2009). Culture and power. In S. Clegg, M. Haugaard (Eds.), *The SAGE Handbook of Power* (pp. 210–238). London: SAGE Publications.

Feinstein, D. (2006). Senator Feinstein warns against proposed revisions to National Park Service Management policies. from http://www.feinstein.senate.gov/public/index.cfm/press-releases?ID=792a0162-7e9c-9af9-75de-6ff377def008

Friends of the Quarantine Station. (1999, 26 January 2012). Welcome. from http://www.manlyquarantine.com/Title.html

Gilmore, J. H., & Pine, B. J. (2007). *Authenticity: What consumers really want.* (Vol. 1). Boston, MA: Harvard Business School Press.

Goldstein, W. (1979). *Australia's 100 years of national parks*. Sydney, Australia: National Parks and Wildlife Service.

Great Barrier Reef Marine Park Authority. (2002). Framework for Management. Cairns, Australia: GBRMPA.

Greider, T., & Garkovich, L. (1994). Landscapes: The social construction of nature and the environment. *Rural Sociology, 59*(1), 1–24.

Hall, C., & Tucker, H. (Eds.). (2004). *Tourism and postcolonialism: Contested discourses, identities and representations*. London: Routledge.

Hardin, G. (1968). The tragedy of the commons. *Science, 162*(168), 1243–1248.

Hillman, W. (2007). Revisiting the concept of (objective) authenticity. *Public Sociologies: Lessons and Trans-Tasman Comparisons.*

Hoskins, I. (2009). *Sydney Harbour: A History*. Sydney, Australia: UNSW Press.

Hughes, G. (1995). Authenticity in tourism. *Annals of Tourism Research, 22*(4), 781–803.

Johnson, N. (2009). Authenticity. In R. J. Johnston, D. Gregory, G. Pratt, M. Watts, & S. Whatmore (Eds.), *The Dictionary of Human Geography* (5th ed., p. 40). Oxford: Blackwell Publishers.

Karskens, G. (2009). *The colony: a history of early Sydney*. Crows Nest, Australia: Allen & Unwin.

Kern, C. L. (2006). *Demarketing as a tool for managing visitor demand in national parks: an Australian case study*. University of Canberra.

Klingle, M. W. (2003). Spaces of consumption in environmental history. *History and Theory, 42*(4), 94–110.

Kotler, P., & Levy, S. J. (1971). Demarketing, yes, demarketing. *Harvard Business Review, 49*(6), 74–80.

Lindberg, K. (2001). Protected area visitor fees overview. Retrieved 1 Jan, 2006, from www.ecotourism.org/onlineLib/Uploaded/ Protected%20Area%20Visitor%20Fee%20(Country).pdf

MacCannell, D. (1973). Staged authenticity: Arrangements of social space in tourist settings. *American Journal of sociology, 79*(3), 589–603.

McKercher, B., Ho, P. S., & du Cros, H. (2005). Relationship between tourism and cultural heritage management: Evidence from Hong Kong. *Tourism Management, 26*(4), 539–548.

McKercher, B., Weber, K., & du Cros, H. (2008). Rationalising inappropriate behaviour at contested sites. *Journal of Sustainable Tourism, 16*(4), 369–385.

PBS. (2009). The national parks: America's best idea. from http://www.pbs.org/nationalparks/

Pearce, P. L., & Moscardo, G. M. (1986). The concept of authenticity in tourist experiences. *Journal of Sociology, 22*(1), 121–132.

Proudfoot, P. R. (1996). *Seaport Sydney: The making of the city landscape*. Sydney, Australia: University of New South Wales.

Q Station. (2015). Welcome to the Q Station.

Ramakrisha, P. (2003). Conserving the sacred: The protective impulse and the origins of modern protected areas. In D. Harmon & A. Putney (Eds.), *The full value of parks: From economics to the intangible* (pp. 27–42). Lanham: Rowman and Littlefield.

Reisinger, Y., & Steiner, C. J. (2006). Reconceptualizing object authenticity. *Annals of Tourism Research, 33*(1), 65–86.

Ross-Bryant, L. (2005). Sacred sites: Nature and nation in the US national parks. *Religion and American Culture, 15*(1), 31–62.

Runte, A. (1977). The national park idea: Origins and paradox of the American experience. *Forest & Conservation History, 21*(2), 64–75.

Runte, A. (1997). *National parks: The American experience*. Lincoln, NE: University of Nebraska Press.

Runte, A. (2002). Why national parks?, from http://www.georgewright.org/192runte.pdf

Sax, J. L. (1980). *Mountains without handrails, reflections on the national parks*. Ann Arbor, MI: University of Michigan Press.

Sellars, R. W. (2009). *Preserving nature in the national parks: A history; With a new preface and epilogue*. New Haven, CT: Yale University Press.

Sharpley, R., & Pearce, T. (2007). Tourism, marketing and sustainable development in the English national parks: The role of National Park Authorities. *Journal of Sustainable Tourism, 15*(5), 557–573.

Shultz, C., & Holbrook, M. B. (1999). Marketing and the tragedy of the commons: A synthesis, commentary, and analysis for action. *Journal of Public Policy Marketing, 18*(2), 218–229.

Steckenreuter, A., & Wolf, I. D. (2013). How to use persuasive communication to encourage visitors to pay park user fees. *Tourism Management, 37*, 58–70.

Steiner, C. J., & Reisinger, Y. (2006). Understanding existential authenticity. *Annals of Tourism Research, 33*(2), 299–318.

Thur, S. M. (2010). User fees as sustainable financing mechanisms for marine protected areas: An application to the Bonaire National Marine Park. *Marine Policy, 34*(1), 63–69.

Tongson, E., & Dygico, M. (2004). User fee system for marine ecotourism: The Tubbataha Reef Experience. *Coastal Management, 32*(1), 17–23.

Uyarra, M. C., Gill, J. A., & Ct, I. M. (2010). Charging for nature: Marine park fees and management from a user perspective. *Ambio, 39*(7), 515–523.

Van Sickle, K., & Eagles, P. F. (1998). Budgets, pricing policies and user fees in Canadian parks' tourism. *Tourism Management, 19*(3), 225–235.

Veal, A. J. (2002). *Leisure and Tourism Policy and Planning*. Wallingford, UK: CABI Publishing.

Wang, N. (1999). Rethinking authenticity in tourism experience. *Annals of Tourism Research, 26*(2), 349–370.

Wearing, S., & Darcy, S. (1999). Ecotourism options in coastal protected area management: A case study of North Head Quarantine Station, Australia. *Environmentalist, 18*(4), 239–249.

Wearing, S., Schweinsberg, S., & Tower, J. (2016). *The marketing of national parks for sustainable tourism*. Clevedon, UK: Channel View.

Wearing, S. L., McDonald, M., Ankor, J., & Schweinsberg, S. (2015). The nature of aesthetics: How consumer culture has changed our national parks. *Tourism Review International, 19*(4), 225–233.

Wilson, E., Nielsen, N., & Buultjens, J. (2009). From lessees to partners: Exploring tourism public–private partnerships within the New South Wales national parks and wildlife service. *Journal of Sustainable Tourism, 17*(2), 269–285.

World Tourism Organisation (UNWTO). (2015, 7 December). Press release – United Nations declares 2017 as the International Year of Sustainable Tourism for Development. from http://media.unwto.org/press-release/2015-12-07/united-nations-declares-2017-international-year-sustainable-tourism-develop

15 Let it all fall down

Delighting in anti-heroes, alternative heritage and ruination

Anthony Patterson

The unhappiest place on Earth

I deeply mourned the death of my favourite anti-hero, A.A. Gill. His *Sunday Times* column was always dazzlingly inventive. Back in the day, its sparkle was the only reason I bought the paper. Adrian's writing stood out from that of his fellow journalists. He had an artful way with prose that few could emulate, and he was funny as hell. Moreover, his nihilistic outlook chimed well with my own once wantonly destructive sensibility. Prophetically, in his drink-sodden autobiography, *Pour Me a Life*, he claimed that he "prayed humbly and sincerely and without regret for an irrevocable death sentence. I didn't ask from rage or irony, not to shake a fist at the uncaring heavens, but with honest sincerity. I prayed like a self-mortifying hermit for terminal cancer." (Gill 2015, p. 26) In a cruel stroke of misfortune his prayers were answered.

What also appealed to me about Adrian was his love of the forlorn, for all that is sad and sorry in this world. His tendency to savour the worst that life can offer is best exemplified in his description of The Lindsey, a dilapidated underground drinking club in the west end of London where, by his own admission, he spent too many hours relishing its alternative heritage.

> The place was coated with nicotine and despair. It was the most hopelessly sad and lonely room I've ever known. There were glazed windows with curtains, behind which was painted a Home Counties landscape, a wry trompe l'oeil that twisted the truth—we were in a cellar, a burrow, a tomb where the wounded, sodden, failed and frightened came to hide. On the wall there was a reproduction of a painting of eighteenth-century huntsmen enjoying a tale and a tincture in some amiable country hostelry. They were the bucolic English yeomen of yore, ruddy and true, loyal, jolly, prosperous and sturdy. The picture was a slap, a caution, a reminder of how far from the ideal of manhood and society I had fallen. All the coy sentimental attempts to cheer up the bar, tranquilize it with kitsch, the plastic flamenco dancers and china poodles, became the malevolent props of a horror movie…I loved it. I loved it because it was so perfectly tailored to me—a room I could look in the eye and know that it loved me right back.
>
> (Gill 2015, p. 9–11).

Curiously though, dilapidation, unless rendered in hyperreal retroscape style (Brown and Sherry 2003), is something neither heritage nor marketing – and by heritage, I mean, the practices and policies that organise our relationship to the material past – normally celebrate. Marketing's obsession, after all, has ever been with the new and improved (Tedlow 1990; Patterson *et al.* 2008). Its thrust is often the creation of fantastic and amazing experiences that enchant and delight (Kawaski 2011). Lamentably, this usually entails being on trend with the contemporary whims of fashion and technology, even if the abiding concern is the preservation of heritage. The zeal to embrace augmented reality to showcase how things once were is just one such example. Having digested a lifetime's exposure to such thinking, a marketer might well be set on entrancing consumers with a multi-sensory experience where service exceeds expectations and the customer is King. The tacit goal, it seems, is to aspire to Disneyland's credo of creating new spaces that each aspire to be 'The Happiest Place on Earth'. For their part, when heritage advocates deem something historic to be of value their default instinct is to preserve and conserve. DeSilvey (2017, p. 2) vividly describes how the heritage industry might attempt to save a crumbling building. Actions are enacted to "strip off the ivy, repoint the mortar, clear the base, and install an informational plaque with a potted history to justify the expense of intervention. The structure would be infilled with official memory and asked to perform as an object of heritage".

Only on the scholarly fringes, in the ill-lit shadows, will you find glum contributors to obscure books about cultural heritage fraternising with scholars revelling in the study of dark tourism and other seedy consumption practices (Sharpley and Stone 2009). It is here that we consider the significance of atypical consumers exemplified by the dear departed A.A. Gill, those who prefer to elope from the sterility of business-ready units in favour of lamentably dishevelled venues like The Lindsey, whose grimy authenticity they find more appealing. The faux distressed wood in a hipster barber shop, the exposed network of metal pipes in the ceiling of a trendy eatery or the fake water-stained rings on a theme pub's tables are anathema to them. These wretched few belong in the 'Unhappiest Place on Earth' where perversely they will be content or at least more content than they would otherwise have been.

Nonetheless, the question of why this should be so has been little addressed. While critical heritage studies in relation to alternative heritage tend to focus on the much worthier subject of the plight of the marginalised and disenfranchised (Winter 2013), this chapter seeks purely to explain its allure. Taking advantage of the freedom that writing a book chapter allows, it in part focuses on a literary consideration of its popularity by periodically reflecting on the musing of Gill and others. Ultimately, I suggest that those appreciative of alternative heritage have three qualities in common: an interest in *retroscendence*, *impoverished enrichment* and *catharsis*. I conclude by hoping that the 'heritage industry' will in future, on occasion at least, just let it all fall down (Hewison 1987).

Retroscendence

I first encountered the concept of 'retroscendence' while reading Will Self's (1993) fabulously off-kilter debut novel, *My Idea of Fun*. Appropriately enough, much like the heritage hovels celebrated in this chapter, it could easily offend pusillanimous readers. There is a shockingly graphic scene in the opening few pages, much too vulgar to recount in these well-mannered pages, that might leave you questioning your choice of reading material. Written in the *Bildungsroman* tradition, the book tells the tale of how an impressionable young apprentice is schooled in marketing's dark art by a wily grandmaster, none too charmingly called 'The Fat Controller'. One of the memorable lessons he teaches is the 'fun' activity of retroscending. While not without an uncanny otherworldly dimension, akin to travelling back through time, the concept essentially "enables us to take any element in our visual field and, as it were, unpack its history" (p. 110). He further elaborates that the technique makes it "possible to enter into the very history of a product, any product, the Porsche or the crisp packet, and flow down its evolutionary folkways, zoom back to the point where it was as yet undifferentiated, unpositioned, unintentional, and therefore not about anything" (p. 212).

While reflecting on Gill's strong kinship with The Lindsey, it struck me that he calls forth on something like retroscendence. He certainly reflects deeply on its convoluted history. Declaring, for instance, "the Lindsey hadn't always been like this, it too had a past, had aspirations. Once it was a theater club, a soigné stage for amateur and professional rising talent. The young Dirk Bogarde had played the Lindsey, the yellowing poster was here to prove it." (p. 11) His ability to retroscend, to appreciate the complete weight of its history and its interwoven concatenations, partially explains why it means so much to him. Its current state of shabbiness is made more poignant when armed with full knowledge of its once illustrious past. Its corrosion also parallels the breakdown of his own body which age, time and ill-treatment have withered. Being in such a place can thus initiate a dichotomous process of moving from the past to the present wherein spatial and bodily memories collide. This, in turn, prompts a deep yearning and sense of profundity that can be quite agreeable to the contemplative sensorium (Robinson 2005). And if that all seems too much like abstract metaphysical babble, well then do not take my word for it. Read instead how the poet Shelley perfectly evokes the bittersweet wistfulness of such affectivity:

> We look before and after,
> And pine for what is not:
> Our sincerest laughter
> With some pain is fraught;
> Our sweetest songs are those that tell of saddest thought.

Elsewhere it has been noted that retro-consumption in retroscapes produces retro-flection, but until now the interplay between memory and emotion provoked by retroscendence has perhaps been understated (Patterson and Brown 2003).

Impoverished enrichment

Understanding what I prefer to call *impoverished enrichment*, otherwise identified as the 'slumming it' movement, can also help explain the attraction of alternative heritage settings (Frenzel *et al.* 2012; Frenzel 2016). Controversially, authentic 'slummers' literally seek to experience the thrill of spending time in the slums of places like Brazil and India. While such behaviour can be beneficial to the residents by perhaps bringing badly needed revenue into the community, often the incursion of mostly white Northern tourists casts them as "victims of the voyeuristic tourist gaze" (Frenzel 2016, p. 12). The continued existence of the Pom Mahakan community in the centre of Bangkok serves as an example of just such an ambiguous co-existence between residents and tourists. The Bangkok Metropolitan Authority consider the place a slum and have been trying to bulldoze it for years to make way for the creation of a new heritage zone in the city. Interest shown by tourists is the only remaining obstacle that stops this from occurring. While the residents would perhaps like to get on with living their lives, to ensure that this alternative heritage site is not destroyed, they must continually sustain the tourist impulse by organising festivals and guided tours (De Cesari and Herzfeld 2015).

My concept of impoverished enrichment though is less bound up with the notions of colonialism or postcolonial reclamation. For me, it encapsulates the rise of DIY global backpacking tours where little is preplanned. You might sleep in a hostel one night and under the stars on another. The term describes the on-the-edge amateurs who undertake life-threatening mountain climbs. Though it is not just about near-death adventures. It can also capture the essence of what it is like to spend time in a grim ramshackle pub. The Urban Dictionary (2018) details a humorous first-person, though not altogether unproblematic, example of slumming behaviour: "Went incognito up to the council estate and visited a public house doing Karaoke. Smoked forty fags, sang five songs, ate fish and chips and made out with a single parent mother."

Impoverished enrichment also has some affinity with what Douglas Copeland (1991, p. 137) labels, 'Underdogging'. In *Generation X* he describes it as "the tendency to almost invariably side with the underdog in a given situation. The consumer expression of this trait is the purchasing of less successful, 'sad', or failing products." This is certainly something that everyday consumers do. Intent on exploring this theme, recently I asked in an online forum whether anyone had ever bought something they felt sorry for. Among the many emotive responses was this delightful example:

> I have quite often bought the last item of something from a shop simply because it "looked lonely". I did it the other day with some croissants. I wanted to buy four, but that would have meant there was one left on the display. I couldn't bear the thought that I had taken away all its friends and it would be left there all alone, so I bought the 5th one too!
>
> I know it's irrational, and I can see how it's a (blatantly obvious) projection of my own concerns. And yet these feelings continue to affect me.

While impoverished enrichment might seem far away from the moral quandary of whether or not to buy a lonely croissant, there is a high probability that it will place you in the vicinity of other destitute objects or people. And rather than turn away from them, often our natural human instinct to protect the vulnerable and weak will kick in. By way of illustration, Gill tells a moving story in his autobiography about meeting a boy who:

> sidled up to me in the lobby of the Hotel Nacional in Havana and asked if I wanted to buy a bootleg tape of Cuban music… I didn't want the tape, but I asked the boy if he would like dinner and to tell me about his life here. He'd never eaten a steak before. All his school friends had piled onto an oil drum raft during the small window that a petulant Castro had offered to people who wanted to leave Cuba to get to Florida, ninety miles away. The boy had got as far as the shore, but didn't go with them because he lost his nerve and worried about his mother. "It was the worst decision of my life," he said. Now he spent hours on his bed feeling his life drift away and listened to American radio and dreamed about the parallel existence that might have been his in America.

A tendency to rejoice in ruinscapes also resonates with the notion of 'ironic consumption', where the idea is that 'the place is so bad that it's good'. It might have a detestable component, something that singles it out as being, what Thompson (2002, p. 133) describes as, "the absolute, epiphanic apogee of awfulness", but it is appreciated and loved all the more for it. In a memorable line from the movie *Ghost World*, a central character's appreciative comment about a naff 50s diner perfectly epitomises the sentiment: "This is so bad it's gone past good and back to bad again". In relation to bad experiences that are paradoxically good, Gill (2015, p. 9) found the extremely poor customer service he experienced in the Lindsey not so much objectionable as endearing. Affectionately, he notes that "Rita [the club owner] was permanently disapproving; she despised her customers as failed, pathetic specimens". Putting up with such a lot contradicts normal everyday expectations to such a degree that, amid the general ruination and ill-treatment, the few serendipitous purple moments that are gleaned become extremely precious, exclusive and therefore sought after.

Catharsis

Life in the First World, where most readers of this book live, is no picnic. The news is invariably grim. Daily we hear of the suffering that exposure to neoliberal ideals engenders among consumers. Regression with little in the way of progression is the story of our times. For its part, consumer and marketing research often characterises life as a scavenge through loveless lulls and days best forgotten (Shankar et al. 2006). As such, consumers are viewed as hedonists seeking to eke out of life what little joy and happiness they can muster (Holbrook and Hirschman 1982). Unsurprisingly, research of a managerial bent is thus firmly intent upon creating customer experiences that are typically described as 'super', 'fun', 'excellent', 'unforgettable' and 'brilliant'.

All of this is true.

And yet, there are those among us who prefer something deeper, more profound. Trite experiential marketing goals like those listed above, do not begin to capture the experience that some seek. There are those among us who actually enjoy wallowing in the misery of modern life. Eagle-eyed media commentators have begun to call such folk aficionados of "grief porn" (Warhurst 2014). They are said to have intensely emotional reactions to artworks – say a painting by Rothko, or a movie like the much-loved but tear-inducing opening scene in Pixar's *Up* (Elkins 2001). By the same token, they are likely to come over all lachrymose upon succumbing to the social media 'clickbait' that proliferates, such as the legion of cute animal videos on Facebook.

Such people are not emotional wrecks on the verge of mental breakdown. Really, what they seek are cathartic moments. Aristotle's concept of catharsis describes the cleansing or 'purification' of the mind that crying by means of witnessing an enacted tragedy can induce. Catharsis, as a concept, it should be said, does not just refer to emotional release brought on by tragedy. It can also help explain our love of horror movies and the like, which admittedly are not for everyone, or the rise of 'dark tourism' where people find perverse pleasure in learning about the anguish that has been wrought on mankind at various historical junctures. Cue the stream of tourists at Nagasaki Atomic Bomb Museum, or at the House of Terror in Budapest. In addition, at the opposite end of the cathartic continuum, it can refer to the emotional release that elicits from the subversions of comedic entertainment.

It is well-documented that heritage sites, especially those that are commercially orientated, can offer significant opportunities to experience a heightened sense of emotional release. Research by Schramm (2007), for instance, who studied the effects of

African-Americans returning to Ghana, noted the cathartic nature of their experience when they visited commemorative slave sites. Gill (2015, p. 45) recounts a similarly cathartic moment while visiting a museum:

> There is in all classical exhibits an overall, overwhelming sense of brokenness. Everything is a bit of something or is missing a bit. The recurring theme is not of creation but of destruction—you constantly try to repair the damage in your head, replace noses and arms, put back handles and spouts. We walked into a room and I burst into tears without warning. I was utterly overcome by sensation.

Ruminating in the aesthetics of such places heightens our susceptibility to the effect of affect (Weiss and Beal 2005). It can remind us of our mortality, the temporality of flesh and blood and all material objects. By helping to dislodge intransigent life perspectives that overlook such thoughts, we experience catharsis.

Exit through the gift shop

It is unfortunate that mainstream consumer and marketing researchers are not better acquainted with consumers who like to tarry in less than salubrious surrounding in search of retroscendence, impoverished enrichment and catharsis. Their natural disposition is to cater to the myth of normalcy (i.e. the mass market), where all reasonable, well-adjusted consumers are thought to reside. Theoretically at least, they espouse a wholesome 'clean living' ideology that marketers seek to mollify by creating a 'decaffeinated' reality, brimful of bland products like beer without alcohol, butter without butter and, of course, coffee without caffeine (Žižek 2002). Disciplines like heritage studies, whose latter-day push to become marketing-orientated, have likewise become similarly smitten by the myth of catering to moderately minded folk whose idea of fun is none is rather temperate (Misiura 2006). Thus, by osmosis, the demonstrable focus of much of the thinking of marketing's confrères frequently dwells on creating the inoffensive and bland. Consider, for instance, how Dickens World, which celebrated the life and work of Charles Dickens, was presented to its customers. The managing director placed the emphasis firmly on entertainment. He is quoted as saying: 'Visitors are not going to come here to be depressed so our role is to entertain them. We're not going to have starving babies crawling around on the cobblestones' (Lukas 2008, p. 166). Consequently, the experience on offer was empty and anodyne. Little wonder it is now defunct.

The existence of such an insipid consumer world is self-evident, but as Diken (2009, p. 3) rightly contends it is "paradoxically accompanied in our culture with a 'passion for the real', a carving for passion and excitement… The imperative 'Moderate'! goes hand in hand with another one, a desire for excitement, to feel life as vibrantly as possible". Being aware that some consumers wish to occupy this space led the prankster artist, Banksy, to create a parody of Disneyland – Dismaland. Hailed in its promotional blurb as "the UKs most disappointing new visitor attraction", this temporary installation is worth contemplating in light not only of how it skewers "utopian images depicting consumerist, neoliberal fantasies [which] substitute for reality in the modern world" (Moser 2017, p. 1046), but also for how it revels in its 'aesthetics of ruin' (Trigg 2009). I had the pleasure of visiting this artwork, and in the gift shop at the end, I eavesdropped on one visitor's summation of the experience. He was evidently thrilled by the unvarnished grimness of the various installations saying, as I recall: 'This is rubbish. I love it'.

Conclusions

This chapter serves as a counterpoint to those that assume cultural heritage is something that should necessarily sparkle and gleam with vitality. Its interest in always sprucing itself up with a lick of paint and a makeover and in protecting the public from the ugly reality of history can sometimes be self-defeating. Heritage should stay true to its decrepit and sometimes distressing core. For as Wilson (2012, p. 4) states: "We are enamoured of ruin. The deeper the darkness is, the more dazzling. Our secret and ecstatic wish: Let it all fall down".

References

Coupland, D. (1991). *Generation X: Tales for an Accelerated Culture*. St. Martin's Press.

De Cesari, C. and Herzfeld, M. (2015) "Urban Heritage and Social Movements", in Meskell, L. (ed.) *Global Heritage: A Reader* (pp. 171–195), Chichester: John Wiley & Sons.

DeSilvey, C. (2007). "Salvage memory: constellating material histories on a hardscrabble homestead", *Cultural Geographies*, 14(3), 401–424.

De Silvey, C. (2017) *Curated Decay: Heritage Beyond Saving*, Minneapolis, MN: University of Minnesota Press.

Diken, B. (2009) *Nihilism: Key Ideas*, London: Routledge.

Elkins, J. (2001) *Pictures and Tears: A History of People Who Have Cried in Front of Paintings*, London: Routledge.

Frenzel, F. (2016) *Slumming It: The Tourist Valorization of Urban Poverty*, London: Zed Books.

Frenzel, F., Koens, K. and Steinbrink, M. (2012) *Slum Tourism: Poverty, Power and Ethics*, London: Routledge.

Gill, A.A. (2015) *Pour Me: A Life*, London: Weidenfeld and Nicolson.

Hewison, R. (1987) *The Heritage Industry: Britain in a Climate of Decline*, London: Methuen Publishing Ltd.

Holbrook, M.B. and Hirschman, E.C. (1982) "The Experiential Aspects of Consumption: Consumer Fantasies, Feelings, and Fun", *Journal of Consumer Research*, 9(2), 132–139.

Kawaski, G. (2011) *Enchantment: The Art of Changing Hearts, Minds, and Actions*, London: Penguin Books.

Lukas, S. A. (2008) *Theme Park*, London: Reaktion Books.

Misiura, S. (2006) *Heritage Marketing*, Oxford: Butterworth-Heinemann.

Moser, K. (2017) "Exhuming the "Dismal" Reality Underneath Banal Utopian Signs: Banksy's Recent Parody of the Disneyfication of the Modern World", *The Journal of Popular Culture*, 50(5), 1024–1046.

Patterson, A. and Brown, S. (2003) "Comeback for the Craic: A Literary Pub Crawl", in: Brown, S. and Sherry, J. F. Jr., (eds.) *Time, Space, and the Market: Retroscapes Rising*, London: ME Sharp, 75–94

Patterson, A., Bradshaw, A. and Brown, S. (2008) "'Don't Forget the Fruit Gums, Chum': Marketing Under Erasure and Renewal", *Marketing Theory*, 8(4), 449–463.

Schramm, K. (2007) "Slave Route Projects: Tracing the Heritage of Slavery in Ghana", in de Jong, F. and Rowlands, M. (eds), *Alternative Imaginaries of Memory in West Africa*, (pp. 71–98). London: Left Coast Press.

Self, W. (1993). *My Idea of Fun*. NY Atlantic Monthly.

Shankar, A, Julie Whittaker, J. and Fitchett, J.A. (2006) "Heaven knows I'm miserable now", *Marketing Theory*, (4), 485–505.

Sharpley, R. and Stone, P. (eds.) *The Darker Side of Travel: The Theory and Practice of Dark Tourism*, Bristol: Channel View.

Robinson, J. (2005) *Deeper Than Reason: Emotion and its Role in Literature, Music, and Art*, Oxford: Oxford University Press.

Tedlow, R.S. (1990) *New and Improved: The Story of Mass Marketing in America*, London: Heinemann Professional Publishing.

Trigg, D. (2009) *The Aesthetics of Decay: Nothingness, Nostalgia, and the Absence of Reason*, New York: Peter Lang.

Weiss, H. M., & Beal, D. J. (2005). "Reflections on Affective Events Theory", in Askanasy, N. M., Zerbe, W., & Hartel, C. E. J. (eds.), *Research on Emotion in Organizations: The Effect of Affect in Organizational Settings* (Vol. 1, pp. 1–21). Oxford: Elsevier.

Warhurst, M. (2014) Tearjerker videos of cute animals: the new 'grief porn'. *The Guardian*, http://www.theguardian.com/lifeandstyle/2014/jul/16/tearjerker-videos-of-cute-animals-the-new-grief-porn

Winter, T. (2013) "Clarifying the Critical in Critical Heritage Studies". *International Journal of Heritage Studies*, 19(6), 532–545.

Žižek, S. (2002) *Welcome to the Desert of the Real*, London:Verso.

16 Conservation and looting of the Tam Ting caves and its impact on Lao heritage values[1,2]

Brian Egloff and Thongsa Sayavongkhamedy

Introduction

The focus of this paper is upon the conservation and subsequent looting of the Tam Ting caves in the Luang Prabang Province of the Lao People's Democratic Republic (Laos) and places those events within the context of the trade in illicit cultural property in South-East Asia. The Tam Ting caves are a relatively unique example as the assemblage of sculptures underwent conservation and an inventory was compiled between 1992 and 1997 with the extent of the looting being documented in 2011. The conservation and research at the Tam Ting caves provide empirical data that documents the massive scale of the illegal trade in cultural property and adds to an understanding of the nature and extent of trafficking networks in South-East Asia (Mackenzie and Davis 2014; Yates, Mackenzie and Smith 2017).

Although a better understanding of the nature and extent of the illicit traffic in cultural property is emerging, after decades of effort to control the trade there have been notable successes, but the overwhelming picture is one of frustration and failure. Christine Alder, Duncan Chappell and Kenneth Polk (2009: 132–133) in *Perspectives on the organization and control of the illicit traffic in antiquities in South East Asia* point out that 'one of the unique aspects of the traffic in antiquities is that the sale of antiquities has not been criminalized in most market nations', and that responses have been 'various laws which are aimed at prohibition of that traffic in the source environments'.

The authors quote Simon Mackenzie (2002: 160–161) that 'Ineffective prohibitions by source States combined with complex and hugely expensive civil mechanisms for recovery of looted artefacts, all amount to a system of legal governance which is demonstrably failing to stop the plunder'. Adler, Chappell and Polk are correct in that the trade is flourishing. Breaches of the national cultural property law in Laos and reports from neighbouring states indicate that looting is widespread, shifting in its geographical focus and is spurred on by substantial profits. Reports indicate that the looting of ancient sites and the breaking and entry into storerooms and religious buildings is rampant throughout much of Southern Asia (Pandy 2003; Thorosat 1999, 2001). Chhay Visoth (2011: 101–116) provides descriptions of the looting of archaeological sites in the vicinity of Angkor, Siem Reap Province while Phon Kaseka (2011) describes examples from the outskirts of Phnom Penh and at other sites throughout Cambodia. It is with reference to the north-west where extensive looting has occurred, that Kaseka (2011: 138) writes:

> Sadly, the impetus for looting still exceeds the efforts of the government and foreign interest groups to put a stop to it. Lack of time, money and trained professionals constitute a large part of the problem.

Seldom do researchers publish articles that describe in detail violations of national cultural property legislation, present contemporary investigative reports or review successful prosecutions. Generally speaking, prosecutions are not based upon cultural property legislation but upon criminal laws pertaining to theft.

Tam Ting conserved and then looted

Colleagues and students from the University of Canberra and the Lao Department of Heritage carried out conservation work between 1992 and 1997 at the Tam Ting caves in Laos (Johnson 1997). The looting that took place after the closure of the project and up to 2011 offers a picture of the extent of the taking and removal of cultural property where virtually all of the monumental and ancient pieces were stolen, some 666 sculptures. Tam Ting is the place where it is believed that the animistic religions of the distant past, featuring a water spirit of the Nam Kong, were brought together peacefully in the 14th century with the newly introduced Buddhist religion under the epic leader Fa Ngum (Fa Ngoum). Theravada Buddhism was in Lao before that time but it was Fa Ngum who promoted the widespread diffusion of the religion (Condominas 1970: 14). Tam Ting, also known as the Pak Ou Caves or Grottos, represents the national spirit of Lao; being one of peace and reconciliation, rather than of conflict and argument (see Figure 16.1).

Tam Ting, as one of thirty listed National Heritage places, is comprised of two separate but once contiguous limestone karst caves and the immediate landscape on the western bank of the Nam Kong (Mekong River) opposite the confluence with the Nam Ou and the riverside community of Ban Pak Ou. The caves are in an uninhabited locale, said to be occupied by spirits, but are easily accessed by river traffic. The lower cave, immediately above the Nam Kong, like the upper cave, includes stupas, shrines and numerous carved images of Lord Buddha in various sizes from circa ten centimetres to

Figure 16.1 Lower cave and walkway to upper cave of Tam Ting from a distance with the Nam Kong (Mekong River) in the foreground (photograph by Egloff April 2011).

near life-size. Brick and concrete walkways connect the upper and lower cave to the river landings and to each other.

The upper cave is deep and cathedral-shaped, being dominated by a reconstructed large stupa. In front of the stupa is the platform where the Lao regent and royal party venerated the shrine on auspicious occasions. Numerous large and small images of Buddha have been placed on the various altars. An ornate set of decorated wooden doors and carved surrounds that once closed the opening to the upper cave is present but fixed open with a relatively recently constructed metal grille closing the doorway. Outside of the upper cave is a heroic-sized seated sculpture of Kaccyana, a contemporary of Lord Buddha who it is said was similar in appearance while living but is represented as being overweight to distinguish him from Lord Buddha. An incidence of the desecration of the shrine at Tam Ting is recorded in charcoal on the limestone wall at the rear of the statue of Pakudha Kaccayanu, 'head of one of the six heretical sects during the time of Buddha' (Malalasekera 1937: 89), that in Lao records that 'In 1948 Phraksak has come to repair the Buddha'. Ban Pak Ou residents recount that the damage was done during the Second World War by Japanese soldiers searching for treasure.

The brick and mortar stupas and platforms in the upper and lower caves remain intact to this day with the upper cave stupa being partially rebuilt from 1992 to 1997 during the joint Lao and Australian conservation project. A conservation plan was drafted and an inventory compiled of the objects that were conserved between 1992 and 1997 and circulated in 1997. Almost 6,000 ancient sculptures or images were recorded as being in the two caves. The moveable religious objects had been cleaned and placed in their regular locations or upon the rebuilt portion of the stupa. All objects in reasonable condition had been recovered from the fallen debris as it was cleaned away. At that time only a count of the objects in each of the groups of the upper cave and the lower cave was made (see Figures 16.2 and 16.3).

As the project closed in 1997, it was apparent that tourism was multiplying and that there was a rapidly growing religious interest in the Tam Ting shrine, both of which were likely lead to an increase in theft. Security needed to be improved at the national heritage

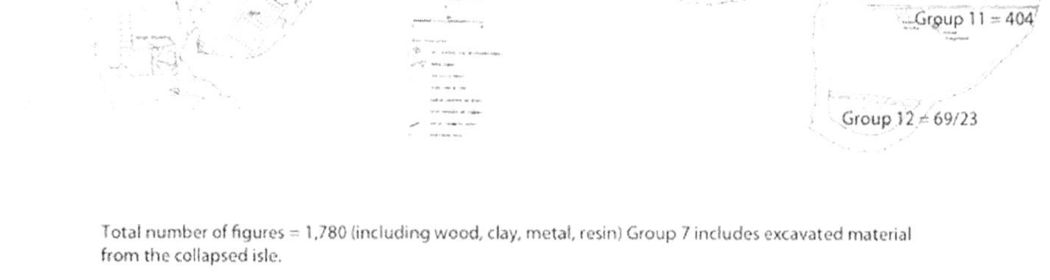

Figure 16.2 Upper cave with the distribution and count of 1,780 sculptures of Lord Buddha as of December 1997 (base drawing by Kelvin Officer 1993).

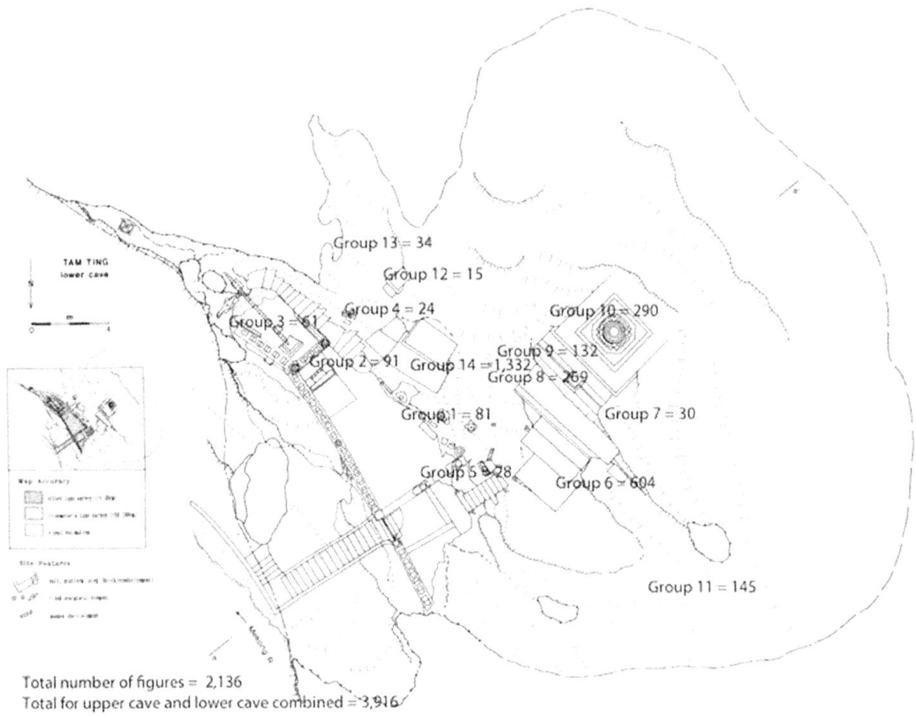

Figure 16.3 Lower cave with the distribution and count of the 2,136 statues of Lord Buddha as of December 1997 (base drawing by Kelvin Officer 1993).

site or objects would be pilfered and sold. The lower cave is more open than the upper cave, naturally lit and relatively easy to deal with in terms of safety and security during tour visits. The upper cave is another matter. It is deep and dark with the main stupa and the majority of the statues at the far end of the cave in all but complete darkness. Conservation work from 1992 to 1997 focused on the conservation of objects and the rebuilding of collapsed shrines and infrastructure. That work was guided by a conservation management plan that was amended annually for the duration of the project. Egloff (1998; also 2001) in 'Practicing archaeology and the conservation of Tam Ting, Lao People's Democratic Republic' considers measures that were taken in the conservation of the national heritage place. Of particular interest today are actions that were not taken including the installation of metal grilles that were advocated by ICOMOS Thailand along with electricity to illuminate the upper cave (Krataithong 1997). Conservation advice stated that the construction of a museum standard security door at the entry to the upper cave would impede air flow, leading to a change in the environment. Any change in humidity could lead to a marked deterioration of the objects, particularly if the lighting increased heat levels within the upper cave. Also, there was a misconception on my part and that of the Lao heritage authorities that as the spiritual value of the place was restored that guardianship would be more stringent and limit the theft of sacred objects.

Between 1997 and 2011, infrastructure maintenance and construction had taken place at Tam Ting, in particular, an additional landing, walkway and exterior platforms at the upper cave. However, no substantial conservation measures or curatorial work has been undertaken since the close of the project in 1997. By all accounts, the staff at the caves were not trained and security was minimal. Tam Ting presents a particular set of challenges that individually may have been dealt with at heritage sites elsewhere in Laos, but when combined required extraordinary measures that were beyond the means of the local provincial or village authorities.[3] Ban Pak Ou, the village directly across the Nam Kong from Tam Ting was connected early in the 2000s to the main north to south paved highway by a secondary unpaved road. It is likely that the ease of access contributed to the vulnerability of Tam Ting to theft.

As of December 1997, there were 5,834 moveable statues (including recognisable fragments) of Lord Buddha in the upper and the lower caves at Tam Ting. In 2011, an inventory indicates that some 666 pieces were missing, including all of the complex composite large-sized sculptures. Refer to Figure 16.4 and Table 16.1 for the comparison of the upper cave main altar that in 2011 is bare of all ancient sculptures. At least seven of those sculptures once positioned on the main altar of the upper cave are life-size. The estimated net loss is some 666 pieces or fragments of sculptures that were there in 1997 as distinct from those that have been brought into the cave post-1997. An interesting feature of the worship at Tam Ting is that there are 1,241 new sculptures and religious offerings, such as amulets, that have been brought to the caves in recent years.

A comparison of the few remaining large-scale statues with the photographs taken from 1992 to 1997 is being undertaken. Missing items will be entered into a database. An illustrated volume dedicated to the loss of sacred sculptures from Tam Ting has been published in Thailand (Egloff and Kelly 2015).

An account of the theft of sculptures

It proved to be difficult to discuss the theft of the sculptures with the Ban Pak Ou villagers as they seemed hesitant and uncertain how to respond to my interests in the breaking into the upper cave and the theft of 666 sculptures from both caves. I knew from living in the village for five field seasons that criticism and controversal subjects were not easily discussed. After being in the village for four days I found myself sheltering from a rain storm in a rest shelter at the Tam Ting caves with a respected elder. He named the three thieves from Ban Pak Ou and described the nature of the theft, the subsequent arrest and conviction (refer to Egloff and Kelly 2015: 81–82). The reason given for the theft was that not all villagers had been included in the management and returns from the caves and three were so upset that they stole the sculptures. One of the thieves who was convicted was a valued member of the conservation team; he is pictured in the 1997 conservation plan and lived only a short distance from where the conservation team was housed and, as such, we regularly met with him and his family in the evenings. As of 2011, the sculptures had not been recovered and new arrangements had been made for the caretaking of the caves that involved 17 families from Ban Pak Ou and other neighboring villages. The situation was far from ideal with only one guardian at the upper cave entrance renting flashlights with perhaps six or more villagers at the lower cave selling tickets as well as flowers and incense.

Japan–Lao conservation initiative at Luang Prabang

The year 2010 was the tenth anniversary of the Minobusan University 'Restore the Buddha Statues' project that focuses upon the deterioration and theft of statues of Buddha from the temples in Luang Prabang, the provincial capital.[4]

Figure 16.4 Stupa of the upper cave in 1997 on the left and in 2011 on the right. The shifting and loss of statues are obvious (photographs by Egloff 1997 and 2011).

Table 16.1 Distribution of sculptures of Lord Buddha in 1997 and 2011 showing an overall loss of some 666 figures

Upper Cave	*1997*	*2011*	*Lower Cave*	*1997*	*2011*
Group 1	1	17	Group 1	81	103
Group 2	28	47	Group 2	91	91
Group 3	18	28	Group 3	61	97
Group 4	372	728	Group 4	24	67
Group 5	64	76	Group 5	28	42
Group 6	136	17	Group 6	604	807
Group 7	395		Group 7	30	21
Group 8	119	229	Group 8	269	227
Group 9	85	70	Group 9	132	224
Group 10	35	934	Group 10	290	223
Group 11	404	547	Group 11	145	37
Group 12	69+23	122	Group 12	15	89
Group 13	31	14	Group 13	34	14
			Group 14	1,332	297
Archaeology 1994	1,340				
Total	3,120	2,829		2,714	2,339
Loss		**291**			**375**

> Students of Minobusan University in Minobucho, Japan are helping restore the Buddhist statues of this site. These are wooden Theravada Buddhism statues made in the 14th century or later, and are of high historical value. Originally the number requiring work was not precisely known, so in 2001 they began a survey of the statues and in 2007 reported to the Laotian government that the study had confirmed the presence of 1,174 statues. In the past few years, more than a tenth of them have since been stolen, presumably by illegal artefact hunters for collection or for sale to collectors both inside the country and abroad. A survey conducted in 2009 revealed that 100 statues were missing from 35 temples. In 2010, another 20 statues were found to be missing. While monks at the temples have begun keeping guard over the statues by sleeping at the temples, Minobusan University students have distributed brochures at the Luang Prabang National Museum to sound the alarm over the property loss and to call for increased security in the city.

The above is but one of many similar reports, in just one locale, indicating that thefts nation-wide must be so numerous that they are virtually beyond comprehension and numeration. For instance, there is an anecdotal account of 700 statues being taken in one incidence where a 'Thai' man arrived at a temple in a truck and spoke with the monks about making a donation of a 'glass Buddha figure' to the temple. While they were talking, the attention of the monks was diverted and accomplices hiding in the truck took the objects. The thieves quickly left the scene of the crime and were not apprehended. The sacred figures have not been recovered.

Spirituality of sculptures

Materiality in a country where a substantial part of the population follows the paths of animism and Buddhism, is politically communist, is economically capitalist and is marked by poverty and inequality is complex, to say the least. Anna Karlström, looking at materiality and immateriality in flux, writes 'Moving between canonical Buddhism, where materiality is a matter of no concern, through animism that holds the idea that things are essential, materiality is indeed important in popular Buddhism' (Karlström 2009: 152). Into the complex equation of beliefs must be added the notion of merit. There are many ways of gaining merit with giving as one of the more obvious means. In practice, this amounts to daily food offerings and other donations as well as more substantial contributions at particular events. Prodigious quantities of sculptures and other religious objects have been brought to the Tam Ting caves over the past decade in acts of merit. There also is the notion that destruction, particularly by passive means, makes space for new spiritual values and merit can be gained by filling the void. Denis Byrne (1995: 266–281; also 1999), in the context of the looting and trade of amulets in Thailand, writes that certain structures having divine power are protected by a fiery energy and:

> The fact that caches of amulets were sealed inside many Buddhist stupas in early times has been responsible for thousands of *stupas* being broken open both historically and in present day. The breaking open and looting of *stupa* is an act of desecration but it is motivated by belief in the spiritual power in the amulets contained in the *stupas.*

Whether it is the spiritual power or the economic value of the amulets is a point that needs to be clarified. However:[5]

> The concept/notion of looting of sacred images as releasing them from worn out context does not sit very well with the fundamental Five Precepts of Buddhism. The third one states that 'with observance and practice of the Dhamma, one should refrain from taking what is not given (e.g., stealing)'. And thus doing so (taking what is not given) is considered committing a bad Karma. It is religiosity against greed for materialism.

Digging for antiquities that have either or both a spiritual and monetary value has been described in a number of contexts including situations in Latin America (Matsuda 1998) and in North America (Hollowell 2006) where the indigenous people excavate ancient sites to provide both an income and a connection with the past. This is similar to Byrne's description of the search for amulets in temple ruins but not at all comparable to forced entry, intimidation and theft of religious statues from temples.

Framework for heritage protection in Laos

Lao's 'Seventh Socio-Economic Plan 2011-2015'[6] places considerable emphasis on the expansion of tourist infrastructure and the development of additional heritage places for visitor use:

> Aim to increase the inflow of tourists to about 2.8 million people, discover and expand natural, cultural and historical sites, and aim to have two more world heritage sites. [page 14]

There is no acknowledgement in the plan of a need to take extraordinary measures to protect National Heritage places and no mention is made of the necessity to provide financial support for programs that counter the theft of national heritage, but cultural programs and awareness are mentioned.

Some 24 pages in length, the *Law on National Heritage* is comprehensive and includes both natural and cultural, and tangible and intangible, heritage with an emphasis on the following:

> The responsible authorities shall pay attention to monitor the cases where it is discovered that the national heritage has been encroached on, destroyed or damaged by human or natural causes, for which immediate protective measures shall be laid down in coordination with the local administration where the heritage is located, followed by notification to the information and culture sector for an immediate solution.
>
> (Article 44)

All levels of government are responsible for the administration of the law including the Ministry of Information and Culture; information and culture divisions at the provincial and city level; information and culture offices at the district and municipal level; and village administrations. The legislation calls for:

> Regular systematic inspections, which are carried out based on the operational plan, on a regular basis and at a specified time.
>
> (Article 69)

Key issues that need to be faced are where does the budget cash flow and the expertise come from to undertake the enforcement of the act and the regular inspection of the 30 National Heritage places. The law stipulates that:

> To assure the protection, conservation, restoration and rehabilitation of national heritage in a sustainable and better-developed manner, it is necessary to establish the national heritage fund . . .

Although the Act requires that there will be a fund to support the administration of the law, recurrent funding is not available to the same extent as it is when dealing with World Heritage places, environmental impact assessments, developmental programs and research projects that are funded externally. Efforts gravitate to projects with additional external funding that facilitates national participation. Article 71 states that individuals or organisations that have violated the provisions of this law shall be re-educated, fined or subject to civil liability or criminal punishment, as determined on a case-by-case basis.

Theft of temple antiquities

An article titled 'Lao Buddha images under threat' by Phonesavanh Sangsomboun (2010)[7] in the *Vientiane Times* offers a perspective on the extent of the theft of ancient Buddha figures throughout Lao and maintains that:

> Growth in the illegal trade of ancient Buddha images out of Laos is threatening the national heritage of many local temples, according to a National Heritage Department spokesperson. Countless numbers of images have been stolen from provinces across Laos in recent years, with very few ever returned, said the Department's Deputy Director General, Mr Viengkeo Souksavatdy. "Over a period of just two or three months, countless figures have been stolen, and their likelihood of recovery is only quite small," he said. In just one night last year, more than 300 images were stolen. Of

them, none have been recovered. Hardest hit by the rising trade have been Khammuan, Savannakhet and Champassak provinces, though thefts have been reported throughout the rest of Laos.

In the past, illegal trading was mainly isolated to smaller statues but, more recently, smugglers have grown bolder and started targeting large images as well, most notably the revered Ongsaen image in Attapeu province.[8] "The smugglers' operations have spread widely, which makes it difficult to control.

It is understood that, as of 2011, no case has been successfully prosecuted in Laos under the *Law on National Heritage of Lao PDR* 2005 but individuals have been prosecuted for theft.

At risk recent finds[9]

Attempts are being made to inventory and monitor the situation of chance finds.[10] One of the key challenges is the lack of trained, energetic, funded and motivated staff at the national and provincial level along with the need for a substantial budget to support their activities. The staff would have to be able to not only deal with internal matters but to also work effectively with national cultural property officers in adjacent ASEAN countries.

As an example, an instance of chance finds vulnerable to theft was in Khammoun Province; the find made by hunters in 2011 revealed 114 statutes of wood, silver and gold, 1 bronze drum and 1 ceramic pot, which was reported in the daily newspaper.[11] Another location of finds was about 50km distant where 229 statues again were found by hunters searching for bats. The find comprised of 64 bronzes; 133 silver; 14 wooden; 1 stone; 1 lead and 16 gold statues. In 2011, small Buddha statues with resin cores and embossed coverings of sheet silver were readily available in the antique shops in Vientiane and some were being donated to the national museum by individuals who expressed concern at their purchase in the local shops.

Incidents of theft at Wat Prao Keo Museum and Sisaket Museum

In 2004, police at the Presidential Palace apprehended a person, said to have stolen widely from Luang Prabang to Vientiane. The thief was in the act of removing a statue of Buddha that weighed 40 kilograms from the adjacent Wat Prao Keo Museum.[12] The break and entry was accomplished with a bolt cutter. The thief fled with the statue and when attempting to climb over the security fence into the adjacent Presidential Palace, and not surprisingly, was apprehended. The Director of Wat Prao Keo Museum, Mr Khochone Keomanivong, filed a report of the incident but knows little of what happened afterward. It is believed that a Thai trader ordered the theft of the Buddha and was waiting in a vehicle outside of Wat Prao Keo Museum to spirit the statue away. This is the third time in recent history that Wat Prao Keo has been broken into. In 1978 the police shot a thief and in 1988 Wat Prao Keo was broken into and at the same time Wat Sisiket, which lies across a main street from Wat Prao Keo, was burgled.

Theft at Vilabouly temple

Following a burglary at Ban Muang Luang, Vilabouly District, Savannakhet Province in southern Lao, a thief was apprehended and on 23 September 2010, photographs of the villain, his break and entry tools, motorbike and the stolen artefacts were taken (Figure 16.5).

Figure 16.5 Thief apprehended following a burglary at Ban Muang Luang, Vilabouly District (photographer not known).

'Buddha lost and found at Vilabouly case' demonstrates that in some situations individual actions can make a substantial difference in the protection of national cultural property. Vilabouly in the south of Lao is in a region that is particularly rich in cultural heritage resources. The anecdotal account of the case is as follows. A member of the local police militia suspected that one of his fellow officers was robbing temples. The 'good cop' asked the 'bad cop' if he could join with him in his thefts and share from the profits. One day they broke into the temple at Ban Muang Luang and stole statues and coins. On departing from the scene of the theft, the 'good cop' used his cell phone to call the militia and the 'bad cop' was apprehended. The 'bad cop' was cuffed with his own handcuffs and the cultural property seized along with the motorbike, tools and his cell phone.[13]

Photograph of the stolen property suggest that the thief was not aware of the qualities of ancient sculptures as a substantial number of the artefacts that were taken are modern in origin being made of clear, coloured or multi-coloured glass.[14] Perhaps the temple had been broken into earlier and the older and larger pieces stolen, leaving only a few small ancient objects remaining.

Mechanisms to mitigate the illicit trafficking

Community processes are viewed as being a valuable mechanism in the mitigation of the illicit trade in cultural property. Some of the considerations are listed below:

- engagement and awareness-raising activities will lessen illicit impacts on cultural property within a multitude of contexts such as development, misadventure, vandalism and theft (Hoffman 1991: 254–259; Huffer 2009: 92–100; Jameson Jr 2004);

- community archaeology and related heritage projects will increase respect for cultural heritage property thereby self-regulating the trade in antiquities (Moser et al. 2002);
- education will enhance the cultural value of heritage, reducing participation by locals in illicit activities (Green 2008: 388; Hoffman 1991; Sabloff 1990); and
- through the power of social marketing illicit activities will be moderated (Jennings and Rand 2008).

The Tam Ting conservation project sought to increase heritage values through the widespread participation of local villagers in the conservation activities. Unfortunately, once the program closed, there was no further monitoring by national heritage authorities and the provincial heritage office was unable to control illicit activities.

Illicit cultural property trafficking in Asia

Where descriptions of the theft of cultural property stolen from places in South-East Asia are provided, the reader is overwhelmed with the enormity of the devastation. It is manifestly apparent that much, perhaps even the greater part, of the ancient heritage of South-East Asia has been stolen and considerable destruction of national cultural heritage has taken place in the process. Jürgen Schick in *The Gods are Leaving the Country: Art Theft From Nepal* provides documentation for more than 160 cases with before and after graphic comparisons of the impact of theft on temples and shrines (Schick 1998). As much of the national cultural property was outdoors and not in museums, it was particularly vulnerable. Schick states that the systematic plundering had started years earlier but by the 1980s had reached a scale that no one previously had thought possible. Bronze sculptures were the first to be removed along with portable painted images. This was followed by wooden and stone sculptures, some of which were architectural elements such as the struts of buildings that when removed the roofs collapsed.

Theft of stone sculptures from the royal conservation depot at Angkor between 9 February and 7 April 1993 has been documented (ICOM 1993, 1997). In some instances, only the heads were taken, leaving behind the shattered remnants of the sculpture. Thieves had targeted the storerooms as early as the 1970s. *Pillaging Cambodia: The Illicit Traffic in Khmer Art* by Masha Lafont provides a broader and more recent overview with a chapter devoted to the demand side of the traffic of stolen objects. Lafont states that it is the demand side that is propelling the trafficking of cultural property. Demand being stimulated by economics and fashion pays little respect to universal laws of ownership and in doing so encourages and directly supports criminal activity. In conclusion, Lafont (2004: 63) writes that:

> The analysis in the previous chapters showed that all the models and measures that were introduced against illicit trafficking in art to date have proven to be powerless and ineffective against the constant increase of art smuggling in Cambodia and elsewhere.

David J. Murphy (1995) offers insights into the traffic of illicit objects that include case studies of prosecutions as well as descriptions of a plethora of instances of national cultural property violations in China, particularly large-scale incidents in Hong Kong. C. Franklin Sayre (1986) advances India and Japan as examples of source and consumer countries while Murphy (1995: 2) observes that the latter has more success at preserving property, evidencing heritage value more than does the former. Murphy considers that a key factor propelling the illicit trade is the strictness of the cultural property legislation. And he goes on to stress that 'Merryman has described this 'cultural nationalism' as an 'unsophisticated form of market aversion' (Murphy 1995: 3 quoting John Henry Merryman: 1988: 481). Assertions are made that if only there were free trade there would be no looting along with claims that archaeologists are their own worst enemies (Merryman 2000). It should be noted that the *Law on National Heritage of Lao PDR* 2005 does allow for the legal export of cultural property if a permit is obtained. The same is true for the *National Cultural Property (Preservation) Act* of Papua New Guinea (Busse 2013; Craig 1992; Egloff 2008). The crucial point that is overlooked by Merryman is that substantial profits are to be made by exporting rare antiquities in excellent condition that most likely would not receive a permit.

Murphy (1995: 172–173) reiterates the assertion that retentive hoarding policies are a driving factor in the illicit trade in artefacts. In a similar vein Murphy (1995: 6–7) quotes de Varine (1985: 155):

> Most of the poorest countries in the world today happen to be the richest in cultural terms, by virtue of both of the complexity of their still vital spiritual and human values and of the stratification of civilisations . . .

The complexity of the illicit trade in national cultural property in China is intensified by its close proximity to the transit states of Hong Kong and Macau, and by what Murphy (1995: 58–59, 65) refers to as 'institutional vulnerability heightened by a lack of funds'. As in other places in Asia, antiquities in China are held to be a hedge against inflation (Murphy 1995: 17).[15]

More than a decade ago, Neil Brodie, Jennifer Doole and Peter Watson (2000), of the McDonald Institute for Archaeological Research in Cambridge, in *Stealing History: The illicit trade in cultural material* presented an overview of the impact of the illicit international trade on archaeological heritage. In a regional-specific paper titled the 'Illicit Antiquities: The Situation in South-East Asia', Brodie (1999) paints a grim picture. Masayuki Nagashima (2002) in *Lost Heritage: The reality of artefact smuggling in Southeast Asia* provides some details on successful prosecutions and reconstructs the transfer routes for artefacts from Cambodia, Lao and Thailand to Singapore and then in some instances back to markets in Bangkok and Chang Mai (Lafont 2004: 56–59).

Trafficking networks documented

It is widely recognised that dealing with the supply side of the illicit trade in artefacts will only have a limited impact unless there is greater control exerted over the demand side of the traffic, profits are controlled and socio economic imbalances are addressed in the source states (Gerstenblith 2009; Kersal 2007; Kersal and Kletter 2006).

Considerable emphasis is placed upon the masquerade where recently stolen goods are sold in apparently legitimate circumstances as objects that were acquired at some time in the past or at times are misrepresented as chance finds (Mackenzie 2005: 4–5, 17–18). In doing so, Mackenzie discusses the strength of the community of dealers who regard the activities of the group as a whole to be legitimate yet the group is not strong enough or willing enough to condemn the actions of any offender (Mackenzie 2005: 251). What Alder, Chappell and Polk propose are 'initiatives that are both focused on the demand end of the market chain (rather than the supply end), and on those approaches that give emphasis on "persuasion" rather than punishment and prohibition' (Alder et al. 2009: 119).

Criminology and its intersection with archaeology are expanding fields of enquiry that consider transnational crime, the harm to cultural resources and the failure of systems to control the trafficking (Mackenzie and Green 2009: 1–2; Mackenzie 2011; Mackenzie and Yates 2016). International networks have been delineated 'using oral history interviews' in Cambodian and Thailand (Mackenzie and Davis 2014: 722; also Byrne 2016; Yates, Mackenzie and Smith 2017). The research indicates that organised crime is involved, the trafficking 'overlaps' with fakes entering the market, the various stages in the movement of illicit artefacts can be delineated and the few end public sales points identified.

Conclusions

The primary task of the Australian National Commission for UNESCO funded project for Stage Two of the conservation of the Tam Ting caves was to obtain construction plans and cost estimates to proceed with an application for infrastructure funding (Egloff and Sayavongkhamedy 2011). A cursory examination of the upper cave indicated that a substantial quantity of sculptures had been removed. This impression was confirmed by a detailed count that established that 666 sculptures were missing, including all of the large complex sculptures, from both the upper and lower caves. As the quotations were being prepared by the construction company, enquiries were made into the nature of the illicit traffic in cultural objects. It was found that instances of breaking and entry and theft were numerous across Lao and virtually unchecked. Further reports indicate that new finds of sculptures in distant locations were also at risk. A few cases of the theft of objects had been reported and information was obtained on those instances. No prosecutions had been made under the *Law on National Heritage of Lao PDR* 2005.

It is doubtful if there has been any major advance in controlling the illicit traffic in Asia over the past decades, although there is a better understanding of the complexity of the trade. Given that there are persuasive links between development and the illicit trade in artefacts, and South-East Asia as a region is experiencing rapid change, there is every possibility that the already flourishing illicit trade in artefacts will accelerate in force until there are few artefacts of cultural significance or monetary value left in ASEAN countries outside of national museums and an untold number of archaeological sites will be destroyed as looting continues unabated.

Acknowledgements

The host family of Suntan Corpolit and Chansamai Sukpajan of Ban Pak Ou are to be thanked for their generous hospitality in sharing their home with the field team and providing magnificent food and drink. From the offices of the Department of Information and Culture in Luang Prabang, the work of the conservation team was facilitated by On Chan, Director General, and Som-Ock Phanthavong, Deputy Director General. The 2011 conservation team was comprised of the following: Samlane Luangaphay, Deputy Director, Archaeology Unit, Department of Heritage, Ministry of Information and Culture, Vientiane; Bounyavat Singha, Officer, Cultural Unit, Luang Prabang; and, Kahm Oun Loi Van, Officer, Pak Ou District. The work at Ban Pak Ou was facilitated by the District Office of Chansouk Hatsady. Dr Vongmany Mounthisone, Director of Antiquities Division, Department of Heritage, Ministry of Information and Culture provided information and newspaper articles on recent finds. The author's gratitude is extended to my esteemed colleague Benita Johnson, of the University of Canberra, and the Lao team members representing the federal and provincial departments of the Ministry of Information and Culture during the 1992 to 1997 conservation work as well as the people of Pak Ou who good-naturedly welcomed the project staff into their community.

Denis Byrne, Anna Karlström and Ken Polk provided insightful comments on an early version of this paper.

Notes

1 A preliminary version of this paper was presented at the Institute of Advanced Studies workshop on the 'Illicit traffic of cultural objects: Law, Ethics and the Realities', The University of Western Australia, 4–5 August 2011. A shortened revision of the paper was presented in October 2014 at the ICAHM Conference, Jishou University, Hunan Province, China. An illustrated account of the theft of the Tam Ting sculptures is published in *Sacred Caves of Tam Ting (Pak Ou), Luang Prabang, Laos: Mystery, Splendor, and Desecration* by White Lotus Press (Egloff and Kelly 2015).
2 The Tam Ting Caves Heritage Management Project was supported by the Commonwealth through the Australian National Commission for UNESCO, Department of Foreign Affairs and Trade.
3 Tam Ting was listed as an endangered site on the Monuments Watch list of 100 Most Endangered Sites. http://www.wmf.org/watch.html.
4 https://buddhistartnews.wordpress.com/2010/03/19/where-is-the-stolen-buddha-heritage-of-l-aos-ending-up/. Accessed 28 September 2017. Refer also to Berliner 2012: 238 for a consideration of the nostalgia of heritage in Luang Prabang.
5 Thong Poumirath, email of 19 October 2014.
6 Lao People's Democratic Government 2010; *Vientiane Times* 85 B3, 08 April 2011.
7 Also on https://groups.google.com/forum/#!topic/laochf/wSJNTEeA09c. Accessed 29 September 2017.
8 A picture of the bronze image of Buddha is provided on http://www.tourism-laos.org/khammuane/heritage_site/Tham_Pha_Bang_cave.html. Accessed 1 September 2017.
9 Information is from Dr Vongmany Mounthisone, Director of Antiquities Division, Department of Heritage, Ministry of Information and Culture.
10 Information is from Dr Vongmany Mounthisone.
11 *Pathetlao Daily,* 10.01.2011, vii 2.572, 01.02.2011 viii 2.588, 11.01.2011 viii 2.573 - 16/2004/6.
12 Interview with Director (4th generation) of Wat Prao Keo, Mr Khochone Keomanivong, Director of Ancient Museum.
13 Information as relayed to Thongsa Sayavongkhamedy.
14 Images supplied by Thongsa Sayavongkhamedy.
15 Refer also Wilhelm G. Solheim II, "Potsherds and potholes: Philippine archaeology in 1974." *Archipelago* 2(June 1974/1975): 8–15; also in *Geography, Archaeology, Psychology and Literature.* Dekalb, Illinois, Center for Southeast Asian Studies, Northern Illinois University, Special Report 10, 15–33.

References

Alder, Christine, Duncan Chappell and Kenneth Polk. 2009 "Perspectives on the organisation and control of the illicit traffic in antiquities in South East Asia." Paper presented at 'Organised Crime In Art and Antiquities', Courmayeur, Mont Blanc, Italy, 12–14 December, 2009.

Berliner, David. 2012 "The politics of loss and nostalgia in Luang Prabang (Lao PDR)." In *Routledge Handbook of Heritage in Asia*, eds. Patrick Daly and Tim Winter. London: Routledge. pp. 234–246.

Brodie, Neil. 1999 "Illicit antiquities: The situation in South-East Asia." Paper presented at 'Art Crime, Protecting Art, Protecting Artists and Consumers', Australian Institute of Criminology, Sydney, 2–3 December 1999.

Brodie, Neil, Jennifer Doole and Peter Watson, eds. 2000 *Stealing History: The Illicit Trade in Cultural Material.* Cambridge: McDonald Institute for Archaeological Research.

Busse, Mark. 2013 "The National Cultural Property (Preservation) Act." In *Protection of Intellectual, Biological & Cultural Property in Papua New Guinea*, eds. Cathy Wimp and Mark Busse. Canberra: ANU Press, 81–95.

Byrne, Denis. 1995 "Buddhist Stupa and Thai Social Practice." *World Archaeology* 27(2): 266–281.

Byrne, Denis. 1999 "The nation, the elité and the Southeast Asian antiquities trade." *Conservation and Management of Archaeological Sites* 3: 145–153.

Byrne, Denis. 2016 "The problem with looting: An alternative perspective on antiquities trafficking in Southeast Asia. *Journal of Field Archaeology* 41(3): 344–354.

Condominas, Georges. 1970 "The Lao." In *Laos: War and Revolution*, eds. Nina S. Adams and Alfred W. McCoy. New York: Harper & Roe, 9–27.

Craig, B. 1992 "National cultural property in Papua New Guinea: Implications for policy and action." *Journal of the Anthropological Society of South Australia* 30(2): 1529–1554.

Egloff, Brian. 1998 "Practising archaeology and the conservation of Tam Ting, Lao People's Democratic Republic." *Conservation and Management of Archaeological Sites* 2: 163–175.

Egloff, Brian. 2001 "Tam Ting Conservation Project: a decade of collaborative heritage practice in the Lao People's Democratic Republic." *Historic Environment* 15: 20–34.

Egloff, Brian. 2008 *Bones of the Ancestors: The Ambum Stone: from the Highlands to the Antiquities Market to Australia*. Lanham, MD: AltaMira Press.

Egloff, Brian and Thongsa Sayavongkhamedy. 2011 "Tam Ting Caves Heritage Management Project, Stage 2, 2011." A report to the Australian Commission for UNESCO Grants Program, Donald Horne Institute, University of Canberra and the Department of Heritage, Ministry of Information and Culture, Vientiane.

Egloff, Brian and Kristin Kelly. 2015 *Sacred Caves of Tam Ting (Pak Ou), Luang Prabang, Laos: Mystery, Splendor, and Desecration*. Bangkok: White Lotus Press.

Gerstenblith, Patty. 2009 "Increasing Effectiveness of the Legal Regime for the Protection of the International Archaeological Heritage." In *Cultural Heritage Issues*, eds. James A.R. Nafziger and Ann M. Nigorski. Leiden: Martinus Nijhoff, 305–322.

Green, Thomas J. 2008 "Cultural Resource Management." In *Handbook of Archaeological Theories*, eds. R. Alexander Bentley, Herbert D. G. Maschner and Christopher Chippendale. Lanham: AltaMira Press, 375–394.

Hoffman, Teresa. 1991 "Stewards of the Past: Preserving Arizona's archaeological resources through positive public involvement." In *Protecting the Past*, eds. George S. Smith and John E. Ehrenhard. Boca Raton: CRC Press, 253–259.

Hollowell, Julie. 2006 "Moral arguments on subsistence digging." In *The Ethics of Archaeology: Philosophical Perspectives on the Practice of Archaeology*, eds. Christopher Scarre and Geoffrey Scarre. Cambridge: Cambridge University Press, 69–93.

Huffer, Damien. 2009 "Conserving the past through play: Educational gaming and anti-looting outreach in Cambodia." *Indo Pacific Prehistory Association Bulletin* 29: 92–100.

ICOM 1993 *Looting in Angkor: One hundred missing objects/cent objets disparus: Pillage a Angkor*. Paris: ICOM.

ICOM 1997 *Looting in Angkor/Pillage a Angkor*. Paris: ICOM.

Jameson Jr., John H. 2004 "Public archaeology in the United States." In *Public Archaeology*, ed. Nick Merriman. London: Rutledge, 21–58.

Johnson, Benita. 1997 "Conservation survey of the Tam Ting Caves." In *Conservation of Ancient Sites on the Silk Road*, ed. Neville Agnew. Los Angeles: Getty Conservation Institute, 67–81.

Jennings, Justin and Adrienne Rand. 2008 "Stemming the tide: How social marketers can help in the fight against looted antiquities." *SAA archaeological record* 8(3): 28–31.

Karlström, Anna. 2009 "Preserving Impermanence: The Creation of Heritage in Vientiane, Laos." *Studies in Global Archaeology* 13. Uppsala: Uppsala Universitet.

Kaseka, Phon. 2011 "Archaeology and cultural resource management south of Phnom Penh, Cambodia." In *Rethinking Cultural Resource Management in Southeast Asia: Preservation, Development and Neglect*, eds. John N. Miksic, Geok Yan Goh and Sue O'Connor. London: Anthem Press, 123–142.

Kersel, Morag. M. 2007 "Transcending borders: Objects on the move." *Archaeologies: Journal of the World Archaeological Congress* 3: 81–98.

Kersal, Morag and Raz Kletter. 2006 "Heritage for sale? Case study from Israel." *Journal of Field Archaeology* 31(3): 317–327.

Krataithong, J. N. 1997 "Report on Museum Security and Selected Sites in Lao People's Democratic Republic." National Museum Bangkok. The Fine Arts Department Ministry of Education, sponsored by UNESCO (Thailand), Bangkok.

Lafont, Masha. 2004 *Pillaging Cambodia: The Illicit Traffic in Khmer Art*. Jefferson, North Carolina: McFarland.

Mackenzie, Simon. 2002 "Illicit Antiquities, Criminological Theory and the Deterrent Power of Criminal Sanctions for Targeted Populations." *Art Antiquity and Law* 7(2): 125–161.

Mackenzie, Simon. 2005 *Going, Going, Gone: Regulating the Market in Illicit Antiquities*. Leicester: Institute of Art and Law.

Mackenzie, Simon. 2011 "Illicit deals in cultural objects as crimes of the powerful." *Crime, Law and Social Change* 56: 133–153

Mackenzie, Simon and Tess Davis. 2014 "Temple looting in Cambodia: Anatomy of a statue trafficking network." *The British Journal of Criminology* 54: 722–740.

Mackenzie, Simon and Penny Green. 2009 "Introduction: A context for the engagement of criminology in archaeology." *Criminology and Archaeology: Studies in Looted Antiquities*. Hart Publishing: Oxford and Portland Oregon, 1–10.

Mackenzie, Simon and Donna Yates. 2016 "Trafficking cultural objects and human rights." In *The Routledge International Handbook of Criminology and Human Rights*, eds. L. Weber, E. Fishwick and M. Marmo. New York: Routledge, 220–230.

Malalasekera, Gunapala Piyasena. 1937 *Dictionary of Pāli Proper Names*. London: John Murray.

Matsuda, David. 1998 "The ethics of archaeology, subsistence digging, and artefact looting in Latin America: Point, muted counterpoint." *International Journal of Cultural Property* 7: 87–97.

Merryman, John Henry. 1988 "The retention of cultural property." *University of California at Davis Law Review* 21: 477–513.

Merryman, John Henry. 2000 "Archaeologists are not helping." In *Thinking About the Elgin Marbles: Critical Essays on Cultural Property, Art and Law*. The Hague: Kluwer Law International, 280–283. Originally published in *The Art Newspaper* 55, January 1996, p. 26.

Moser, Stephanie, Darren Glazier, James E. Phillips, Lamya Nasser el Nemr, Mohammed Saleh Mousa, Rascha Nasr Aiesh, Susan Richardson, Andrew Conner and Michael Seymour. 2002 "Transforming archaeology through practice: strategies for collaborative archaeology and the Community Archaeology Project at Quseir, Egypt." *World Archaeology* 34(2): 220–248.

Murphy, J. David. 1995 *Plunder and Preservation: Cultural Property Law and Practice in the People's Republic of China*. Hong Kong: Oxford University Press.

Nagashima, Masayuki. 2002 *Lost Heritage: The Reality of Artefact Smuggling in Southeast Asia*. Bangkok: The Post Publishing Plc.

Pandy, Alka. 2003 "Illicit traffic in heritage properties." In *Illicit Traffic in Cultural Property*, Workshop Prevention of Illicit Traffic in Cultural Property, Workshop Proceedings, 25 July 2003, New Parliament House Annexe, ed. Neeru Misra, New Delhi, 27–29.

Sangsomboun, Phonesavanh. 2010 "Lao Buddha images under threat." *Vientiane Times* 26 May 2010.

Sayre, C. Franklin. 1986 "Comment, Cultural Property Laws In India And Japan." *U.C.L.A. Law Review* 33(25): 851–890.

Schick, Jürgen. 1998 *The Gods Are Leaving the Country: Art Theft from Nepal*. Bangkok: White Orchid.

Solheim II, Wilhelm G. "Potsherds and potholes: Philippine archaeology in 1974." *Archipelago* 2 (June 1974/1975): 8–15; also in *Geography, Archaeology, Psychology and Literature*. Dekalb, Illinois, Center for Southeast Asian Studies, Northern Illinois University, Special Report 10, 15–33.

Thorosat, Rachanie. 1999 "The destruction of the cultural heritage of Thailand and Cambodia." In *Illicit Antiquities: The Destruction of the World's Archaeological Heritage*. Cambridge: Macdonald Institute of Archaeological Research, 102–112.

Thorosat, Rachanie. 2001 "Report from Southeast Asia." *Culture Without Context* 8(Spring): 18–21.

de Varine, Hughes. 1985 "The rape and plunder of cultures: An aspect of the deterioration of the terms of cultural trade between nations." *Museum* 35: 152–157.

Visoth, Chhay. 2011 "Conservation of the Thnal Mrech Kiln Site, Anlong Thom, Phnom Kulen." In *Rethinking Cultural Resource Management in Southeast Asia: Preservation, Development and Neglect*, eds. John N. Miksic, Geok Yan Goh and Sue O'Connor. London: Anthem Press, 101–116.

Yates, Donna, Simon Mackenzie and Emiline Smith. 2017 "The cultural capitalists: Notes on the ongoing reconfiguration of trafficking culture in Asia". *Crime Media Culture* 13(2): 245–254.

17 Re-thinking places

From dark heritage sites to socially symbolic scapes

Audrey Gilmore and Roxana Magee

Introduction

There is a close relationship between people and place. A place is a social construction where the physical and social environment is moulded by the people who occupy it. Often there is an emotional bond that individuals or groups develop towards their environment; place shapes personal experiences (Rubinstein and Parmelee, 1992). Therefore, in the context of tourist spaces such as dark heritage sites, both site managers and visitors assign meaning to place.

Tourism regions and heritage sites require careful management; sites need to attract visitors and they need to be managed sustainably. They also need to provide a unique setting so that they can secure visibility to the outside and reinforce local identity to the inside (Columb and Kalandides, 2010). There are many challenges for the managers of dark heritage sites, both in terms of managing sites sustainably and providing a meaningful experience for visitors to the site.

Sites associated with natural or man-made disasters or atrocities have become not only places of remembrance, but also tourist attractions in themselves (Stone, 2006). Many scholars have found that there is a growing fascination with sites of death, disaster and atrocities (Cohan 2007; Logan and Reeves, 2009; Stone and Sharpley, 2008) and dark tourism has emerged as a field of academic study and a topic of media parlance (Foley and Lennon, 1996a, 1996b; Ryan and Kohli, 2006; Sharpley and Stone, 2009, Stone, 2006). Foley and Lennon (1996a, 1996b) first introduced the term 'dark tourism' and used it for the title of their widely cited book. Since then, dark tourism has been defined in a variety of ways and is a rather emotive label (Stone 2006). For example, it has been defined as: the act of travel to sites associated with death, suffering and the seemingly macabre (Stone, 2006); visitations to sites associated with death, disaster and depravity (Lennon and Foley, 2000) and sites of death, disaster and depravity (Miles, 2002); visitations to places where tragedies or historically noteworthy death has occurred and that continue to impact our lives (Tarlow, 2005). It has also been defined as heritage that hurts (Uzzell and Ballantyne, 1998), places of pain and shame (Logan and Reeves, 2009), difficult heritage tourism and heritage that the majority of the population would prefer not to have (Macdonald, 2006). However, there is no overall accepted definition and some argue that the term remains poorly conceptualised (Jamel and Lelo, 2009). Dark tourism is associated with sites linked to the aftermath of Nazism, fascism, communism, genocide, terrorism, slavery, apartheid and extreme poverty (Knudsen, 2011). The literature also refers to dark tourism as thanatourism, using the two terms interchangeably by making use of Seaton's (1996) definition of thanatourism as travel to a location wholly or partially motivated by the desire for actual or symbolic encounters with death (Magee and Gilmore, 2015). Miles (2002) distinguishes between places or sites *associated* with death, disaster and depravity and sites *of* death, disaster and depravity, drawing attention to the temporal and spatial distance from original events, thus constructing a 'dark-to-darker tourism' continuum where sites associated with death belong to the dark end of the spectrum while sites of death belong to the darker end (Magee and Gilmore, 2015). However, a more positive perspective of dark tourism is that it is a way of relating to and establishing a dialogue with the past (Antze and Lambek, 1996) and remembering the past, activating lived or prosthetic memories (Knudsen, 2011; Knudsen and Waade, 2010).

This chapter investigates dark tourism in the context of four dark heritage sites (former concentration camps) where death, genocide, events of the Holocaust and Nazi Germany atrocities occurred during the Second World War, especially in relation to the Jewish people. These are unique heritage sites and deathscapes as they are inherently dissonant (Ashworth and Tunbridge, 1996) and intertwined with interpretation and meaning (Beech, 2009). Large numbers of visitors are attracted to these sites and increasingly they are young and non-Jewish. In addition, visitors spend long periods of time within the physical environment of sites. Given that the dimensions of dark tourism consumption are not clear, scholars have called for the exploration of dark tourism using an inter-disciplinary lens, taking account of tourism and business management concepts (Biran and Hyde, 2013). This discussion evaluates dark heritage sites as places by applying the servicescape (Bitner, 1992) framework to dark tourism site management. The focus of the chapter is to consider dark heritage servicescapes and evaluate the marketing management of dark heritage tourism within the context of contemporary perspectives on distant dark events.

Visitor motivations at dark heritage sites

In order to consider what site managers need to provide in terms of a servicescape and how best to facilitate visitor interaction and engagement at dark heritage sites, it is useful to consider visitor motivations. There is a significant body of work regarding the investigation of visitor motivations (Biran et al., 2011; Cohen, 2007; Logan and Reeves, 2009; Poria et al., 2006; Seaton, 1996; Stone and Sharpley, 2008) and a range of visitor motivations, perceptions and sought benefits when visiting heritage sites has been identified (Biran et al., 2011). This discussion seeks to shed some light on what sites can provide to facilitate these motivations by providing the opportunity for a range of interactions between the visitor and dark heritage sites. Biran et al. (2011) identified three categories of visitors to heritage sites. The first group of visitors are 'ordinary' tourists, who do not have a personal attachment or connection with the site. The visit is seen as leisure and visitors seek education and knowledge. The second category of visitors are those with personal connections to the site where the site carries personal meaning and heritage, the visit is not seen as leisure and these visitors are considered to be identity reinforcers. The third group of visitors are 'ambivalent' visitors who display some similar characteristics to the first category, often visiting a site 'to see it to believe it'.

Visitors to heritage sites seek both personal and social identity. The value embedded in a visitors' onsite experience can be developed through communication with the physical site and interactive experiences that can help them expand their own worldview, and to try to understand different worldviews in relation to how they respond to history and present-day relevance. This has implications for how sites are managed in terms of providing the setting for visitor experience and allowing visitors to learn from the past while acknowledging that not everyone can or will learn in a similar way. Thus the site managers' role will involve trying to facilitate the complex process where visitors and staff can be encouraged to learn from each other and experience a sense of belonging (Magee and Gilmore, 2015).

Dark heritage sites as 'servicescapes'

Bitner (1992) developed the servicescape framework to illustrate the importance of the role of the physical environment in consumers' and employees' behaviour in a service setting. The effect of atmospherics and physical design in a physical environment where service experiences occur can impact upon internal cognitive, emotional and physiological responses in both customers and employees. This is particularly evident for service settings such as heritage sites, as the service is usually produced and consumed simultaneously, that it is the visitor who is 'in the factory' (Bitner, 1992, p.57). The physical environment is rich in cues and may be very influential in how consumers and employees behave and respond within a specific setting. Conceptualising the heritage site as a servicescape where visitors seek to understand and interpret past events is a useful way of recognising the complexity of the visitor's total experience and the challenge for site managers in providing a servicescape that can deliver a continuum of experience.

The *physical* environmental elements that impact upon both customers' and employees' behaviour, as identified by Bitner (1992), are: ambient conditions, spatial layout/functionality and signs, symbols and artefacts. Ambient conditions, for instance, temperature, air quality, noise, music, visual factors like colour, shape and cleanliness are generally the most obvious and easiest environmental factors to identify and include controllable observable stimuli (Bitner, 1992). Space and functionality refer to how layout, equipment and furnishings contribute to the consumption experience (Harris and Ezeh, 2008). Signs, symbols and artefacts include a combination of what can be described as rudimentary, but still necessary, systems of signs (i.e. giving directions), as well as more complex symbols that can create particular types of impressions (Bitner, 1992). These signs and symbols can relate to both the intended meaning from the site manager's perspective, as well as the personal meaning constructed subjectively by consumers (Rosenbaum, 2005).

Most importantly, Bitner's (1992) servicescape model illustrates the importance of the physical site where the service delivery occurs and its impact upon visitor experience. Responding to Bitner's (1992) call to move beyond a consumption setting's physical dimension and to consider the less tangible dimensions present within a consumption setting, Rosenbaum and Massiah (2011) conceptualised an expanded servicescape framework that adopts a multi-disciplinary approach to take account of other environmental stimuli and components that influence customer behaviour and social interaction. It comprises of four environmental dimensions: physical, social, socially symbolic and natural. These four categories of stimuli may enhance or constrain employee and customer approach or avoidance decisions and social interaction behaviours. Rosenbaum and Massiah's (2011) framework develops the original servicescape framework to a more advanced position (while retaining Bitner's core concept); the extended servicescape model treats the consumption setting holistically, as comprising of not only the setting's physical, built and manufactured dimension already reviewed by Bitner (1992), but also of the social (i.e. human), socially symbolic and natural dimensions that together 'act in unison to influence customer behaviour'

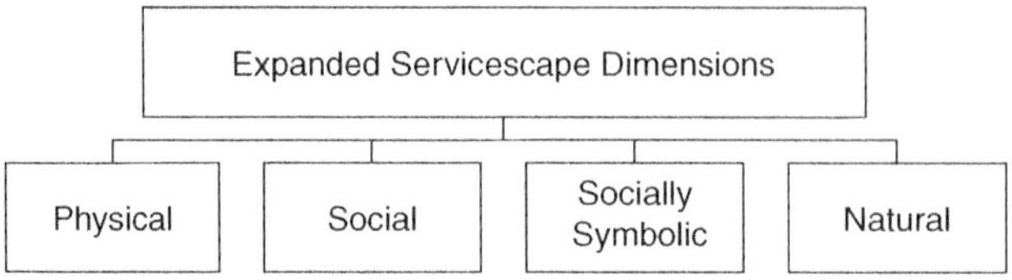

Figure 17.1 Expanded servicescape (adapted from Rosenbaum and Massiah, 2011).

(Rosenbaum and Massiah, 2011, p.481). Figure 17.1 illustrates a simplified adaptation of the expanded servicescape framework advanced by Rosenbaum and Massiah (2011).

The *social* dimension incorporates the complex human dimensions that are evident at dark heritage sites linked to crimes of death, genocide, suffering and tragedy. As stated by Proshansky (1978, p.150), 'there is no physical setting that is not also a social, cultural, and psychological setting'. Basing their social dimension on previous research (Rosenbaum and Montoya, 2007), Rosenbaum and Massiah (2011) conceptualised the social dimension as being comprised of: consumers, employees, along with their density in the setting and their expressed emotions. For dark heritage sites, the social dimension gains multiple other facets, as it includes the humanistic dimension defined by additional stakeholders, in addition to visitors and employees. There are several groups and unique sets of social connections that require careful investigation and examination in terms of site-management implications. Centrally, the victims and the historical evidence manifested in comprehensive biographical research and statistical data that support the human stories have enabled a differentiated portrayal of the multinational victimised collective often referred to as 'prisoner society' (Perz, 2013). Some of the victims are also survivors, another significant stakeholder category, whose testimonies and power of influence has been and continues to be significant, on many levels, representing a legacy for future generations to come. Victims' and survivors' families are another category, often actively involved in the present life of the site, especially through education, communication and commemorative activities.

A new and challenging dimension within the overall social spectrum that seeks to capture all of the humanistic components is the emergence of the 'perpetrators' society' (Durr et al, 2013) which 21st century memorial education requires to be revealed, deciphered and communicated, adding a new, unique, challenging, yet essential perspective to the already multi-layered, multifaceted narratives at sites of death, genocide and human suffering. This is an equally sensitive and challenging part of the continuously evolving narrative present at dark heritage sites (Gluck, 2013), and a specific example of atrocity heritage (Ashworth and Tunbridge, 1996, p.21).

The *socially symbolic* dimension relates to the understanding gained at dark heritage sites and how the various site's own attributes, history and connections with different social and ethnic groups manifest themselves as a source of meaning(s). The potential for 'dissonant heritage' (Tunbridge and Ashworth, 1996) at sites of death, genocide and human suffering is recognised. This relates to how the past, its conserved artefacts and remembered personalities, symbols and associations are related to specific social and ethnic groups and how such connections between the site's evidence and these groups provide specific meaning(s).

The *natural* dimension refers to the natural setting, the geographical and topographical location of each site that are essential for the assessment of the authenticity of the site and its history. The rationale for the inception of the camp or site and the subsequent life of each camp during its existence were often dictated by the geographical position and the proximity to natural resources or other points of economic interest (Geyer et al, 2010). The natural vegetation was and continues to be of significant importance to sites of death and genocide, as often trees and woodland areas provided the camouflage under which heinous crimes took place.

These four servicescape dimensions are key components of heritage sites. While acknowledging the fundamental importance of the physical aspects of a site, the combination of the social, socially symbolic and natural dimensions are crucial to the visitor experience and to the management of dark heritage sites. Site managers have the opportunity to design servicescapes that offer unique and enlightening service interactions and experiences for visitors, with the potential to make visitors more sensitive to human suffering and aware of threats to humanity so that they can be prevented in the future. The sites can only speak to the visitors if they are assessable and legible through explanatory labelling, clear communication and interpretation.

Re-thinking dark heritage site servicescapes

The chapter draws on a recent study of the nature and role of servicescapes at four dark heritage sites of death, genocide and human suffering which were former concentration camps during the Second World War (Magee and Gilmore, 2015). These sites were chosen because they are sites of death and dark events and, until recently, the majority of visitors were people with strong personal ties to the sites. The new challenge for site management is to re-think the existing perception of these places as dark heritage sites so that they can engage with new, younger visitors who have no personal ties with sites.

The four sites that were investigated were the Auschwitz-Birkenau memorial and museum in Poland, Dachau concentration camp and Sachsenhausen concentration camp in Germany and Mauthausen concentration camp in Austria. Auschwitz-Birkenau memorial and museum is located in Poland, near the town of Oswiecim, 42 miles from Krakow. It was established in 1940 for political prisoners and became an extermination camp until it was liberated at the end of the Second World War in 1945. The site is divided into two parts, Auschwitz 1 and Auschwitz 11-Birkenau, which are situated 2 miles from each other, in a total area of 472 acres. Today the memorial and museum include the original camp blocks, guard towers, walls and places where prisoners were executed, remnants of four crematoria and areas where human ashes were deposited (Auschwitz-Birkenau Memorial and State Museum Annual report, 2012, 2013; Auschwitz-Birkenau State Museum in Oswiecim Guide book, 2012). Mauthausen Concentration Camp memorial is located in Austria on the outskirts of Mauthausen village, 13 miles from the city of Linz. It was established in 1938 for political prisoners and became an extermination camp until it was liberated at the end of the Second World War in 1945. The site is close to granite quarries, where inmates were enlisted to work in the armaments industry from 1942. Today the memorial site includes the sick camp and quarry, reconstructed with original structures, a modern visitors' centre and a cemetery. It is surrounded by meadows and countryside landscape with views of the nearby village and the site is visible to local townspeople (The Concentration Camp Mauthausen 1938–1945).

Dachau Concentration Camp memorial is located in Germany, in the town of Dachau near Munich (approximately 13 miles away). It was established in 1933 for political prisoners and became an extermination camp until liberation at the end of the Second World War in 1945. Today it is a memorial site with some original and reconstructed buildings, crematoria, exhibitions, religious monuments and memorials. A visitor centre with a reception area, information desk, café and bookstore opened in 2009 (Dachau Concentration Camp, 2010; text and documents CD, 2005; Dachau Concentration Camp – 'Scripts for walk and tours', 2010). Sachsenhausen concentration camp is located in Germany, 22 miles north of Berlin. It was established in 1936 primarily for political prisoners and became an extermination camp during the Second World War. It was liberated in May 1945. The site is positioned in an industrial area with workshops where prisoners were forced to work. It became Sachsenhausen National memorial in 1961 when many original buildings were removed. Today the camp is a museum and memorial. Several buildings and structures have been reconstructed, including guard towers, crematory ovens and camp barracks (Sachsenhausen Concentration Camp 1936–1945, Events and Developments', 2011).

The key characteristics, main mission and purpose of each site were investigated. Prior to site visits, detailed analysis of site-related documentation (reports and website material) was carried out. The documents analysed included annual reports from each site; the Auschwitz-Birkenau 'preserve authenticity' project summary (2012); Auschwitz-Birkenau Memorial and State Museum Annual report (2012; 2013); Auschwitz-Birkenau 'the past and the present' brochure; the Auschwitz-Birkenau State Museum in Oswiecim Guide book (2012); Auschwitz-Birkenau 'the place where you are standing' album (2013); the Dachau Concentration Camp Memorial Site 1933-1945 text and photo documents CD; the Dachau Concentration Camp Script for Walks and Tours on the Grounds of Dachau Concentration Camp (2010); Dachau Concentration Camp Memorial Site (2013); the Mauthausen Memorial website, the Concentration Camp Mauthausen 1938-1945 catalogue (2013); the Durr et al's (2013) Mauthausen Bulletin, the Mauthausen Concentration Camp, the crime scenes of Mauthausen – searching for traces, room of names; Sachsenhausen concentration camp 1936-1945, Events and Developments (2011); Sachsenhausen Memorial and Museum Guide Website.

Observations of the site topography, natural and physical environment and artefacts were carried out during site visits. Face to face and online interviews were carried out with managerial decision makers, including site managers, heads of education, press officers, site spokespersons and site guides. These interviews explored management perspectives and priorities for each site servicescape and how they engage with visitors. Semi-structured interviews were carried out with a total of sixty visitors (across the four sites) regarding their perceptions of the site servicescapes and their experiences on site. Interviews were recorded and transcribed in full. The Rosenbaum and Massiah (2011) expanded servicescape framework components of physical, natural, social and socially-symbolic were used to guide the research and are used to present and illustrate the challenges for site managers at these dark heritage places today.

The physical and natural environment

The physical and natural dimensions are closely intertwined at dark heritage sites. Each site encompasses expansive areas of land which provide the physical and natural servicescape for the entire visitor experience. Observations at these sites and interviews with both managers and visitors regarding the role of the physical and natural environment revealed that the place itself was vitally important to both visitors and managers. Site managers indicated that attention to the physical and natural servicescape was often their prime focus and it was sometimes a struggle to maintain the authenticity of sites because of the size of the sites and the number of buildings that need to be maintained. The main function of each site is to preserve the physical structures and remnants of the site that remain from the past and to use these to underpin research and education initiatives. The natural environment includes areas which are mass graves containing human ash. Visitors are exposed to the topography and the elements when on site, therefore the vegetation and weather conditions contribute to the overall ambience.

Both site managers and visitors recognised the fundamental value of place authenticity associated with the different roles of dark heritage sites. They are memorial sites, they commemorate the dead and suffering, they are sites of mourning and are witness to painful and cruel events. Site managers focus on the authentic physical and natural dimensions of the site to ensure that they have meaning for visitors, explicitly in terms of the tangible aspects and artefacts and also in relation to the meanings and historical narratives that underpin the sites. Conservation of authenticity is one of the most important challenges site managers need to address as it is perceived to be the underlying motive behind personal and community group visits to dark heritage sites. Place authenticity is also difficult to encapsulate as it is closely embedded in remembrance and commemoration; the physical site is linked to the importance of where specific dark events occurred. As memorial sites, they need to be managed as authentic physical and natural sites; and they need their meaning to be communicated to visitors both as individuals and as communities.

At Auschwitz-Birkenau, the 'natural environment is very important as mass graves and areas containing human ash are located in various places … which makes the site beyond all other functions a cemetery, a resting place' (Press Officer, Auschwitz-Birkenau). At Sachsenhausen, managers indicated that the original buildings and structural remains of the concentration camp were 'guarantors of the memory', therefore it is important to preserve them. At Dachau, managers emphasised that the original aim of the site was closely linked to the victims, survivors and their relatives, therefore the place is important as it is an address where they can remember and mourn the dead and the suffering; 'a tangible address for the victims, survivors and their relatives' (Dachau site manager). The physical and natural environment was described as a site of mass murder, a crime scene at Mauthausen where the former concentration camp is a 'stone witness' to past events. Visitors stated that the physical and natural environment and exhibitions were central to their experiences on site; for them, it was important to visit the site where real historical events took place.

The artefacts were also important in illustrating the story and authenticity of each site. Artefacts include the exhibits that were prisoners' personal effects, these enable visitors to make an empathetic connection between this site, the victims of the work camp and their own life, now in the present (Head of Education, Dachau). These include objects, photographs and documents that belonged to the victims. Artefacts evoke empathy with the victims, for example when they see baby clothes and toddlers pushchairs (Auschwitz-Birkenau), they tend to imagine their own families. The buildings and site remnants testify to the tragic history and make it possible for visitors to try to imagine life within a concentration camp. Visitors commented that the physical environment and the use of authentic artefacts which previously belonged to victims and survivors were particularly poignant in their overall understanding of what happened at these sites. For example, 'I saw the scale and intensity of wrongdoing..' (visitor at Sachsenhausen Site); 'this is so much more than what you learn from books, what you learn here in a day and seeing it with your own eyes, you will never forget' (visitor at Sachsenhausen site); 'walking through the woods and seeing the mass graves made me realise the extent of the horror' (visitor at Dachau site).

Social and socially symbolic dimensions

In recent years, site management have been re-thinking their approach to interpretation, communication and visitor interactions on site. The challenge for site managers is in ascertaining how best to draw meaning from the past for visitors with different backgrounds and perspectives. Today there is an increased focus on education and interpretation, and to provide a servicescape that will encourage visitors to co-create their own unique experience at these sites. The aim is to build on the site's authentic characteristics by providing a relevant and engaging experience. Given that many visitors today have no personal attachment to the sites and may be seeking a 'see it to believe it' or knowledge-seeking experience, site managers recognise the importance of interpreting the meaning and history of the sites and that there are some larger contextual issues to be explained. In particular, the historical, social, political and economic context of each site's existence and why they were created. This has led to a wider management agenda in re-thinking the interface with visitors and the social and socially symbolic dimensions of sites.

As the distance in time grows since the atrocities were committed, there is a noticeable difference in visitor profiles at these sites. Many visitors are younger than those in the past and many have no personal attachments to sites in contrast to times past when many had emotional ties to specific sites. In addition, visitors today represent a wider range of ethnic backgrounds than previously; for example, people from Asian countries not directly affected by National Socialism and the Nazis such as Japan and South Korea, now visit the sites in large numbers. This lack of visitor familiarity with the specific history of sites has led to the need for more explanation regarding how sites could have existed within a populated region, relatively unhidden from local people. Site managers have recognised that more explanation is needed and that the narrative has changed since the 1950s when local people perpetuated the story that they did not see anything or know what was going on at concentration camps. Today the narrative at sites recognises that both perpetrators and victims were recruited from society and without society's knowledge and active support the camps could not have existed. To achieve this, communication at the sites relate to the changing need of visitors in terms of their familiarity with the history and context of the sites, the nature of interpretative methods and educational material.

Each site offers tours for visitors from different backgrounds and levels of knowledge with the aim to provide a dynamic, interactive educational experience for visitors. There are different types and lengths of tours, visitors have the opportunity to visit many places of interest. For example, the standard tour at Auschwitz-Birkenau takes three hours, and the extended tour takes 6 hours. There is also a tour offering an enhanced educational experience with a high level of interpretation and educational activities. Each site offers tours specifically tailored for school groups. Developmental work on the pedagogical concept is on-going. The education concept is based on the interaction of three components: documentary evidence, topography of site and visitors perspectives. Visitors are presented with the whole human spectrum of perspectives: victims, perpetrators, collaborators and bystanders. For example, at the Sachsenhausen site, visitors can identify with the individual biographies, they can see similarities between their own lives and that of the prisoner, they can guess how sad and tragic it had been for that person (Site guide, Sachsenhausen site). Tour guides are the interface between the site and the visitors. They are trained to use questions as a way to incorporate the visitor into the tour and to make it more interactive where possible. For example, at Dachau, visitors are invited to be active participants, to ask questions and they are guided to observe artefacts. At Auschwitz-Birkenau, visitors walk the actual path where victims stepped down from the trains and follow it to the crematoria where victims were murdered. Each site endeavours to have well-trained guides who can tailor the message to suit groups with different backgrounds and level of knowledge about the site. Site managers stated that the aim was to change site guides into educators (Head of educational projects, Auschwitz-Birkenau).

The role of the tour guides is vital to visitors' on-site experiences. For example, at the Dachau site, a visitor commented that 'our guide was amazing, she transported us to the days when terror lived in that place'. Visitor perceptions of the interpretation and social interaction at sites was central to their experiences, and the observation of artefacts illustrated that the victims were normal people with normal lives before they were deported to concentration camps. A visitor at Sachsenhausen commented that the visit 'made me think of myself and my family, what if something like this happened to us?' Visitors' engagement with site artefacts and social interactions on-site helped them realise the extent of the horror and sadness of the historical events.

Challenges for management at dark heritage sites

All the site managers emphasised that they wanted their dark heritage site to be about sensitive heritage rather than dark tourism. They did not like the term 'dark' heritage sites and did not see their role in relation to dark events but rather to enlighten visitors and to help society learn from the past and reflect on social morals. The Senior Officer at Mauthausen emphasised that the site was not a place of dark tourism, but that it was about providing a cognitive understanding of the world. The aim was to take a step away from a defensive understanding of history and move towards an active engagement with the past. Similarly, the Director at Auschwitz-Birkenau indicated that it was important to explore the Auschwitz tragedy to help people get to know the world better, but also to present the entire sphere of human hope, challenges and threats. Site managers would prefer the sites to be managed as sensitive heritage sites. The aim of all levels of management at the sites was to trigger the visitor to reflect on 'what has this is to do with me?' (Head of Education, Dachau). The story of each site indicates that there is a permanent danger, the negative potential of human beings to do harm and the sites' aim is to alert visitors to the dangers of mankind's inhumanity to mankind. Site managers also aim to focus on the stories of survival and how society can learn from the sites rather than being fascinated by dark or macabre events. The educational messages that underpin the importance of learning from past atrocities are designed so that they can be absorbed both on a personal level and on a wider communal level, so that people may contribute to their own communities and to help build a better world. Fundamentally, many visitors wanted to focus on how to transform tragedy into survival and focus on the value of life, rather than having a negative experience based on stories of sacrifice, loss and tragedy. The overall message from these sites was aimed at encouraging people to go forward with a reinforced belief that empathy, respect and humility are vitally important human values.

Managing these dark heritage servicescapes involves managing the physical and natural components for the site while recognising that interactive communication and education is important in underpinning the social and socially symbolic dimensions. Visitors are not passive recipients of information but have social, psychological and cognitive baggage and different perspectives regarding distant historical events. Traditionally site managers' have focused on maintaining the physical environment and original artefacts as this has been important in maintaining evidence of dark events, remembering the past and commemorating the dead. Although this continues to be important today (as the authenticity of the servicescape is a fundamental component for visitors' experiences at dark heritage sites), the social and socially symbolic meaning experienced at the sites are equally important. Today, heritage sites want to disassociate themselves from concepts and labels of 'dark tourism'; and instead, they want to focus on maintaining authenticity and the original purpose of the sites while making them meaningful and relevant for today's visitors.

The social dimensions relate to site interpretation and the role of guides in providing the historical background and making sense of the sites for visitors. Both the social and socially symbolic dimensions are vitally important in connecting visitors with a site. On-site experience can be created and embedded in the visitor's experience through communications with guides and artefacts in addition to the physical environment. These aspects of site experience have been developed and expanded in recent years. Site managers view education and interactive communication as vitally important in reaching a new generation of visitors, to tell the whole story from victims, survivors and perpetrators perspectives within the historical context. A new generation of visitors are less likely to have an emotional link to the sites, but want to understand what happened at these sites and why it was allowed to happen. Today, these sites increasingly focus on education and interpretation and they aim to provide a servicescape where different types of visitors can engage. The socially symbolic dimensions are integral to facilitating the creation of both personal and societal meaning, the interactive experience encourages visitor engagement at sites. Whether visitors have personal attachment or not, significant or little knowledge of this period of history, servicescapes aim to offer an authentic site (physical and natural dimensions) in tandem with the interpretative (social) and socially symbolic dimensions (place meaning) that facilitate visitor engagement.

Site managers recognise the different visitor motivations and aim to deliver a dynamic mix of site authenticity and enhanced interpretation that will facilitate socially symbolic meaning. To this end, dark heritage site servicescapes provide the backdrop for the co-creation of visitor experiences. Thus, dark heritage sites can be symbolic sites that deliver authenticity, interpretation, social interactions and meaning so that visitors can engage and co-create their own unique experiences; and use these experiences to contribute to societal values in the wider context. In an ideal world, individual visitors can learn and reflect on the site narrative; and they can contribute to society by endorsing social change, global citizenship and community cohesion.

Figure 17.2 illustrates the interrelationships between the expanded servicescape dimensions at dark heritage sites. The physical and natural aspects of the servicescape provide the setting for the on-site social interactions between the site employees and visitors.

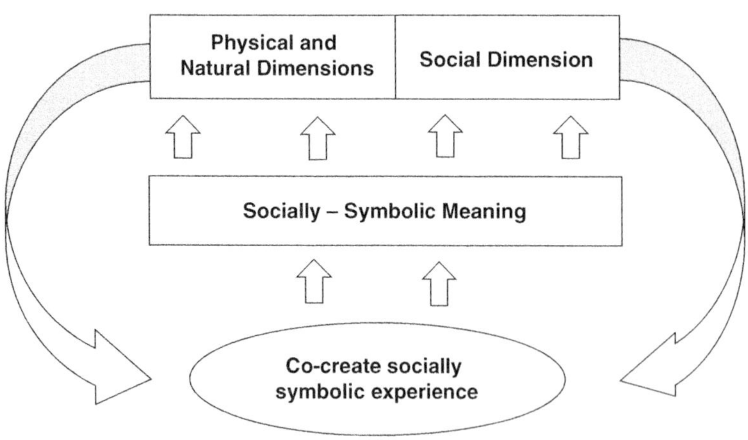

Figure 17.2 Socially symbolic experience.

These interactions and experiences help visitors to co-create socially symbolic meaning and learning onsite. Together these interactions contribute to both site managers and visitors' ability to develop empathy, understanding and meaning in relation to the tragic historical events.

Conclusions

Overall, dark heritage sites offer society a place where it can consider moral codes and issues, the role of such sites is to enlighten society about the atrocities of the past and strengthen society's commitment to humanitarian values. These sites aim to become established places of learning, where the public are invited to view the historical remains and to visit explanatory exhibitions in order to understand events. Currently, heritage sites have an increased focus on education and interpretation and are moving from a focus on managing physical sites to the co-creation of experience between site and visitor. Site managers want to disassociate themselves from 'dark' tourism and be more closely involved in enlightening a new generation of visitors.

There has been growing scepticism of the pertinence of the connection between the history of the Holocaust and issues of human rights. Some argue that there is a danger of distorting history when it is used as a means to acquire ethical lessons. To arrive at certain educational goals, the symbolic meaning of past atrocities may be misused, depreciating and contradicting the true meaning of the events. Thus, there is a need for a sensitive approach to managing sites and providing the setting for visitor experience. A sensitive approach needs to balance the need to learn from the past while acknowledging that not everyone can or will learn in a similar way. It is a complex process and people should be encouraged to learn and draw socially symbolic meaning from each other; site managers and visitors with different backgrounds, culture and histories can contribute by facilitating the process and scene setting.

The value and role of the servicescape in relation to dark tourism sites are to engage with visitors and be cognizant of the growing scepticism and different perspectives regarding past events. In re-thinking the role of dark heritage sites, managers increasingly adopt the role of facilitator and co-creator of social communication, cooperation and socially symbolic meaning The success of each site relies on the visitors' engagement and power to co-create a meaningful experience for themselves, others and society.

References

Antze, P. and Lambek, M., (1996) *Tense Past.* New York: Routledge.

Ashworth, G.J. and Tunbridge, J.E. (1996) *Dissonant Heritage: Management of the Past as a Resource.* Chichester: Wiley.

Auschwitz-Birkenau Memorial and State Museum Annual report, (2012, 2013).

Auschwitz-Birkenau Memorial, "Preserve Authenticity" report, (2012).

Auschwitz-Birkenau Memorial, "The past and the present" brochure, (2012).

Auschwitz-Birkenau State Museum in Oswiecim Guide book, (2012).

Auschwitz-Birkenau, "The place where you are standing" Album, (2013).

Beech, J. (2009) 'Genocide tourism'. In: Sharpley, R. and Stone, P. eds. *The Darker Side of Travel. The Theory and Practice of Dark Tourism.* Bristol: Channel View Publications.

Biran, A. and Hyde, K. (2013) Guest editorial: New perspectives on dark tourism. *International Journal of Culture, Tourism and Hospitality Research.* Vol 7 No.3 pp.191–198.

Biran, A., Poria, Y. and Oren, G. (2011) Sought experiences at (dark) heritage sites. *Annals of Tourism Research.* Vol. 38 No.3 pp. 820–941.

Bitner, M.J. (1992) Servicescapes: The impact of physical surroundings on customers and employees. *Journal of Marketing.* Vol. 56 No.1 pp. 57–71.

Cohen, E. (2007) "Authenticity" in tourism studies. *Tourism Recreation Research.*Vol. 32, No. 2 pp. 75–82.

Columb, C. and Kalandides, A. (2010) 'The '*be* Berlin campaign': old wine in new bottles or innovative form of participatory place branding?', in G. Ashworth, and Kavaratzis, M. eds. *Towards Effective Place Brand Management: Branding European Cities and Regions.* pp. 173–90. Cheltenham/Northampton, UK: Edward Elgar.

Dachau Concentration Camp Memorial Site (2013) Introduction. Available from: http://www.kz-gedenkstaette-dachau.de/index-e.html [Accessed on 17 August 2013].

Dachau Concentration Camp Memorial Site 1933-1945, text and documents CD (2005).

Dachau Concentration Camp – "Script for walks and tours on the grounds of Dachau concentration camp", (2010).

Dachau Memorial Site, Bavarian Memorial Foundation Guidebook.

Durr, C., Lechner, R., Wahal, N. and Wensch, J. (2013) 'The New Exhibitions at the Mauthausen Memorial. Concept and Curation'. In: Holzinger, G and Kranebitter, A. eds. *Mauthausen Bulletin. The Mauthausen Concentration Camp. The Crime Scenes of Mauthuasen – Searching for Traces. Room of Names.* Mauthausen: Federal Ministry of the Interior. pp.17–22.

Foley, M. and Lennon, J. (1996a) Editorial: Heart of darkness. *International Journal of Heritage Studies.*Vol. 2 No. 4 pp. 195–197.

Foley, M. and Lennon, J. (1996b) JFK and dark tourism: A fascination with assassination. *International Journal of Heritage Studies.*Vol.2 No.4 pp. 198–211.

Geyer, N., Franke, M. and Foch, P. (2010) "Script – Walks and Tours on the grounds of Dachau Concentration Camp Memorial Site". Dachau: Bayerische Gedenkstatten.

Gluck, B. (2013) 'Introduction'. In: Holzinger, G and Kranebitter, A. eds. *Mauthausen Bulletin. The Mauthausen Concentration Camp. The Crime Scenes of Mauthuasen – Searching for Traces. Room of Names.* Mauthausen: Federal Ministry of the Interior. pp.10–11.

Harris, L.C. and Ezeh, C. (2008) Servicescape and loyalty intentions: An empirical investigation. *European Journal of Marketing.*Vol. 42 Nos. 3–4 pp. 390–422.

Jamal, T., and Lelo, L. (2009) Exploring the conceptual and analytical framing: From darkness to intentionality. *Tourist Experiences: Meanings, Motivations, Behaviours Conference,*April 2009. University of Central Lancashire, United Kingdom.

Knusden, B.T. (2011) Thanatourism: Witnessing difficult past. *Tourist Studies.*Vol. 11 No. 1 pp.55–72.

Knusden, B.T. and Waade, A.M. (2010) 'Performative authenticity in tourism and spatial experience: Rethinking the relations between travel, place and emotion.' In: Knusden, B. T. and Waade, A.M., eds. *Re-Investing Authenticity: Tourism, Place and Emotions.* Bristol: ChannelView Publications. pp.1–19.

Lennon., J. and Foley, M. (2000) *Dark Tourism: The Attraction of Death and Disaster.* London: Continuum.

Logan, W. and Reeves, K. (2009) *Places of Pain and Shame. Dealing with Difficult Heritage.* Oxon: Routledge.

Macdonald, S. (2006) Undesirable heritage: Fascist material culture and historical consciousness in Nuremberg. *Journal of Heritage Studies.*Vol. 12 No. 1 pp. 9–28.

Magee, R. and Gilmore, A. (2015) Heritage site management: from dark heritage to transformative service experience? *The Service Industries Journal.*Vol. 35, Nos. 15–16 pp. 898–917.

Mauthausen Memorial website: http://en.mauthausen-memorial.at/index_open.php

Miles, W. (2002) Auschwitz: Museum interpretation and darker tourism. *Annals of Tourism Research,*Vol. 29 No. 4 pp. 1175–1178.

Perz, B. (2013) 'Exhibiting the Concentration camp. Old and New Historical Exhibitions at Mauthausen'. In: Holzinger, G and Kranebitter, A. eds. *Mauthausen Bulletin. The Mauthausen Concentration Camp. The Crime Scenes of Mauthuasen – Searching for Traces. Room of Names.* Mauthausen: Federal Ministry of the Interior. pp. 23–29.

Poria, Y., Reichel, A. and Biran, A. (2006) Heritage site management: Motivations and expectations. *Annals of Tourism Research.*Vol. 33 No. 1 pp. 1172–1188.

Proshansky, H.M. (1978) The city and self-identity. *Environment & Behaviour.*Vol. 10 No. 2 pp. 147–169.

Rosenbaum, M.S. (2005) The symbolic servicescape: Your kind is welcomed here. *Journal of Consumer Behaviour.* Vol. 4 No. 4 pp. 257–267.

Rosenbaum, M.S. and Montoya, D.Y., (2007) Am I welcome here? Exploring how ethnic consumers assess their place identity. *Journal of Business Research*. Vol. 60 No. 3 pp. 206–214.

Rosenbaum, M.S. and Massiah, C. (2011) An expanded servicescape perspective. *Journal of Service Management*. Vol. 22 No. 4 pp. 471–490.

Rubinstein, R.L. and Parmelee, P.A., (1992) 'Attachment to place and the representation of the life course by the elderly'. In: I. Altman and Low, S.M. eds., *Place Attachment*. New York: Plenum Press, pp. 139–163.

Ryan, C. and Kohli, R., (2006) The buried village, New Zealand – An example of dark tourism? *Asia Pacific Journal of Tourism Research*, Vol. 11 No. 3 pp. 211–226.

Seaton, A. (1996) Guided by the dark: From thanatopsis to thanatourism. *International Journal of Heritage Studies*. Vol. 2 No. 4 pp. 234–244.

Sachsenhausen concentration camp 1936-1945, "Events and Developments" (2011).

Sachsenhausen memorial and museum guide – English version (2012).

Sachsenhausen memorial and museum guide website: http://www.stiftung-bg.de/gums/en/index.htm

Sharpley, R. and Stone, P. (2009) *The Darker Side of Travel. The Theory and Practice of Dark Tourism*. Bristol: Channel View Publications.

Stone, P. (2006) A dark tourism spectrum: Towards a typology of death and macabre related tourist sites, attractions and exhibitions. *Tourism: An Interdisciplinary International Journal*, Vol. 54 No. 2 pp. 145–160.

Stone, P. and Sharpley, R. (2008) Consuming dark tourism: A thanatological perspective. *Annals of Tourism Research*. Vol. 35 No.2 pp. 574–595.

Tarlow, P.E. (2005) Dark tourism: The appealing "dark" side of tourism and more. In: Novelli, M. ed. *Niche Tourism: Contemporary Issues, Trends and Cases*. Amsterdam: Elsevier.

The concentration camp Mauthausen 1938-1945 Catalogue, (2013).

The concentration camp Mauthausen 1938-1945, "The crime scenes of Mauthausen, searching for traces rooms of name" Bulletin, (2013).

Tunbridge, J.E. and Ashworth, G.J., (1996) *Dissonant Heritage: The Management of the Past as a Resource in Conflict*. Chichester: Wiley.

Uzzell, D. and Ballantyne, R. (1998) Heritage that hurts: Interpretation in a postmodern world. In: Uzzell, D. and Ballantybe, R. eds. *Contemporary Issues in Heritage and Environmental Interpretation*. London: The Stationary Office.

Index

Note: Page numbers in italics indicate figures. Page numbers in bold indicate tables.